Praxis Framework

An integrated guide to the management of projects, programmes and portfolios

a Williams Lea company

Published by TSO (The Stationery Office), part of Williams Lea, and available from:

Online
www.tsoshop.co.uk

Mail, Telephone & E-mail
TSO
PO Box 29, Norwich, NR3 1GN
Telephone orders/General enquiries: 0333 202 5070
E-mail: customer.services@tso.co.uk
Textphone: 0333 202 5077

© Praxis Framework Limited 2023

The rights of Adrian Dooley to be identified as the author of these materials/publication/work (collectively the 'Work') has been asserted by them in accordance with the Copyright, Designs and Patents Act 1988 (as amended) and any applicable laws worldwide; all rights remain reserved by the author.

No part of the materials in this Work including graphics and/or logos, may be copied, photocopied, reproduced, translated or reduced to any electronic medium or machine-readable form, in whole or in part, without specific permission in writing from TSO.

Applications to reuse, reproduce and/or republish any material in this Work should be sent in writing to TSO at 18 Central Avenue, St Andrew's Business Park, Norwich, NR7 0HR with an email to: commissioning@williamslea.com

Notice of Liability

The contents in this Work and anything contained in it is distributed 'As Is,' without warranty of any kind, either express or implied, including but not limited to implied warranties for its quality, performance, merchantability, or fitness for any particular purpose. Neither Praxis Framework Limited, Adrian Dooley nor the publisher, its employees, agents, dealers and/or distributors shall be liable to any end user(s) and/or third parties with respect to any liability, loss and/or damage caused and/or alleged to have been caused directly and/or indirectly by the contents of this material or any parts thereof, and the aforementioned parties disclaim all such representations and warranties and assume no responsibility for any errors, inaccuracies, omissions, or any other inconsistencies herein.

This Work may include hyperlinks to third-party content, advertising and websites, provided for the sake of convenience and interest. Neither Praxis Framework Limited, Adrian Dooley nor the publisher endorse any advertising and/or products available from external sources and/or any third parties.

Trademarks

PRINCE2® is a registered trade mark of the PeopleCert group.

First edition 2023
ISBN 9780117094208
J003964108

Contents

Preface and acknowledgements — viii

Foreword — x

Introduction — 1

Part 1 Knowledge — 5

  1.1 Overview — 6
  1.2 Context — 7
      1.2.1 Setting — 7
          Environment — 8
          Projects, programmes and portfolios — 9
          Complexity — 11
      1.2.2 Governance — 13
          General — 13
          Projects, programmes and portfolios — 14
          Project, programme and portfolio management — 15
          Life cycle — 17
          Sponsorship — 24
          Support — 26
         Knowledge management — 28
          Capability maturity — 29
      1.2.3 Professionalism — 32
          Communities of practice — 33
          Competence — 34
          Ethics — 35
          Learning and development — 36
  1.3 Management — 37
      1.3.1 Interpersonal skills — 38
          Communication — 39
          Conflict management — 41
          Delegation — 43
          Influencing — 46
          Leadership — 47
          Negotiation — 50
          Teamwork — 52
      1.3.2 Delivery — 54
          Integrative management — 55
          Organisation management — 57
          Stakeholder management — 61
          Business case management — 64
          Planning — 66
          Control — 68

Information management...71
Assurance 73
Scope management 75
Requirements management....................................... 80
Solutions development 83
Benefits management... 85
Configuration management...................................... 88
Change control 91
Schedule management 93
Time scheduling 96
Resource scheduling 98
Financial management... 100
Investment appraisal 102
Funding 105
Budgeting and cost control 108
Risk management..111
Risk context 113
Risk techniques 115
Change management...118
Resource management 120
Procurement 123
Contract management... 126
Mobilisation 129

Part 2 Method   133

2.1 Overview 134
2.2 Project and programme processes 135
2.2.1 Identification process 137
2.2.2 Sponsorship process 140
2.2.3 Definition process 144
2.2.4 Delivery process... 148
Boundaries process 153
Development process 156
2.2.5 Benefits realisation process 158
2.2.6 Closure process.. 161
2.3 Portfolio processes 164
2.3.1 Initiation process 164
2.3.2 Governance process.. 167
2.3.3 Management process... 170
2.3.4 Co-ordination process 173
2.4 Documentation... 175
2.4.1 Management plans... 176
Organisation management plan 176
Stakeholder management plan 178

  Control management plan 180
  Information management plan 181
  Assurance management plan. 183
  Scope management plan. 183
  Benefits management plan 185
  Schedule management plan. 187
  Finance management plan 189
  Risk management plan 190
  Change management plan 192
  Resource management plan. 193

 2.4.2 **Scope documents** **195**
  Mandate 195
  Vision statement. 195
  Specification. 196
  Product documents 196
  Relationships 198
  Blueprint. 200
  Benefits map 201
  Benefit profile 201
  Business case 203
  Brief 204

 2.4.3 **Delivery documents**. **205**
  Definition plan. 205
  Communication plan 205
  Stakeholder register. 205
  Risk register 206
  Delivery plan. 209
  Issue register 210
  Lessons log 211
  Daily log. 212
  Change log 212
  Progress report 213
  Event report 215
  Follow-on actions report. 216

Part 3 Competence 217

 3.1 **Overview** **218**
 3.2 **Management competencies** **219**
 3.3 **Delivery competencies**. **219**
  3.3.1 **Provide assurance**. **220**
  3.3.2 **Manage the organisation** **221**
  3.3.3 **Manage stakeholders** **222**
  3.3.4 **Manage the business case** **223**
  3.3.5 **Plan governance** **225**
  3.3.6 **Plan delivery** **226**

	3.3.7	Exercise control	227
	3.3.8	Manage information	228
	3.3.9	Manage scope	229
		Manage requirements	230
		Develop solution	231
		Manage benefits	232
		Control scope change	233
		Manage the configuration	234
	3.3.10	Manage the schedule	235
	3.3.11	Manage finance	236
		Develop investment appraisal	237
		Manage funding	238
		Develop budgets and control costs	239
	3.3.12	Manage risk	240
	3.3.13	Manage change	241
	3.3.14	Manage resources	242
		Procure resources	243
		Manage contracts	244
		Mobilise resources	245
3.4	**Interpersonal competencies**		**246**
	3.4.1	Communicate	246
	3.4.2	Manage conflict	247
	3.4.3	Delegate	248
	3.4.4	Lead	249
	3.4.5	Influence	250
	3.4.6	Negotiate	251
	3.4.7	Work within a team	252
3.5	**Process competencies**		**253**
	3.5.1	Identify a project or programme	253
	3.5.2	Sponsor a project or programme	254
	3.5.3	Define a project or programme	255
	3.5.4	Deliver a project or programme	256
		Develop products	257
		Manage boundaries	258
	3.5.5	Close a project or programme	259
	3.5.6	Realise benefits	260
	3.5.7	Initiate a portfolio	261
	3.5.8	Govern a portfolio	262
	3.5.9	Manage a portfolio	263
	3.5.10	Co-ordinate projects and programmes	264

Part 4 Capability maturity — 265

4.1	Overview	266
4.2	Capability	268
	4.2.1 Generic goals	269

		Level 2	269
		Level 3	269
		Generic attributes	269
	4.2.2	**Assurance**	**271**
	4.2.3	**Support**	**272**
	4.2.4	**Organisation management**	**273**
	4.2.5	**Stakeholder management**	**274**
	4.2.6	**Business case management**	**275**
	4.2.7	**Control**	**276**
	4.2.8	**Information management**	**277**
	4.2.9	**Scope management**	**278**
		Requirements management	279
		Solutions development	280
		Benefits management	281
		Change control	282
		Configuration management	283
	4.2.10	**Schedule management**	**283**
	4.2.11	**Financial management**	**285**
		Investment appraisal	286
		Funding	287
		Budgeting and cost control	288
	4.2.12	**Risk management**	**289**
	4.2.13	**Change management**	**290**
	4.2.14	**Resource management**	**291**
		Procurement	292
		Contract management	293
		Mobilisation	294
4.3	**Maturity**		**295**
	4.3.1	**Maturity levels 2 and 3**	**296**
		Generic attributes	296
		Identification process	297
		Sponsorship process	298
		Definition process	299
		Delivery process	300
		Development process	302
		Boundaries process	303
		Closure process	304
		Benefits realisation process	305
		Governance process	306
		Management process	307
		Co-ordination process	308
	4.3.2	**Maturity levels 4 and 5**	**309**

References — 311

Index — 315

Preface and acknowledgements

For much of my working life I have been involved in developing project and programme managers, and consulting with organisations who want to improve their project delivery.

Over the years, I felt I was spending too much time explaining the differences between various bodies of knowledge, methods and other guides. These were rarely fundamental differences of principle and most people I worked with saw many irritating inconsistencies that simply added an unnecessary layer of confusion. All they wanted was to understand the basic concepts of good practice and apply them in as efficient a way as possible.

Eventually in 2012, after a couple of years working on version 6 of the Association for Project Management's (APM) *Body of Knowledge*, events provided the opportunity to create the *Praxis Framework*. Starting with a blank sheet of paper, I took the tried and tested practices of numerous guides and reworked them so that they fitted together seamlessly – or at least as seamlessly as seemed practical.

The process made me think long and hard about a few areas that are treated slightly differently in the *Praxis Framework*: the nature of projects, programmes and portfolios, and the nature of capability maturity being the main ones.

The world that the *Praxis Framework* was born into is very different from that of the 1980s and 1990s, when most of the current well-known practice guides first came into being. The Framework is freely available online at www.praxisframework.org. Publishing online doesn't only make the information highly accessible, it also makes it open for all practitioners to comment and contribute.

The Framework has evolved to be community driven, with frequent and regular updates that reflect how projects, programmes and portfolios are actually managed. One of the great successes has been the flood of volunteers who have given up their time to translate the framework into eight languages (with more on the way).

With the great support of Richard Pharro (APM Group Ltd) and Donnie MacNicol (Team Animation) we have also been able to build the Praxis Pathway – an approach that helps individuals, teams and organisations embed the framework and pragmatically address the factors that lead to so many failed initiatives.

As the framework is community driven the list of contributors grows constantly. An acknowledgements page in print would soon become out of date, so a regularly updated list of all those who have helped us to build and continue to expand and refine the framework can be found at **www.praxisframework.org/resource-pages/contributors**.

However, even the best of websites doesn't have the tactile quality of a book. The opportunity to leaf through pages, highlight text and make margin notes still appeals to most of us. So I would like to thank everyone at TSO for showing faith in the *Praxis Framework* concept and publishing this book.

Finally, in the greater story that led to this day, there are too many people to thank individually so apart from everyone at The Projects Group (TPG) who stuck by me for 25 years and put up with my constant stream of bright (and not so bright) ideas, I will pick out two names.

My thanks go to the late Geoff Reiss who turned up on a building site in Salford on a drab Autumn day in 1979 with an Apple II computer that could perform critical path analysis – and completely changed the course of my career. I'd also like to thank my long-suffering wife Elizabeth, who now has a vague idea of why I 'spend so much time in the study'.

Adrian Dooley
Surrey, January 2023

Foreword

Projects change the world. Projects make impossible dreams possible.

The behavioural and social sciences endorse the idea that a few ways of working and collaborating are particularly motivating and inspiring for people working on a project. A project should have ambitious goals, a higher purpose and a clear deadline. You have probably noticed that what people tend to remember most clearly from their careers is the projects they work on – often the successful ones and the failed ones.

According to recent research, the number of individuals working in project-based roles will increase from 66 million (in 2017) to 88 million (forecast 2027). I describe this as the 'project economy', a term I conceived in 2018 when working on my earlier book, *The Project Revolution: How to Succeed in a Project-Driven World*.[1]

The emergence of projects as the economic engine of our times is silent but incredibly disruptive and powerful. And this massive disruption is not only impacting the way organisations are managed. Every aspect of our lives is becoming a set of projects. In the project economy we are all project managers.

And yet far too many projects and programmes still fail to deliver the promised benefits. The team at *Praxis Framework* have set out to address the root causes of this and have started by producing the integrated guide to the management of projects, programmes and portfolios set out in this publication. It combines knowledge, processes, competence and capability into a single, coherent and integrated framework – a vital contribution to the professional literature.

The framework is just the starting point for an approach called the Praxis Pathway, which seeks to address many of the factors that prevent good practices being properly understood and embedded in corporate culture.

Whether you are a project manager, programme manager or portfolio manager, this guide is a timely resource full of practical tools and real examples that will help you build the knowledge and skills to thrive in a project-driven world. It is also the foundation of an approach that can greatly improve the effectiveness of teams and the capability maturity of organisations.

If you are working in projects or someone eager to learn about modern project management practices, I highly recommend reading this book.

Antonio Nieto-Rodriguez
Advisor, HBR Author, Professor, PMI Fellow and Past Chair

---

1 Project Management Institute (2017). *Project Management Job Growth and Talent Gap Report* 2017–2027.

Introduction

Knowledge (Part 1) reflects the content of the guides that are often called bodies of knowledge. Its component functions are the building blocks of the project, programme and portfolio (P3) management discipline. These functions are integrated in processes that correspond to the phases of the life cycle.

The processes are combined with documentation standards to form the Praxis method (Part 2), as shown in Figure 0.1.

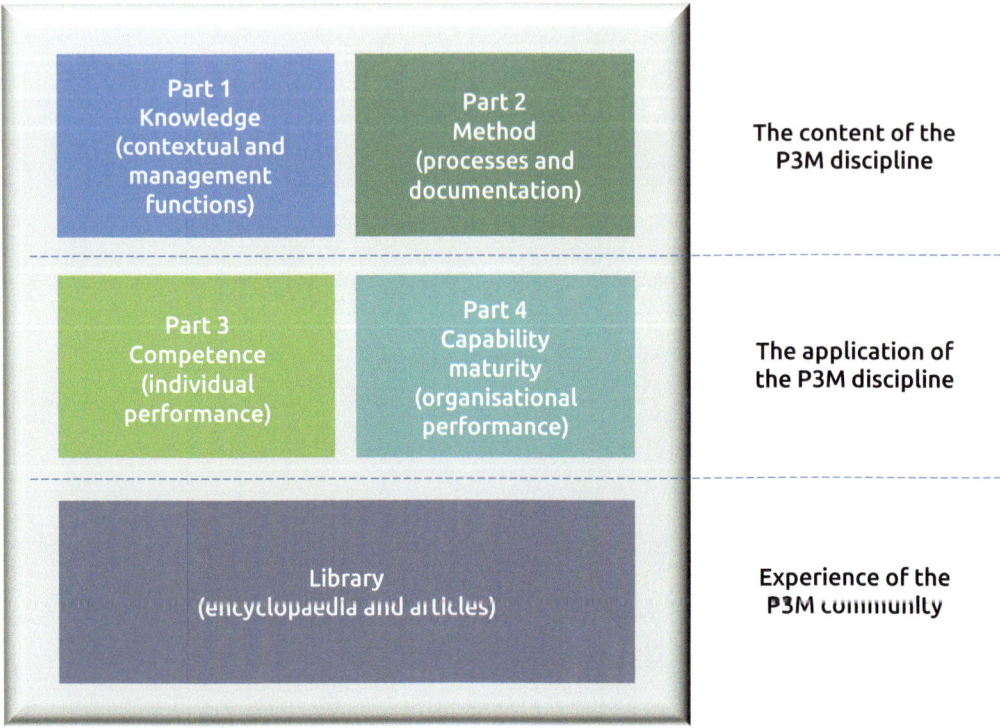

Figure 0.1 Elements of P3 management

Competence (Part 3) defines the required abilities of individuals who apply the functions and methods.

Capability maturity (Part 4) describes the stages of organisational development that ultimately lead to a culture of effective and efficient application of functions and methods.

These four aspects are well served with existing and popular guides or frameworks that address one or two of the four elements. This narrow focus sometimes leads to an approach that does not facilitate integration or reflect latest thinking. Praxis provides the first all-encompassing framework that not only integrates the four elements but also combines this with latest thinking in areas such as complexity and capability maturity.

But a structured framework is only the beginning. There is a wealth of knowledge and experience in the community at large. The Praxis library is an accumulation of information from a wide variety of sources that complements Parts 1 to 4 with additional detail and thought-provoking debate.

Praxis is just a starting point. In order that it can be tailored for use in many, widely varied contexts, it avoids going into too much detail. The framework is supported by a wealth of detailed information that will develop over time to create a knowledge base that will help practitioners manage projects, programmes and portfolios in their own context.

Note: the text refers to commonly used models, tools and techniques such as Monte Carlo analysis, MoSCoW prioritisation, and Delphi. These are explained in detail on the Praxis website at **www.praxisframework.org/en/library/encyclopaedia**. The References section at the end of this publication lists the publications cited.

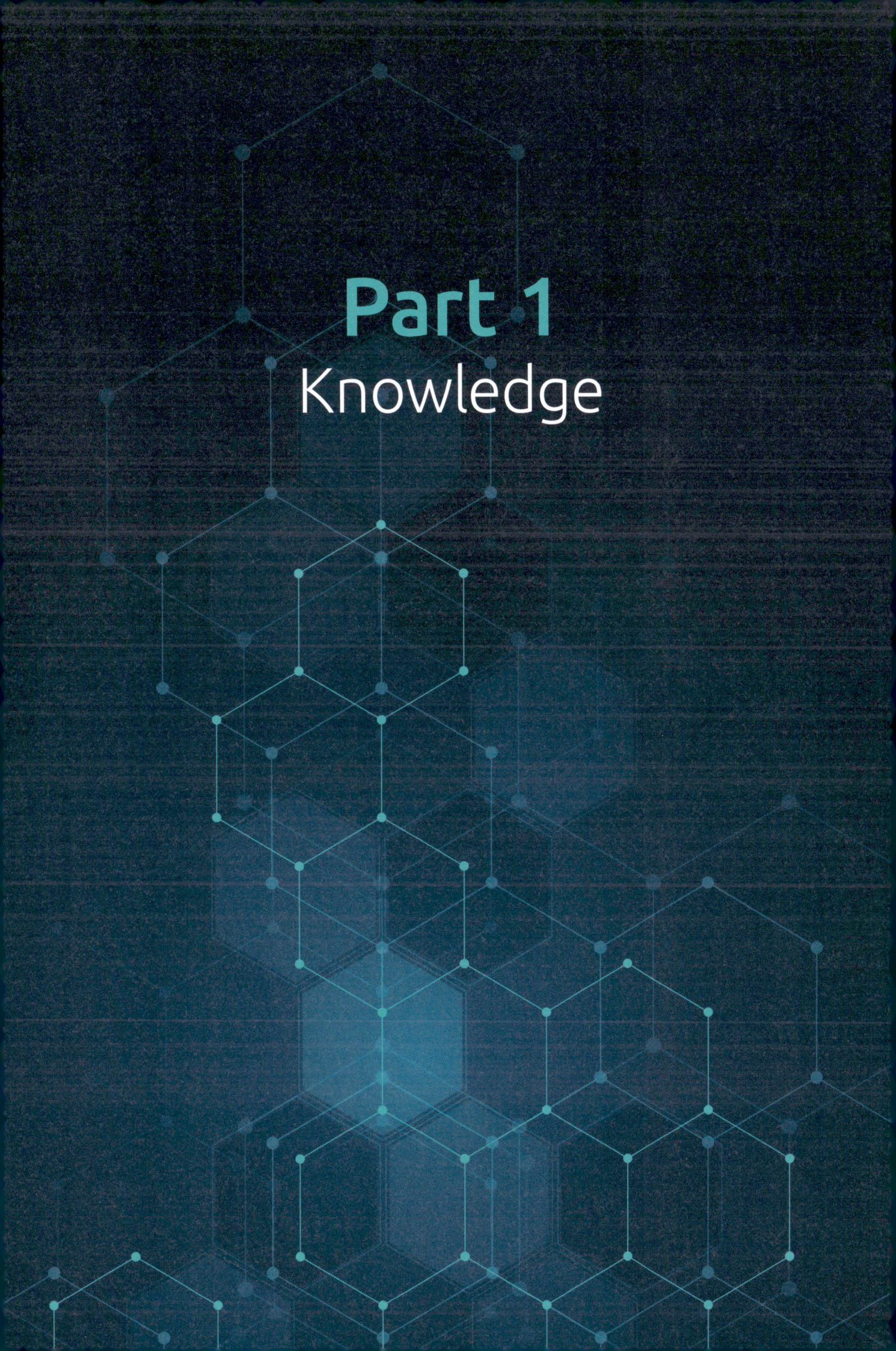
Part 1
Knowledge

1.1 Overview

Part 1 is called Knowledge because it aligns with guides that are frequently referred to as bodies of knowledge. The aim is to define the building blocks of the discipline of P3 management and is based on the concept of a functional analysis. The functions described in Part 1 are split between context and management.

Contextual functions are not directly responsible for achieving project, programme or portfolio objectives but are part of the context which supports that endeavour.

Management functions are the ones that are applied in the completion of projects, programmes and portfolios.

A key concept of Praxis is that the dividing lines between projects, programmes and portfolios are blurred. Some ventures will exhibit characteristics of all three. The underlying principle is that the terms 'project', 'programme' and 'portfolio' simply represent points on a continuum that is described by the complexity of the work being managed. Therefore, wherever appropriate, a function is described in terms of its general application and then by its adaptation to increasing complexity.

Part 1 integrates with Parts 2, 3 and 4, as shown in Figure 1.1. Each function describes the procedures, tools and techniques that can be used in management processes. In return Part 2, Method, provides a structure for the use of the functions within the life cycle.

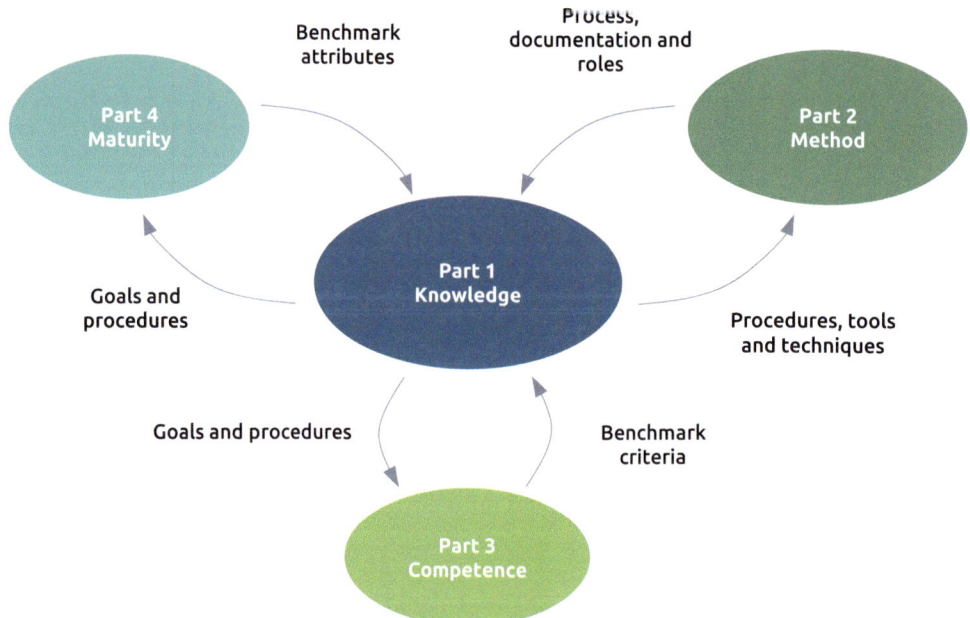

Figure 1.1 Functional framework relationships

The management functions also provide the structure and specific goals for the capability aspect of maturity. The procedures described in each function are used as the basis for defining different levels of capability and the attributes described in the maturity model provide benchmarks for the organisational implementation of the function.

The goals and procedures described in the functions form the basis of the knowledge and performance criteria listed for each competency. In return these provide benchmarks for the individual performance of the function.

1.2 Context

The P3 management context has two aspects that can be likened to nature and nurture.

The nature aspect is referred to as the setting. This deals with factors that define the properties of a project, programme or portfolio. Some of these are concerned with the inherent nature of the work and others with the nature of the surrounding environment. It also addresses the complexity of the work being managed. The setting is the primary factor that decides how the work will be governed.

For those involved in P3 management at a strategic level, the setting is created by external factors and is the starting point for them to nurture both the governance of specific projects, programmes and portfolios, and the profession that will deliver them.

Hence, context comprises three components: setting, governance and professionalism, as shown in Figure 1.2.

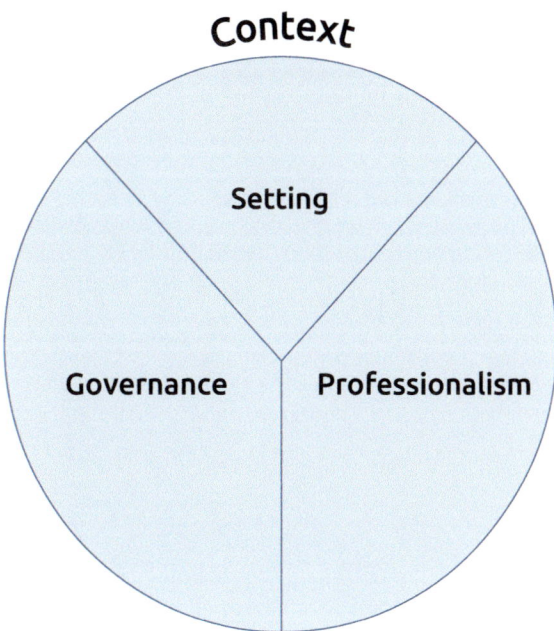

Figure 1.2 The three components of context

1.2.1 Setting

The inherent nature of a project, programme or portfolio is derived from its objectives and how they will be achieved. Some objectives are clear and well defined, and are produced using tried and tested methods and technology. Other objectives are ambiguous and the way they should be produced is uncertain due to unfamiliarity or innovative technology.

These factors are collected together under the title of complexity. This broadly equates to a measure of how difficult the work will be to manage and therefore influences the methods that should be used and the necessary competence of the management team.

The external factors that influence the nature of the work include commercial, organisational and geographical ones. These collectively form the environment.

Whether to govern the work as a project, programme or portfolio is a decision made early in the life cycle and is closely associated with complexity. Once that decision has been made it then forms part of the context in which the Praxis knowledge functions, processes and competencies are applied.

Environment

The way a project, programme or portfolio is governed and managed will depend upon many different external factors. These must be understood by the P3 sponsor and manager at the outset so that the work is managed in an appropriate manner.

The relationships between the host organisation and its component projects, programmes and portfolios have multiple layers. A portfolio will always sit within a 'host organisation'; for example, a company, government department or charity.

Some organisations may provide no co-ordination across projects and programmes at all, in which case each project or programme stands alone within the organisation. Some programmes will be part of a portfolio and some projects will be within a programme, as shown in Figure 1.3. Other projects may simply be part of the portfolio.

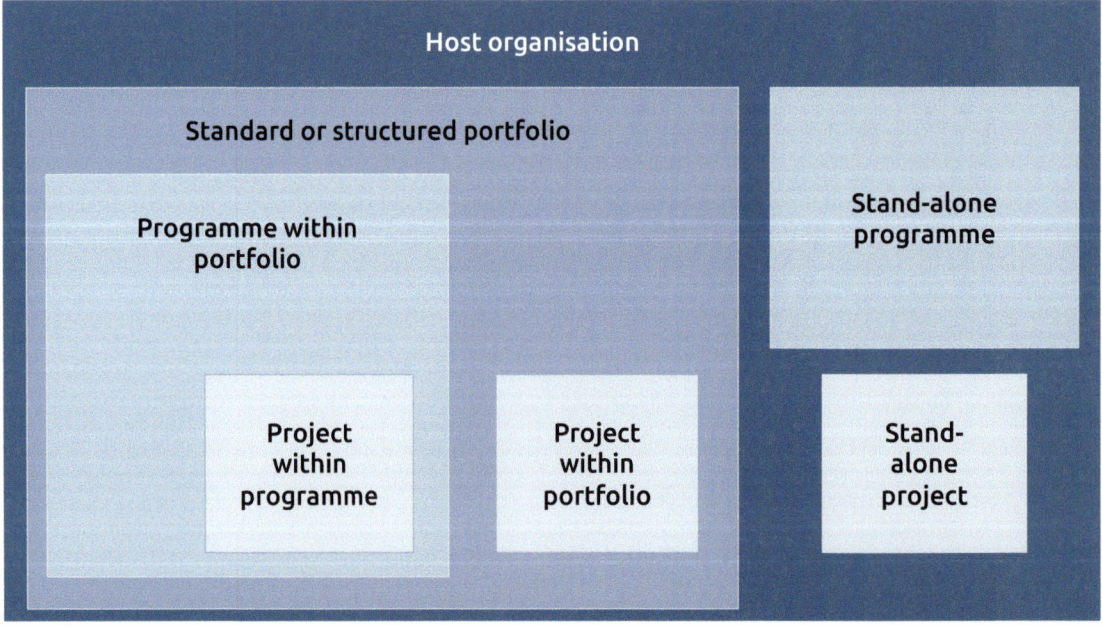

Figure 1.3 Relationships between the host organisation and its projects, programmes and portfolios

From a contractual point of view, projects are often delivered by a contracting organisation on behalf of a client. The contracting organisation is given a contract to deliver an output and its involvement ends with the handover of the completed deliverables. The contractor's project may well be a subset of the client's project or programme. In such circumstances a project may be part of two separate portfolios: the client's and the contractor's.

Large, complex projects or programmes may be beyond the capability of any one organisation and require the creation of a joint venture. This can make funding, apportionment of benefits and stakeholder management much more complex.

Projects, programmes and portfolios exist in both the public and private sectors and may be for commercial or not-for-profit organisations.

All these aspects of the environment have a significant influence on how risk, innovation and value are perceived.

These are just a few of the many factors that make up the P3 environment. Others may include:

- the commercial sector; for example, construction, IT, ship building and pharmaceuticals
- multinational work with different geographical locations and operational languages
- regulated environments where outputs, outcomes, benefits and the way work is performed must conform to published standards
- the particular needs for accountability and transparency in the public sector.

These factors can combine in a myriad of ways to create unique influences on the way a project, programme or portfolio is governed and managed.

The management team needs to assess the environment as early as possible in the life cycle. A typical technique for this assessment is PESTLE, which stands for political, economic, sociological, technical, legal and ecological factors.

As well as considering the effect that the environment has on the project, programme or portfolio, it should also consider the impact of the work on its environment. This principle is inherent in functions such as stakeholder management and change management.

As the work progresses its interactions with its environment will develop and change. The management team must monitor this and identify issues and opportunities that arise.

Projects, programmes and portfolios

Project, programme and portfolio are terms used to describe typical combinations of complexity and environment that require distinguishable approaches to governance.

The terms have been used in various ways since the origins of modern project management in the 1950s. Many argue that there is no need to distinguish between the three and that the term 'project' is sufficient to cover the entire range of initiatives that an organisation may undertake.

The use of the three terms is a useful mechanism for describing three points in a continuous range, much as it is sometimes useful to refer to 'colour' and at other times useful to refer to the primary colours of red, blue and yellow. The world is seen as a vast number of colours that are combinations of the three primaries. So it is with P3 management. Different initiatives and undertakings are combinations of project, programme and portfolio. The art of P3 management is to combine the characteristics of the three to suit each individual situation. This happens when competent people work in a mature organisation.

> A company's head office staff are spread across multiple offices. This is seen as inefficient and the objectives for changing the situation may be expressed in different ways.
>
> An output could be a new corporate HQ building with the outcome being staff co-located and operational in the new HQ. The resulting benefits would include reduced staff travel between offices and reduced facilities management costs.

Projects, programmes and portfolios (P3) are discrete packages of work that are managed in order to achieve defined objectives. The way a package of work is managed depends upon its context.

Organising a small exhibition shares the same basic principles as organising the Olympic Games but these events present very different managerial challenges. Delivering a construction project to a client will need a different approach to internally managing an acquisition.

The key distinguishing factor between a project, a programme and a portfolio is the complexity of the scope. The scope of projects, programmes and portfolios is initially expressed as a set of objectives. These may be expressed as outputs, outcomes or benefits, although outcomes are primarily a stepping stone from outputs to benefits rather than an end in themselves.

Work leading to a single output (i.e. low complexity of scope) is typically referred to as a project. Work that combines multiple projects with change management to deliver benefits (i.e. higher complexity of scope) is considered to be a programme.

Projects and programmes are similar in that they are unique, transient endeavours, undertaken to achieve planned inter-related objectives. This similarity is reflected in the fact that Praxis defines common life cycle processes that can be used in both cases.

> A pharmaceutical or utility company may have a regulated portfolio and a non-regulated portfolio. Either portfolio could be standard or structured.
>
> A construction company may have a portfolio of client projects and another of internal projects. The client portfolio will probably be a standard one while the internal one may be structured.

Portfolios are different in that they are collections of projects and programmes whose objectives may be completely independent or related only at a strategic level. Praxis defines two types of portfolio:

- **A standard portfolio** comprises a set of independent projects and/or programmes. The main objective of co-ordinating a standard portfolio is to ensure that the component projects and programmes are managed in a consistently effective way.
- **A structured portfolio** comprises a set of projects and/or programmes that are united by a set of common strategic objectives. Structured portfolios have many more inter-relationships between the component projects and programmes and governance must be more rigorous. An example of a structured portfolio would be an organisation that repeatedly implemented the objectives of its strategic planning cycle through a rolling portfolio life cycle.

An organisation may have multiple portfolios distinguished by environment, geography or operating division.

The key to achieving capability maturity in P3 management is to tailor the approach to each set of circumstances. The first step is to choose the overall governance approach based on the complexity of the scope. Within this, the procedures, techniques, documents and competencies should be adapted to suit each individual set of circumstances.

Complexity

Complexity is an indicator of the inter-relationships within a project, programme or portfolio that affect the way it will be managed and the skills needed to manage it. Since all projects, programmes and portfolios are made up of many inter-related functions and processes they are all, by the dictionary definition, complex. But of course some are more complex than others.

There is recognition that degrees of complexity require different managerial approaches and skills but there is no absolute scale of measurement. To a large degree complexity is in the eye of the beholder.

While there are attempts within the profession to define complex and non-complex work in a binary way, Praxis takes the view that complexity is a continuous scale applicable to different areas of P3 management. Degrees of complexity influence the way that functions, methods and competencies are tailored.

Projects and programmes exhibit differing degrees of complexity. Portfolios have a degree of inherent complexity due to their scale but mainly reflect the complexity of their component projects and programmes.

Commonly identified areas of complexity for projects and programmes include:

- **Scope**

    This perhaps is the most obvious area of complexity. It can range from the production of a single output to the delivery of a complex concoction of inter-related outputs, outcomes and benefits and all points in between.

    Complexity of scope should not be confused with that of scale. The construction of a major road may take a long time and cost a great deal but be less complex (in terms of scope) than a much smaller exercise in business change, with associated technology and social change.

    It is the complexity of scope that is most influential in the choice of life cycle and method. In short, the choice as to whether a piece of work will be managed as a project or programme is primarily based on the complexity of the scope.

- **Uncertainty**

    All projects and programmes are, by definition, uncertain. Project and programme management is, therefore, designed to manage uncertainty. This can sometimes give the impression that the discipline is trying to remove uncertainty before embarking on a project or programme. That is not the case. If no endeavour was ever undertaken without removing uncertainty then very little would be done.

Project and programme management embraces uncertainty but must be tailored to ensure that the methods, techniques and resources used are appropriate for the level of uncertainty inherent in the work.

> One way of managing uncertainty of scope is to use a parallel rather than a linear life cycle so that objectives can evolve throughout the life cycle.

Uncertainty may relate to initial assumptions, predictability of outcomes, stability of specifications and a host of other factors.

- **Change**

    Some non-complex projects do not involve any management of change at all. Other projects and programmes will require individuals and groups to change the way they live or work, permanently or just for the duration of the work.

    The amount of change can be viewed in terms of its breadth and its depth. The breadth of change relates to the number and range of people who will be required to change. The broader the change, the larger the stakeholder community and the wider the range of support and opposition to the work. The work may only affect a small number of people in a single department or a large community covering multiple disciplines or organisations on an international scale.

    The depth of change refers to the degree to which people have to change, or the impact it has upon them. Examples of significant change are where business change leads to loss of jobs or an infrastructure project displaces people from their homes.

- **Innovation**

    Innovation can be in the technical approach to the work or in the management methods.

    Technical innovation is the more obvious. In a world where technology moves at an ever-increasing pace, there will always be projects and programmes that either create the new technology or are the first to put it into practice.

    It is also important to consider 'innovative' as a relative term. What is innovative for one organisation may not be so for another. An organisation that is very mature at delivering projects may have never delivered a programme before, so to that organisation, programme management is an innovative approach and is therefore complex.

- **Dynamics**

    The degree of complexity in a project or programme is, of course, subject to change. The web of inter-relationships will vary over the life cycle. Some work operates in a stable environment while some is subject to many kinds of external change, whether it be political, social, technical or so on.

Any attempt to categorise so many inter-related aspects of a project, programme or portfolio is bound to be purely illustrative. Different sources list different areas of complexity and there is no definitive model. In fact, attempting to define a general and definitive model is a somewhat pointless exercise since complexity itself is so complex. Where complexity models can work well is in a closed environment; for example, an organisation may develop a complexity model for its own range of work. This can help with decisions like matching a project with a suitably experienced project manager or how much investment should be made in the governance infrastructure.

Ultimately the point of understanding complexity is to know the diversity of work that can be tackled with P3 management and the need to tailor all aspects of the discipline to specific circumstances.

1.2.2 Governance

General

The word 'governance' clearly derives from the practice of governing a political state by its government.

In recent years the concept of corporate governance has taken the term and applied it to the commercial world. There are many different definitions of governance but they all include certain key elements, all of which can be adapted and applied to the governance of projects, programmes and portfolios. The goals of P3 governance are therefore to:

- provide a system of good practice by which projects, programmes and portfolios will be managed
- balance the differing needs of all stakeholders
- monitor the actions of management to mitigate the risk of inappropriate actions
- clearly define roles and responsibilities and ensure they are performed by competent people
- ensure ethical behaviour and promote transparency.

P3 governance is a necessary component of corporate governance. This is increasingly demanded by shareholders, clients and government. Many organisations have to comply with external regulations and legislation (e.g. the UK Corporate Governance Code and Sarbanes-Oxley in the USA).

Initially, governance may appear to be another layer of managerial bureaucracy but the benefits of good governance include the optimisation of investment, avoidance of common reasons for failure and motivation of staff.

Good governance minimises the risk arising from change and will help maximise the benefits. It also promotes the continued development of the discipline and profession of project, programme, and portfolio management.

All topics within the Praxis framework contribute towards good governance. However, the key areas covered in this section are:

- **P3 management** the methods that deliver projects, programmes and portfolios
- **Knowledge management** the organisation's ability to capture, develop and improve its capability and maturity
- **Life cycle** the structure underpinning delivery
- **Capability maturity** the development of increasing levels of effectiveness and efficiency
- **Sponsorship** the link between P3 management, strategic management and business as usual.

Important functions from other sections include:

- **Stakeholder management** Although this is usually discussed in the context of specific projects and programmes the principles can equally be applied to stakeholders in the P3 management process.
- **Ethics** Ensuring that all members of the P3 organisation act in the best interests of stakeholders.

Governance begins with the host organisation whose board must ensure that P3 management is visibly and proactively promoted.

Many different organisational structures may be created to 'own' P3 management (or aspects of it). Terms such as project management office (PMO), project, programme and portfolio support office (P3O), project services, centre of excellence (CoE) or community of practice (CoP) are all in common use.

The name often reflects the scope of responsibilities. For example, a project support office (PSO) provides predominantly administrative support to a project; a centre of excellence will usually concentrate on improving capability maturity and continuing professional development (CPD), while a PMO may effectively be the same as a portfolio management organisation.

Projects, programmes and portfolios

The application of the principles of governance is not dependent on having a corporate approach. Just because a less mature organisation does not have an established P3 governance structure, projects and programmes are not exempt from applying good governance.

Where centrally driven governance is not in place, the project or programme team should take responsibility for governance itself.

The sponsor is responsible for ensuring that governance mechanisms are in place. Periodically checking that these are being applied is referred to as assurance. This should be performed by someone external to the management team who reports directly to the sponsor.

The path to capability maturity for most organisations will start with inconsistent governance across the informal portfolio of projects and perhaps programmes.

As the organisation develops its P3 capability, programmes will be formed that include projects with different approaches to governance. Similarly, portfolios will be formed from projects and programmes with different approaches. The risk of allowing component projects or programmes to continue unchanged has to be balanced against the benefits of adopting a consistent approach across the programme or portfolio.

Some organisations will develop one portfolio comprising all the programmes and projects it undertakes. The governance of the portfolio will then drive the governance of all component projects and programmes.

Large organisations may have multiple portfolios and there may be good reasons for having different governance frameworks, perhaps due to geographical, political or regulatory contexts.

However, the core values should be consistent across the organisation and compatible with organisational governance.

Governance can be tricky where two or more organisations with different cultures combine in a joint venture to run a portfolio. In cases such as this there should be carefully agreed:

- arrangements covering decision-making and joint authority for managing contacts with owners, stakeholders and third parties
- business cases that reflect the apportionment of risk and reward
- arrangements that recognise existing governance arrangements and the technical strengths and weaknesses of the co-owners
- approval mechanisms that give the owners the opportunity to re-evaluate their participation
- procedures for reporting, independent reviews and dispute resolution.

Project, programme and portfolio management

General

Project, programme and portfolio management (P3 management) is the application of methods, procedures, techniques and competence to achieve a set of defined objectives.

The goals of P3 management are to:

- deliver the required objectives to stakeholders in a planned and controlled manner
- govern and manage the processes that deliver the objectives effectively and efficiently.

Investment in effective P3 management will provide benefits to both the host organisation and the people involved in delivering the work. It will:

- increase the likelihood of achieving the desired results
- ensure effective and efficient use of resources
- satisfy the needs of different stakeholders.

A consistent approach to P3 management, coupled with the use of competent resources is central to developing organisational capability and maturity. A mature organisation will successfully deliver objectives on a regular and predictable basis.

Project and programme management

Projects and programmes are very similar in that they are unique, transient endeavours, undertaken to achieve a set of stated objectives. The distinction between a project and a programme is mainly made in order to accommodate different degrees of complexity of scope. The differences in project management and programme management mirror this distinction.

The central elements of both project and programme management are:

- having a clear reason why the work is necessary
- capturing requirements, specifying objectives, estimating resources and timescales
- preparing a business case to explain that the work is desirable, achievable and viable

- securing funding for the work
- developing and implementing management plans
- leading and motivating the management and delivery teams
- monitoring and controlling scope, schedule, finance, risk and resources
- maintaining good relations with stakeholders
- closing the project or programme in a controlled manner when appropriate.

Components that relate to scope complexity, and are therefore typical characteristics of programme management, are:

- project co-ordination: identifying, initiating, accelerating, decelerating, redefining and terminating projects within the programme
- managing inter-dependencies between projects, and between the change management activity of the projects
- transformation: taking project outputs and managing change within business as usual so that outputs deliver outcomes
- benefits management: defining, quantifying, measuring and monitoring benefits.

The sponsor and manager share responsibility for these elements with the sponsor being ultimately accountable for achievement of the business case.

The manager is responsible for the day-to-day running of the project or programme and needs to be competent in the six aspects of delivery:

- scope management
- schedule management
- finance management
- risk management
- resource management
- if relevant to the scope of the work, change management.

Competence in interpersonal skills such as leadership, influencing, communication and conflict management is also vitally important.

Where the scope of work includes benefits that include organisational change, business change managers are responsible for successful transition and benefits realisation.

Portfolio management

In a standard portfolio, portfolio management will focus on increasing the effectiveness and efficiency of project and programme management across multiple projects and programmes with independent objectives.

The core components of standard portfolio management are:

- establishing an infrastructure to support projects and programmes
- defining management procedures and processes to be used consistently across projects and programmes

- co-ordination of limited resources, by matching demand and supply and optimising allocation of available resources.

In addition to this, a structured portfolio co-ordinates projects and programmes that collectively realise a host organisation's strategic objectives. The goal is to balance the implementation of change and the maintenance of business as usual while optimising the return on investment.

The additional core elements of structured portfolio management are:

- maintaining a balanced portfolio aligned with strategic objectives in changing conditions
- improving delivery of projects and programmes through a co-ordinated, portfolio-wide view of risk, resources, dependencies and schedules
- co-ordinating the need for change with the capacity of different parts of the organisation to absorb change
- reducing costs by removing overlapping and poorly performing projects and programmes.

The management of a structured portfolio must constantly review the balance of investment and benefit, creating and closing projects and programmes as necessary.

Life cycle

General

A P3 life cycle illustrates the distinct phases that take an initial idea, capture stakeholder requirements, develop a set of objectives and then deliver those objectives.

The goals of life cycle management are to:

- identify the phases of a life cycle that match the context of the work
- structure governance activities in accordance with the life cycle phases.

Projects and programmes are the primary mechanisms for delivering objectives, while portfolios are more focused on co-ordinating and governing delivery of multiple projects and/or programmes. As a result the project and programme life cycles have many similarities and follow the same basic approach.

The simplest life cycle is a project life cycle that is only concerned with developing an output, as shown in Figure 1.4.

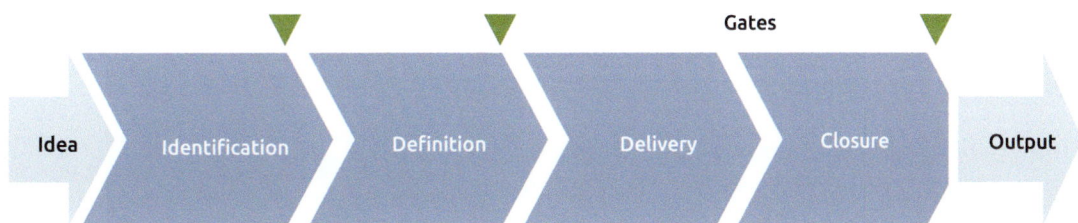

Figure 1.4 Simple project life cycle

It all starts with someone having an idea that is worth investigation. This triggers high-level requirements management and assessment of the viability of the idea to create a business case. At the end of the phase there is a gate where a decision is made whether or not to proceed to a more detailed (and therefore costly) definition of the work.

If the idea is good enough, the work will continue to a detailed definition that produces a full justification for the work. Once again this ends in a gate where a decision is made whether or not to proceed to the delivery phase. Once the output has been produced it is usually subject to an acceptance process before being formally delivered to its new owner. The life cycle comes to an end with the closure of the project.

All outputs are intended to deliver benefits and this can be shown as an additional phase, as shown in Figure 1.5.

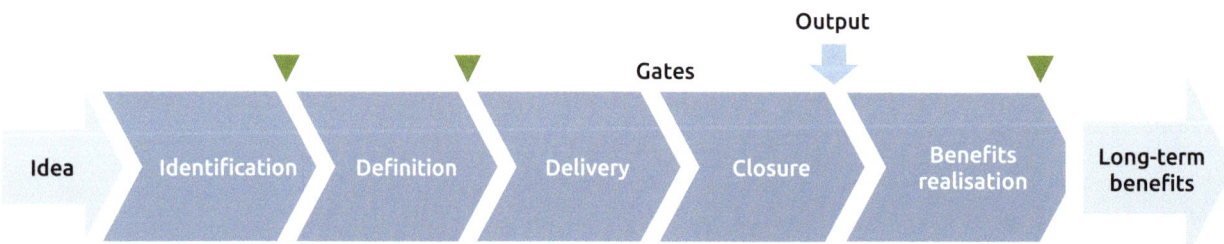

Figure 1.5 The benefits realisation phase

These basic life cycles can be adjusted to many different contexts; for example, in circumstances where the work:

- is performed by a contractor on behalf of a client
- is a project that is part of a programme
- has a scope that can be defined early or scope evolves as the work progresses.

The life cycle is also greatly influenced by the complexity of the scope of work; for example, where the work:

- includes the achievement of outcomes and benefits
- is extensive and needs segmentation.

These more complex contexts require more sophisticated life cycles and these are generally referred to as programmes.

The phased structure of life cycles facilitates the creation of governance mechanisms, such as:

- **Defined processes** The management of each phase can be described as a process made up of a number of relevant activities.
- **Stages and tranches** The delivery phase can be subdivided into packages of work, typically called 'stages' on projects and 'tranches' on programmes.

> Each life cycle phase described in this topic has a corresponding entry in the method, competence and capability maturity sections of Praxis.

- **Gate reviews** These are conducted at the end of a phase, stage or tranche. The sponsor will consider performance to date and plans for the next phase, stage or tranche before deciding whether the business case remains viable, practical and achievable.
- **Post-reviews** Learning from experience is a key factor in maturity. Post-project and post-programme reviews document lessons learned for use in the future.
- **Benefit reviews** These measure the achievement of benefits against the business case.

The two main approaches to the life cycle phases are serial and parallel. The fundamental difference between these is whether requirements and solutions can be defined up front or can evolve throughout the life cycle.

Two factors influence whether a serial or parallel life cycle will be used:

- Firstly, where the deliverables can, or need to be, substantially specified before work starts on delivery, the life cycle will be predominantly serial. Where a specification evolves as work proceeds, the life cycle will be parallel.
- Secondly, even if the work could be fully specified in advance, it can reduce the overall duration of a project or programme if specification work and delivery are run in parallel. This is often called 'fast tracking'.

Parallel life cycles facilitate delivery methods such as agile and concurrent engineering.

Development life cycles work in conjunction with the P3 life cycle. These focus on the specific technical context of the work and how it will be performed, as distinct from how the overall project, programme or portfolio will be managed. Commonly quoted development life cycles include waterfall and 'V'.

Project

The scope of a project life cycle can take various forms to suit the context. Some projects will be part of a programme and will only be concerned with delivering outputs (the traditional project life cycle). Some projects will be expected to incorporate the management of change and realisation of benefits (the extended project life cycle). A few applications (e.g. whole-life costing) may consider the full product life cycle but this is outside the scope of Praxis.

Where a contractor is working for a client, the contractor's 'project' may simply be the development, handover and closure phases of the client's project that includes identification, definition and benefits realisation.

A typical serial project life cycle is shown in Figure 1.6.

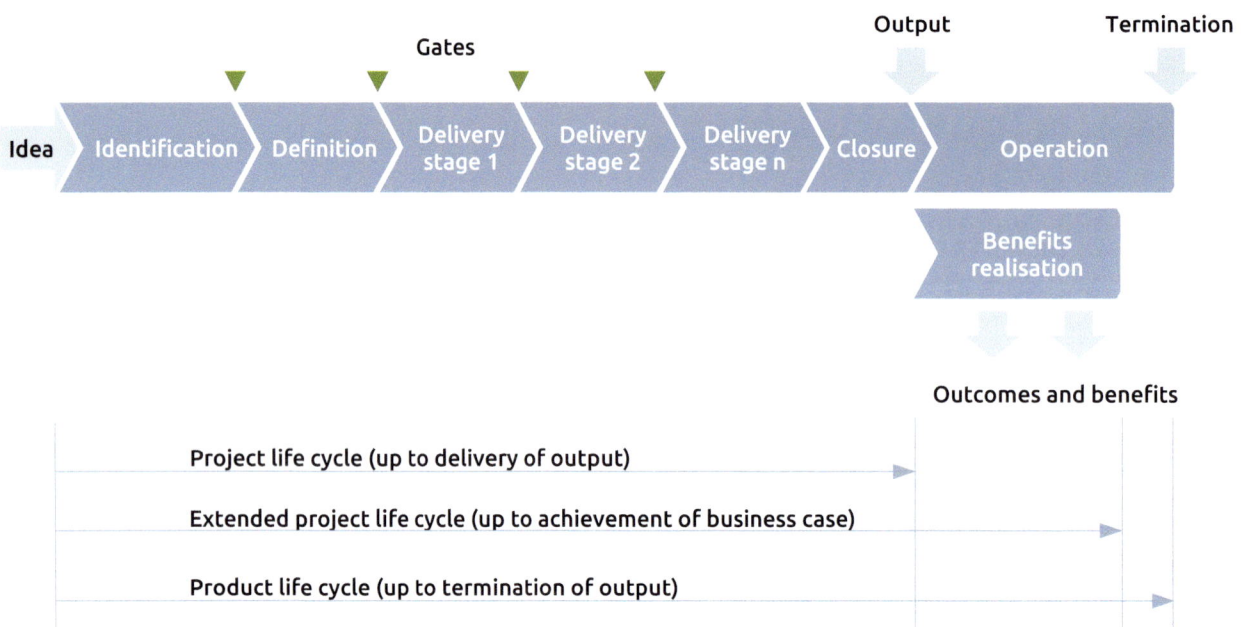

Figure 1.6 Extended life cycles

- **Identification** In this phase the initial idea is developed and a project brief is created. A sponsor is appointed and, if possible, a project manager. Sufficient analysis must be performed to enable senior stakeholders, led by the project sponsor, to make two decisions:
  > Is the project likely to be desirable, achievable and viable?
  > Is it worth investing in the definition phase?
- **Definition** In this phase the requirements are assessed in greater detail and the preferred solution specified. The management plans, delivery plans and business case are developed and these have to be approved by the sponsor before progressing to the next phase.
- **Delivery** This phase may be further broken down into stages. At the end of each stage the continuing justification for the project is be reviewed.
- **Handover and closure** The project outputs are handed over and accepted by the sponsor, client or users as required.
- **Benefits realisation** Where appropriate, a project may include a benefits realisation phase. This is typically done where there is a non-complex, one-to-one relationship between an output and the benefit.

The full product life cycle also includes:

- **Operation** continuing support and maintenance
- **Termination** closure at the end of the product's useful life.

In a parallel project life cycle (see Figure 1.7), most of the phases overlap and there may be multiple handovers of interim deliverables prior to closure of the project.

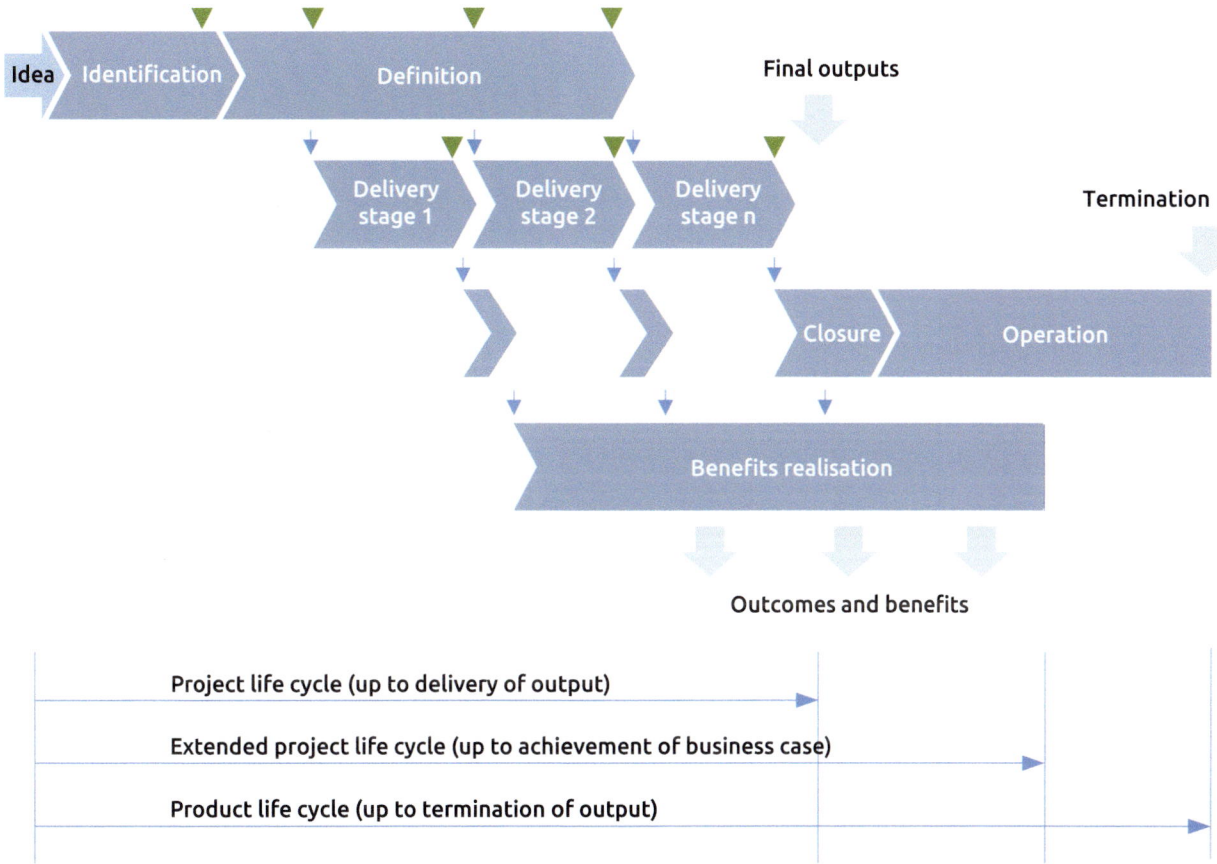

Figure 1.7 Parallel life cycles

The significant characteristic of a parallel life cycle is the feedback between phases. The delivery of the initial work to be defined influences the next piece of definition. Similarly, the experience of handover, benefits realisation and operation may all feed back into prior phases to create a series of iterations. Rather than show a parallel life cycle in chronological terms, it can be illustrated as an iteration that is repeated as often as necessary to deliver the output, after which the project is closed (see Figure 1.8).

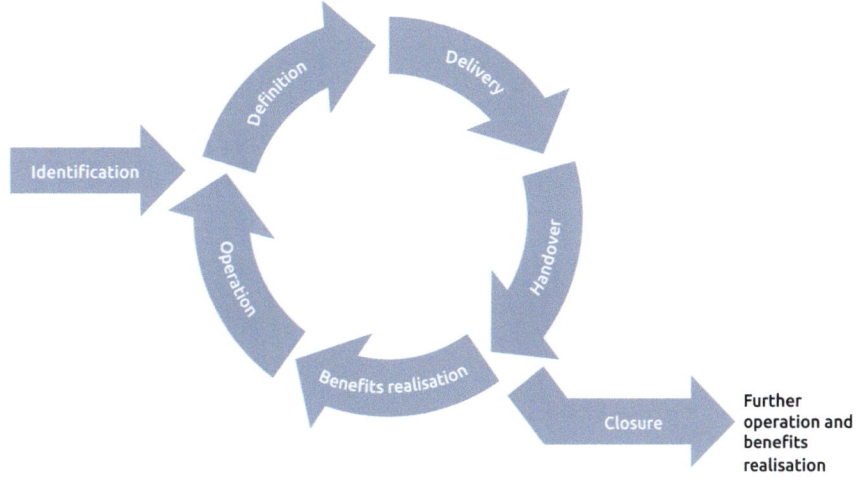

Figure 1.8 Parallel life cycle shown as an iteration

The idea of iterative or parallel working is taken to its logical conclusion in the agile methods commonly used in IT systems development.

Programme

A typical programme life cycle is shown in Figure 1.9.

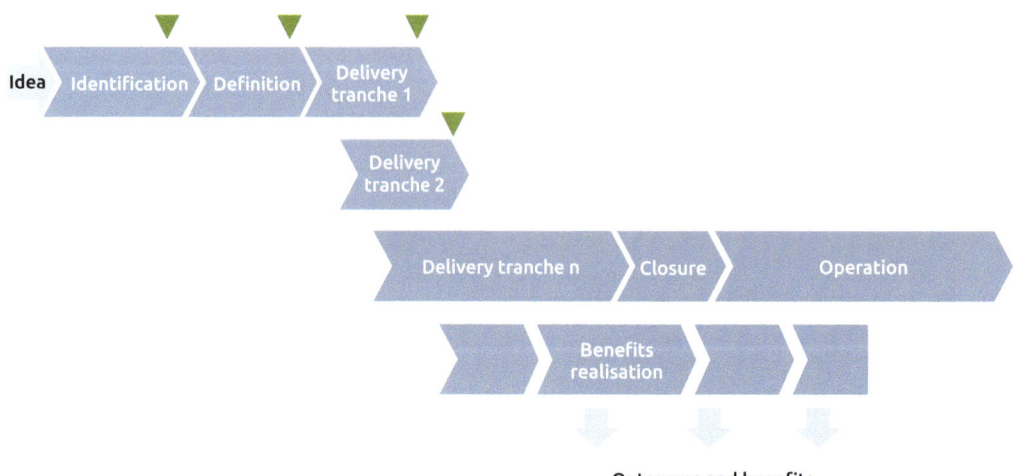

Figure 1.9 Programme life cycle

- **Identification** The vision and outline business case for the programme are created in this phase. A sponsor is appointed to oversee the phase and provide a mechanism for approvals. The expected benefits are outlined and a programme brief is prepared. Sufficient analysis must be performed to enable the main stakeholders, led by the programme sponsor, to make two decisions:
  > Is the programme likely to be viable?
  > Is it definitely worth investing in the definition phase?
- **Definition** The vision is developed into a detailed description of the end state of the programme, often referred to as a blueprint. The management plans, delivery plans and business case are developed so that the sponsor and key stakeholders can make an informed decision whether to proceed with the programme.
- **Delivery** This phase is usually broken into groups of projects, called tranches, that each deliver beneficial change in their own right. A review at the end of each tranche assesses the continuing justification for the programme.
- **Benefits realisation** As new outputs are delivered by projects, transformation work has to be done to ensure new ways of working become embedded in business as usual. Benefits will be measured and compared with the baseline in the business case. This phase is segmented to reflect the fact that the change management necessary to realise benefits is not constant and will fluctuate in level.
- **Closure** Of the last projects, of budgets and demobilising the programme management and delivery teams.

The realisation of benefits will usually continue after the closure of the programme. Some members of the programme team (typically the programme sponsor and business change managers) will continue in their roles to ensure that benefits are realised as required by the business case.

Programme life cycles are inherently parallel. Although the definition phase will produce sufficient detail to authorise delivery, each tranche and project will instigate further detailed definition. As each project delivers outputs, benefits realisation will run in parallel with the programme delivery phase.

Portfolio

Unlike projects and programmes, portfolios are less likely to have a defined start and finish. Portfolio management is a more continual cycle co-ordinating projects and programmes, as shown in Figure 1.10. It may, however, be constrained by a strategic planning cycle that reviews strategy over a defined period. If an organisation has, for example, a three-year strategic planning cycle, then the portfolio cycle will have compatible time constraints.

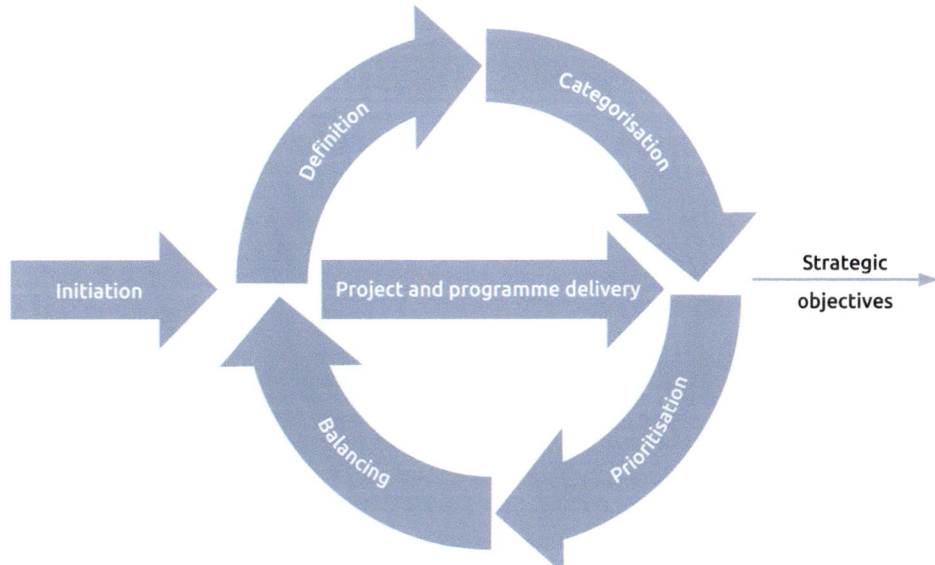

Figure 1.10 Portfolio management as a continual cycle

The aim of the portfolio is to co-ordinate projects and programmes:

- **Initiation** This is a one-off phase that represents the point at which the host organisation decides to set up a portfolio. It is where the infrastructure is created that enables the portfolio cycle to operate.

The portfolio life cycle is inherently parallel. At any point in time the emphasis may be on one phase or another, but aspects of all will be undertaken simultaneously:

- **Definition** The projects, programmes and change to business as usual required to meet portfolio objectives are identified and evaluated in a selection process that maximises the effectiveness and efficiency of the portfolio.
- **Categorisation** The projects and programmes may be organised into 'sub-portfolios' or groups that share certain characteristics, such as alignment with particular strategic objectives.

> In the Praxis process model these four parallel phases are combined within the portfolio management process.

- **Prioritisation** Priorities can be set by strategic objective, return on investment or any other chosen metric. On the assumption that no organisation has sufficient resource to do everything it wants, the prioritisation process forms the basis of the next phase.
- **Balancing** The portfolio must be balanced in terms of risk, resource usage, cash flow and impact across the business.

Portfolio management incorporates the overall governance of projects and programmes within the host organisation. The portfolio management team may be responsible not only for co-ordinating the projects and programmes to deliver strategic objectives, but also for improving the maturity of P3 management.

Sponsorship

General

Sponsorship provides ownership of, and accountability for, the business case and ensures that the work is governed effectively.

The goals of sponsorship are to:

- provide ownership of the business case
- act as champion for the objectives of the project, programme or portfolio
- make go/no-go decisions at relevant points in the life cycle
- address matters outside the scope of the manager's authority
- oversee assurance
- give ad-hoc support to the management team.

There are various names given to the role that provides sponsorship, such as: executive, senior responsible owner or client. In Praxis the role is referred to as the sponsor.

A common failure in less mature organisations occurs when the role of sponsor is not taken seriously. It must be an active role, fulfilled by someone who is committed to performing the activities set out in the sponsorship process.

It will depend upon the context of the work whether sponsorship is provided by an individual alone or with the support of others.

Where a sponsor is supported by other managers they are commonly referred to as a project or programme board. Within a board the sponsor retains ownership of, and accountability for, the business case.

While the sponsor's primary role is to ensure that the business case continues to justify the work throughout the life cycle, this would not be possible without an effective working relationship with the project or programme manager. To the extent that, if the business case ceases to justify continuing investment, the sponsor needs to work with the manager to redefine or prematurely close the project or programme.

This relationship is illustrated by the links between the sponsorship process and the other processes. In fact there is a close relationship between those links and each of the sponsorship goals.

The sponsor usually has responsibility to others within the host organisation or perhaps an external client. This responsibility includes ensuring that the work is being managed effectively. The sponsor does this through assurance, which is an independent review of the management of the work.

A sponsor must be someone who:

- has the credibility to provide leadership that crosses corporate and departmental boundaries
- is genuinely enthusiastic about the objectives of the project or programme
- is able and willing to commit time and energy to the fulfilment of the role.

Although sponsors do not have to be ex-project or programme managers, their job will be a great deal easier if they have a good understanding of the manager's role.

Projects, programmes and portfolios

The role of the sponsor must reflect the context and complexity of the work. Ideally, the sponsor will be appointed soon after the issue of the mandate. The role then continues through until the end of the life cycle. On non-complex projects this will be once the final output has been completed and handed over. On projects and programmes that include benefits within their scope the sponsor will typically remain in post until the benefits realisation process is complete and the business case has been achieved.

Where a project is performed by a supplier organisation on behalf of a client, it is often the case that the sponsor is from the client organisation and the manager is from the supplier. In this situation it can be useful to have a senior representative of the supplier working with the sponsor on a project or programme board.

The stakeholder environment on a project or programme is independent of the complexity of its scope. Even small projects can have difficult stakeholders to deal with. The seniority and credibility of the sponsor must reflect the complexity of the stakeholder environment. Excellent communication and influencing skills will be needed, especially where there is opposition to change.

In the programme and portfolio environment an individual may combine sponsorship and managerial roles. For example, a programme manager may act as sponsor to the programme's component projects. In fact, on a large complex project, the relationship between the overall project manager and the project managers of supplier 'sub-projects' is very similar to the sponsor-manager relationship.

At portfolio level the sponsorship role usually expands to cover broader aspects of governance. Hence the corresponding process is called the portfolio governance process.

While it is very unusual for a portfolio to have a single, focused business case, the sponsor of a portfolio is accountable for the overall effectiveness of the component projects and programmes. This is as much about supporting and promoting the discipline and profession of P3 management as it is about the objectives of individual projects and programmes.

A portfolio sponsor must ensure that the portfolio performs consistently in order to deliver the host organisation's strategic objectives. One way of achieving this is by using the capability maturity framework as a catalyst for improvement.

Support

General

Support is a set of specialist and administrative services carried out on behalf of project, programme or portfolio managers. A support infrastructure can be constituted in many different ways, with many different roles within the realm of P3 management. A definitive set of goals for support is impractical but they are generally drawn from the following broad list:

- provide administrative support to P3 managers
- support the governance of P3 management
- provide specialist technical support
- conduct assurance.

Routine administration is required on all projects, programmes and portfolios. On small projects this may be performed by the project manager, but on medium to large projects and all programmes and portfolios a P3 manager needs support in handling day-to-day administration.

Some projects, and most programmes and portfolios, also require specialist skills in areas such as risk, quality or finance.

An administrative support function can operate at different levels depending upon how it is constituted. It may provide:

- administrative help in areas such as planning, risk management and change control
- the secretariat for meetings and logistical services for members of the management team
- technical support including collecting, analysing and presenting progress information, managing inter-dependencies and handling communications with stakeholders
- assurance of governance structures and standard P3 management practices through audits, health checks and phase end reviews.

A more sophisticated support function may also cover:

- provision of subject matter expertise to ensure that there is access to all necessary tools and techniques
- training, coaching and mentoring for the project, programme or portfolio management team
- maintaining the infrastructure, momentum and drive to support communities of practice
- improving, embedding and measuring capabilities to achieve higher levels of maturity
- owning and deploying standard tools and techniques.

The P3 support infrastructure may range from a single person to a large team containing many different roles and specialists including, among others:

- planners and schedulers
- cost engineers
- subject matter experts
- assurance staff
- configuration managers.

The overall infrastructure may be divided into multiple offices, some temporary and some permanent. For example, a support office might provide administrative support to a specific project or programme. This is then disbanded once the work is complete. In contrast, an organisation-wide support office has a permanent support role independent of the creation and completion of any individual piece of work.

The shape of the infrastructure will reflect its context, but its component groups must always have a clearly defined purpose and scope. The roles and levels of authority of these groups must be communicated to the delivery team(s) and reinforced periodically.

Projects, programmes and portfolios

Where a project is part of a programme or portfolio, the project support function will usually be provided by the programme or portfolio office.

On smaller, stand-alone projects that cannot justify the overhead of a support organisation, the administration work will fall on the project manager's shoulders. This can lead to a reaction against 'bureaucracy' when the project manager is asked to spend a lot of time producing standard documentation. Some organisations will have central functions for planning, financial management, procurement, etc., that may be able to provide assistance in these circumstances.

With the support of the sponsor, the project manager of a small, stand-alone project should seek as much help with day-to-day administration as possible. Taking shortcuts in the administration of even the smallest project is often a cause of failure.

Beyond day-to-day management of the project, the project manager should be provided with other types of support. This may include CPD through communities of practice, career advice or managing the transition between one project and the next. It is this broad support for the profession and discipline of project management that is provided by the governance infrastructure.

Programmes or large complex projects are large enough to carry the overhead of a support function and may also have access to a central support function. Programme support functions must have the expertise to cover the additional services required. These typically include supporting change management, benefits management and project interfaces.

The programme management team decides how to constitute the support organisation across the programme; for example, whether one support function will serve the programme and all its component projects, or whether some, or all, projects will have separate project support functions.

Some organisations will have multiple departmental or regional portfolios, while others might have a single, organisation-wide portfolio. In the latter case, the portfolio and the governance infrastructure are effectively the same thing. This is often referred to as a PMO and is a permanent organisational structure with its remit being decided by whether the portfolio is standard or structured.

Knowledge management

General

Knowledge management involves the systematic identification, recording, and distribution of insights and experiences that enable their adoption in new situations.

The goals of knowledge management are to:

- capture useful knowledge from the management of projects, programmes and portfolios
- make tacit knowledge from experienced practitioners available to all
- support capability maturity management and continuous improvement in P3 management.

The most common examples of useful knowledge in P3 management are 'lessons learned'. These should be recorded throughout the life cycle in a lessons log with a particular focus on capturing them during reviews at the end of a stage or tranche.

Reviewing lessons learned from previous projects and programmes is an activity during the identification process. Failure to use the experiences and insights from previous work will often lead to a repeat of past mistakes.

Knowledge management is an important element in developing an organisation's capability maturity. Capturing lessons learned is an attribute of maturity level 3 capability, while implementing an integrated and structured knowledge management system is an attribute of level 4.

Knowledge is usually described as taking one of two forms: tacit and explicit.

Tacit knowledge is the sum of experiences, insights, observations and communications that every person holds in their memory. Clearly, experienced P3 managers, sponsors, business change managers and others will have large amounts of tacit knowledge about P3 management that they use every day to successfully deliver projects and programmes.

A key role of knowledge management is to capture this tacit knowledge and convert it into explicit knowledge. This simply means that it is expressed and recorded in a way that is accessible by those who wish to develop their knowledge and learn from the experience of others.

The users of this explicit knowledge will range from novice project managers to experienced portfolio managers facing new challenges. A mature organisation will foster a culture of learning and development with knowledge management being one of its tools.

> This aspect of knowledge management is the essence of what Praxis is designed to achieve. The taxonomy of Praxis is the foundation on which tacit knowledge from the P3 management community at large can be recorded and made explicit in a highly accessible way.

There are many theories and models of knowledge management, with Nonaka and Takeuchi's being a common example.

Within the P3 management organisation the steps involved in establishing knowledge management include:

- ensuring senior management commitment to the principles of knowledge management
- assurance of the elements of the P3 method that capture and utilise knowledge
- implementing and maintaining a system for storing and maintaining knowledge.

Capturing lessons learned is only one way of creating explicit knowledge and is primarily based on the tacit knowledge available within the organisation.

This should be supplemented with external sources of knowledge through involvement with broader communities of practice including professional bodies.

Knowledge management reduces the inherent risk involved in the management of projects, programmes and portfolios through the use of proven methods and techniques and avoidance of known pitfalls.

It can also motivate management team members who see a vehicle for them to help improve P3 management at an organisational level through their personal contributions.

Projects, programmes and portfolios

In a more mature organisation there should be an existing knowledge management system that all projects, programmes and portfolios can access.

Without this, an individual project has limited opportunity to implement knowledge management unless it is large and complex. Smaller stand-alone projects in less mature organisations rely on individual management team members to apply their tacit knowledge.

In these situations, the host organisation risks losing its capability to manage projects when skilled staff leave. Simple actions to mitigate this risk can include the use of project diaries retained by the organisation and provision of time in which project managers can get together to exchange experiences.

By definition, a programme comprises multiple projects and has the opportunity to record lessons learned from earlier projects so that they can be applied to later projects. It will be down to the programme management team to provide that continuity.

The greatest opportunity for developing robust knowledge management lies within a portfolio. At this level the management team should secure funding for a knowledge management system if it does not already exist within the host organisation as a whole. This would typically be done during the initiation process.

Capability maturity

General

Capability and maturity are usually represented as a model against which an organisation's performance can be measured and improved. Usually referred to as capability maturity models, they describe the essential elements of effective processes and work on the premise that the quality of a system or product is highly influenced by the quality of the process used to develop it.

The goals of capability and maturity management are to:

- assess the ability of an organisation to perform P3 management effectively and efficiently
- identify how the organisation can improve its P3 management
- promote the improvement of P3 management against an independent standard.

The idea of a capability maturity model that describes an organisation's increasing effectiveness in sequential stages was popularised by the Software Engineering Institute (SEI) at Carnegie Mellon University in the USA.

Since the SEI Capability Maturity Model was first published in 1993, the concept has been replicated for many areas of business, including P3 management.

The current version of the SEI model is the CMMI (Capability Maturity Model® Integration). This identifies two scales: one for capability and one for maturity. Capability addresses individual process areas whereas maturity addresses the overarching integrated processes.

> Praxis adapts and applies the principles of CMMI® to the functional and process elements of P3 management.
>
> In the Praxis capability maturity model, knowledge functions are assessed on the capability scale and life cycle processes (which integrate the functions) are assessed on the maturity scale.

The capability scale runs from levels 0 to 3:

- **Level 0 Incomplete** The function is not performed or is partially performed. The goals of the function are not achieved.
- **Level 1 Performed** The function is performed and the goals are partly achieved but the procedures and application are inconsistent.
- **Level 2 Managed** The function is managed in accordance with policy. It is performed by competent people with adequate resources to produce controlled outputs. The function is monitored for adherence to its description.
- **Level 3 Defined** The function is consistently managed using tailored versions of the organisation's standard approach. Lessons are captured and contribute to organisational knowledge.

The maturity scale identifies the stages in an organisation's development from its initial chaotic attempts to manage projects, programmes and portfolios, to a point where most initiatives succeed and the organisation has the ability to improve continuously:

- **Level 1 Initial** Processes are ad hoc and occasionally chaotic. The organisation does not provide a stable environment to support functional capability and success depends upon individual effort and heroics. Maturity level 1 organisations often deliver the project, programme or portfolio objectives but frequently exceed budgets and schedules. They have a tendency to overcommit, abandon their processes in times of crisis and be unable to replicate their successes.
- **Level 2 Managed** The relevant functions are managed to capability level 2. The overall life cycle-based process ensures that functional procedures are maintained during times of stress and progress is visible to management at defined points.
- **Level 3 Defined** The relevant functions are managed to capability level 3. Projects, programmes or portfolios tailor functional procedures and perform these within a centrally defined but tailored set of life cycle based processes. The organisation improves processes and procedures.

- **Level 4 Quantitatively managed** Performance metrics are gathered and used to control future performance. Quality and performance is understood in statistical terms.
- **Level 5 Optimising** Continuous process improvement is enabled by quantitative feedback from the process and from piloting innovative ideas and technologies.

The two scales overlap as shown in Table 1.1.

Table 1.1 Overlaps between the capability and maturity levels

Level	Capability levels (functions)	Maturity levels (processes)
0	Incomplete	
1	Performed	Initial
2	Managed	Managed
3	Defined	Defined
4		Quantitatively managed
5		Optimising

The aspiration of most organisations is to achieve maturity level 3, which represents the 'effective organisation'. The return on investment for achieving level 3 is provided by a reduction in time and cost over-runs, greater predictability in the achievement of objectives and a more robust (and therefore less risky) delivery environment.

Levels 4 and 5 are concerned with becoming more efficient; i.e. the benefits of achieving level 3 are retained but less effort is expended in maintaining them.

> The Praxis approach to maturity is similar to the ISO 9000 approach to quality, in that an organisation defines its own required scope of capability maturity against which it will benchmark and improve.

Maturity is sensitive to the context of projects, programmes and portfolios. It should not be necessary to achieve capability or maturity in functions or processes that an organisation does not normally perform.

Any given level of maturity indicates the level of performance in those areas that are appropriate to the organisation's context.

Projects, programmes and portfolios

Projects are the basic building blocks of both programmes and portfolios. It is highly unlikely that an organisation could start to develop a mature approach to delivering programmes and portfolios without first establishing a consistent way of managing projects.

Ideally, programmes are initiated in an organisational environment where project management is already well established and consistent. However, it is not uncommon for an organisation to be managing projects in an inconsistent manner and then collect these together in a programme.

In this instance the programme management team has an opportunity to develop programme-wide governance mechanisms for the component projects (if this has not already been done at portfolio level). In this way, programmes can not only deliver defined organisational change and benefits, but also act as a catalyst for improving the maturity of project management, which in itself leads towards programme management maturity.

In a standard portfolio the emphasis is on developing maturity of projects and programmes through standardised methods and functions. This is sometimes known as 'management of projects'. This approach can achieve maturity level 3; i.e. the overall portfolio of projects and programmes is managed to achieve higher levels of project and programme management maturity.

> A contracting organisation's portfolio is made up of projects and/or programmes performed on behalf of clients. This portfolio is driven by the ability to win contracts rather than the delivery of strategic internal change. This type of standard portfolio may only aspire to level 3 maturity.

Progression to level 5 maturity requires the application of a defined portfolio management process in addition to achieving corresponding levels of maturity for component projects and programmes.

1.2.3 Professionalism

There is a constant and often heated debate within the community about whether P3 management is a profession or not. Those who argue against it are talking about a Profession with a capital 'P' where 'Professionals' need a licence to practise and can be sued for negligence. Doctors, lawyers, accountants, among others, fall into this category of professional.

But there are many other definitions of the term professional, the simplest being that someone is paid to do a job in contrast to an amateur who is not.

P3 management meets many of the requirements of a profession, such as:

- it can be a full-time occupation
- there are university courses for different aspects of P3 management
- associations exist at local, national and international levels
- codes of professional ethics exist and are adhered to
- schemes exist to verify knowledge and competence to practise.

This debate is largely academic. What is important is the attitude of people who manage projects, programmes and portfolios, and no-one would argue that that attitude should not be 'professional' – even if it does only have a small 'p'.

This section of context addresses different aspects of creating a professional attitude among everyone involved in projects, programmes and portfolios. Not just the managers, but team members, sponsors and stakeholders. In Praxis, references to 'the profession' mean those who practise the discipline of P3 management with a professional attitude, where 'the discipline' is the set of methods, tools and techniques employed by the profession.

To promote professionalism, this section describes:

- **Communities of practice** groups of people who come together to exchange knowledge and develop both themselves and the profession
- **Competence** the means by which an individual can understand what they need to do and how roles can be defined
- **Ethics** understanding acceptable behaviour for a professional
- **Learning and development** how competent professionals need to be trained and continuously developed.

Communities of practice

Communities of practice (CoPs) are groups of people who share an interest in P3 management or an aspect of it. The goals of these communities are to:

- share information that helps individuals to develop their skills
- help the profession to collectively evolve and improve.

There are three aspects of a community of practice:

- the domain
- the community
- the practice.

The domain is the common interest. It could simply be P3 management, but there are many examples of more specialised communities of interest, such as risk management or value management. The domain may also refer to a business sector (e.g. construction, IT, local government or pharmaceuticals) or one large organisation.

The community refers to where the CoP draws its members from. There are international, national, regional and local communities of interest. Obvious examples of these are the national and international professional bodies, such as the International Project Management Association (IPMA), the Project Management Institute (PMI®) and the Association for Project Management (APM). Some communities are loosely bound by their membership of social media groups.

The practice is the way that the community shares information on its chosen domain. This could range from formal knowledge management within an organisational CoP to loose discussion groups on social media. In between these two are all manner of communities that may meet to exchange views, organise CPD events, publish newsletters or even offer accreditations.

The nature of CoPs varies widely but all share the objective of transferring knowledge and developing skills. Other benefits of a community include:

- promoting the professionalism of P3 management
- providing a focus for professionals who are often isolated from day-to-day contact with fellow professionals
- the motivational effect of being part of a community of like-minded individuals
- innovative thinking that comes about through shared experience.

It is all too easy for communities to be set up with enthusiasm and then fade away through lack of support. Where an organisation sets up a community of practice as part of its commitment to the discipline and profession of P3 management, it must recognise that the community will need corporate support and ongoing commitment in terms of financial support and allowing P3 managers time to take part.

Competence

Dictionary definitions of competence are relatively straightforward and are simply concerned with an individual's ability to perform a job or role successfully. A competent project manager is, therefore, someone who is able to successfully manage a project. A competent programme manager is someone who can successfully manage a programme.

In the context of the Praxis framework, the goals of competence are to:

- define criteria that enable competence to be identified
- provide a means of integrating functional and process competencies to support capability maturity.

The competence of, for example, a project manager is not a guarantee that a project will be delivered successfully. There are too many other factors at play, not least the competence of the sponsor and members of the management and delivery teams. It is not unreasonable to say that the competence of influential stakeholders is also important – and that is in terms of their competence in the role of stakeholder as opposed to their actual job.

Clearly, successful projects, programmes and portfolios are dependent upon the competence of a wide range of people. That is why the deployment of competent people is a characteristic of capability maturity at level 2.

> Because the deployment of competent people is a characteristic of level 2 capability maturity, the competencies defined in Praxis describe how an individual should perform in an organisation at that level.

Beyond the basic definition as an ability to perform a role, competence is variously defined as being made up of knowledge, experience, performance and behaviour in different combinations and perceived importance.

The idea of an individual being competent leads inevitably to the question, 'What does competent look like?' Many organisations seek to answer this question through a competency framework. This is a structured set of competencies, where a competency is a definition of attributes that an individual must have, or acquire, to perform effectively.

Competencies are defined for topics that make up a discipline. So in the case of the Praxis competency framework, the management functions in the knowledge framework and the processes in the method are the topics for which competencies are defined.

Competency frameworks can be used for a variety of purposes such as:

- defining role descriptions
- competency-based interviewing
- competency assessment to determine learning and development needs
- competency-based appraisals.

In theory, competencies can be defined in terms of knowledge, experience, performance and behaviour. For example, in the function of risk management, the following could be defined:

- **Knowledge** 'Know and understand techniques for assessing threats and opportunities'.
- **Experience** 'Has managed others practising risk assessment on complex projects'.
- **Performance** 'Able to assess the probability and impact of risk events'.
- **Behaviour** 'Prepared to take calculated risk to achieve worthwhile objectives'.

Experience and behaviour are more sensitive to the environment in which the competency is applied, so generic competencies are more often defined in terms of knowledge and performance, leaving experience and behaviour to be added as part of a full role description.

The competencies for every project, programme, portfolio and role within them will vary according to the environment of the work to some degree. The key benefit of a competency framework is that individual competencies can be combined in different ways to create different roles that are appropriate to any given environment.

Therefore, competence for a particular role in a specific environment is a combination of competencies taken from the framework. Even then, the competencies may need to be tailored to suit specific situations.

Ethics

Ethics are the moral principles that govern someone's behaviour or the way they perform an activity. Ethical behaviour could be said to be the cornerstone of competence in a professional environment. For that reason, most professional bodies have a code of conduct and all members must commit to adhere to it.

In the context of Praxis, the goals of ethics are to:

- encourage ethical behaviour in the practitioners of the P3 management discipline
- raise the standards of professionalism by which P3 managers are judged and thereby raise the status of the profession.

One of the inherent problems with ethical behaviour is that it is subjective. What is considered moral and ethical in one culture is not the same as that which is considered moral and ethical in another. As well as professional codes of conduct, there are some statutory requirements in different jurisdictions; for example, the Bribery Act in the UK.

A P3 manager needs to understand the moral values of different stakeholders, as well as the relevant national and international laws. Sometimes, different sets of guidelines may conflict. While legislation clearly takes precedence, a P3 manager must also be aware of where professional codes and company codes may differ. If a professional believes there are conflicts or differences in the various codes, then advice or direction should be sought from a relevant authority.

Behaving ethically is not just about following guidelines and keeping within the law. It permeates all the competencies of P3 management. Obvious connections can be made to areas such as influencing and negotiation where someone will very quickly lose trust and respect if they are seen to act unethically.

The need for ethical behaviour is not limited to the manager; a project, programme or portfolio's values, or code of conduct, must be clearly articulated, understood and maintained by all. This can be achieved through training, specific guidance and assurance.

It is not just the management processes that need to be considered. The P3 manager should also be aware of the impact of the outputs, outcomes and benefits of the work. One important example of this is the focus on environmental sustainability in all aspects of project, programme and portfolio delivery.

With society in general demanding increasing transparency and expecting professionals to behave in an ethical manner, the P3 manager needs to be able to take and explain ethical decisions in a way that maintains the commitment of all stakeholders.

Learning and development

Learning and development encompass the continual improvement of competence at all levels of an organisation. The goals of learning and development in an organisation are to:

- develop competent individuals
- encourage an environment of continual professional development
- promote the contribution of learning and development to the capability maturity of the organisation.

Within an organisation, learning and development needs are set by performance management. This determines the relationship between people's ability levels and the aspirations and expectations of the organisation. Identification, application and monitoring of learning within projects, programmes and portfolios develops the organisation's delivery capability.

> Praxis promotes the idea that an organisation should aspire to capability maturity. The Praxis competencies list performance and knowledge criteria that align with the capability maturity definitions. This allows development of individuals and development of the organisation to progress simultaneously.

The gap between expectation and ability is normally addressed by planned learning and development programmes. These might involve a short-term response, such as a one-day course, or a long-term approach, such as a three-year, part-time MSc.

The skills that need to be developed might be specifically job-related, as in the use of a software tool or a management process, or aimed at a specific project, programme or portfolio-related qualification. In the P3 environment, learning and development also often take the form of courses that lead to professional qualifications.

Organisations vary widely in their ability to deliver learning and development. The 'blue chip' approach may involve the creation of an 'academy' or 'university' offering a wealth of courses and qualifications. A small organisation, however, will rely more on internal support and mentoring and provision by external providers.

The scope and timescale of individual work commitments will directly affect the nature of learning and the type of development activity. Most organisations will use a variety of approaches, selecting the right one for their needs and those of their staff.

P3 managers have a role in providing an environment that supports the learning and development of staff. Individually, they will also be involved in performance reviews and suggestions for future career development.

P3-based organisations and their managers realise the need to have a well-educated and skilled workforce. However, this does not mean that individuals can abrogate responsibility for their own CPD. An organisation's performance management system will typically encourage individuals and their supervisors to identify gaps in knowledge and skills.

Individuals may be part of a project, programme or portfolio for several years and their welfare needs to be managed accordingly. This requires appropriate staff induction, career development plans, skills needs analysis, and development and training.

Organisations need to recognise that CPD for staff remains an overarching principle. P3 managers must recognise the need for individuals to undertake CPD to keep pace with changing standards, legislation, tools, techniques and methods.

CPD in its most basic form involves:

- identifying current and future needs
- setting specific learning objectives
- planning activities to support development
- recording activities and achievements.

Professional bodies play an important role by maintaining records of attendance and dossiers of CPD certificates for their members. These can be used to both structure personal development plans and highlight an individual's commitment to the profession.

The learning and development needs of organisations, teams and individuals are in a constant state of flux as they attempt to meet the challenges and competitive forces of the marketplace. This requires a dynamic approach to learning and development, using all the tools available.

1.3 Management

While section 1.2, Context, includes a functional breakdown of the landscape of P3 management, this section deals with how people and work are managed to achieve objectives. Management is split into interpersonal skills and delivery.

Interpersonal skills are the functions that are least specific to P3 management. They are life skills that are used in all walks of our personal and professional lives. The descriptions in this section draw upon many behavioural models that were not originally devised in the P3 management context but are relevant. Each function is described as it applies to P3 management in general and the Praxis framework in particular.

Section 1.3.2, Delivery, addresses those areas that are traditionally thought of as being the essence of P3 management. They are all about the mechanics of converting ideas into reality and dealing with the many difficulties that lie along that path.

Every management function has a corresponding competency definition in Praxis. Every delivery function also has a corresponding capability.

1.3.1 Interpersonal skills

When the complexities of human behaviour are subdivided into distinct functions it can inevitably become somewhat artificial and theoretical. But P3 sponsors, managers and team members need to understand the mechanisms by which people relate to, and interact with, other people. Simple models such as the ones referenced in this section are a useful starting point for each individual as they build their own interpersonal skill set.

The wheel in Figure 1.11 shows the seven interpersonal skills covered by Praxis. They can be loosely arranged into those that are primarily team oriented and those that are primarily stakeholder oriented.

Figure 1.11 The seven interpersonal skills of managers

The wheel takes the P3 manager as its starting point, hence leadership appears at the top.

A manager needs to lead and motivate their management team and delivery teams. This will be through visionary leadership (ensuring people are committed to the objectives of the work) and managerial leadership (delegating work and developing teamwork).

The manager must also lead the stakeholder community, who do not collectively form a team and to whom delegation is rarely appropriate. When dealing with stakeholders, influencing and negotiation are more relevant. If the stakeholders are particularly senior or vital to the achievement of objectives, the P3 manager will inevitably call upon the support of the sponsor.

Whether the manager is delegating work to a team or influencing stakeholders, conflict will inevitably arise in some form. The manager will need to have conflict management skills no matter how well honed their other interpersonal skills may be.

Naturally, at the heart of all human interactions is communication.

If a manager can apply these skills with professionalism and within an ethical framework, they will engender trust and respect.

The fundamental principles of interpersonal skills do not vary across the range of projects, programmes and portfolios. However, the context and organisational structures do change and this leads to different challenges and different emphases in their application.

Communication

General

Communication is the means by which information is exchanged and a common understanding achieved. Its goals are to:

- impart relevant information
- ensure the information is understood.

In the P3 environment these basic goals are a means to:

- ensuring that members of the management team understand the objectives and their role in achieving them
- building relationships with stakeholders
- minimising conflict by avoiding misunderstandings
- developing confidence and trust
- maintaining the commitment of stakeholders and team members
- effective control of the work throughout the life cycle.

Communication comes in many forms. The obvious primary forms are written, verbal and body language but these are modified by many other factors, such as whether they are formal or informal; active or passive; conscious or unconscious.

Models such as Berlo's provide simple structures from which an understanding of the many complex aspects of communication can be developed.

In its basic form, communication involves the person who originates a message; a channel for communicating that message; and a person who receives the message.

Looking at the P3 manager and sponsor as the primary sources of communication, the first thing these people must do is decide what needs to be communicated and to whom. This principle is embodied, for example, in stakeholder management, where a great deal of time is spent in seeking to understand who needs to have what information and when. How that translates to different messages given to different people is embodied in the communication plan.

The way someone creates a message and the way someone else receives that message will depend on numerous factors, such as their personal values, vested interests, frame of mind and even their personal 'learning style' (someone's learning style indicates whether they respond better to auditory, visual or kinaesthetic channels of communication).

The P3 manager and sponsor must take all these factors into account when deciding on the content and structure of their communications.

The range of available channels of communication is increasing all the time. Traditional channels such as paper, telephone and face-to-face are being supplemented and often replaced by email, social media and tele-conferencing. Every new channel brings its own opportunities and challenges for communication.

All communication will encounter barriers. This could be as simple as different languages in international teams or trying to be heard in a noisy environment. Habitual use of acronyms and jargon can make communication more efficient but can alienate those who are not familiar with it. Hidden barriers can include a history of conflict or lack of trust. All of these must be considered as part of the communication process.

As with any framework for managing projects, programmes and portfolios, Praxis contains many document definitions and associated templates. These are vehicles for communication but should not be seen as a means of shortcutting the principles outlined above. While consistency of documentation is very useful it must not become the primary objective. If a particular message needs to be structured and presented in a different way, the standard document must be tailored or even disregarded in favour of something more effective.

This is why capabilities and maturities at level 2 often use phrases like 'standard reports are distributed at regular intervals' and at level 3 use phrases like 'standard documentation is adapted to suit the context'.

Anyone performing assurance or assessment of capability maturity needs to understand this. Since communication is the means by which tacit knowledge is converted to explicit knowledge, it is also useful to view this in the context of the broader knowledge management function.

Projects, programmes and portfolios

The basic principles of communication are exactly the same regardless of the complexity of the project, programme or portfolio. However, the way those principles are applied will be greatly affected by the context of the work.

On small, non-complex projects it may well be that most communication is verbal. This is fine as long as key decisions are documented and communicated in a form that relies less on memory and interpretation.

As projects become bigger and more complex, the use of standard documentation becomes more important. This makes it easier for more people to be involved in preparing and receiving consistent information; subject, of course, to appropriate tailoring to suit the context.

On large, complex projects with many components, or on programmes with multiple projects, the audiences for communications become large and diverse. Careful planning of communication becomes ever more important, as does the co-ordination of different messages to ensure consistency. At this point the P3 manager may have to supervise others who are doing the bulk of the communication, perhaps as part of a dedicated support team within the project or programme.

Programmes and portfolios will create large amounts of communication using multiple channels: some formal but most of it informal.

The management of the formal information can be handled through formal information management procedures. The effectiveness of the informal communication depends upon the competency of individuals, the leadership of the P3 managers and the maturity of the organisation.

At portfolio level, the management team needs to focus on co-ordination of communication but also, perhaps more importantly, creating a culture of effective communication within an ethical framework.

Conflict management

General

Conflict is most usually perceived as something that is negative and almost invariably having a detrimental impact on the achievement of the project, programme or portfolio objectives. Some aspects of conflict can be used positively and it is important to recognise the difference between conflict management and conflict resolution. The latter is only one aspect of the former.

The goals of conflict management are to:

- utilise the positive aspects of conflict
- resolve organisational and interpersonal conflict
- minimise the impact of conflict on objectives.

The P3 environment is one where people come together on a temporary basis, in new and changing situations, in order to work together to produce a set of objectives. It is a situation that is almost designed to create conflict.

Thamhain and Wilemon investigated what aspects of projects create conflict and identified seven main sources, including schedules, priorities and costs. They also noted how these vary in terms of the intensity of the conflict they create during the project life cycle.

While issues of schedule, priority and cost etc. may be contentious, it takes people to cause a conflict. Disagreements can involve any number and variety of parties to the work. It could be two members of the management team, someone in the management team and a supplier, or two stakeholders.

Disagreements generally arise through a host of factors, including:

- conflicting working styles
- unspoken assumptions
- conflicting perceptions
- differing personal values
- emotions such as stress, fear and uncertainty
- conflicting roles
- miscommunication.

There is clearly great potential for conflict to adversely affect the achievement of the objectives. While a P3 manager may be skilled in conflict resolution it is important that conflict management is applied to pre-empt and avoid conflict before it occurs.

Maccoby and Scudder describe a five-step process for conflict management with 'resolution' being the final step. Given the nature of P3 management, it is not surprising that the steps in this procedure have echoes throughout many other functional procedures.

The P3 manager should anticipate conflict but not necessarily seek to avoid all of it. Some degree of conflict is seen as a necessary part of building a high-performing team as illustrated by the 'storming' stage of team development in Tuckman's model. Facilitating healthy disagreement can help develop the individuals and provide learning experiences. This must be carefully managed to prevent it becoming counter-productive.

When negative conflict does inevitably occur it needs to be resolved to minimise the damage caused.

Individual conflicts can emerge suddenly or gradually; they can be a single event or the accumulation of many small events. The intensity of conflict is usually described in terms of the magnitude of the event(s) and their frequency.

Typical indicators of an emerging conflict include hostility, lack of co-operation or an obvious direct challenge. Hidden conflict may be indicated by changes in style or communication, opting out of team activity, passive obstruction or subversive behaviour.

Conflict can be damaging if left unresolved. It creates uncertainty, affects morale and undermines the effectiveness of a team. Eventually this can result in a delay, or even failure, to deliver the objectives.

When attempting to resolve conflict it is useful to distinguish its different components. As Furlong points out, a resolution is easier to find if conflict resolution focuses on factors such as data and structure rather than values and relationships.

For some forms of conflict, a mediator may be useful. This could be a question of authority (such as where the sponsor may mediate between the manager and a senior stakeholder) or of expert knowledge (such as where expert knowledge of employment issues is necessary).

A mediator must focus on the issues rather than the personalities. They must have the ability to listen actively and facilitate negotiation towards a resolution.

Typical actions for the resolution of interpersonal conflict can include:

- careful choice of venue – a neutral, comfortable and accessible space
- clear time management, guidance on acceptable conduct and objectives for each session
- identification of facts and distinguishing assumptions
- recognising the different levels of power and influence among the participants
- assessing the potential impact of personal values and opinions
- reflecting perspectives, expectations, antagonisms and emphasising areas of agreement
- defined escalation routes if resolution is not possible.

Conflict resolution is a complex skill but identifying specific techniques or approaches helps to understand what is involved and develop the right competences.

There are many models for describing different aspects of conflict resolution. A particularly useful one for the P3 manager is the Thomas-Kilmann instrument based on Blake and Mouton's managerial grid. This is designed to identify someone's natural style for responding to conflict. Different styles are needed in different circumstances but everyone has their own preferred style.

Perhaps the hardest skill in conflict resolution is adopting a style that is personally unnatural but is the right one for the circumstances.

Projects, programmes and portfolios

The overall intensity of conflict will increase as the complexity of the work increases. As projects increase in size and complexity the number and diversity of people involved will increase as will the number of products and targets.

Some projects and all programmes will include change management that must be successful if benefits are to be achieved.

Greater complexity is synonymous with larger numbers of inter-dependencies (e.g. between projects within a programme) and inter-relationships.

As projects grow into programmes and programmes grow into portfolios, the effort spent on conflict management also grows. The effect will primarily be seen as investment in areas such as stakeholder management, teamwork, risk management and the early stages of the life cycle where most conflict originates.

In programmes and portfolios the management team will have to co-ordinate conflict resolution within the component parts. It may be that a single stakeholder is in dispute with two projects within a programme and these are being resolved differently. A programme or portfolio management team needs to maintain an overview of conflicts being addressed.

Delegation

General

Delegation is the practice of giving a person or group the authority and responsibility to perform specific activities on behalf of another. The act of delegation does not transfer accountability and the person who has delegated the work remains accountable for its results.

The goals of delegation are to:

- allocate work effectively to individuals, teams and suppliers within the project, programme or portfolio
- use delegation as a motivation and development tool.

In many ways, delegating a work package or task is a microcosm of the wider P3 environment. There are many shared principles, as illustrated in Figure 1.12.

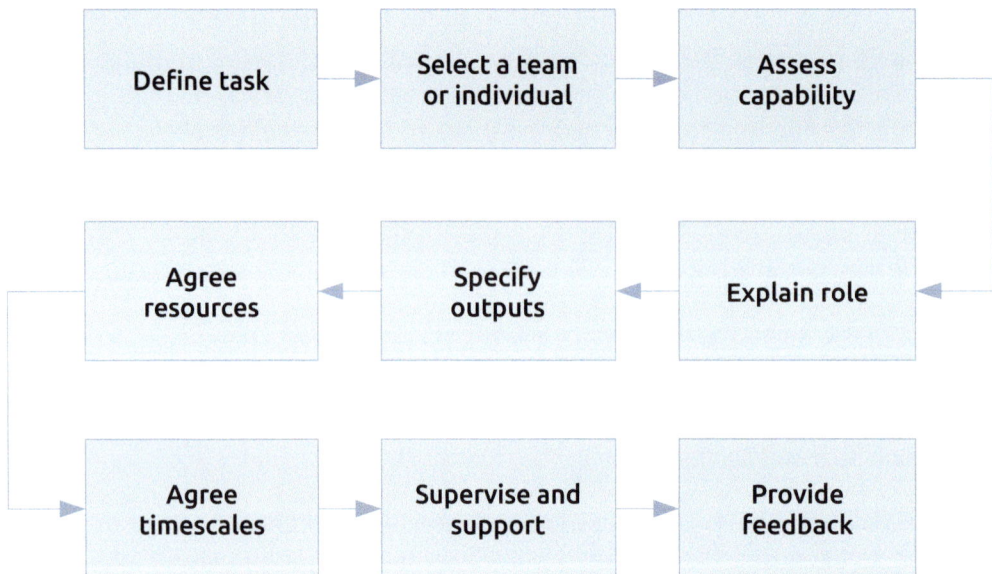

Figure 1.12 Principles of delegation

The first step is to define the task or work package and confirm that it is something that can be delegated. A team or individual can then be selected, but their capability to do the work should be assessed and any training needs identified.

The transfer of the work will clearly require the manager to specify what needs to be done, but it is not only the production work that is being delegated. Some degree of responsibility and authority is also being transferred, so the manager must explain the role as well as the outputs.

At this point, in P3 terms, the delegating manager has simply provided the scope of the work. The next two steps cover discussions about the resources needed and the required timescales for delivery.

Once the work is underway, the manager should exercise a suitable degree of supervision and provide support as required.

Feedback is useful throughout the procedure but is shown at the end where the feedback on the end result is delivered.

Delegation is primarily a means of distributing work around the various P3 contributors, but it is also a means of motivating teams and individuals to realise their full potential. Delegation underpins a style of management that encourages project team members to use and develop their skills and knowledge.

Models that illustrate the relationship between leadership and teamwork often make reference to delegation in the context of skilled leaders and high-performing teams. For example, the Tannenbaum and Schmidt continuum illustrates the relationship between the P3 manager's use of authority and the freedom available to the delegated resources.

There are numerous potential obstacles in the path of effective delegation, including:

- complex lines of authority in a matrix organisation
- the ability of the P3 manager to select the members of their teams
- a blame culture where there is intolerance of mistakes, making people reluctant to accept responsibility
- reluctance to delegate ('By the time I've explained it, I could have done it myself').

Delegation is an essential component of developing high-performing teams and a competent P3 manager will need to develop skills to overcome all these personal and organisational obstacles.

Projects, programmes and portfolios

The principles of delegation are at the heart of any project, programme or portfolio method.

Portfolios delegate work to programmes and projects; programmes delegate the production of outputs to projects and change management to business change teams; projects delegate work packages to suppliers and sub-projects.

In organisation management the different managerial levels are defined, along with the flow of delegation. On a small, non-complex project this may only extend to a sponsor, a manager and a delivery team. As size and complexity increase, so do the levels within the organisation.

One of the effects of this is that people become both delegators and delegatees. A programme manager may receive delegated authority from the programme sponsor but then acts as the sponsor of projects – and delegates to project managers accordingly.

Anyone who is a link in this chain must consider carefully what can and cannot be delegated. This is why the first step in the delegation procedure refers to the need to confirm that the task is 'something that can be delegated'. A simple example of this is where the sponsor will delegate the preparation of a business case to the manager but cannot delegate the authority to approve the business case.

The Praxis processes reflect the principles and procedure of delegation in many ways. The simplest example is the relationship between the development process and the delivery process.

An important element of delegation in the P3 environment is the effect of changes to objectives and delivery plans. While a task may be defined and delegated it is inter-related to many other tasks within a project, programme or portfolio, and therefore subject to change.

Everyone within the P3 environment should expect change. What will counter the beneficial effects of delegation is uncontrolled change. At project level change control will address changes to scope, and at portfolio level the co-ordination process will communicate the effects of links between delegated parcels of work.

At all levels of complexity between these two extremes, the delegator must keep the delegatee informed. That means explaining the reasons for change in the delegated work as well as the changes to the work itself.

Influencing

General

P3 managers will often be in a position where the exercise of direct authority is either inappropriate or impossible. In these situations the manager must seek to affect the behaviours and actions of others through influence rather than authority. The goals of influencing are to:

- develop and maintain a high-performing team
- persuade stakeholders to support the objectives
- persuade stakeholders to support the achievement of the objectives.

Models of leadership, such as Hersey and Blanchard, mirror models of teamwork, such as Tuckman. One of the strong themes of these models is that as the team develops, the manager's style must change from authoritative to supportive. In a high-performing team with a supportive manager, one of the manager's key skills will be influencing. In this relationship, the manager is not so much telling the team members what to do as influencing them to do the right thing.

While influencing is a useful skill to back up authority, it is an essential skill when the P3 manager does not have the necessary authority. Stakeholder management identifies numerous people that the P3 manager needs to influence. This influence may be required to overcome objections, provide resources or even help influence others.

Models for the nature and practice of influencing include Cialdini, and Cohen and Bradford. These have many common features and emphasise two common themes:

- understand the people you wish to influence
- understand what you can do for them in return for what you want them to do for you.

To achieve this, a successful influencer will:

- understand their own behaviour and how it relates to others
- have a clear vision of what the work involves and how it affects others
- communicate effectively using all appropriate means
- negotiate to find mutually acceptable solutions to issues
- understand context, including cultural, social and political factors
- behave ethically at all times.

A P3 manager's ability to influence is often based on different sources of power as described by Montana and Charnov. A manager must understand their sources and levels of power so that they can be used constructively and certainly not abused.

If influencing is successful, it will result in changes of attitude and behaviour of those being influenced. The result will be acceptance of, and support for, the objectives of the work.

Influencing can take many forms. It can be deliberate or accidental, overt or discreet, focused or widespread. The P3 manager must be aware of all these aspects, both beneficial and detrimental. The manager's actions to positively influence one person may negatively influence another; effort in influencing a delivery team may create enthusiasm that positively influences others. As with all aspects of P3 management, the P3 manager must habitually consider the consequences of their actions.

While an individual's ability to influence will be based largely on their personality and behaviour, it is also dependent on their position in the organisation. Sometimes even the most skilled P3 manager will need support from their sponsor simply because the influencing skills need to be backed up by the kind of authority or credibility that is linked to seniority in the organisation.

Projects, programmes and portfolios

A P3 manager has nominal authority over the members of their management and delivery teams, but since many projects and programmes operate in a matrix organisation, those same team members will have other allegiances. As a result, team members will be subject to different, and sometimes conflicting, influences. The P3 manager needs to understand this context and probably influence other managers in the matrix so that they act in support of the project or programme.

Programmes, and some projects, will include work to realise benefits, which will incorporate change management. Implementing and embedding change is not something that can be done through authority alone. People in the affected business-as-usual parts of the host organisation must be encouraged to accept and support the proposed change and value the predicted benefits, all of which require influencing skills.

As the work becomes more complex, so do the relationships between all the various stakeholders. On a programme, one stakeholder may be affected by multiple projects and a programme manager needs to ensure that attempts to influence stakeholders by different project managers are not counter-productive. The programme-level co-ordination of stakeholder management will include co-ordinated communications aimed at influencing the stakeholder. The programme manager must balance the needs of multiple projects and focus the communication in a way that has the greatest net benefit to the programme.

At the upper end of the complexity scale, portfolio management requires the involvement and support of executive teams and management boards throughout the host organisation. Strong leadership is required at the very top of the organisation to provide a background of authority for the portfolio objectives. Strong influencing skills will be required to address a complex web of interests in the portfolio.

This does not necessarily stop at the boundaries of the host organisation. A portfolio is the most visible aspect of P3 management to the outside world and if the host organisation wishes to gain support from shareholders, public bodies, customers etc., then influence must be available at the highest level.

Leadership

General

The verb *to lead* is derived from the word *laed*, a term common to ancient Northern European languages such as Anglo-Saxon, Dutch and Swedish. It means a path, road, journey or course of a ship at sea. By implication a leader is one who guides those travelling the path.

Leadership has many definitions because it is exercised in so many different contexts. In simple terms, in the context of P3 management, leadership is best defined by its goals, which are to:

- provide focus and promote commitment to objectives
- inspire team members to successfully achieve the objectives.

Leadership theory revolves around the relationship between the leader and those who follow. The most basic managerial relationships were described by McGregor with his description of Theory X and Theory Y managers and these evolved into the idea of transactional and transformational leaders.

A transactional leader ensures that requirements are agreed and that the rewards and penalties for achievement, or lack of it, are understood. It is an exchange process to do with setting objectives, communicating plans and explaining what team members or suppliers will receive in return for their effort. This approach primarily addresses the first goal of leadership and is reflected in many areas of P3 management, such as requirements management, the definition process and contract management.

A transformational leader is one who does everything possible to help people succeed in their own right and become leaders themselves. They help those people to transform themselves and achieve more than was intended. This approach primarily addresses the second goal and is reflected in the many leadership models that link the style of the leader to the development of the team being led.

The P3 environment is, by definition, temporary. Teams come together to achieve objectives and are disbanded once the work is complete. Models of teamwork describe how teams go through certain development stages and many leadership models such as Hersey and Blanchard, and Blake and Mouton, show how the leader's style must adapt in parallel with the progression of the team. This is often referred to as situational leadership.

Of course, teams are made up of individuals and different individuals are motivated by different things. The basic principles of motivation are explained in models such as Maslow and Herzberg and the P3 manager needs to understand both the individuals in the team and their collective development.

Another variable that is unique to the P3 context is the life cycle. Different types of team may be required at different phases of the life cycle and teams that span different phases may react differently to them. A key skill of any leader is conflict management and the nature of conflict is also affected by the progression of the work through the different life cycle phases.

These aspects of what a leader needs to address were brought together in Adair's model of action-centred leadership, which looks at how the different components of task (objectives), team and individual need to be balanced.

Ultimately, the position of leader is 'granted' by followers who make the decision to follow. That decision will be influenced by the leader using an appropriate style of leadership that takes account of both the situation and the readiness of people to follow.

A team member's readiness to follow a leader will depend to a degree on their perception of the leader's 'power'. This is not as purely transactional as it sounds and, as described by Montana and Charnov, is equally applicable to transformational styles of leadership.

Every individual has their own preferred style of leadership. This is the style they will instinctively exhibit in most situations. It will lie somewhere between McGregor's extremes of Theory X and Theory Y. By far the hardest part of leadership for a P3 manager is having to exhibit different styles of leadership for different teams at different phases of the life cycle, most of which will not be their preferred style.

Projects, programmes and portfolios

The relationship between a leader and their team takes time to develop, so small projects with a small team are a difficult situation for the prospective leader. The project manager of a small, non-complex project has to develop a relationship with the team very quickly. This situation is often compounded by the fact that, in such situations, the project exists in a matrix organisation where the team members have other departmental managers. These departmental managers have the default 'legitimate power' and most of the 'reward power' described by Montana and Charnov. The project manager must therefore seek to develop their own legitimate power alongside 'expert power' and possibly 'referent power'. This latter authority to lead comes from having a strong sponsor who is visibly committed to the objectives.

The value of willing followers should not be underestimated, particularly in the context of small projects. The host organisation's capability maturity can be significant for these small-project environments because in a mature organisation the team members are more familiar with the project management context and have higher levels of what Hersey and Blanchard call 'follower readiness'.

As projects become more complex there will be more time to develop the leader-follower relationship. Teams have time to develop according to the various teamwork models and the P3 manager has the opportunity to apply the principles of situational leadership.

While leaders require followers, they must also themselves be able to follow. Many projects will be part of a programme or portfolio that also has its leader. A project manager will need to be a strong leader but must also be able to be an effective team member in respect of the programme or portfolio.

On programmes, portfolios and larger projects the primary leadership issue becomes one of scale rather than time. The P3 manager may be more detached from some individuals or entire teams. While some of the more managerial aspects of leadership will be delegated, there will still need to be high-level visionary leadership for the project, programme or portfolio as a whole. This is an aspect of leadership that the P3 manager shares with their sponsor and a visibly effective partnership will greatly increase the chances of success.

The nature of a programme also influences leadership style. In the programme setting:

- the objectives are more visionary and fluid than in the project setting
- many of the people who need to be led are themselves leaders
- change management affects a wide range of stakeholders.

A vision is more difficult to communicate than a set of product specifications. A programme manager is less likely to gain credibility and authority through expert power than through visionary leadership (charisma power) that is visible to all programme and project team members.

A programme manager needs to develop strong leadership skills to establish credibility with a team of project managers and business change managers who are leaders in their own right. This is especially true where actions that best serve the programme are in conflict with what a project manager believes are in the best interests of the project or a business change manager believes are not in the best interests of business as usual.

Leadership of a structured portfolio is the most visionary in nature as the single purpose of the portfolio is to deliver the host organisation's strategy. Clearly, referent power is important here and developing follower commitment to the vision of the portfolio is almost synonymous with commitment to corporate vision and strategy. This kind of connection is typical in a mature organisation.

Negotiation

General

Negotiation is a collective term for various mechanisms that seek to resolve differences between individuals, groups or companies. Its goals are to:

- find solutions to issues involving two or more parties
- develop beneficial relationships between two or more parties.

The principles of negotiation are used in many different contexts. Two obvious applications are in conflict management and procurement. These two examples illustrate the breadth of situations where negotiation skills need to be applied. Addressing personal conflict often involves emotional and cultural issues, whereas procurement negotiation is usually about contractual terms and conditions.

Whatever the context, there are common factors that exemplify a good negotiator:

- the ability to describe common goals and boundaries
- emotional control and equal treatment of all parties
- good listening and communication skills
- thorough knowledge of bargaining tactics
- an ability to close a negotiation in a way that secures the outcome.

A negotiation is often described as having one of two flavours: competitive or collaborative.

Competitive negotiation is about getting the best deal for one party regardless of the needs and interests of the other. This can easily become a battle where the winner takes all and while competitive negotiation should be avoided, this may not always be possible.

Collaborative negotiation seeks to create a scenario where all parties involved get part or all of what they were looking for from the negotiation. This approach tends to produce longer-term solutions and minimise the opportunity for future conflict.

Every individual has a natural preference for the way they negotiate; Shell's model combines collaborating and competing with three other personal preferences based on Blake and Mouton's managerial grid.

Regardless of whether the negotiation is competitive or collaborative, it usually follows a typical procedure as shown in Figure 1.13.

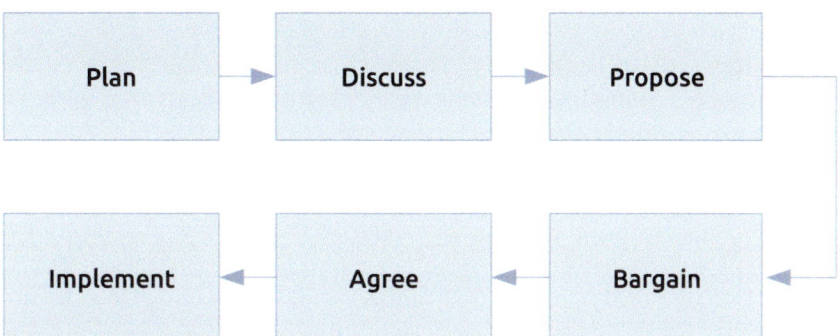

Figure 1.13 Negotiation procedure

- **Plan** All parties should prepare thoroughly. This includes gathering as much information as possible; setting goals for the outcome and agreeing an escalation route if the negotiation is unsuccessful. Each party should attempt to understand the cultural, commercial and ethical background of the others.
- **Discuss** Set the scene, identify the key issues and communicate the objectives. Listen, question and feed back regularly to confirm understanding.
- **Propose** Suggest a solution that is clear and unambiguous.
- **Bargain** Discuss the proposal; communicate personal boundaries and areas of flexibility.
- **Agree** Reach agreement on the core issues; document what has been agreed; and record any peripheral, outstanding items with timescales for resolving them.
- **Implement** Communicate the outcome of the negotiation as necessary; update any related P3 management documentation.

Negotiation is easy to get wrong. The cardinal sin is to enter into negotiations unprepared. This can easily lead to mistakes such as making opening offers that are clearly unacceptable to the other parties. Pressure to conclude negotiations and get on with the project or programme can result in rushed discussions that produce difficult-to-implement outcomes. It is important when bargaining to stay calm and know when to take a break. Whenever it takes place, the result of a negotiation will have repercussions throughout the remainder of the life cycle, so it is worth the investment to get it right (or as right as reasonably possible) before moving on.

Projects, programmes and portfolios

Project managers are often most involved in negotiation as they have direct involvement with the teams that deliver the project.

In the identification and definition phases of the life cycle, requirements are being captured and initial plans produced. The project manager will need to balance the time, cost and scope requirements by negotiation with stakeholders and with support from the sponsor.

During mobilisation and procurement, the project manager will need to negotiate internally with line managers in the matrix organisation and conduct more formal contract negotiations with potential suppliers. As the project progresses, conflicts between team members will arise and the project manager will need to negotiate solutions to conflicts.

In some cases there may be specialist help available from a support office. Even if there is not a dedicated support office, it is important to know when to ask for help from specialists; for example, the host organisation's HR or legal departments.

In portfolios, programmes and more complex projects the range of negotiating scenarios gets broader and broader. P3 managers in these more complex situations need to understand negotiation in the context of delegation.

In particular, where a programme or portfolio is made up of multiple layers of management teams with delegated authority, a balance must be struck between removing autonomy from one level and gaining an advantage by collectively negotiating on behalf of the programme or portfolio as a whole.

The hierarchy of management teams also provides a mechanism for escalation should a negotiation at a lower level be unsuccessful. This should be explained in the relevant management plans; typically the resource management plan.

Teamwork

General

Teamwork is how a group of people come together to collaborate and co-operate in achieving common objectives. The goals of teamwork are to:

- create a team from a collection of individuals
- develop and maintain the performance of the team.

Teams exist in all walks of life, from working teams to sporting teams. The difference between a team and a group of individuals is the team's collective commitment to agreed objectives. All teams are made up of individuals and regardless of the context of the team, human nature means that they go through similar stages of development and suffer from the same problems.

The main distinguishing factor of project, programme and portfolio teams is their temporary nature. A P3 manager needs to build a team as quickly as possible and maintain its performance against the backdrop of impending demobilisation. It helps considerably if the individuals who make up the team are comfortable with, or actively enjoy, the dynamic environment of projects, programmes and portfolios. Familiarity with the nature of project, programmes and portfolios throughout an organisation is something that naturally arises from the development of higher levels of capability maturity and functions like communities of practice in particular.

Models of teamwork tend to address two aspects. Firstly, the nature of the individuals who make up the team and, secondly, the developmental stages of the team as a whole.

Belbin and Margerison-McCann illustrate how different personalities work together to create a working team. Each personality has its strengths and weaknesses. Ideally, within the team, one person's strengths will balance other people's weaknesses. Individuals will perform better in a team context if they are given a role that plays to their strengths.

P3 managers are rarely in the position of the manager of a sports team who can select in-form players from a squad to suit the demands of the next game. A P3 management team is more typically made up of people who are available at the time. Such teams are unlikely to form an ideal combination of Belbin team roles and the manager must work with individuals to develop behaviours that may not be their natural style.

Once assembled, teams do not become high-performing simply because they have been given a common objective. They typically go through a series of development stages as illustrated by Tuckman or Katzenbach and Smith. P3 managers must be aware of where a team is in the development cycle and adjust their leadership style to suit.

The team cycle and the project or programme life cycle are related. At the simplest level (i.e. one team working on one project) Thamhain and Wilemon showed how varying levels of conflict in the project life cycle follow a similar pattern to varying levels of conflict in a team cycle such as Tuckman's. Awareness of models such as this help P3 managers understand how their leadership and conflict management skills need to be applied; for example, in the definition phase of the life cycle with a team that is going through its 'storming' phase.

Once established, a P3 manager is responsible for the continued cohesion of the team. They should strive to keep individuals motivated and support them in their personal and career development aspirations. In a matrix organisation this means the P3 manager must have a good working relationship with the team member's line manager.

A common focus on well-defined objectives is an important tool for developing a team, but in the P3 context it can also be a weakness. The objectives of projects, programmes and portfolios are susceptible to change. Sometimes this is due to unavoidable external factors, but often it will be due to changing requirements from stakeholders. If a team is focused and committed to well-defined objectives, frequent and uncontrolled change can be demotivating.

In environments where change is common, or requirements need to be flexible, P3 managers may choose an agile approach. This requires a team with a different mind-set as agile teams are often self-organising and may use techniques such as time boxes and MoSCoW prioritisation.

In many contexts the P3 manager faces the additional challenge of maintaining a sense of teamwork among members who are not physically co-located. In the digital age virtual teams may not just be spread across different offices but across different continents and time zones.

Projects, programmes and portfolios

Within the P3 environment there will be a hierarchy of different teams. The obvious example is a project management team within a programme, a programme management team within a portfolio, and the overall portfolio management team.

Projects are where the most close-knit teams will be found. In a traditional project the objectives are well defined and often broken down into a series of well-specified products providing a clear focus for the team's efforts. The project manager will communicate the objectives and explain how they will be achieved so that team members understand their role. While functions such as scope management, planning and communication are presented as core P3 management functions, they are also, in effect, team development functions.

As projects become more complex and develop into programmes, the P3 manager will delegate portions of the work to team managers or sub-project managers. By implication, the P3 manager is delegating responsibility for team development as well as delivery, but must retain an overview of performance.

In programmes there will be a number of sub-teams that the manager needs to develop as well as the central management team. These could include, for example, a 'team' of project managers or a 'team' of business change managers. While each member of these teams has their own objectives they need to work together to achieve the overall vision. The team working approach can also be applied to groups who do not typically regard themselves as a team but who could benefit from an element of team culture; for example, 'teams' of suppliers or stakeholders.

All sub-teams will need to be developed concurrently to support the achievement of the programme's vision and component benefits. The levels of responsibility of the team members may mean that a collaborative working group approach is more relevant. While individual managers will take responsibility for the development of their own teams, the programme manager must create a team ethos for the programme as a whole. Inevitably there will be a significant turnover rate within programme teams as projects are instigated and closed or as business-as-usual units deliver changes to their way of working.

The principles of team working are not as visible in the portfolio context. Other than in the core portfolio management team, the levels of interaction associated with team working are not present. Wider groups of individuals with responsibility to deliver different parts of the portfolio are, in effect, a collaborative team, but that is not immediately obvious to those involved.

It is in the interest of the portfolio that the appropriate type of team working is encouraged and exploited at all levels to maximise portfolio effectiveness. Collaborative and co-operative working within the portfolio with a shared vision of the strategic objectives should be encouraged.

Maintaining a team ethos across these broad, diverse and changing communities will require excellent communication and leadership skills on the part of the P3 manager, closely supported by the sponsor.

1.3.2 Delivery

This area is about the functions that are immediately concerned with the delivery of outputs, outcomes and benefits. Six of the sections deal with components that are fundamental to every project, programme and portfolio:

- **Scope** What are the objectives and scope of the work?
- **Schedule** How long will it take to achieve?
- **Finance** How are necessary funds acquired and costs managed?
- **Risk** What threats and opportunities are involved?
- **Change** What areas of business as usual must be changed to realise benefits?
- **Resource** How will the necessary resources be acquired, mobilised and managed?

Some functions operate across these fundamental components and are collected together under the general title of integrative management.

Most functions in this section contain a procedure that describes the typical steps that should be followed. These are often iterative and a generic form of procedure is shown in Figure 1.14.

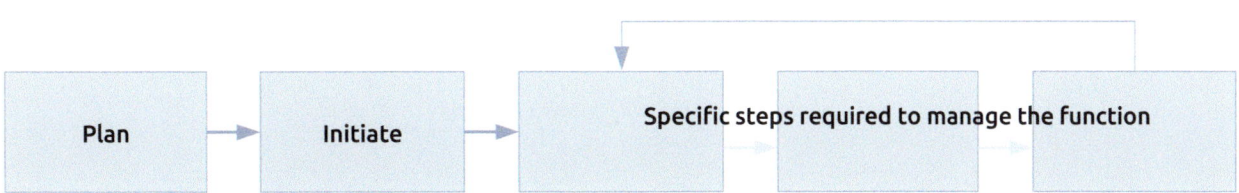

Figure 1.14 Generic procedure

Functional procedures will be repeatedly performed in each of the life cycle phases but must be adapted to the circumstances. Depending upon the life cycle phase, the focus will be on different procedural steps.

Common to all procedures are the 'plan' and 'initiate' steps. The planning step involves creating a management plan for the function that describes the policies, procedures, tools and techniques that should be used to manage the function. The initiation step covers the mobilisation of resources required to perform the procedure.

> Performing procedures in a way that is appropriate to the life cycle phases is a common element of competencies and an attribute of level 3 capability.

Although the plan and initiate steps are shown separately for each function they will largely be performed collectively for all functions.

The planning step is normally part of preparing governance documents in the definition process. The initiation step will be divided between the latter part of the definition process and the beginning of the delivery process.

The specific steps relate to work that is unique to each function, such as estimating costs or identifying risk, and these are repeatedly performed throughout delivery. However, the specific steps will also be performed at a high level in the identification process to produce the brief and the definition process to produce the definition documentation.

Integrative management

The topics in this section do not directly address the fundamental components of delivery; i.e. scope, schedule, cost, risk, change and resource. They are integrative functions that act across those components.

The overall goals of the integrative management functions are to:

- plan all aspects of the work
- develop and maintain the justification for the work
- monitor and control performance
- ensure information is accurate, current and accessible
- establish and maintain a management team
- identify and communicate with people affected by the work
- ensure that the management of the work is relevant and effective.

Each integrative function brings together aspects of the fundamental delivery components, as shown in Figure 1.15.

Figure 1.15 Fundamental components of delivery

The planning function has two purposes. Firstly, it sets out the policies for managing the fundamental components. Secondly, it defines and estimates what needs to be done, how it should be done and when it should be done. Every delivery procedure has an explicit 'plan' step but replanning is implicit throughout.

The control function takes the outputs of planning as a baseline and tracks what actually happens against what was planned to happen. Control methods are normally focused on dealing with deviations from plan and attempting to return to plan. However, control also involves assessing whether to terminate work that is no longer justifiable. Control is implicit with the specific steps of each delivery procedure.

The planning and control functions create a large amount of information covering the content and governance of the work. This needs to be created, updated and communicated effectively for planning and controlling the work through formal information management.

The business case is the key document for projects and programmes. It states why they are worth the investment. Preparing a business case requires the summarisation and integration of information from all the fundamental components.

There are many people involved in a project, programme or portfolio, and while some are directly involved in managing or performing the work, others are simply affected by it. Organisation management describes the management team and its roles and responsibilities while stakeholder management explains how people who are involved in, or affected by, the work in any way must be identified and engaged.

As part of the sponsorship role, a sponsor has to ensure that the work is being managed according to the policies and procedures set out when the work was approved. This is achieved through assurance.

Organisation management

General

Organisation management is concerned with creating and maintaining a management structure applicable to the project, programme or portfolio and the context in which it operates. Its goals are to:

- design an organisation appropriate to the scope of work to be managed
- identify and appoint members of the management team
- maintain and adapt the organisation throughout the life cycle.

The procedure for managing the organisation is a simple one, as shown in Figure 1.16.

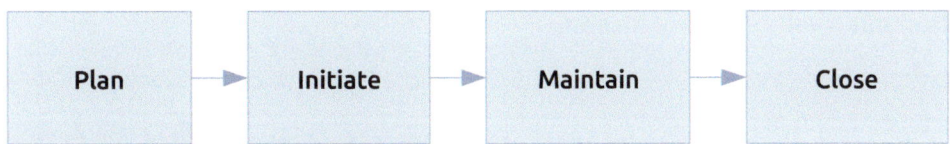

Figure 1.16 Organisation management procedure

Planning for organisation management includes the design of an organisation structure that will match the context and scope of the work. This will include the description of policies for appointing staff and cross-reference the relevant host organisation HR policies.

The initiate step involves making appointments and delivering any necessary training.

The demands on the organisation structure will usually change during the course of the project or programme life cycle. The organisation must be amended to take these changing requirements into account.

> There is a strong correlation between the initiate and close steps in organisation management and the mobilise and demobilise steps in mobilisation.
>
> The difference is simply that organisation management deals with the management team and mobilisation deals with delivery resources.

Finally the organisation is closed down and disbanded.

The organisational structure of individual projects, programmes and portfolios will vary according to the context and specific needs of each situation. In broad terms the organisation will always have four main levels, as shown in Figure 1.17.

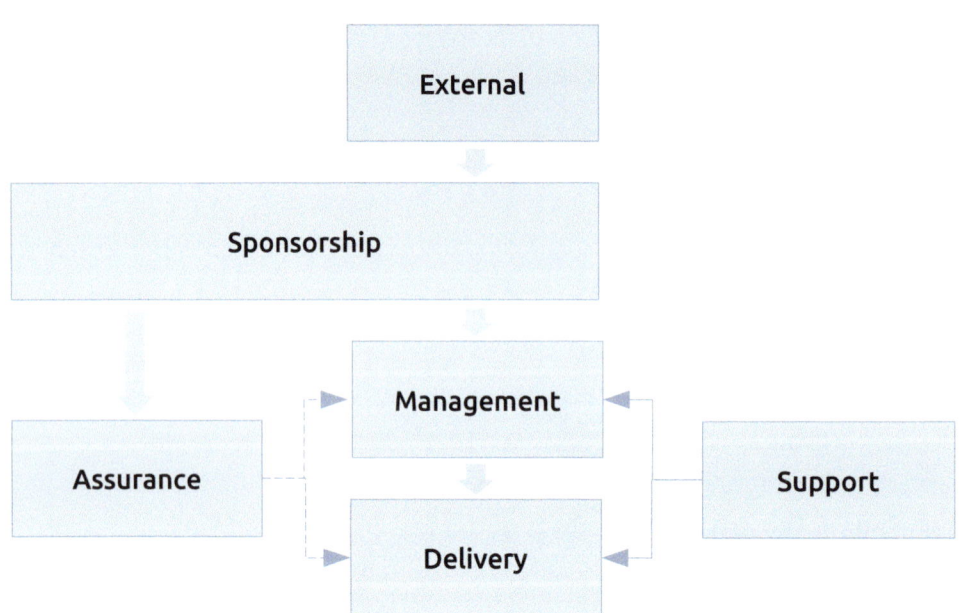

Figure 1.17 The four levels of an organisation

The external level in the organisation represents the body that first mandated the work. This could be a company mandating a portfolio; a client mandating a project; a programme mandating a project; or a department mandating a programme. Whatever the nature of the external organisation it delegates responsibility for looking after its interests to the sponsorship level.

The sponsorship function, in conjunction with the sponsorship process, provides the link between the management and external levels. The sponsor champions the work and owns the business case.

The management level is where the day-to-day responsibility for managing the work resides. The sponsorship and management levels form the management team, whether it be a project, programme or portfolio management team.

The delivery level represents the staff, contractors and suppliers involved in the delivery process.

All the levels are relative and context sensitive. For example, the day-to-day management of a programme includes the provision of sponsorship to component projects. The programme management team will see the project management teams as its delivery teams. From the project management team's point of view, the programme management team is their sponsor and it has delivery teams of staff and suppliers creating outputs and reporting to it.

The whole structure depends upon good delegation and control systems that ensure the appropriate level of management is involved in key decisions.

> The context sensitive nature of the levels is important when Praxis makes observations about the relationships between the levels. For example, in the delivery process, Praxis states that 'Each delivery team will provide the management team with regular progress reports'.
>
> This is true regardless of whether it involves a project delivery team reporting to a project management team or a project management team acting as a delivery team to a programme management team.

Alongside the main four-level structure are assurance and support. An assurance team reports to the sponsor and provides confidence that the management and delivery of the work are being conducted effectively and appropriately, which will include adherence to the various management plans.

The support function provides administrative and technical services to both the management and delivery levels.

Some project-based organisations, typically in construction or engineering, will have people working exclusively on a particular project or programme, but most host organisations are based around a departmental structure overlaid with projects and programmes known as a matrix organisation.

In a matrix organisation, delivery resources, and sometimes management resources, report both to their line manager and to the project or programme. This can create conflict between the two sources of authority and should be recognised by the host organisation.

The organisation will evolve during the life cycle. During the identification process and definition process, specialist structures may be employed, some of which may continue into the delivery process, but not necessarily so. Different stages or tranches of work may require different organisational designs.

Projects, programmes and portfolios

Adapting the standard structure for a project results in the organisation shown in Figure 1.18.

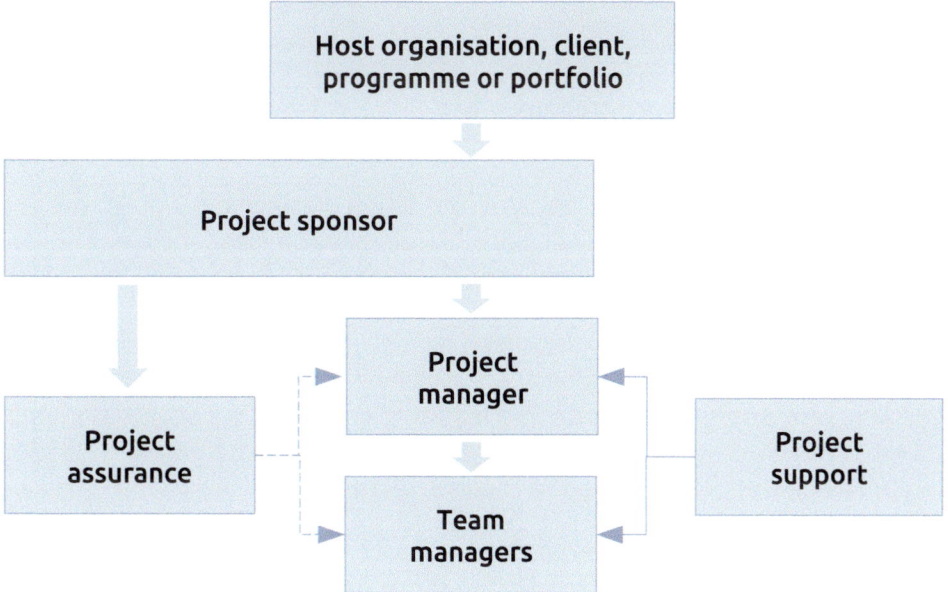

Figure 1.18 Adapting the standard structure for a project

The sponsor is an individual who may be supported by other senior managers in larger, more complex projects. Such a group may be known as a project board or steering group. This is the level that is most context sensitive. For example, where the project is within a programme, the programme manager may also take the role of project sponsor. In the case of a project involving a contractor and client organisation, a project board may include representatives of both.

On small projects, the support and team manager responsibilities will be taken on by the project manager. As the scale of the work increases, there will be a need for separate support resources and team managers who look after specific work packages.

The structure of the project organisation showing contractors, departments, teams and sometimes individuals is often represented by an organisational breakdown structure (OBS), as shown in Figure 1.19. This can be combined with a work breakdown structure to produce a responsibility assignment matrix (RAM).

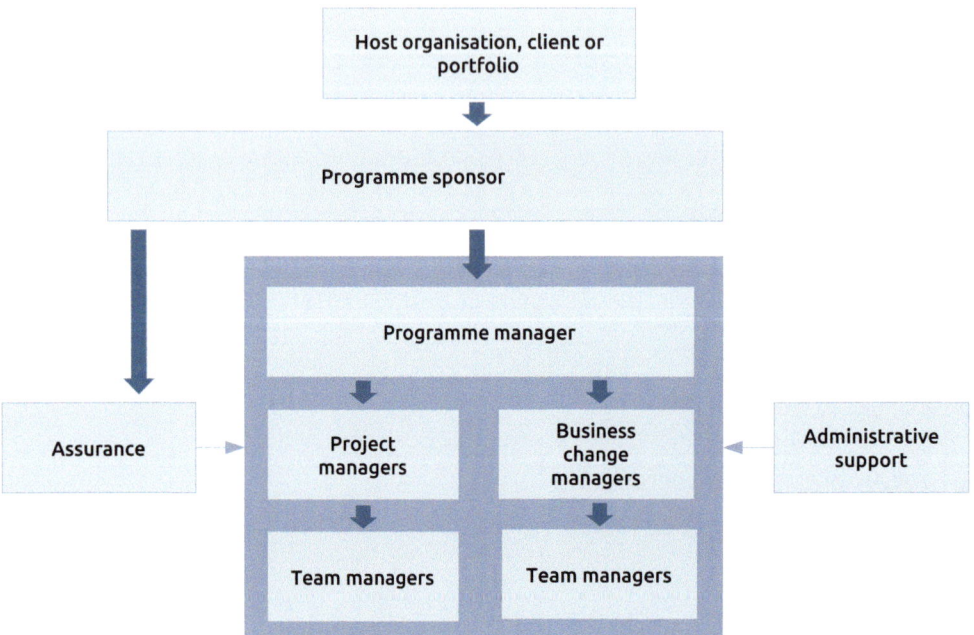

Figure 1.19 Organisational breakdown structure

The main addition to the basic organisation structure when managing programmes is the role of business change manager (BCM). BCMs focus on change management and benefits management to achieve the benefits set out in the business case.

The programme sponsor will usually be supported by a group of senior managers, although the sponsor will still be ultimately accountable for the business case. These senior managers are sometimes known as the sponsoring group and it should comprise the senior managers from the business units most affected by the programme. This supports a close working relationship and understanding between the programme and those affected by it.

In a portfolio there are typically only three organisational levels, since the external and sponsorship levels are, in effect, one and the same thing, as shown in Figure 1.20. This external/sponsorship level is usually accountable not only for the delivery of the portfolio's objectives but also the development of the discipline and profession of P3 management. This is described in the portfolio governance process and has parallels with the way other professional departments within a company are governed.

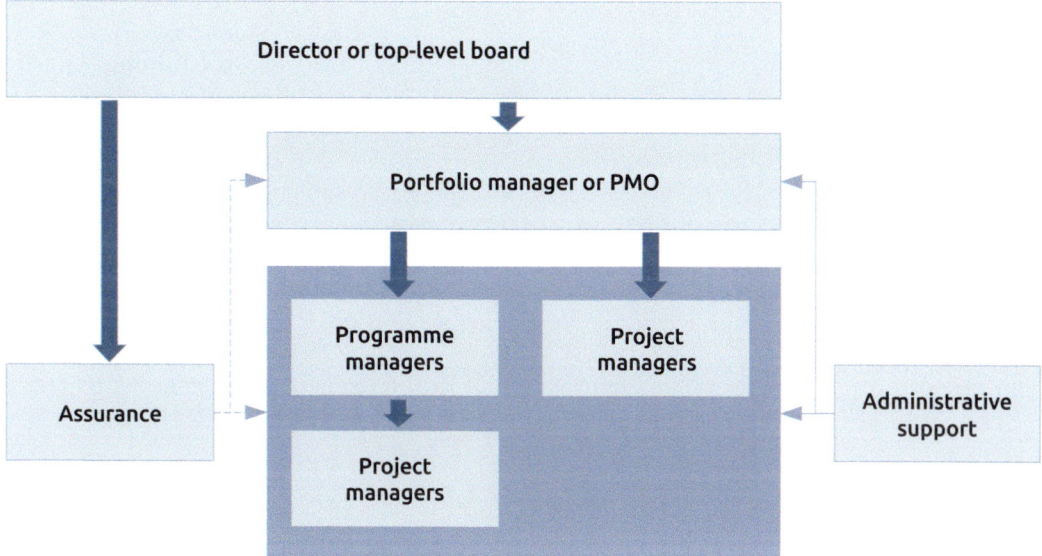

Figure 1.20 Role of the portfolio management office

Ideally, someone on the main board of the organisation will represent P3 management. This will effectively make that person the sponsor of the portfolio.

The management of a portfolio is sometimes handled by a group known as a project management office (PMO). The PMO manages the portfolio and may also be responsible for the overall development and promotion of P3 management in the host organisation.

PMOs can be constituted in many different ways but in this context the PMO is synonymous with the portfolio management team.

Stakeholder management

General

Stakeholder management ensures that stakeholders are appropriately involved in all aspects of the project, programme or portfolio. Its goals are to:

- ensure that the views and attitudes of all stakeholders are understood
- influence stakeholders to be supportive of the work wherever possible
- maximise the impact of supportive stakeholders
- minimise the impact of unsupportive stakeholders.

Stakeholders are individuals or groups with an interest in the project, programme or portfolio because they are involved in the work or affected by the outcomes.

Most projects, programmes and portfolios will have a variety of stakeholders with different and sometimes competing interests. These individuals and groups can have significant influence over the eventual success or failure of the work.

Working with stakeholders is a vital component of many functional procedures. For example, requirements management is based on stakeholders' wants and needs, and risk context (and therefore risk management) is based on understanding stakeholder appetite for, and attitude to, risk.

The stakeholder management procedure has six steps (see Figure 1.21). It starts with the planning step that defines the scope and objectives of stakeholder management and results in the stakeholder management plan. The initiation step is performed once the work is approved and the resources needed to manage stakeholders are mobilised.

> Given that an understanding of stakeholders is so important to other functions, it is worth investing significant effort on this during the identification process, Identify a project. This will ensure a more robust brief and a more efficient start to the definition process.

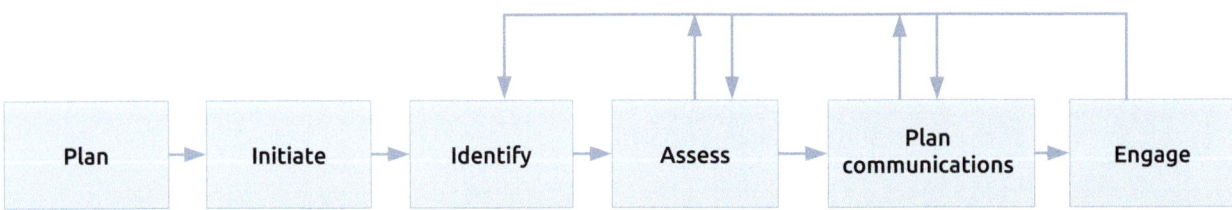

Figure 1.21 Stakeholder management procedure

The identification of stakeholders can involve, for example, interviews, brainstorming, checklists and lessons learned. Understanding the relationships between stakeholders and their different areas of interest is usually achieved through stakeholder mapping. Common types of stakeholder include:

- staff, contractors and suppliers who are performing the work
- individuals and groups who are affected by the creation of outputs or outcomes
- owners, customers or funders of the host organisation
- statutory, regulatory and governmental bodies.

More detailed stakeholder maps will assess each stakeholder in terms of their interest in the work and influence over the way it is performed. Those with an ability to directly affect the objectives are sometimes highlighted as being the key stakeholders.

Typical issues to consider when assessing each stakeholder are:

- How will they be affected by the work?
- Will they be openly for, against or ambivalent to the work?
- What are their expectations and how can these be managed?
- Who and/or what are the primary influences on the stakeholder's view of the project?
- Who would be the best person to engage with the stakeholder?

Once the stakeholders have been assessed, plans can be put in place to communicate with them with a view to addressing their interest and influence. The principles of how stakeholders will be approached are described in the stakeholder management plan, while the detailed communications are set out in a communications plan.

Plans for communication with stakeholders who have high levels of interest and influence will be different from those who have low levels of interest and influence. Similarly, communication with stakeholders who are naturally positive about the work will be different from those who are negative.

The communications planning will identify the ideal people to engage with each stakeholder. In many cases the P3 manager will take on the task, but it is also useful to call upon peers, senior managers or others who may be better placed. Engaging with more senior stakeholders is often the role of the sponsor.

Stakeholder management becomes more complex when stakeholders' views, roles or allegiances etc. change throughout the life cycle. For that reason, the stakeholder management steps must be repeated throughout the life cycle.

Projects, programmes and portfolios

On a small project, the project manager will probably be able to identify who all the stakeholders are, perhaps with help from the sponsor. A simple stakeholder map will suffice and the communications activities may be included in the project plan. Stakeholder management is an important activity, even on the smallest of projects. Project managers can make a big difference to the eventual success of the project simply by ensuring they understand their stakeholders and taking time to engage with and influence them.

In programmes and large projects stakeholder maps should be created at different levels and will be the responsibility of the project managers and programme manager respectively. Stakeholders should only appear on maps where they have an identifiable interest or influence. Those with an interest in a project should be on the project-level map. Those with an interest in multiple projects, or the business as usual being affected by the projects, should also appear on the programme-level map. Where stakeholders have an interest in multiple projects, the programme-level map must clearly differentiate their interests and influence in each. This ensures that stakeholders appear in only one communication plan and avoids the danger of mixed messages.

Programme support will maintain the stakeholder documentation and may include a communication specialist. It will also liaise, as appropriate, with either corporate communications or a portfolio support function where one exists.

In a structured portfolio the management team needs to co-ordinate the stakeholder management activity of all component projects, programmes and business-as-usual areas within the portfolio. They must also maintain a portfolio-wide stakeholder management plan which needs to cover aspects such as:

- the overall stakeholder management policy, including key stakeholder groups and interfaces
- how the stakeholder management policy will be monitored
- how stakeholder management at project and programme level will be co-ordinated and supported
- gathering and publicising senior management support for the portfolio processes and portfolio content.

Stakeholder management can be one of the most challenging activities within structured portfolios. Change management across the portfolio can be undermined if there are local areas of an organisation with poor stakeholder commitment.

Business case management

General

Business case management is the function concerned with developing, communicating and maintaining the business case. Its goals are to:

- summarise context and delivery in a single document
- explain the desirability, achievability and viability of the proposed work
- develop the primary document that will be used to support a go/no-go decision at all gates in the life cycle
- update and maintain the business case throughout the life cycle.

All projects and programmes must have a business case that demonstrates the value of their objectives.

In the identification process an outline business case is incorporated into the project or programme brief that is used by senior management to assess whether to give the go-ahead for the definition process. A detailed business case is prepared during the latter process and then used to decide whether full approval for the work should be given.

> Unlike most other delivery functions there is no procedure to describe the development of the business case. Its management is adequately covered by activities in the Praxis process model.

Once approved, the business case must be kept up to date, reflecting approved changes. In this way, it can be used as the primary document at gate reviews (e.g. at the end of a tranche or stage) to determine if the work should continue.

A business case typically includes sections on the:

- **Context** The background of the project or programme and why it is needed
- **Delivery summary** A top-level view of the stakeholders, scope, schedule, finance, risk, resource and change involved
- **Justification** An explanation of why the work should be undertaken.

Justification comprises three tests; i.e. is the work:

- **Desirable?** This is determined from requirements management which demonstrates that the objectives of the work are required by the stakeholders.
- **Achievable?** Benefits management defines achievable benefits, solutions management specifies achievable outputs and planning establishes the practicality of the work (within any time and resource constraints).
- **Viable?** Investment appraisal assesses the financial return on investment and risk management assesses the exposure to risk in performing the work.

The business case is owned by the sponsor, who has ultimate accountability for ensuring that the benefits are achieved.

Projects, programmes and portfolios

A business case must include a value of benefits as well as the costs of producing the output, but some projects are only concerned with delivering an output.

If the project is performed by a contractor on behalf of a client, the assumption is that the client has assessed the value of the benefits and agreed a price for the output with the contractor. The contractor's business case will be based simply on the profit element of the contract, whereas the client's business case will be based on the cost of the output and the value of the benefits. Where the two partners in the project have different business cases this can be a source of conflict. Each party must be realistic and understand the driving factors in each other's business case.

Where the project is delivering an output from which business as usual or a parent programme will realise benefits, the business case may not have been produced by the project manager. However, the project manager will probably be responsible for updating the business case and ensuring that plans for realising benefits remain achievable and viable.

Programmes are usually broken down into tranches and it is useful to have a business case for each tranche. This ensures that each tranche can be justified in its own right and if a programme needs to be terminated early, the completed tranches will have produced a financial return. If the first tranche of the programme is fairly short, it also ensures that stakeholders see some early benefits or 'quick wins' as they are sometimes known. This helps promote stakeholder commitment, which may wane if the first benefits take a long time to materialise.

Problems affecting one project in a programme may have a knock-on effect on the business case of another. As part of the delivery process, the programme management team must monitor the effect of inter-dependencies between business cases.

Since a portfolio is not a stand-alone enterprise, but rather a collection of programmes, projects and business-as-usual elements, the portfolio does not require its own business case. The programmes and projects within it each have their own.

The co-ordination of business cases within a programme or portfolio is far easier if there is consistency of approach. In more complex environments, guidance should be provided on how all the component business cases will be structured and the preferred techniques to be used. This is particularly important when preparing financial appraisals that will be consolidated.

In a structured portfolio the component business cases are derived from the strategic objectives that the portfolio is designed to achieve. The portfolio management team will then use the business cases to categorise, prioritise and balance the portfolio in line with the strategic objectives during the portfolio management process.

Planning

General

Planning determines what is to be delivered, how much it will cost, when it will be delivered, how it will be delivered, who will carry it out and how all this will be managed. It occurs broadly at two levels: governance and delivery.

> In Praxis, management planning and delivery planning are covered by separate competencies.
>
> The corresponding capabilities (from the Capability Maturity model) are deemed to be included in the other functional capabilities.

The goals of management plans used in governance are to:

- describe the principles that should be used to manage the work
- provide consistency with flexibility across multiple projects and programmes.

The goals of delivery planning are to:

- describe the objectives of the project, programme or portfolio
- define the work required to achieve the objectives and describe how it will be performed
- estimate the resources and finance needed to perform the work
- document the plans and update them throughout the life cycle.

At the governance level a series of management plans sets out the principles of how each aspect of the work will be managed. These plans include documents such as the risk management plan, scope management plan and financial management plan.

These governance-level plans set out policies and procedures for each aspect of management. They list preferred techniques, including templates for documentation and defined responsibilities. These plans ensure the quality of the P3 management processes and deliverables. Therefore, developing the governance-level plans could also be termed 'quality planning'.

Delivery plans address seven questions:

- **Why?** Everyone involved in, or affected by the work, should understand why it is being done. At the highest level, this would be a vision of the key elements and benefits of the work. As more detailed information is developed the question is answered in the business case.
- **What?** The work will have objectives that are determined in requirements management. These will be described as outputs, outcomes and/or benefits in documents such as a specification, blueprint or benefit profile.
- **How?** There are often different ways of achieving the stated objectives. Solutions development determines the best way and this is stated in the business case and embodied in many other detailed delivery plans.
- **Who?** This covers the management organisation and the delivery resources as defined in organisation management and resource management respectively. Who will do the work is clearly closely associated with how the work is done and is also addressed in the detailed delivery plans.
- **When?** Schedule management determines the timing of milestones, stages, tranches, work packages and individual activities.

- **Where?** While many projects are in one physical location, more complex projects, programmes and portfolios are spread across many locations and often time zones. The impact of this needs to be reflected in all delivery plans.
- **How much?** Naturally, the cost of the work is an essential component of the business case. Financial management determines how much the work will cost and how it will be funded.

The life cycle of projects and programmes is designed to answer these seven questions in stages. Outline documentation is developed during the identification process and, subject to approval through the sponsorship process, is used to produce the detailed delivery plans during the definition process.

All delivery plans originate from estimates. These will be based on whatever data is available together with expertise in its interpretation and application. The more information available, the more accurate the estimates. Inevitably, in the early phases of a project or programme, there is less information available than in the later phases. This results in a funnel where the range of estimates narrows throughout the life cycle, as shown in Figure 1.22. The estimating funnel covers a normal life cycle but the same principle applies to extended life cycles.

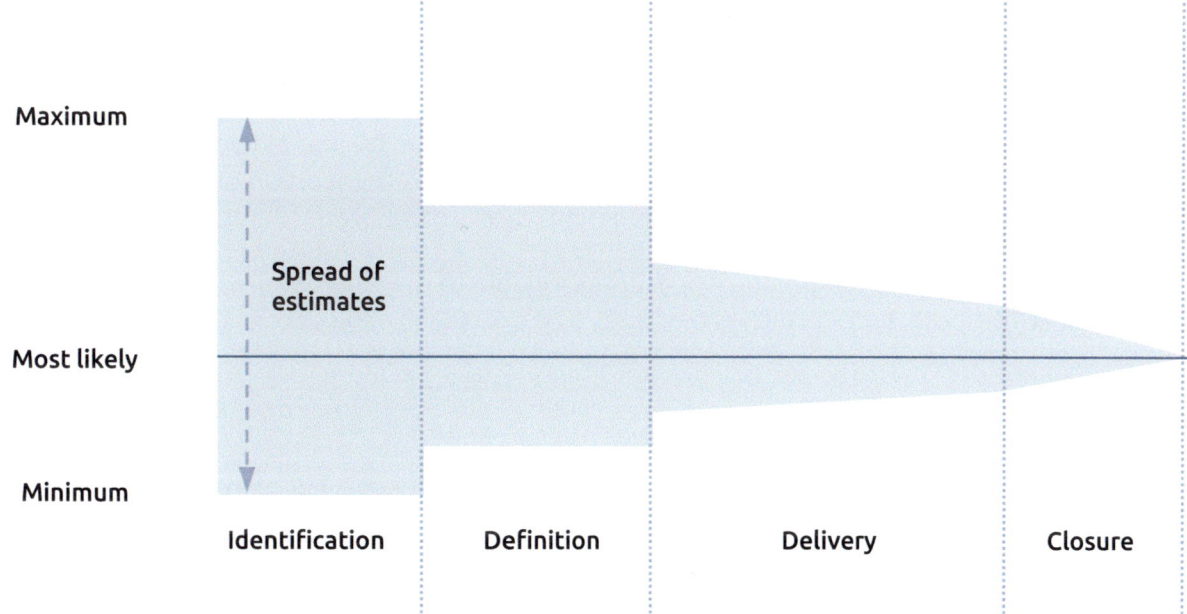

Figure 1.22 The estimating funnel

This inherent uncertainty in plans is often ignored or misunderstood by key stakeholders who interpret estimates in line with their personal requirements rather than practical realities. That is why techniques such as Monte Carlo in scheduling and the use of reserves as part of budgeting and cost control should be used as evidence of the effects of the estimating funnel.

The P3 manager owns the management and delivery plans but they should be developed with the wider team. Some specialist planning expertise may be provided by a support function. This removes ambiguity, sets expectations and develops commitment to the plan.

Once agreed at the end of the definition process, delivery plans provide baselines which are periodically reviewed and updated. These form the basis of reviews during the boundaries process where the continuing justification of the work is assessed.

Projects, programmes and portfolios

Small projects rarely have the opportunity to invest in the development of management plans. Good management practices will depend on the skill and experience of the project manager. In a more mature organisation there may be standard management plans available that can be tailored to suit.

Where a project is part of a programme or portfolio, the parent body should provide management plans and guidance on the production of delivery plans. The exception to this is where a standard portfolio comprises contracted projects for different clients. Each client may specify the use of their own standard approaches. The portfolio management team must therefore concentrate on supporting management teams in their use of varied documentation standards.

> Many approaches to P3 management are very specific about differences between project, programme and portfolio planning documents. Praxis defines many planning documents that serve various purposes and can be applied to any degree of complexity by a competent manager. Look at the purpose of a document and decide if it is useful to your work regardless of whether you call it a project, programme or portfolio.

Too much planning can be as damaging to a project as too little. All planning documents must be tailored to the context of the work. For example, a simple stakeholder map or risk register is far better than none at all, but time spent making them overly complicated can be a distraction.

On larger projects and all programmes, it is unreasonable to develop detailed delivery plans for the entire life cycle. Later tranches or stages of work will be subject to change as a result of altered requirements and performance in the earlier stages. It is common to apply the principle of rolling-wave planning where earlier stages and tranches are planned in more detail than the later ones.

Programmes and portfolios will have central plans and delegated delivery plans. For example, a programme may have a high-level schedule where each project and change management work package is represented as a single bar in a Gantt chart. Each project will then have its own detailed schedule. The challenge for planners is to enable information to flow between the higher and lower levels of plan while preserving the planning autonomy of the project manager and business change managers.

Control

General

Control involves monitoring performance against approved baselines, updating delivery documents and taking corrective action as necessary. Control is required throughout the life cycle but this explanation is primarily aimed at controlling the delivery process.

The goals of control are to:

- review performance against baselines
- evaluate the effect of actual performance on future plans
- take action as required to achieve planning targets or agree revised targets.

Control techniques fall into one of three broad categories: cybernetic, go/no-go and post-control.

Cybernetic control is part of the day-to-day management of the work; go/no-go control is applied at the key decision points in the life cycle; and post-control is concerned with learning from experience so that P3 management is continuously improved.

The term 'cybernetic' is derived from the Greek for helmsman and a P3 manager uses cybernetic control to 'steer' the project, programme or portfolio on a day-to-day basis. The work of the P3 manager is, strictly speaking, first-order cybernetic control and the relationship between the P3 manager and sponsor is second-order cybernetic control.

> Cybernetic control is focused on the delivery process. Go/no-go control is focused on the reviews between life-cycle phases and the boundaries process. Post-control is primarily addressed in the closing process with a link back to the review previous lessons activity in the identification process.

The key element of cybernetic control is feedback. A system is monitored, feedback is provided and compared to a norm. Action is taken to align the system with the norm. In P3 management, the baseline plans are the norm; monitoring provides the feedback on performance and the P3 manager takes action to adhere to the baseline plans. Tolerances are acceptable deviations from the baselines. If performance is outside, or predicted to be outside, the agreed tolerances, this is classed as an issue that must be escalated to the sponsor. The sponsor and manager will then agree on the appropriate corrective action. If the result is a major change to the work, then a new baseline may be agreed against which future performance is monitored.

Go/no-go control is used at key decision points built into the life cycle. These are typically found at the end of a phase, stage or tranche of work and involve a major review of what has been delivered.

At these decision points, the sponsor considers the available information and decides whether to proceed with the remaining work. In extreme cases a project, programme, or possibly even portfolio may be terminated because it is no longer justifiable.

Post-control is entirely retrospective. It is concerned with learning from experience through, for example, post-project or post-programme reviews.

Specific control methods are used according to the nature and complexity of what is being controlled. For example, a common method of illustrating schedule performance are RAG reports (Red, Amber, Green). Green status means performance is within tolerances and predicted to remain there. Amber is within tolerances but predicted to exceed them. Red indicates performance has exceeded tolerances.

All six components of delivery need to be controlled. Some techniques, such as change control and quality control, are specific to one of the elements, such as scope. Others, such as earned value management (EVM), bring together multiple elements (e.g. schedule and cost).

In the context of creating outputs, control of scope is effectively the same as quality control. It has the most diverse range of techniques, covering inspection, testing and measurement. It verifies that the deliverables conform to specification, are fit for purpose and meet stakeholder expectations. Example techniques include: crushing samples of concrete used in the foundations of a building; reviewing user interfaces of computer applications; x-raying welds in a ship's hull; and following the test script for a new piece of software. Inspection often produces empirical data, and tools such as scatter diagrams, control charts, flowcharts and cause-and-effect diagrams all help to control the quality of deliverables.

Controls can also be regarded as event-driven or time-driven. Go/no-go and post-control are event-driven and events could be life cycle-based (the conclusion of a phase, stage or tranche) or feedback-based (when tolerances are exceeded).

Time-driven controls are more typical of cybernetic control and involve weekly or monthly reports, periodic reviews or regular progress meetings. It is the P3 manager's responsibility to collect progress data and prepare reports, highlighting areas that need attention. In some cases this work will be done by a support function, freeing the manager to concentrate on decision-making and implementing corrective action.

No work will ever progress strictly according to plan. A good plan will contain elements of contingency and management reserves that will cushion the effect of issues. Some of these reserves will be in the control of the P3 manager and others within the control of the sponsor.

Projects, programmes and portfolios

The way progress data is collected and reported will depend on the planning techniques used to develop the baseline.

On a small project, the schedule baseline may have been prepared and presented as a simple Gantt chart; in which case schedule progress may be shown as a slip chart.

As projects become more complex and schedules are based on network diagrams, these models can be used for more sophisticated control techniques such as earned value management (EVM) or critical chain.

The more sophisticated the method of recording and analysing progress, the more accurate the predictions of future performance. For example, where a simple slip chart based on critical path analysis (CPA) may not predict a future breach of tolerances, a forecast based on EVM will show a breach. This is because CPA assumes future rates of progress will be in accordance with the original plan, whereas EVM assumes future rates of progress will be in accordance with historical rates of progress.

While control systems for traditional projects tend to focus first on time and cost, agile projects focus on scope. In the agile environment products are delivered in short time-boxed sprints and control techniques such as Kanban are more appropriate when controlling the flow of work. Over a number of sprints, burndown charts are often a better way of illustrating progress than Gantt charts.

In programmes and portfolios there will be multiple levels of cybernetic control. A project manager on a project will gather regular feedback on progress and take corrective action as required. Where the project is part of a programme, the programme manager may take the role of project sponsor and provide the second level of control. If the programme is part of a portfolio there is a similar relationship that introduces a third level of control.

This does not mean that there are three people controlling the project on a day-to-day basis. Each level of control deals with a different degree of detail and has a different span of control. Within larger projects or programmes and portfolios the control system (possibly laid out in a control management plan) must, for each level, explain how:

- tolerances will be set
- progress data will be gathered and reported
- inter-dependencies between different plans will be monitored
- progress information will be consolidated upwards
- decisions will be communicated downwards.

As the work becomes more complex it is vital to focus on key performance indicators (KPIs) rather than monitor everything in great detail. The role of a project, programme or portfolio support office will be indispensable as complexity increases and managers need timely and accurate information to make good decisions.

Information management

General

Information management is the collection, storage, dissemination, archiving and eventual destruction of information. Its goals are to:

- capture data accurately and consistently
- develop usable information from raw data
- maintain information securely and accessibly during its useful life
- support effective decision making and communication.

Large amounts of data will be collected during the course of a project, programme or portfolio. The management teams need to take the raw data and generate information through analysis and interpretation. A typical information management procedure is shown in Figure 1.23.

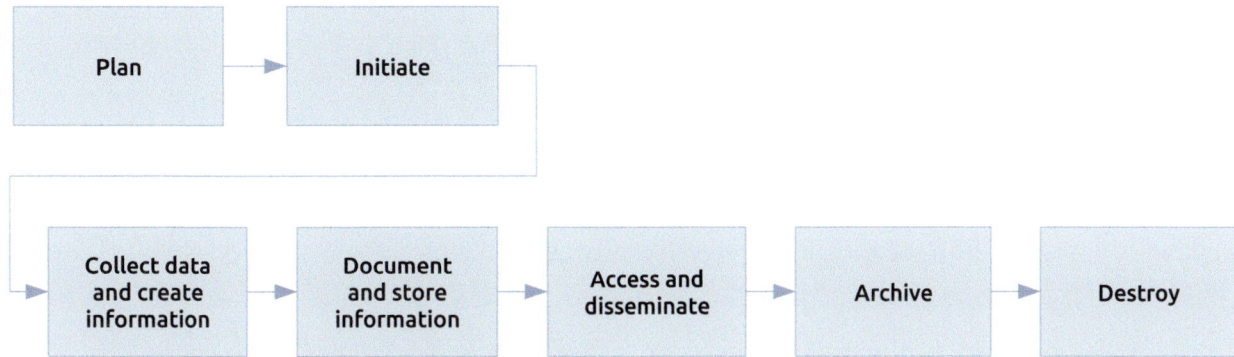

Figure 1.23 Information management procedure

The creation of data starts as soon as the mandate is issued so information management procedures and responsibilities need to be defined early in the life cycle. These will usually conform to organisational standards, but any adaptations may be necessary for particular contexts such as regulatory or security requirements. The standards will be set out in an information management plan.

The initiation step will ensure the necessary resources are mobilised and IT infrastructure is in place.

In the early phases of the life cycle data collection will focus on requirements management and solutions development. It will then move on to the creation of management and delivery plans showing how the solution will be delivered. As the work progresses, performance data will be collected to support control.

Data must be collected consistently and accurately so that it may be transformed into usable information for the P3 management team and stakeholders. This is much easier if standard techniques are adopted to capture and analyse the data and standard documents used to present the resulting information.

> It is important not to see standard document definitions as being fixed. One of the generic attributes of level 3 capability is that all documentation is based on organisational standards but has been tailored to suit the context in which it is being used.

P3 management methods such as those described by Praxis define a suite of standard documents and many organisations develop electronic templates to ensure consistency. Key documents will be subject to configuration management and the information management plan will define how information is classified and stored. Storage must be designed with accessibility, security and confidentiality in mind.

The expected distribution of documents will be set out in many relevant management plans with the stakeholder management plan being of particular significance. The timing of distribution may be set out in a communications plan and the information management system must be able to support this.

Most of the information on a project, programme and portfolio is transient; i.e. it is superseded with time. This does not mean it should be destroyed. Certainly for the duration of the life cycle, superseded information should be archived in case it is needed in the future. This is particularly relevant in the case of contract documentation that may be called on in the event of a dispute. Organisational policies often dictate the period for which archives should be maintained and these will reflect statutory obligations in areas such as financial accounting.

Some information contains a different intrinsic value characterised by the lessons learned. Some material from the information management system will become part of a knowledge management system that enables individual managers to learn from others and the organisation to develop its capability maturity. It makes sense if these systems work in a similar and compatible way.

Ensuring that a project, programme or portfolio is capturing relevant data and maintaining appropriate documentation is an important part of the assurance function.

Projects, programmes and portfolios

On small projects, information management will be part of the project manager's role and will probably be seen as something that takes time away from the important job of managing the project.

Documentation is a bit like insurance. Until it is needed to solve a problem it is not missed if it is not there. How an organisation supports its managers in this area is a key indicator of its capability maturity. A mature organisation will have standards and resources in place to lighten the administrative burden, particularly on the managers of small projects, and will ensure that all project managers understand the importance of good information management.

Programmes, portfolios and larger projects will be able to justify additional staff to help with information management, often as part of a support office.

Programmes and portfolios need to address three particular factors:

- consistency of information management across all component projects, programmes and business as usual
- co-ordination of information management across the programme or portfolio
- distinguishing between portfolio, programme and project level information as appropriate.

Consistency is important for both data and information and requires a common system for recording and distributing data. This should allow individual management teams to have access to relevant information across the portfolio or programme to better manage their component part. For example, this would ensure that all projects in a multinational programme report costs in the same currency, using the same mechanism for calculating exchange rates. Without consistency it is impossible to aggregate information automatically to create an overall picture.

The portfolio management team is likely to have responsibility for both knowledge management and development of capability maturity. Since information management is closely linked to both these areas the portfolio management team must take a long-term view to ensure that good practice is embedded in the organisation.

Assurance

General

Assurance is the set of systematic activities intended to ensure that the objectives and management processes of a project, programme or portfolio are fit for purpose.

The goals of assurance are to:

- review management planning
- monitor effectiveness of functions and processes
- give stakeholders confidence that the work is being managed effectively and efficiently.

The targets of assurance can be split into two simple categories: the objectives of the work (outputs, outcomes or benefits) and the processes (project, programme or portfolio) designed to achieve them.

Objectives will usually be the subject of quality control techniques, which will be defined in the appropriate management plans. The role of assurance is to audit the management plans to ensure appropriate standards have been set and check that the results of quality control have been acted upon.

Processes and procedures should also be set out in the management plans. The assurance function should check that the appropriate management plans are in place, the processes and procedures are fit for purpose and competent resources are applying them.

> The term assurance is commonly used in the context of 'quality assurance'. Praxis does not separate out quality as a function since quality, in all its forms, is built into the entire framework. Quality is an inherent characteristic rather than a separate function. Therefore quality planning is covered in the planning function and quality control is covered in the control function. The fourth aspect of quality, continual improvement, is encompassed within capability maturity.

Assurance is the responsibility of the P3 sponsor. Anyone performing assurance must be independent of the management and delivery teams, and report directly to the sponsor. Assurance resources will often come from a dedicated support organisation or project management office (PMO). It is the sponsor's responsibility to use the results of assurance to address any issues and instil confidence in the management team.

Performing assurance is a key indicator of an organisation's level of capability maturity. It is accepted as a key function in developing the quality of P3 management but is not without its problems.

Thamhain and Wilemon identified that 'procedures' are one of the main sources of conflict in projects. This can be interpreted in different ways, but when independent auditors arrive to check that certain procedures are being followed, it can definitely cause concern among the management team and potentially lead to conflict.

Therefore, the sponsor should not only accept responsibility for ensuring assurance happens but also that it visibly makes a positive contribution. There are various ways that this can be achieved; for example:

- Assurance should be risk-based. This means that it concentrates on the riskier areas of what is being assured. If a project has particularly difficult stakeholder issues or is implementing highly innovative technology, then assurance should focus on those areas and not go through a laborious box-ticking exercise in straightforward areas of management. If a programme is being managed by a less experienced programme manager, that would be a focus of risk-based assurance.
- Assurance should assist as well as check. Conflict is more likely to arise if the people doing the assurance simply turn up, check procedures and leave. The assurance role should be one of assisting and advising as well as reviewing. People in this role move from project to project and programme to programme. They are in the perfect position to promote good practices and disseminate lessons learned.
- Assurance should be seen as a sign of the organisation's commitment to develop the discipline and profession of P3 management rather than just a means of checking up on people.

The intended approach to assurance, the resources required and scheduled reviews are all set out in the assurance management plan. Since it is the sponsor's responsibility to ensure that assurance is implemented, this plan has to be prepared by the sponsor or delegated to someone not involved in the management of the work being assured.

Projects, programmes and portfolios

For stand-alone projects, it is relatively straightforward to define what constitutes 'independent' assurance, but in programmes it is more complex.

The programme organisation is often responsible for assuring the component projects. Therefore, people who assure the projects may be members of the programme management team. Clearly, they cannot then have responsibility for assuring the programme and other, independent assurance resources must be used.

To add to this complexity, the programme manager often fulfils the role of sponsor for component projects and, in this position, has responsibility for project assurance, while having to remaining independent from programme assurance.

A more mature organisation may collect all its assurance resources in an organisation, such as a PMO, that is independent of all projects and programmes – and potentially independent of any portfolios. This is entirely dependent on the nature of the organisation, the scale and complexity of its projects, programmes and portfolios, its capability maturity and also its environment.

Some more complex environments may need multiple assurance teams. For example, in a regulated environment there may be an internal team that focuses on effective and efficient management and an external team that focuses on conformance with regulations.

In these environments each team will have their own procedures and scope designed to meet the needs of one group of stakeholders. It is possible for the total assurance burden to become onerous and even unworkable. In these circumstances, the sponsor must get the different teams to work in a co-ordinated manner, sharing information where possible and ensuring that all aspects are covered. This approach is known as integrated assurance.

Portfolio sponsors are often part of the organisation's main governing board. At this level assurance provides a vital link to organisational governance. Usually, the organisation's audit committee has a general duty for ensuring that the board has the assurance that it needs. In a mature organisation, this means that the assurance of projects, programmes and portfolios ultimately flows through the organisation to the body responsible for corporate governance.

Scope management

General

Scope management identifies, defines and controls objectives, in the form of outputs, outcomes and benefits. Its goals are to:

- identify stakeholder wants and needs
- specify outputs, outcomes and benefits that meet agreed requirements
- maintain scope throughout the life cycle.

Scope is the totality of outputs, outcomes and benefits that should be delivered. The complexity of the scope is the main distinguishing factor between work that is managed as a project, a programme or a portfolio.

The way in which scope is managed depends upon three things: the nature of the objectives (outputs, outcomes or benefits), the definability of the objectives, and the complexity of the work.

The scope of a project will typically only include outputs but, where complexity is low, may be extended to cover benefits. The scope of a programme invariably covers benefits realisation and the resulting change management. The scope of a standard portfolio is defined by its component projects and programmes, whereas the scope of a structured portfolio is defined by the strategic objectives it is designed to achieve.

> A key element in the identification process is to decide whether achievement of the objectives requires changes to business as usual. The management of low-level change may well be achievable using typical project governance structures. More extensive and complex change is an indicator that programme (or in some cases portfolio) governance structures are more appropriate.

Scope management is made up of five main areas that work in unison to identify, define and control the scope:

- **Requirements management** captures and analyses stakeholder views of the work's objectives. Requirements are 'solution-free'; i.e. they describe the stakeholders' wants and needs but do not determine the outputs required to meet them.
- **Solutions development** takes the requirements and investigates how they may be met while providing the best return on investment.
- **Benefits management** takes requirements that have been expressed in terms of benefits and manages them through to their eventual delivery. Benefits management is usually dependent upon change management to convert outputs into outcomes and derive benefits from outcomes.
- **Change control** is a procedure that captures and assesses potential changes to scope. It ensures that only desirable, achievable and viable changes are made.
- **Configuration management** monitors and documents the development of products. It records approved changes and the archival of superseded versions. The information in a configuration management system will help the assessment change requests.

The way that these areas inter-relate varies considerably. A simple scope management procedure could take the form shown in Figure 1.24 ('implement solution' covers both change control and configuration management).

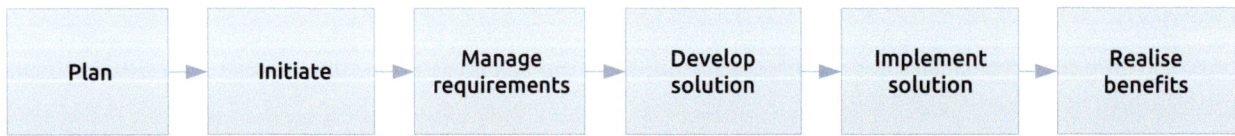

Figure 1.24 Scope management procedure

This describes a linear approach that is appropriate where a small number of outputs supports a small number of benefits; i.e. a piece of work of low complexity that will probably be managed as a project.

In a more extensive piece of work where multiple outputs and benefits have complex relationships, scope management integrates the procedures of its component functions, as shown in Figure 1.25.

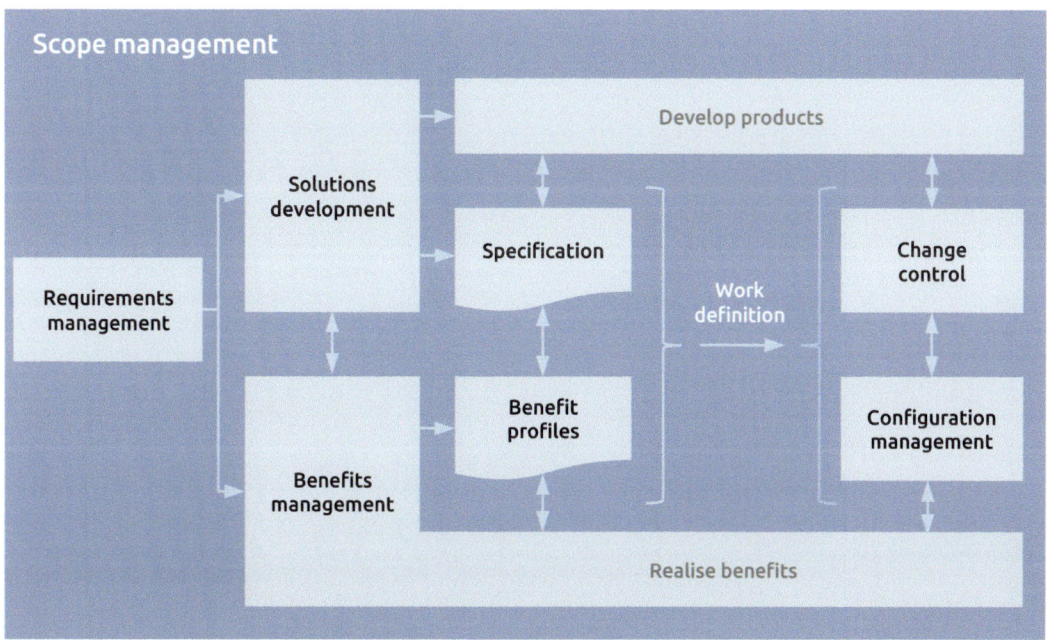

Figure 1.25 Scope management and its component functions

Requirements management will always trigger solutions development, which designs the tangible outputs. If requirements have been defined in terms of benefits the benefits management function will be triggered. Benefits rely on the implementation of outputs so solutions development and benefits management must initially work in parallel.

Once outputs have been documented in a specification and benefits have been defined in benefit profiles, the work has a baseline for what must be delivered. This normally occurs at the end of the definition phase of the life cycle, although some detail may be left for completion at the beginning of stages or tranches.

Definition of the work needed to deliver the specification and benefits is covered as part of schedule management. This work definition will be used to create models of the work that enable time scheduling, resource scheduling, budgeting and cost control.

Once work starts on the delivery phase of projects and programmes any changes to baseline scope must be subject to formal change control and recorded in configuration management along with the results of quality control.

The develop products process covers the conduct of the work that is entirely dependent on the technical content, whether it be construction, software development, pharmaceutical development or any other sector. The detail of this is outside the remit of P3 management except where it interfaces with scope management.

Benefits management continues beyond the production of the benefits profiles to cover the use of change management to realise benefits. This function can be described in a way that is sector-independent and is therefore deemed to be part of P3 management.

The degree to which detailed requirements and solutions can be predicted at the beginning of the project, programme or portfolio will influence how scope is managed.

Where the objective is well understood and has a tangible output (e.g. in construction and engineering projects and programmes) it is usual to define the scope as accurately as possible in the definition phase. Change control then assesses all potential changes to scope, reduces cost escalation and maintains the viability of the business case.

It is also useful to define what is outside of scope to avoid misunderstandings. Clearly defining what is in and out of scope reduces risk and manages the expectations of all the key stakeholders.

Where the objective is less tangible or subject to significant change (e.g. business change or some IT systems), a more flexible approach to scope is needed. A parallel life cycle may be adopted and an agile approach may be taken, where scope is iteratively refined throughout the delivery phase.

An important factor in managing the scope of work is to maximise value for money. The discipline of value management brings together an important set of procedures and techniques that operate throughout the six areas. It ensures that investment in a project, programme or portfolio is optimised for the potential return it can deliver.

> The evolution of P3 terminology has created potential confusion in the terms 'change control' and 'change management'. Change control deals specifically with the control of potential changes to scope. Change management covers the work involved in changing working practices in business as usual.

Projects, programmes and portfolios

Once an output has been specified, work definition determines the individual activities that will be needed to create it and its component products. This information can be presented as a product breakdown structure (PBS) and/or a work breakdown structure (WBS).

Developing a breakdown structure is an iterative exercise. It will initially be done during the definition process in parallel with detailed planning for the other aspects of the project (i.e. time and cost). These three elements of the triple constraint must be balanced, and this may require various adjustments to the detail of the PBS and WBS.

In traditional projects, where there is a reasonably comprehensive specification of the output, the approved breakdown structure is baselined at the end of the definition process. The products in a PBS will become configuration items in a configuration management system, and any proposed changes of scope will go through a formal change control procedure.

Some projects use an agile approach where the scope baseline will initially comprise functional requirements rather than fully specified products. The products that fulfil these functions will be developed in iterations known as time boxes.

Programme requirements are typically described in terms of outcomes and benefits with the associated outputs being delivered by projects. The scope of a programme is therefore specified using a blueprint, benefit profiles and a list of component projects.

The relationship between outputs, outcomes and benefits is rarely one-to-one and there will be multiple dependencies between the outputs, outcomes and benefits. These inter-dependencies must be defined and documented. Effective solutions development, benefits management, change control and configuration management for the programme as a whole will all depend upon understanding these inter-dependencies.

The scope of a programme tends to be more fluid than that of a project. It is unlikely that solutions for all the projects within the programme can be identified at the outset and the business environment may change. A programme management team will have to manage evolving scope throughout the life cycle.

> The terminology of scope has become somewhat blurred in recent years. Praxis takes the following approach to establish some clarity:
>
> - An objective can be an output, outcome or benefit.
> - Most outputs are formally handed over from one party to another – in which case they may be referred to deliverables.
> - A more complex output may be made up of multiple products, some of which may be deliverables in their own right.
> - Some products will also be entered into a configuration management system and defined as configuration items.
> - Products, groups of products and the work to produce them are collectively known as work packages.

A standard portfolio is an accumulation of projects and programmes with unconnected objectives. The primary purpose of a standard portfolio is to create an infrastructure that implements consistent standards and makes optimum use of the organisation's resources. Its scope is flexible and is simply the sum of the projects and programmes it contains.

A structured portfolio is defined by the strategic objectives of its host organisation that it is designed to satisfy. Its scope is the sum of the projects, programmes and change activity required to deliver those strategic objectives.

Scope management of a structured portfolio starts by identifying relevant projects and programmes. It is likely that existing projects and programmes will initially be included, and over the life of a portfolio many ideas for projects and programmes will emerge and compete for inclusion. The scope is regularly reviewed and adjusted by the prioritisation and balancing activities in the portfolio management process. Eligibility criteria need to be established which may be expressed in terms such as required levels of return on investment or acceptable levels of risk.

The portfolio governance process should provide rules for bringing new proposals forward for review with the portfolio manager helping project and programme sponsors to shape their potential entry into the portfolio. While solutions development and benefits management are largely delegated to projects and programmes, the portfolio co-ordination process will ensure that value is maximised.

Requirements management

General

Requirements management establishes stakeholders' wants and needs, and then reviews these to create a set of baseline requirements for use in solutions development and benefits management. Its goals are to:

- ensure that all relevant stakeholders have the opportunity to express their wants and needs
- reconcile multiple stakeholder requirements to create a single viable set of objectives
- achieve stakeholder consensus on a baseline set of requirements.

A clear and agreed expression of requirements and their acceptance criteria is essential for the success of any project, programme or portfolio. Requirements may be expressed as physical deliverables, business benefits, aspirations, functions or technical needs.

The planning step will define the techniques and approaches that will be used to work with stakeholders to capture and agree requirements (see Figure 1.26). The initiation step will ensure the necessary resources are mobilised and requirements management can start.

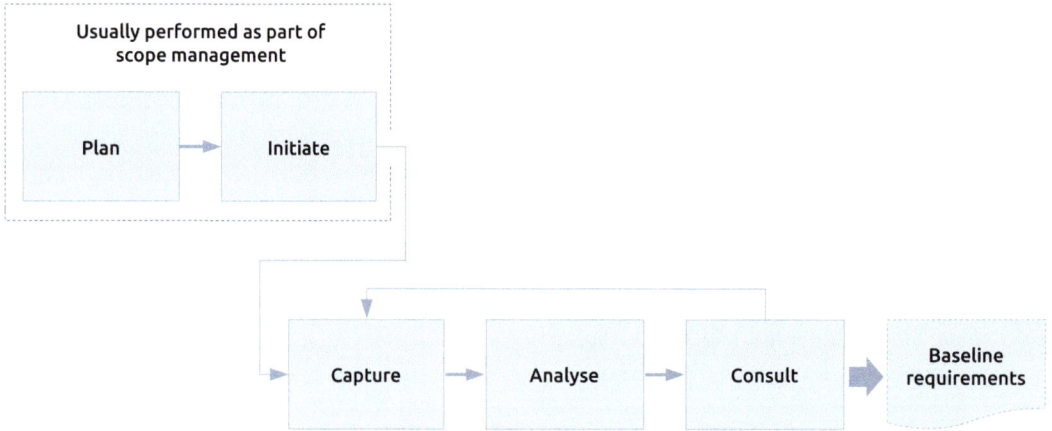

Figure 1.26 Requirements management procedure

The planning and initiation steps are usually performed as part of an overarching scope management procedure but may be separated out where requirements are particularly complex or extensive.

The first specific step in the procedure is to capture all types of requirements. Most will be generated by internal and external stakeholders (such as clients and users) but there may also be a background of legal or regulatory requirements that must also be included.

The requirements must be analysed to ensure they are practical, achievable and define 'what' is required rather than 'how' it will be achieved. A well specified requirement has the following characteristics:

- **Unique** It addresses only one core requirement.
- **Current** It is up to date and relevant to the business need.
- **Consistent** It does not conflict with other requirements.

- **Understandable** It is clear and unambiguous.
- **Verifiable** The compliance of products designed to meet the requirement can be verified through inspection, demonstration or testing.
- **Traceable** The requirement can be traced from the originating need, through the delivery process, to the delivered product.
- **Prioritised** Its importance is understood relative to other requirements.

The remaining steps will be undertaken according to the context of the work. For example, the approach for software development using a parallel life cycle and an agile approach would be different from that using a serial life cycle; managing requirements for business transformation will be different from construction.

Capturing requirements can be done in any number of ways ranging from personal interviews, surveys and workshops, to focus groups, modelling and simulation.

Some development methodologies, including agile, are designed to enable the continuous capture and refinement of requirements on the assumption that the stakeholders may not be sure of their needs at the outset.

Analysing requirements involves looking for any gaps, overlaps or conflicts in what different stakeholders have asked for. It will need some initial high-level solutions development, planning and benefits management to appreciate the implications of the requirements. The result is a thorough understanding of requirements and the way they contribute to the overall objective.

The consult step is primarily about providing feedback to stakeholders and building consensus. The results of the analysis are communicated through individual consultation or group workshops. This leads to a debate about the functionality and alternative ideas.

Consultation may well result in further requirements being captured and analysed. The eventual result is a baselined set of options for functional requirements. These can then be used to examine alternative solutions during solutions development.

One well established technique that addresses requirements management, solutions development and some aspects of benefits management is called value management. While value is a subjective term and means different things to different people, in the P3 environment it is a means of maximising value for money and is represented by the following ratio:

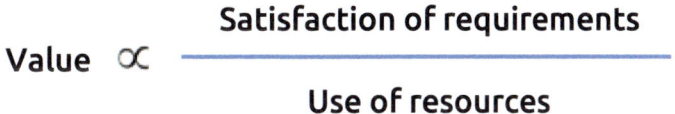

$$\text{Value} \propto \frac{\text{Satisfaction of requirements}}{\text{Use of resources}}$$

The goal of value management is not to maximise the satisfaction of requirements, nor to minimise the use of resources, but to establish the balance that maximises the ratio of the two.

Projects, programmes and portfolios

Initial project requirements are defined during the identification process and only need to be detailed enough to identify the probable solution and complete the brief. Requirements management is performed in detail during the definition process, along with solutions development, in order to complete a full investment appraisal and business case.

On small projects with relatively straightforward objectives this may all be done by the project manager. As the requirements become more complex, specialists may need to be involved. Even on small projects 'failure to fully understand stakeholder requirements' is one of the most common causes of project failure. This is not an exercise that can be done casually.

For projects that are part of a programme or delivered by a contractor to a client, requirements will be derived from the programme requirements or client's brief. They will relate to an output and, depending on how well the requirements are described, may result in a reduction in effort needed.

Where it is intended to use agile techniques, the requirements management procedure must be efficient and dynamic. It must use rigorous prioritisation mechanisms, such as MoSCoW, to ensure that only valuable and justifiable requirements are included in each package of work.

An early matter to resolve is whether the requirements are expressed as outputs, outcomes or benefits. This will govern whether the project includes benefits realisation as part of an extended project life cycle. If the requirements include multiple benefits that involve more than one area of business change and multiple outputs, the work is best governed as a programme rather than a project.

Programme requirements will typically be expressed as a combination of outputs and benefits. These may have quite complex relationships that can be described in a benefits map.

The relationship between requirements management and the subsequent functions of solutions development and benefits management is not entirely sequential. Particularly in the identification process and definition process of the life cycle, stakeholder requirements will need some high-level quantification of benefits and evaluation of solutions before arriving at a baseline set of requirements. The programme management team is responsible for requirements management as it applies to the programme's benefits and the team must decide how much responsibility for requirements management of outputs will be delegated to the project teams.

A useful dividing line between the programme and projects is for the programme to express the functional requirements needed from an output. It is then for the project teams to manage the technical requirements that will deliver the required functionality, as shown in Figure 1.27.

If using value management the programme management team must balance value across the projects. For example, reprioritising and redistributing resources may result in greater overall value across the programme, even though this appears to reduce the value from one particular project.

A standard portfolio is made up of projects and programmes with independent requirements. The requirements of the portfolio are concerned with efficient use of resources for the host organisation and improvement in the discipline of P3 management. Once these requirements are set in the portfolio initiation process they will remain fairly constant.

The initial requirements of a structured portfolio will be expressed in terms of the organisation's strategic objectives. These will be a mixture of stand-alone and inter-related requirements. The requirements management procedure in a structured portfolio assesses the strategic objectives and clarifies them with the executive board.

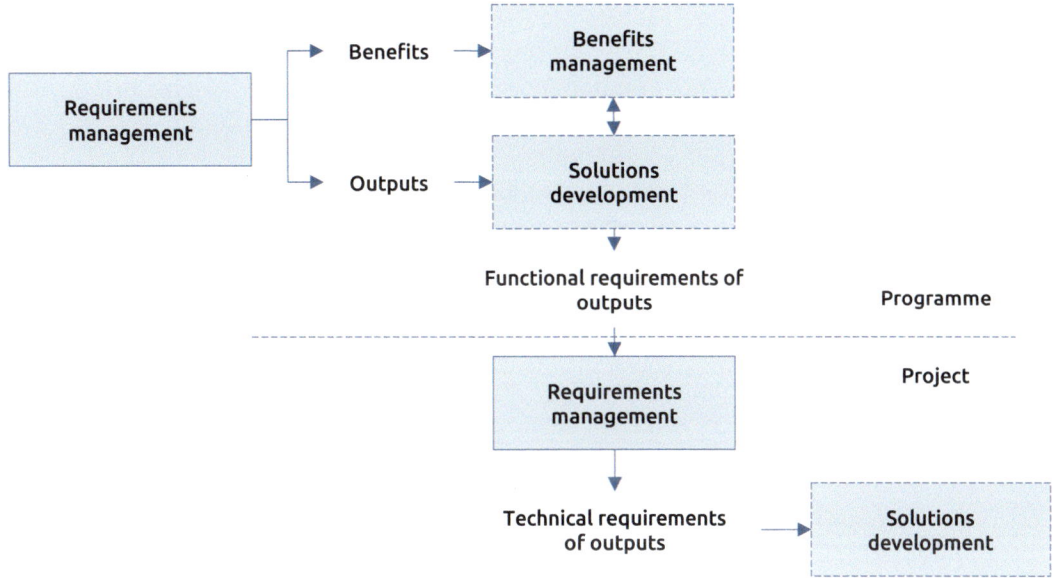

Figure 1.27 Project and programme requirements management

The assessment of requirements will start during the portfolio initiation process. Inter-related objectives should be identified and may be collected into a programme with independent objectives delivered through projects. This design activity will be constantly reviewed as part of the prioritisation and balancing activities in the portfolio management process.

Most requirements management activity will be delegated to the project and programme management teams, but the portfolio management team must perform two key functions.

Firstly, it must act as the interface between the projects and programmes on the one hand and the executive board who own the strategy on the other. On behalf of the executive board, the portfolio management team must ensure that their requirements are accurately translated into projects and programmes. On behalf of the project and programme management teams, it must ensure that the strategic requirements are adequately defined so that the projects and programmes have sufficient information to deliver the right outputs and benefits.

Secondly, it must co-ordinate projects and programmes to ensure that the many, localised requirements management processes work in harmony. This is part of the portfolio co-ordination process and may involve taking central responsibility for dealing with key stakeholders. It will definitely involve vetting detailed project and programme requirements to monitor gaps, overlaps and conflicts.

Solutions development

General

Solutions development determines the best way of satisfying the requirements for an output. Its goals are to:

- evaluate baseline requirements and alternative solutions to achieve them
- select the optimum solution
- create a specification for the solution.

Requirements management produces a clear set of stakeholder requirements but does not explain how to meet those requirements. Solutions development investigates the technical options for meeting the requirements and will work in conjunction with investment appraisal that investigates the financial implications of the different options.

Just like any other function, solutions development needs to be planned and initiated, as shown in Figure 1.28. Since the solutions development steps follow on naturally from those in the requirements management procedure, it would be unusual for it to have separate planning and initiation steps. However, some contractual circumstances may make requirements management and solutions development the responsibility of different organisations; in which case the procedures would be separate.

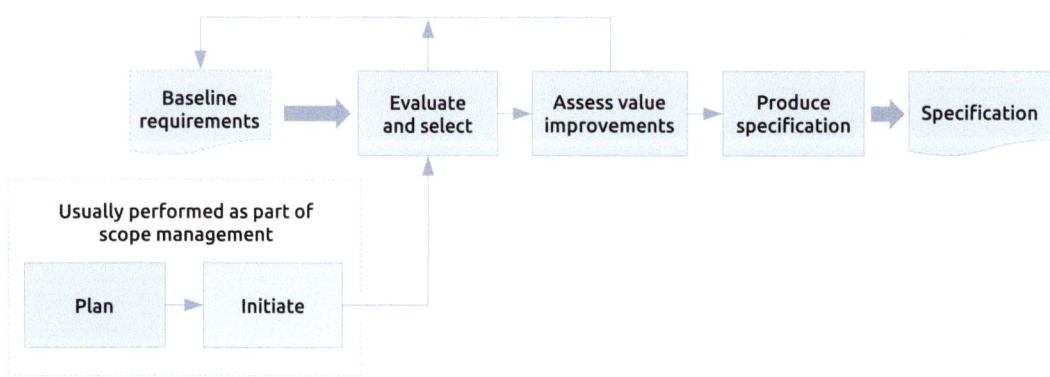

Figure 1.28 Solutions development procedure

Evaluation looks at alternative approaches and assesses how well they will perform against stated criteria, such as capital cost, speed of delivery and degree of risk. The techniques involved range from simple 'make or buy' considerations to the full-blown modelling and simulation of innovative solutions. A value management approach can be used to help select the best-value options.

As one solution emerges from the evaluation and is selected as the optimum solution it will be developed into a specification. In some cases the detailed elements of the specification will only cover the early stages of development, with later stages being refined as the work proceeds. The development of value-improving proposals can occur at any stage of the delivery process.

> Verification of products is part of quality control and configuration management. Validation is similar to the continuing confirmation that the objectives remain justifiable as defined by the business case.

The solution should be regularly checked against the requirements (which may themselves be subject to change). This takes two forms. 'Verification' is the term used to ensure that the solution is being built right; 'validation' is the term used to ensure that the right product is being built. Verification is against specifications; validation is against requirements.

Projects, programmes and portfolios

The great majority of projects are designed to deliver an output and no more. Where the requirements are relatively simple, and use tried and tested technology, the type of solution will be implicitly understood by the stakeholders and management team; for example, 'My requirement is to keep my car dry and off the road' – the solution is to build a garage. Solutions development then simply becomes the production of a specification without the preceding consideration of options such as to rent a garage or to sell the car and travel by bus. The project manager will need to judge the degree to which stakeholder assumptions should be challenged and more radical solutions suggested.

Traditional projects describe the output in a specification. This is contained within the definition documentation and submitted for approval at the end of the definition process. The specification may be supported by additional information such as a product or work breakdown structure.

Agile methods place much less emphasis on the detailed specification of a solution early in the life cycle. Instead, they focus on prioritised functions that are delivered incrementally in a series of time boxes or sprints. The detail of the output evolves during the iterations and addresses the typical problem of IT projects where it is difficult for a stakeholder to accept components of the system until they actually see it in action.

The equivalent of the specification for a programme of business change is the blueprint. This describes the cumulative effect of change on the organisation. It is a picture of all the outcomes created by the programme.

Each project within the programme is aimed at delivering an output that contributes to the blueprint. In most cases the degree of detail in the blueprint will leave ample space for project management teams to consider alternative solutions for the required outputs. However, the programme management team must co-ordinate project solutions and review proposals. There will be elements such as common components and technology platforms that are transferable between projects and the compatibility of solutions proposed by different projects should be checked.

Solutions development is predominantly a project and programme matter but the portfolio management team may set guidelines about innovation and risk that constrain the types of solution considered.

Benefits management

General

Benefits management defines benefits, implements the necessary change and ensures the benefits are realised. Its goals are to:

- define benefits and dis-benefits of the proposed work
- establish measurement mechanisms
- implement any change needed in order to realise benefits
- measure improvement and compare it with the business case.

The realisation of benefits is the driving force behind any project, programme or portfolio. The definition of a benefit is broad – it is simply a positive impact of change. Since any change has the potential to have a negative impact, benefits management also covers the management of dis-benefits. These are negative effects of change that the host organisation is prepared to accept as part of the cost of achieving the positive benefits.

> In many guides, the management of benefits is seen as a function unique to programmes. Praxis maintains that the realise benefits process can be part of a project life cycle when the complexity of scope is low – for example, where one output delivers one benefit.

Some benefits are tangible and some are not. Examples of tangible benefits are 'reduced costs' or 'jobs created'. Intangible benefits are things like 'improved corporate reputation' or 'decreased risk'.

The value of benefits is a vital input to investment appraisal in the business case. The business case is owned by the sponsor who is therefore ultimately accountable for the realisation of the benefits in the business case.

Benefits are derived from outcomes through change management. Day-to-day responsibility for the implementation of change and realisation of benefits lies with one or more business change managers. The relationship between project or programme managers and the business change manager(s) is crucial. The delivery of outputs and the management of change must be closely co-ordinated.

The benefits management procedure has five main steps, as shown in Figure 1.29.

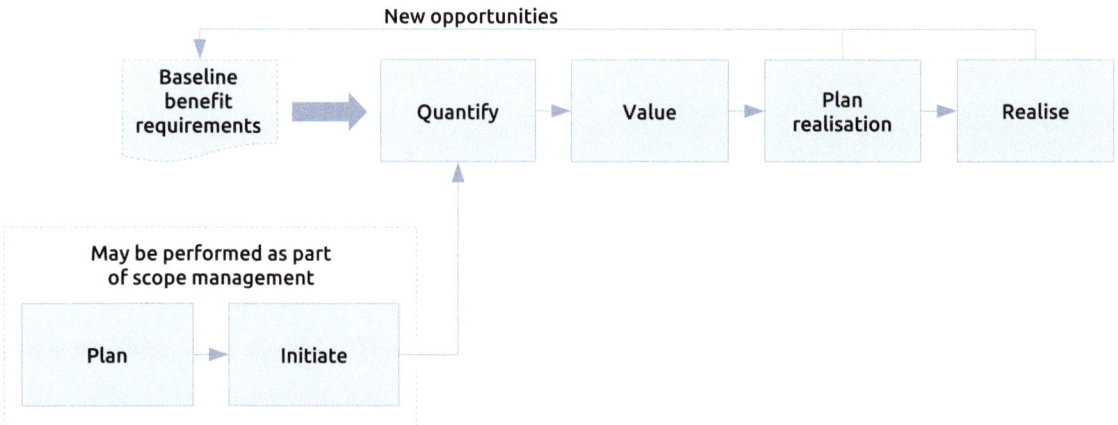

Figure 1.29 Benefits management procedure

Planning explains how benefits will be managed. It sets out policies for aspects such as measurement, roles and responsibilities, priorities and key performance indicators. If the intended approach to benefits management has been defined in a broader scope management plan the planning step may simply involve reviewing and updating the relevant section of that document.

Once the work has been authorised the resources needed to perform benefits management are mobilised so that benefits management work can start. This is the initiation step.

In less complex situations (e.g. a project delivering a single benefit), the planning and initiation steps may be performed as part of an overarching scope management procedure. In programmes, benefits management will justify a dedicated benefits management plan.

Benefits depend on the delivery of outputs and the achievement of outcomes. The inter-relationships between these will have been defined during requirements management using techniques such as benefits mapping. Each benefit (and dis-benefit) then needs to be quantified and valued.

It is very easy to describe a benefit such as 'increased sales' but far less easy to accurately quantify it. Numerous studies have shown a tendency to overestimate the quantity of benefits that will result from a change initiative. This step in the procedure uses techniques such as workshops, pilot studies or Delphi to compensate for individual optimism or organisational pressure.

Value can be expressed in many ways and benefits are often referred to as 'financial' or 'non-financial'. Since most business cases are based on some form of financial investment appraisal, benefits should be valued in financial terms whenever possible. While it may be relatively straightforward to provide a financial value for 'increased sales', it is less simple to calculate the financial value of 'increased efficiency' and difficult to do so for 'improved customer satisfaction'. In an acceptable business case the quantifiable benefits will outweigh the costs. It is very dangerous to rely on the 'feel-good factor' of intangible and unquantifiable benefits in a business case.

This step will apply various techniques to estimate the financial value of benefits so that these can be compared with the financial cost of realising the benefits.

It is important to apply the same rigour when quantifying and valuing dis-benefits as when performing those steps on benefits. Only then is that aspect of the business case robust.

Planning realisation involves capturing baseline measurements and agreeing targets. Baseline measurements identify the current performance of an operation so that improvements can be measured. A benefits delivery plan illustrates the timeline and milestones for realising benefits, including any dependencies on project outputs or interactions between benefits.

Benefits are realised when something changes. This usually involves permanently changing attitudes and behaviours as well as physical changes. The failure to embed new attitudes and behaviours so that they become normal practice is often the greatest risk to the realisation of the benefits in the business case. A strong emphasis on change management is an essential part of the realise step.

> The realise step is synonymous in both the benefits management procedure and the benefits realisation process.

A business change manager needs to ensure that changes are permanent and track realisation of associated benefits. The bulk of the benefits may only be realised after a project or programme is completed. Long-term actions and monitoring for continued realisation should be documented as part of the handover to business as usual.

While implementing change, new opportunities for additional benefits should always be sought.

Projects, programmes and portfolios

The majority of projects conclude with the handover of an output but where the relationship between output and benefit is less complex, the project life cycle may incorporate the benefits realisation process.

If a project is restricted to delivering an output it may or may not require the project manager to be involved in the realisation of benefits in some way.

Where a project is delivering an output to a client under contract the project manager usually has no formal involvement in benefits realisation. However, the project manager should be familiar with the client's business case and may be able to suggest value improvements along the way.

Where a project is delivering an output as part of a programme or portfolio, the project manager must work closely with other members of the programme management team and business change managers in particular.

As objectives become more complex with multiple benefits, outcomes and outputs, the work is clearly in the category of 'programme'. The management of this complex network of objectives is the primary goal of programme management.

A defining aspect of this is the hierarchy of business cases that arise. The overall programme business case may be broken down into tranche business cases and further subdivided into individual project business cases. As with the objectives, these are inter-related in complex ways.

The attribution of benefits to individual project business cases can be a difficult exercise. Double counting of benefits across a programme can arise, particularly where investment approvals are involved. This should be approached in a pragmatic way and resolved through benefits mapping and stakeholder consultation. Where appropriate, the benefit should be attributed to a specific project based on the principle of greatest contribution.

A consistent approach to benefits management must be maintained across the programme, particularly for consistency of measurement. Without this, it is difficult to aggregate benefits across multiple projects and assess their collective impact on business performance.

The benefits of a standard portfolio revolve around the simple fact that projects and programmes managed and co-ordinated in a consistent way are more efficient.

Structured portfolios will have a set of objectives derived from strategic objectives – which it is fair to assume have been deemed to be beneficial to the organisation in some way. Other than the efficient management and co-ordination of projects and programmes, the benefits of the portfolio are delivered entirely through its component projects and programmes. The portfolio's role is to ensure that these collective benefits are consistent with the strategic objectives. Strategy mapping uses the principles of influence diagrams to ensure that investment decisions, and the scope of each project and programme, are driven by the contribution of benefits to achieving the operational, organisational or business strategy.

Just as with programmes, portfolios must ensure that the approach to benefits management is consistent across the portfolio, enabling the prioritisation and balancing activities in the portfolio management process to be effective. A well-defined, flexible, portfolio-wide policy for benefits management will also reduce the work needed to develop management plans at project and programme level.

Portfolios are able to gather and assess longer-term data on the performance of benefits management. This can be used to improve benefits management practices by sharing and applying lessons learned, ideally through a knowledge management system.

Configuration management

General
Configuration management encompasses the administrative activities concerned with the creation, maintenance, controlled change and quality control of products. Its goals are to:

- identify the products that will be treated as configuration items
- support the assessment of change requests and document the results of change control
- maintain the validity of the configuration and the accuracy of the configuration management system.

A configuration is the complete set of functional and physical characteristics of a final deliverable defined in the specification. At its simplest, configuration management is the same as version control.

Configuration management provides control over the development of products. It helps to avoid mistakes and misunderstandings about what a product is required to do and whether it does this. It provides the verification of products as required by solutions development. This function also ensures that adequate procedures are in place to provide continuing maintenance of products for the duration of the product life cycle.

A typical configuration management procedure is shown in Figure 1.30.

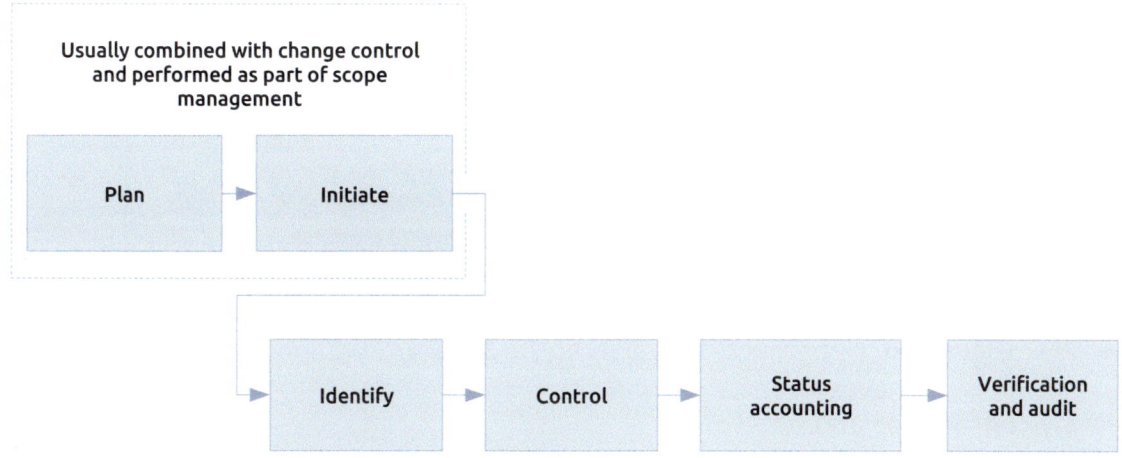

Figure 1.30 Configuration management procedure

A configuration management plan (whether as a separate document or a section of the scope management plan) should describe any specific techniques and the extent of their application during the life cycle. The plan should also identify roles and responsibilities for carrying out configuration management. Initiation will make sure that the required resources, including people, tools and systems, are in place.

Configuration identification involves breaking down the work into component products (configuration items), creating a unique numbering or referencing system and establishing configuration baselines. This aligns closely with the preparation of a product breakdown structure in scope management.

The control step ensures that all changes to configuration items are documented. An important aspect is the ability to identify the inter-relationships between configuration items. This is essential information for the review and assess steps in the change control procedure as the practicality of making a change to scope will be affected by its impact on interconnected configuration items.

Status accounting tracks the current status of a configuration, providing traceability of configuration items throughout their development and operation. Regular status reports will indicate if change requests are being processed in a timely manner and may highlight products that are subject to frequent requests for change or stakeholders who are common sources of change requests.

Verification and audit is used to determine whether a product conforms to its requirements and configuration information. Typically, an audit is undertaken at the end of a phase, stage or tranche.

Configuration audits take one of three forms:

- A physical audit looks at the relevant elements of a configuration item and will confirm that the item meets its specification. It will check the results of quality control and confirm that all the necessary test documentation has been completed.
- A functional audit of a configuration item will check that it performs the function for which it was designed.
- A system audit checks that the configuration management system is working, able to support the planned procedure and perform the necessary functions. This aspect of configuration management is part of the assurance of the function.

A form of configuration management can also be applied to the management documentation. This is mainly about version control but could also include functional audits as part of assurance.

As work is completed, responsibility for maintaining deliverables passes to the client or business as usual. The management team is responsible for ensuring that relevant information management principles have been applied and the configuration is easily transferable to those who will be maintaining the products long after the project or programme has been closed.

Projects, programmes and portfolios

The need for formal configuration management beyond simple version control will depend upon the scale and complexity of the objectives. It will also depend upon the degree to which specification changes are allowed. In a project that has a contract based on a firm price payment method, no change is allowed. In an agile project changes are an inherent part of the method. Both contexts need to track different versions of a product in development and both need to support verification of products against the specification. Configuration management systems have to adapt to very different situations.

Within scope management, work definition produces a product breakdown structure and detailed descriptions of each product. This becomes the configuration and once it is baselined it is subject to formal change control and configuration management.

Some projects are more complex because they include safety-critical, secure or related environments. The larger the project, the more people may be involved in developing, testing and integrating a product. Configuration management has a role to ensure that there are no gaps in the chain of quality control, testing and record keeping for all products, intermediate assemblies and testing regimes that might compromise the final deliverables.

A programme management team needs to ensure that all outputs fit together and function properly in the context of the blueprint. Each project and area of change activity within the programme must adopt a consistent approach to managing configurations. This makes it much simpler to assess whether a change to the products of one project will have any effect on the products of another project, or on the programme's eventual benefits.

A portfolio is unlikely to produce any configuration items other than key management documents, but where different project and programme deliverables come together to meet a strategic objective, the portfolio management team must track the configuration to ensure the final integration achieves the required result.

Change control

General

Change control is the means by which all requests to change a scope baseline are captured, evaluated and then approved or rejected. Its goals are to:

- capture stakeholders' requests to make changes to scope
- ensure that requests are only approved if viable and achievable
- integrate changes into the existing scope.

Where scope is well defined early in the life cycle, it is essential for success that changes to approved baselines are controlled. A rigorous change control procedure must be established and maintained on all projects, programmes and portfolios. It must allow stakeholders to submit their suggestions for changes to scope. A typical procedure is shown in Figure 1.31.

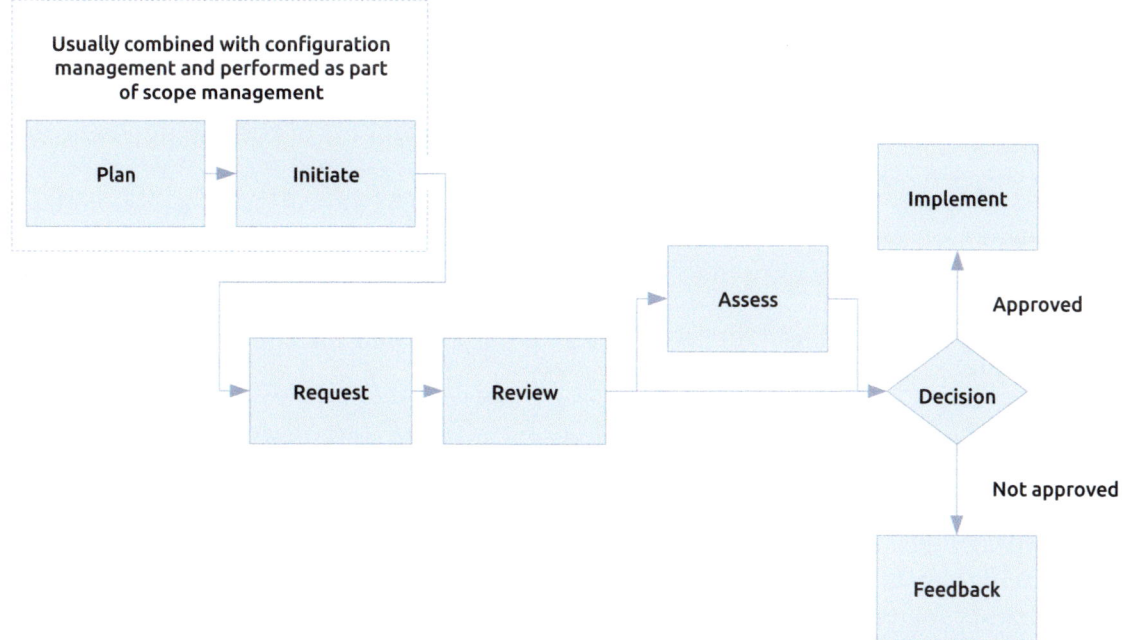

Figure 1.31 Change control procedure

The planning step will define how the management team will work with stakeholders to handle a subject that can be a significant source of conflict. It may include setting limits on the amount of change permissible and must certainly integrate closely with stakeholder management. It may even define which stakeholders are allowed to submit requests, perhaps acting as a point of contact and initial filter for their stakeholder group.

The initiation step will ensure that resources are mobilised that have the necessary competence to deal with the complexity of the scope. This sometimes requires the appointment of a body called the change control authority to ensure that change requests are not only properly assessed but the procedure is seen to be open and fair.

Planning and initiation will often be performed as part of overall scope management and will usually be combined with the corresponding steps in the configuration management procedure.

The first specific step in the procedure is when a stakeholder makes a change request. The stakeholder must provide relevant information about the nature of the change. The request is entered into a change log which records all requests and their status (e.g. pending, approved, rejected or deferred).

The change request is reviewed to determine its high-level impact on outputs, outcomes and benefits. If necessary, further clarification may be sought before deciding if it is worthwhile performing a detailed assessment. The proposed change may be rejected without further evaluation, in which case the reasons for rejection will be recorded and feedback given to the stakeholder.

If a full assessment is justified, all options relating to the change are captured and evaluated. To be accepted a proposed change should be beneficial, practical and affordable.

Beneficial means that it has a positive impact on the business case, or has some other advantage such as reducing risk. Practical means that it will work in the context of the specification and any other changes. Affordable means that funds are available to pay for the change, perhaps through a change budget or management reserve.

The detailed impact on delivery plans is also assessed and a recommendation to approve, reject, defer or request more information is made. Thresholds are set to determine whether the decision can be made by the P3 manager, sponsor or other members of the management team.

The decision is then communicated to the management team and stakeholders, including feedback where appropriate. Recording lessons learned from the assessment can speed up future assessments that have similar technical content.

If the change is approved, relevant delivery plans are updated and the changes are made to existing products, or specifications for future products.

There is always the possibility that urgent changes are imposed or pushed through without due process. These should be retrospectively put through the change control procedure.

Any approved changes need to be fed back into the configuration management system. In some circumstances it may be appropriate to have a change freeze where no further changes to scope will be considered. Where this has been agreed by the sponsor, it should be included as a key decision point in the scope management plan.

Projects, programmes and portfolios

Most change requests relate to the products that make up a project output. Approved changes usually have cost implications and ideally funds will have been set aside in the project budget to cover this. Some projects will be subject to contractual terms that have a significant impact on change control. Payment methods written into the contract may not allow any change to the contracted specification, while others will have a predetermined schedule of payments for authorised changes.

Just like any other budget, a change budget will have limits and tolerances. If the work is predicted to exceed these tolerances the project manager will need to escalate this issue to the sponsor who may have to seek additional funding.

Agile projects take a very different approach and make change an integral part of development. Each iteration starts with a planning meeting that clarifies and prioritises the products addressed in the iteration. Some of these features may be changes to existing features but are considered alongside all the others.

Change control at programme level is concerned with changes that relate to benefits, either because a change request is directly aimed at a benefit profile or because of the indirect effect of project changes on benefits.

The procedure will initially assess the impact of a change request on benefits and then assess the impact on the component projects. Significant change to a project may require a redistribution of resources or funds and may have a knock-on effect on other projects.

Some change requests within one project may have knock-on effects on other projects. The complexity of these interdependencies is something that the programme management team needs to be very aware of.

A structured portfolio is dependent upon corporate strategy for its objectives. This may change to reflect a changing commercial environment, and naturally the portfolio must respond accordingly. The change control procedure does not really apply to 'change requests' emanating from corporate strategy in terms of deciding whether to accept or reject them. Nonetheless, these changes still need to be assessed for their implications on the objectives of the component projects and programmes.

Instead of approving or rejecting a change request, the portfolio version of the procedure may result in reprioritisation, or even cancellation, of some projects or programmes and the identification of new ones.

Schedule management

General

A schedule is a timetable showing the work involved in a project, programme or portfolio. It is a dynamic document that is created and maintained throughout the life cycle. Schedules can be created for different aspects of the work and these are an important means of communication with all team members and stakeholders.

To be realistic, schedules must reflect the impact of resource availability, risk and estimating accuracy on the performance of the work. The goals of schedule management are therefore to:

- determine timescales for the work
- calculate profiles of resource demand
- present schedule reports in a format suitable for different stakeholders.

The schedule management procedure will vary in accordance with the context of the work but a typical high-level procedure will follow the steps shown in Figure 1.32.

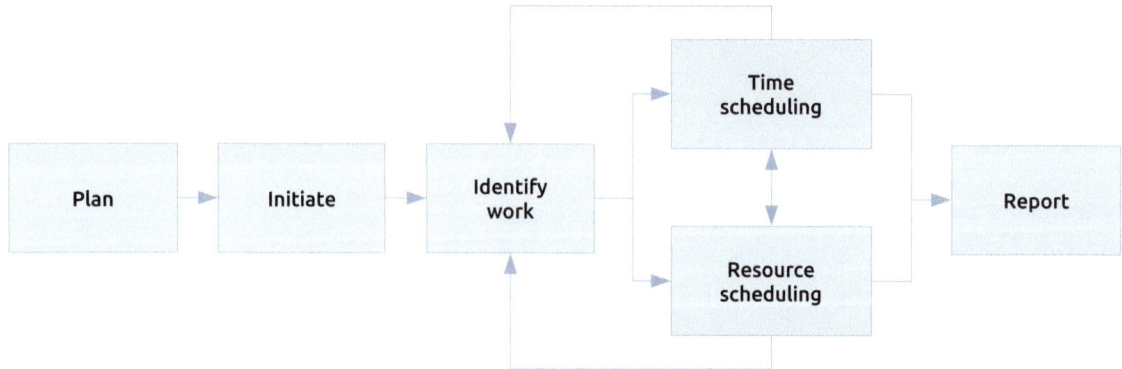

Figure 1.32 Schedule management procedure

The planning step will define the techniques and approaches that will be used to identify, schedule and report. The initiation step will ensure the necessary resources are acquired and mobilised.

Scheduling starts with the identification and definition of the work that is needed to deliver the objectives. Some work definition may have been performed as part of the scope management procedure but that is now developed in more detail.

This identification will be performed both top-down and bottom-up. Within a portfolio or programme, the work will be identified in large components; i.e. the projects and programmes within a portfolio or the projects within a programme. This may identify top-level constraints that are passed down to the component programmes and projects. Detailed scheduling based on analytical models is then conducted at project level, with the results feeding back up to the high-level programme or portfolio level.

> The same top-down and bottom-up principles are also applicable to large projects that may be divided into sub-projects.

Schedule reports range from simple milestone charts to the statistical complexity of Monte Carlo distributions. Which reports to use for different stakeholders can be set out in a schedule management plan or a stakeholder management plan if preferred.

Schedule management is concerned with the time aspect of the triple constraint. It is therefore closely inter-related to the functions that deal with the other two aspects: namely, scope management and financial management (cost).

In some contexts (e.g. traditional construction and engineering) scope is defined first and the time and cost are derived from this. In others, time and/or cost may be the principal constraints with scope being dependent upon the time and cost available. This is known as an agile approach.

The approach to developing schedules has to reflect this relationship between time, cost and scope. In some cases, rigorous techniques can be used to model the work and calculate detailed timings. In other cases, initial broad estimates are made that are constantly refined as more information becomes available.

The more detailed models described in time scheduling and resource scheduling can be used to test different scenarios. During the definition process these may relate to alternative solutions, with the aim of understanding the schedule consequences of achieving the objectives in different ways. During the delivery process different scenarios might test alternative ways of creating an output or responding to a risk event occurring. Testing theoretical scenarios in this way is commonly called 'what-if?' scheduling.

The factors affecting the way in which schedules are presented typically include:

- the level of scheduling detail required
- whether schedule information needs to be combined with resource and/or scope information
- the context of the work
- the audience for the information.

By far the most common way of presenting schedule information is a form of bar chart known as a Gantt chart. This can simply show the performance of activities on a horizontal timescale or it can be combined with logical dependencies between activities, resource usage or progress information. While a schedule is primarily about timing, the combination of time and other information is more commonly referred to as a plan.

Delivery plans are fundamental to control techniques so care must be taken in selecting the modelling and calculation techniques that are most appropriate to the context of the work. There are numerous software tools that enable work to be scheduled and presented in different ways. How scheduling should be performed and which tools should be used will be set out in a schedule management plan if the complexity of the work justifies it.

> Praxis makes a distinction between delivery plans and management plans. The former is about the timing of what will be done while the latter is how the work will be governed.

Projects, programmes and portfolios

Most detailed scheduling takes place at project level where the outputs are produced. Traditionally, project schedules concentrated on the technical activity that created products but more recently, management activity is also being included. As the complexity of the work increases it becomes impractical to maintain a single detailed schedule.

Large-scale projects will often use rolling-wave planning where only short-term work is shown in detail with longer-term work being shown in summary. As the amount of management activity increases it may be useful to create separate delivery plans for different areas, such as a communications plan or a benefits realisation plan.

The need for multiple plans is inevitable as complexity increases. Within a programme, for example, there will be diverse components such as:

- projects in progress that have their own detailed delivery plans
- projects that are not yet initiated
- management activity (e.g. communications, procurement)
- change management activity.

At programme level there should be a delivery plan that summarises the component plans. For this to be effective, the management team must ensure that similar scheduling policies are adopted across the programme. These policies may be set out in a schedule management plan.

In order to avoid the top-level programme plan becoming cumbersome it will contain summary 'activities' that may represent entire tranches or projects. Other information may be represented as key milestones extracted from more detailed plans.

The greatest diversity of planning information exists in a portfolio. Portfolio plans need to be presented in a way that enables stakeholders to understand what information is derived from detailed schedules and what is more speculative.

An important aspect of portfolio management is capacity planning. This ensures that the necessary resources can be procured to deliver the portfolio. It must also avoid bottlenecks and conflicting demands on limited resources. This means estimating the number of resources required and the timing of their utilisation. Schedules must be consistent in the way they estimate activities and allocate resources so that aggregation at the portfolio level is accurate.

The portfolio management process must continuously balance changing resource demands and prioritise the allocation of limited resources. Doing this effectively will depend upon the schedule information aggregated from the component projects and programmes.

Time scheduling

General

Time scheduling techniques are used to develop and present schedules that show when work will be performed and products delivered. The goals of time scheduling are to:

- construct a model for use in numerical analysis
- calculate dates for components of work
- determine where there is flexibility in the schedule.

The time scheduling procedure has three steps, as shown in Figure 1.33.

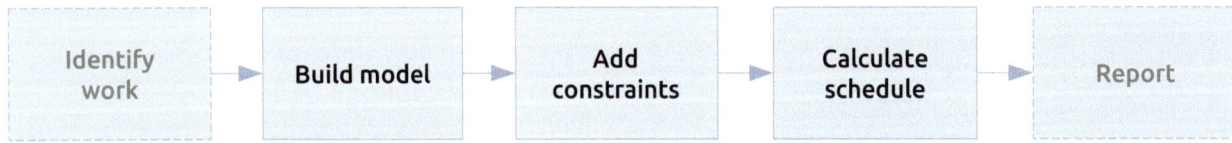

Figure 1.33 Time scheduling procedure

Once the work has been identified a model is built that reflects the sequence of work and the time required to complete each component. This 'logical model' must be supplemented by external constraints such as external decisions (e.g. a regulatory approval or delivery of a procured component). Once the model reflects the internal logic of the work and the external constraints, the schedule is calculated.

In reality these steps are by no means sequential. The model will be adjusted, constraints will be reviewed and the calculation repeated in order to arrive at the optimum schedule.

The range of techniques available to model, schedule and report the work involved in a project, programme or portfolio is very broad. The appropriate choice of technique depends upon the context and how much information is available at the point when the scheduling is being done. For example, factors affecting the choice of technique will include whether the:

- scheduling is taking place in the identification or delivery phase of the life cycle
- scope of the work is well defined or flexible (traditional versus agile approaches)
- schedule represents a summary of other schedules
- output is aimed at members of the delivery team or external stakeholders
- work is inherently innovative or uncertain.

The use of scheduling methods that are inappropriate to the needs of the project, programme or portfolio can cause significant problems. An overly complex approach is just as bad as a simplistic approach, so care must be taken to ensure techniques are appropriate and correctly applied.

The most common mechanism for building a model is a network diagram which is made up of all the interconnected activities required to achieve the objectives. This is the basis for estimating and scheduling work with increasing sophistication. The simplest form of calculating a schedule is critical path analysis (CPA). CPA calculates start and finish dates for all the activities in the network. Some activities will have flexibility (referred to as float) and others will not. The sequence of activities with no float are referred to as the critical path – hence the name.

CPA has two major shortcomings. Firstly, it takes no account of the effect on the schedule of limited resources. This is addressed by further analysis in resource scheduling. Secondly, it assumes a single estimate of the time required to perform each activity. Estimating is an inexact science and it is far more realistic to use a range of duration estimates rather than a single-point estimate. This leads to statistical techniques such as Program Evaluation and Review Technique (PERT) or Monte Carlo.

Whatever the technique used to calculate activity dates, the results are typically represented as a form of bar chart known as a Gantt chart.

The main advantage of the network diagram is that it can be frequently updated with new information and quickly recalculated. This is an ongoing process throughout the life cycle and uses information about actual progress to predict the eventual completion of the work.

Activities in the network diagram may have allocated costs as well as durations. A technique that combines the effect of both time and cost as part of project control is EVM. This measures progress in terms of value delivered rather than elapsed time and is used to provide more accurate predictions of future progress and completion based upon progress to date.

Projects, programmes and portfolios

Network diagrams are most applicable to projects rather than programmes, but even here they are not always the best approach. Network diagrams are ideally applied in a traditional project where there is a specification for a unique output. Two examples of situations where they are not used are:

- projects that produce multiple repetitive products; for example, a project to build a new housing estate. In this case a technique such as line of balance may be more appropriate

- agile projects where the performance of activities is far more fluid and a full specification is not available to model in the definition process. Agile projects focus more on techniques such as time boxes and MoSCoW.

Most time scheduling is performed with the aid of specialist software packages. While these packages provide the ability to build and analyse sophisticated models of a project, they also provide the capacity to build very large models. As projects become larger and more complex there is a great temptation to build ever-larger models because the computing power available today means that analysis is almost instantaneous.

However, the art of P3 management involves having an understanding of cause and effect as it applies to the work being managed. The larger and more sophisticated the model, the harder it is for a manager to have a good feel for cause and effect when making decisions. Sensitivity analysis can be useful in assessing the impact of different factors on the schedule.

Creating a single homogenous model for a programme is rarely successful. Programmes and larger projects need to create multiple schedules that may be linked by a few key milestones or arranged as a hierarchy. Ideally, this series of interconnected schedules will reflect the organisation structure to some degree so that individuals can schedule the work that they are responsible for without their schedule being constantly and automatically changed by updates to someone else's schedule.

Of course, these schedules do not operate in isolation and the interdependencies between them must be accommodated. This is where specialist planning resources come into their own, perhaps as part of a support office. These specialists can assess the impact of one schedule upon another and interpret the implications for the management team.

The logical interdependencies between projects and programmes in a portfolio should be minimal. If there are significant dependencies between two or more projects, for example, the portfolio management team should consider whether these would be managed more effectively as a single project or programme.

Resource scheduling

General

Resource scheduling is a collection of techniques used to analyse the resources required to deliver the work and when they will be required. The goals of resource scheduling are to ensure:

- efficient and effective utilisation
- confidence that the schedule is realistic
- early identification of resource capacity bottlenecks and conflicts.

Resource scheduling is a supplement to time scheduling, not an alternative. The procedure has three steps, as shown in Figure 1.34.

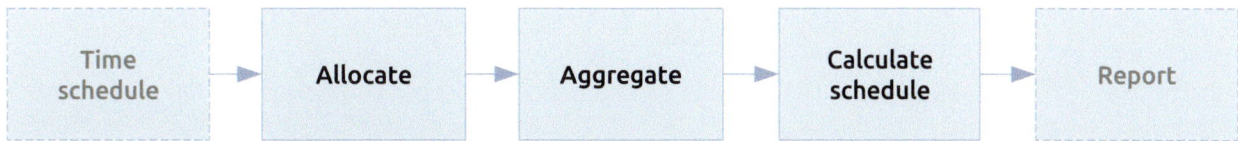

Figure 1.34 Resource scheduling procedure

The model developed in the time scheduling function is used as the basis for allocation of resources to different components of work. This enables the demand for resources to be aggregated over time. This almost inevitably leads to a demand profile that has periods where demand exceeds supply or where resources are idle. The purpose of calculating the schedule, using resource-limited scheduling techniques, is to modify timings in order to deal with these peaks and troughs of demand.

From a scheduling point of view there are two broad categories of resource – consumable and reusable. Consumable resources are typically materials. Reusable resources are people and machinery.

The first step in the procedure allocates resources to activities. This will comprise quantities of consumable resource or the effort required by reusable resources. Once the resources have been allocated and a time schedule calculated, the resources can be aggregated. The results of aggregation are normally presented as a resource histogram. For consumable resources the histogram will normally show cumulative usage (also known as an s-curve). For reusable resources the histogram shows usage period by period (e.g. day-by-day, week-by-week or as required).

The schedule for consumable resources forms the basis of procurement, including detail that may be included in a contract, such as the scheduling of deliveries. The schedule may also reveal issues with materials or components that have to be ordered well in advance. This can sometimes lead to the situation where orders need to be placed before the work is fully authorised (see the 'pre-authorisation work' activity in the definition process).

Reusable resources are rarely, if ever, limitless and the schedule needs to be reviewed to take all limitations into account. There are two approaches to resource-limited scheduling that reconcile resource limits and time constraints: resource smoothing (or time-limited resource scheduling) and resource levelling (or resource-limited scheduling).

Resource smoothing reschedules activities while retaining the finish date calculated by CPA. This results in a resource histogram where the peaks and troughs are 'smoothed out' but not eliminated. A smoothed schedule is useful where it is possible and practical to procure additional resources for periods of time.

Resource levelling ensures that resource demand never exceeds availability. This usually results in an increase in the time taken to complete the work and is more appropriate when there are strict limits on the available resources.

The simple process of smoothing or levelling the whole schedule ('simple' because it is the default approach of most scheduling software packages) does not reflect the true situation. In reality, some resources may have flexibility while others do not, meaning that some need to be smoothed and some need to be levelled. It is also a fact that the schedule will be more sensitive to limits on some resources than others, but this effect is masked when all resources are scheduled simultaneously.

A better understanding of the relationship between resource limitations and the schedule can be achieved through a form of sensitivity analysis where resources are scheduled individually. Alternatively, techniques such as critical chain can be used to address the issues in a different way.

Projects, programmes and portfolios

Most resource-limited scheduling techniques are based on an initial model derived from a network diagram. The drawbacks of scaling up these techniques from projects to programmes and portfolios are explained in the subsection on Time scheduling in section 1.3.2.

Once the overall schedule for a programme or large complex project is broken down into component schedules, each one can be analysed locally. Of course, the problem here is that local decisions may have a wider impact that is then lost. A balance must be found between creating an overly large and detailed schedule that no-one can effectively manage and a series of local schedules that do not reflect all the interdependencies.

Where the work is sufficiently large or complex to warrant multiple schedules the programme or portfolio management team should focus on capacity planning. In general management, capacity is defined as 'the maximum amount of work that an organisation is capable of completing in a given period'.

A programme or portfolio management team must therefore consider the capacity of the resources available to its work. It may adopt a policy of allocating portions of these resources to the component projects where the detailed scheduling is done. The component schedule may then be consolidated for review and the process repeated until a balance of resource distribution is achieved. This is part of the balancing activity in the portfolio management process.

Financial management

General

Financial management covers all aspects of obtaining, deploying and controlling financial resources. The goals of financial management are to:

- estimate the cost of achieving the objectives
- assess the viability of achieving the objectives
- secure funds and manage their release throughout the life cycle
- set up and run financial systems
- monitor and control expenditure.

Financial management is made up of three main areas:

- Investment appraisal is the procedure by which the viability of the work is assessed. This is one of the primary inputs to the business case.
- Funding is concerned with securing the investment required to complete the work and ensuring it supports cash flow.
- Budgeting and cost control estimates costs, predicts cash flow and then applies controls to monitor cash flow.

The management of finance on projects, programmes and portfolios takes many different forms, but a simple procedure is shown in Figure 1.35.

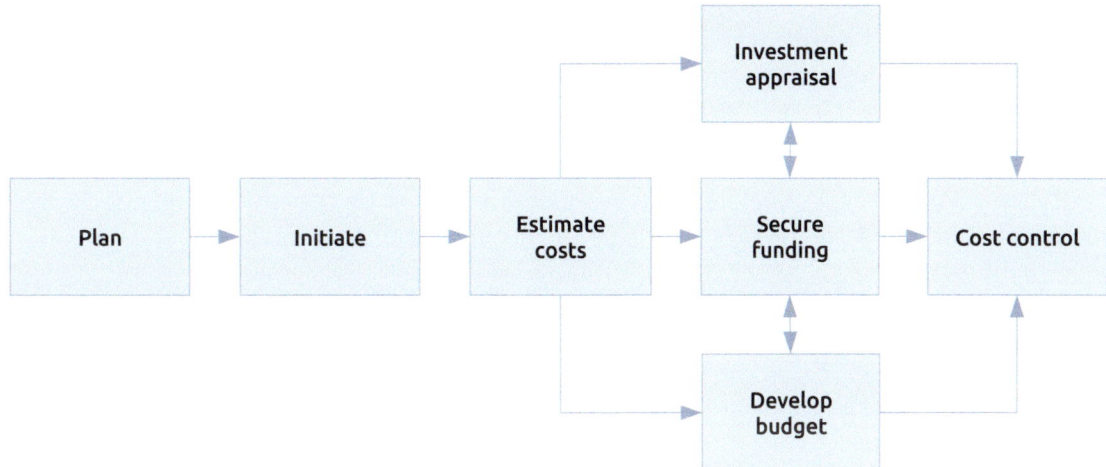

Figure 1.35 Finance management procedure

The procedure starts with the planning step that defines the scope and objectives of financial management and results in the finance management plan. The initiation step is performed once the work is approved and the resources needed to manage finances are mobilised.

The first specific step is to estimate what the work may cost. Cost estimates are made and refined in parallel with other planning procedures that establish the scope of work and estimate schedules, resources and risk.

The estimated costs are balanced against the value of benefits (as calculated in the benefits management procedure) and documented in the business case. Work is approved if it can be shown not only that the benefits outweigh the costs but also that the organisation cannot get a better return by investing the same funds elsewhere.

Estimated costs will be collated onto budgets for different aspects of the work. These are combined with the delivery schedule to create cash flow information. Additional budgets may be created to deal with contingency and a reserve to be held by the sponsor.

The exercise of securing funds continues in parallel with these steps and with the different phases of the life cycle. For example, when a mandate triggers the identification phase of a project or programme, it should come with sufficient funding to complete the identification process. If the brief is approved at the end of the identification process, that approval should be accompanied by sufficient confirmed funds to complete the definition process and sufficient funds in principle to complete the work.

As the work proceeds and the amount of money involved increases, financial control systems need to be implemented that are consistent with the volume and nature of financial transactions. These systems will work in conjunction with schedule management systems to predict cash flow and then track actual expenditure against budget.

The approach to financial management within a project, programme or portfolio is highly dependent upon the policies, procedures and standards used in the host organisation. These, in turn, are affected by the regulatory and legislative environment. At the outset, financial procedures must be set out in the finance management plan that comply with all appropriate standards and enable exchange of information with the host organisation's financial systems.

Projects, programmes and portfolios

Financial management systems need to be appropriate to the scale and complexity of the work. This can range from a small project within a department to a highly complex portfolio of international projects and programmes owned by partner organisations. Regardless of scale and complexity the fundamental principle is always that costs must be controlled and checked to ensure they are not predicted to exceed the value of expected benefits.

Smaller projects will not justify investment in their own financial systems and will use the systems of the host organisation. This can lead to problems where the financial systems are configured to report on an operational basis and do not easily facilitate the type of cost breakdown needed for a project. More mature organisations will ensure that their corporate financial systems can exchange data with project systems for scheduling.

Larger projects and programmes may be able to justify dedicated financial management systems, and portfolios should certainly have this capability. These systems will need to consolidate financial data from different sources, such as the component projects, business-as-usual activity and the top-level management infrastructure. Finance and accounting policies need to be consistent and this is a particular challenge where the work is international, multicompany or both.

Investment appraisal

General

Investment appraisal is a collection of techniques used to identify the attractiveness of an investment. Its goals are to:

- assess the viability of achieving the objectives
- support the production of a business case.

Investment appraisal is very focused on the early phases of a project or programme and is performed in parallel with the early work on management plans and delivery plans, as shown in Figure 1.36. The existence of discrete planning and initiation steps for this function is entirely dependent upon the scale and complexity of the work. In programmes and portfolios these steps are necessary in order to establish consistent appraisal across all component projects and programmes. In projects it is much more likely that any planning and initiation of investment appraisal will be absorbed within the identification and definition processes.

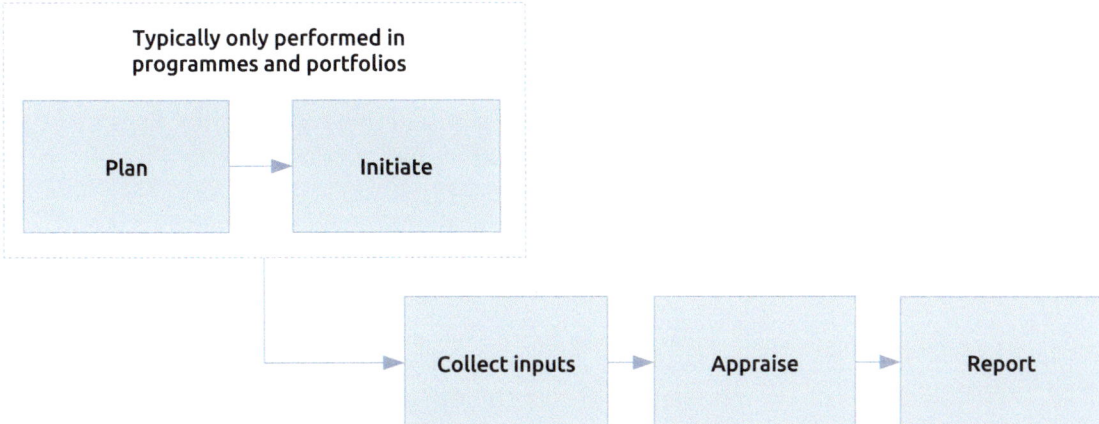

Figure 1.36 Investment appraisal procedure

Most investment appraisals are based on cash flows but there are other factors that may need to be included, such as:

- **Legal considerations** A project that enables an organisation to conform to new legislation may be compulsory if the organisation is to continue to operate. An appraisal based on the return on investment is therefore less appropriate.
- **Environmental impact** The effects of work on the natural environment are increasingly a factor when considering an investment. Environmental impact analysis of infrastructure work is written into legislation in many parts of the world.
- **Social impact** For charitable organisations, return on investment could be measured in non-financial terms such as 'quality of life' or even 'lives saved'.
- **Operational benefits** These could include less tangible elements such as 'increased customer satisfaction', 'higher staff morale' or 'competitive advantage'.
- **Risk** All organisations are subject to business and operational risk. An investment decision may be justified because it reduces risk.

Investment appraisal needs inputs from all these factors. During the identification process of a project or programme these inputs will be 'top-down'; i.e. based on comparative or parametric estimating techniques. In the definition process they will be summaries of detailed delivery planning; i.e. bottom-up.

The first specific step is to collect the relevant information. Depending upon where in the life cycle this is being done it may require the creation of top-down data or the summarisation of bottom-up data. This should be done in conjunction with stakeholders to ensure that all relevant subjective, as well as objective, inputs have been captured.

The next step is to perform the appraisal using suitable techniques. Finally, the results of the appraisal are reported, usually in the form of a business case.

> Subjective dis-benefits are often the biggest point of disagreement among stakeholders. If a new railway line adversely affects a popular rural beauty spot, how is that compared with the economic benefit that the railway creates?
>
> In cases like this the dis-benefit is entirely subjective and even the benefit is difficult to quantify, making comparison very difficult.

At the heart of an investment appraisal lies a comparison between investment and return. Any objective comparison requires both sides to be measured in the same units, such as cash. In many cases the investment side of the equation in projects, programmes and portfolios is easily quantified in terms of cash, with the exception of subjective dis-benefits. The return can also usually be measured in terms of cash but subjective benefits can often be a significant component.

There are numerous techniques for investment appraisal and where there is a significant emphasis on subjective benefits, scoring methods may be most appropriate.

The simplest of the financial techniques is the payback method. This calculates the payback period; i.e. the time taken for the value attributable to benefits to equal the cost of the work. This is a relatively crude mechanism but can be useful for initial screening, especially when reviewing projects and programmes for inclusion in a portfolio.

A better way of comparing less complex investments is the accounting rate of return (ARR). This expresses the 'profit' as a percentage of the costs but has the disadvantage of not taking the timing of income and expenditure into account. This makes a significant difference on all but the shortest and most capital-intensive of projects.

Where there is a significant time difference between the expenditure and the consequent financial return, discounted cash flow techniques are more appropriate. The simplest of these is the calculation of net present value (NPV). This calculates the present value of all cash flows associated with an investment: the higher the NPV the better. A discount rate is used to show how the value of money decreases with time (assuming an inflationary environment).

The discount rate that gives an NPV of zero is called the internal rate of return (IRR). NPV and IRR can be used to compare alternative approaches in solutions development on a number of projects or programmes in the portfolio management process.

When you are appraising capital-intensive work the full product life cycle may need to be considered because of the significant termination costs.

One of the biggest issues with investment appraisal is over-optimistic estimates of the value of benefits. Some appraisal approaches use an adjustment for optimism bias, where opinions on benefit value are reduced before inclusion in a business case.

> An example of the effect of whole-life costing would be a nuclear power station. A full appraisal would include the cost of decommissioning the plant and disposing of waste as well as the construction and operating costs.

The potential for optimism is greatest when the benefits are difficult to quantify and assumptions have to be made about their value. The value of intangible benefits may be quantified by applying a series of assumptions. For example, work that improves staff morale may lead to lower staff turnover and reduced recruitment costs. The reduction in costs then constitutes the financial value of the benefit. Such assumptions need to be carefully documented and reviewed.

Benefits arising from organisational change can give rise to a significant proportion of intangible and non-financial benefits being included in an appraisal. Appraisals should not be overly dependent on non-financial benefits, as anything can be justified through subjective views of value.

Projects, programmes and portfolios

All investment appraisal is based on the relationship between cost and benefit, but many projects have no involvement in the benefits realisation process and are only concerned with delivering an output. If a project hands over an output to business as usual or a programme management team for subsequent benefits realisation, the project management team may have no responsibility for the initial investment appraisal. Even so, the project manager should be familiar with the investment appraisal in the business case and manage the project accordingly. The project manager is usually given responsibility for maintaining the business case and updating the investment appraisal even if this was originally prepared by someone else.

Where the project delivers an output to a client under contract, the contracting project management team may perform a form of investment appraisal that balances the contractual costs and risks against the agreed price and payment terms as part of their own business case.

Programmes will have an overall business case but may also take responsibility for performing separate investment appraisals of component projects. The programme management team must set out standards for the appraisal of component projects and their associated benefits in a finance management plan. This needs to accommodate the fact that a single benefit may be derived from multiple outputs. The full value of that benefit cannot therefore be claimed by any one project.

Consistent and compatible techniques must be used across the programme so that individual project business cases can be aggregated and summarised in the tranche or programme business cases.

In portfolios the management process includes an activity where projects and programmes are selected for inclusion in the portfolio. In a structured portfolio, suggested projects and programmes should have a clear link to fulfilment of the strategic objectives covered by the portfolio. In a standard portfolio it will simply be a matter of whether the project or programme is worthwhile and within the constraints defined for the scope of the portfolio.

The portfolio management team must establish a system for capturing and screening ideas for new projects or programmes. This is where simpler techniques such as payback and ARR may be used. A criterion may be set that requires payback within the financial planning cycle. Any projects or programmes that do not provide payback in that period are discarded. As the higher-potential ideas are captured, they will be subject to more detailed appraisal.

Funding

General

Funding is the means by which the finance required to undertake a project, programme or portfolio is secured and made available to perform the work. Its goals are to:

- determine the best way to fund the work
- secure commitment from the fund holders
- manage the release of funds throughout the life cycle.

Typical steps involved in the funding procedure are shown in Figure 1.37.

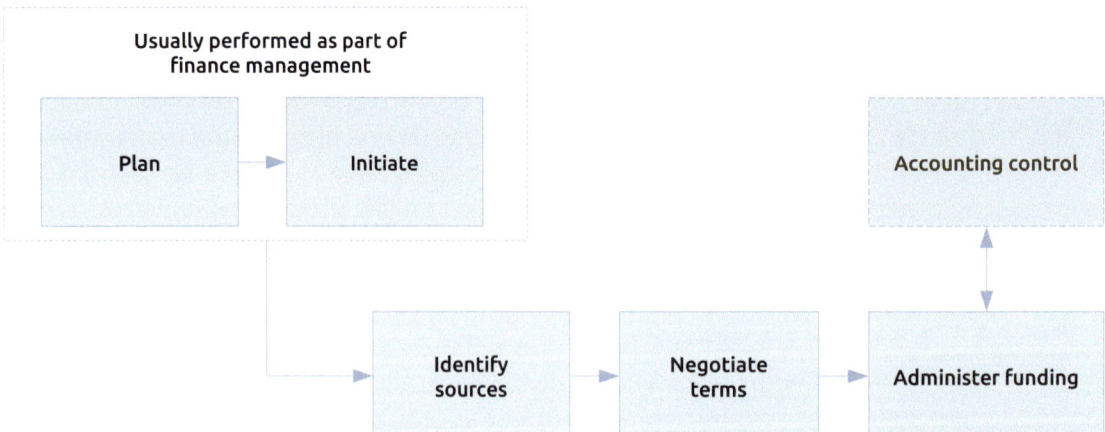

Figure 1.37 Funding procedure

The first step in the procedure is to identify the possible sources of funding. These could be from internal or external sources or a combination of both. The scale of funding may be as simple as allocation of funds from a single departmental budget or as complex as international financing of a joint venture. In some cases the work may be expected to be self-funding, with revenues generated from earlier stages of work providing funds to deliver the later stages.

Internal funding is where all the costs of the work are funded from the host organisation's existing resources in operational and capital budgets. It is unlikely that terms need to be negotiated for internal funding but conditions may be applied and recorded in the finance management plan.

Where funding is provided by an external body such as a bank or by shareholders, terms and conditions will need to be negotiated. This can include interest rates, charges and procedures for release of funds. Complex funding arrangements may need the management team to have access to specialist expertise.

Through the life cycle, as plans are defined in ever-greater detail with increasing levels of confidence, funds will be fully committed and approval given to commence work. Administering funds therefore involves:

- **Initially** Committing funds for the identification process and reserving funds for the definition process
- **At the end of identification** Committing funds for the definition and reserving funds for the delivery process
- **At the end of the definition** Committing funds for delivery, or at least the first stage or tranche of work
- **At each review** Committing funds for the next stage or tranche will be dependent upon a viable business case.

Whether internal or external, recipients of benefits or not, funders must be treated as key stakeholders and managed accordingly.

Projects, programmes and portfolios

Smaller projects tend to exist within departmental boundaries. They will be funded from a single departmental operational budget and the project sponsor may well be the departmental manager who owns that budget. As projects become larger they cross departmental boundaries and draw upon multiple budgets. The project sponsor is then more likely to be someone who is impartial and acceptable to the various budget holders. A project board may be formed to give representation to the key funding providers. Organisation management will take these factors into account when designing the organisational structure.

In situations where a contractor is delivering a project on behalf of a client, the contractor's funding comes from the client (who may well have their own external sources to manage). Payments from the client to the contractor will usually be based on valuations of work done at agreed points, either at key milestones or regular periods. The contractor will often need bridging finance in place to cover the time delay between paying bills and receiving funds based on valuations.

In some countries, there are funding arrangements that have been put in place by government to form partnerships with the private sector for major infrastructure projects. Many of these are principally procurement tools, designed to harness private sector management, expertise and resources in the delivery of public services, while reducing the impact on public sector borrowing. Others are ownership structures in which the government retains an equity stake in the asset.

Build, own, operate, transfer (BOOT) arrangements can be applied to a private sector initiative as well as a public-private sector one. In a BOOT project one organisation is given a concession from the commissioning organisation to fund, build, operate and eventually transfer a facility.

Programmes are very likely to involve multiple internal budgets. Even where a strategic programme may be funded from central corporate resources, there will be change management activity in business as usual that is usually funded by the departments involved.

Having secured funding for the programme, the programme management team is responsible for distributing funds to the component projects. It must always be aware that it is really funding the delivery of benefits; the projects are simply the means of creating the outputs that enable the benefits to be realised. With the focus on the overall business case funds will be allocated and reallocated in accordance with the benefits they create. This may involve moving funds between projects, rescoping projects or even cancelling them in order to use funds more effectively.

Standard portfolios are often made up of projects delivered for clients. Most of the portfolio budget is simply the aggregation of the various project budgets. However, managing the client projects as a portfolio may provide the opportunity to use the cash flow of some projects to bridge the finance for others, thus avoiding the need for more expensive external funds.

A strategic portfolio is funded as part of the business planning cycle. Ideally, the objectives of the portfolio will be delivered within the same time frame. If not, the portfolio runs the risk of having its funding changed in the next business planning cycle and with it the continued funding of projects and programmes.

The prioritisation and balancing of projects and programmes within a strategic portfolio will, to a large degree, depend upon how it is funded. For example, there may be levels of uncertainty regarding future availability of funding. Long-term secured funds should be used for the longer, high-priority programmes, while short-term funds will be matched to shorter-term projects or smaller programmes.

Budgeting and cost control

General

Budgeting and cost control includes the detailed estimation of costs, the setting of agreed budgets, and control of costs against that budget. Its goals are to:

- determine the income and expenditure profiles for the work
- develop budgets and align them with funding
- implement systems to manage income and expenditure.

Typical steps in the budgeting and cost control procedure are shown in Figure 1.38.

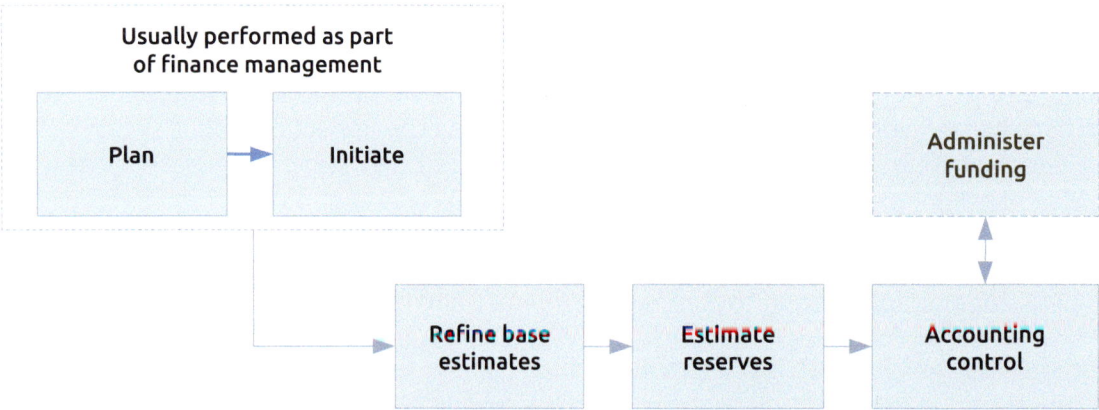

Figure 1.38 Budgeting and cost control procedure

A budget identifies the planned expenditure for a project, programme or portfolio. It forms the baseline against which the actual expenditure and predicted eventual cost of the work is reported.

Initial cost estimates are based on comparative or parametric estimating techniques. These are refined as the achievability and desirability of the work are investigated and a detailed understanding of scope, schedule and resource is developed.

The base cost is the cost of the work according to the schedule. This is typically made up from costs associated with:

- resources such as staff or contractors
- accommodation and infrastructure such as office rental or support for ICT systems
- consumables such as power or stationery
- expenses such as staff travel and subsistence
- capital items such as equipment purchase.

These base costs have two pairs of possible attributes:

- **Direct and indirect** Costs that are directly attributable to the project, programme or portfolio are direct costs, whereas overheads shared with other parts of the host organisation are indirect.
- **Fixed and variable** Fixed costs remain the same regardless of how the work proceeds (e.g. capital costs). Variable costs fluctuate with the amount used (e.g. salaries or fees).

Any cost will be a combination of attributes from these pairs (e.g. variable direct costs or fixed indirect costs).

If the financial systems allow, it is useful to break costs down into a cost breakdown structure (CBS). Costs can also be classified in accordance with the work breakdown structure and organisational breakdown structure. These classifications enable costs to be reported according to any combination of cost type, resource type or section of work.

Risk management will identify the potential cost of dealing with known risk and allocate this to a contingency budget. Even the best risk management cannot foresee all possible causes of additional cost so a further level of reserve is held by the sponsor to cover unforeseen circumstances. This is known as the management reserve.

The greater the chance of unforeseen circumstances, the more management reserve is required; so highly innovative work will need a larger management reserve than routine work.

The three major components of a P3 budget are therefore:

- the base cost estimate
- contingency reserve
- management reserve.

Contingency and management reserves will be owned and deployed according to policies set out in the finance management plan.

Once the costs and reserves have been approved at the end of the definition process they become the budget. The cumulative expenditure of the budget is often shown as an s-curve. This profile can be used in financing and funding. It allows a cash flow forecast to be developed, and a drawdown of funds to be agreed.

As the delivery process gets underway so does accounting control. Actual costs may be recorded directly by the P3 management team, or indirectly through operational finance systems. Where P3 managers are reliant upon information from operational systems, the information needs to be checked to ensure that costs have been posted correctly. Many operational financial systems are not ideal for project or programme-based accounting.

> The 'accounting control' step of this procedure should be closely aligned with the 'administer funding' step of the funding procedure to ensure that funds are ready to be released to meet the costs incurred.

Three types of costs must be tracked:

- **Committed costs** These reflect confirmed orders for future provision of goods and/or services
- **Accruals** Work partially or fully completed for which payment will be due (in accordance with contract terms)
- **Actual costs** Money that has been paid.

The forecast cost is the sum of commitments, accruals, actual expenditure and the estimated cost to complete the remaining work.

No project, programme or portfolio goes exactly according to plan. The profile of actual expenditure will inevitably be different from planned expenditure. Typically, the P3 manager is responsible for managing the base costs. Thresholds will be set that trigger the involvement of the sponsor. These thresholds are known as tolerances and, if expenditure is predicted to exceed tolerances, the manager must escalate this to the sponsor.

Dealing with increased costs may include drawing funds from either the contingency reserve or the management reserve. Alternatively, the work could be reduced in scope to cut the estimated cost to complete the work or additional funds secured. These decisions are made jointly by the manager and sponsor and highlight the importance of this working relationship.

Periodically, the business case must be formally reviewed to ensure the work is still viable. In the latter stages this review must consider sunk costs. These are actual and committed expenditure that cannot be recovered, plus any additional costs that would be incurred by cancelling contracts. Completing an overspent project or programme may be considered worthwhile if the remaining cost to complete the work is less than the eventual value.

Projects, programmes and portfolios

Just as the principles of company accounting are the same regardless of the size of the company, the principles of P3 accounting are common regardless of the scale of the project, programme or portfolio. What does change, in line with the complexity of the work, is the volume and diversity of transactions. While spreadsheet and planning software may be adequate for tracking costs on small projects, international portfolios will need to handle multiple currencies and provide different types of financial reports for many different stakeholders.

As the work becomes more complex, the application of more sophisticated cost control techniques can be justified.

The ways in which cost estimates are produced will become increasingly diverse as the work becomes more complex. These estimates are subject to the same uncertainty as all estimates and techniques used for dealing with time estimating can also be used for costs, such as applying the PERT approach. Alternatively, risk registers may include the calculation of expected value, which is used in the calculation of the contingency reserve.

Where possible the procurement approach may be used to transfer risk to suppliers through fixed price payment methods, which reduces some of the uncertainty in the cost baseline.

Tracking costs can be combined with tracking progress in the technique called earned value management (EVM). EVM takes the budget and uses it to represent the value of the work. The value of work performed at any point during the delivery process can then be compared with the actual cost of performing it and the value of work planned to have been performed at that point. This enables predictions to be made about future performance based on actual performance to date, both for cost and schedule. The overheads of implementing EVM can be significant and it is unlikely that this will be effective on smaller projects unless they are part of a programme or portfolio that is using the technique.

Programme and portfolio management teams must appreciate the need to balance consistency of budgeting and cost control across the component projects and programmes with the need to apply techniques that are appropriate. For example, within a portfolio, some projects may be simple and predictable, while others may be innovative and uncertain; some will have significant capital costs and others will not.

The finance management plan at programme or portfolio level should provide advice on estimating and cost control techniques while ensuring that costs reported by component projects or programmes can be meaningfully aggregated to provide comprehensive financial reporting. The prioritisation and balancing activities in the managing a portfolio process depend upon a good understanding of the costs of the component projects and programmes.

Strategic portfolios are usually aligned with corporate financial cycles. Budgets for these are less concerned with the cost of delivering a specific result, and more to do with what can be delivered within a defined budget.

> Some may see this aspect of portfolio management as being agile project management on a grand scale.

Risk management

General

Risk management allows individual risk events and overall risk to be understood and managed proactively, optimising success by minimising threats and maximising opportunities. Its goals are to:

- ensure that levels of overall risk within a project, programme or portfolio are compatible with organisational objectives
- ensure that individual risks and responses are identified
- minimise the impact of threats to objectives
- optimise opportunities within the scope of work.

Risk is inherent in all projects, programmes and portfolios because each one is a unique combination of objectives, solutions, people and context. Each project, programme and portfolio will have an inherent level of overall risk. This overall risk has two components: risk events and uncertainty.

A risk event is an identifiable event that, if it occurs, will have an impact on the objectives. The key phrase here is 'if it occurs'. Risk management is all about dealing with things that may, or may not, happen.

Uncertainty relates to a form of risk that cannot be identified as a specific risk event. For example, in the use of innovative technology there may be uncertainty about performance or reliability of some components. At a more mundane level every set of plans has a degree of uncertainty because they are based on estimates of varying accuracy.

Risk events are viewed as being either positive or negative. A negative risk (threat) is the one most people are more familiar with. It is something that will have an adverse effect on the objectives if it occurs. A positive risk (opportunity) is something that can enhance the value of the work if it occurs.

The procedure as illustrated in Figure 1.39 starts with the planning step that defines the scope and objectives of risk management and results in a risk management plan. Many risk management plans focus on dealing with risk events because these are more tangible. A more mature organisation will ensure that plans also address uncertainty and make allowances for this difficult-to-quantify aspect of overall risk.

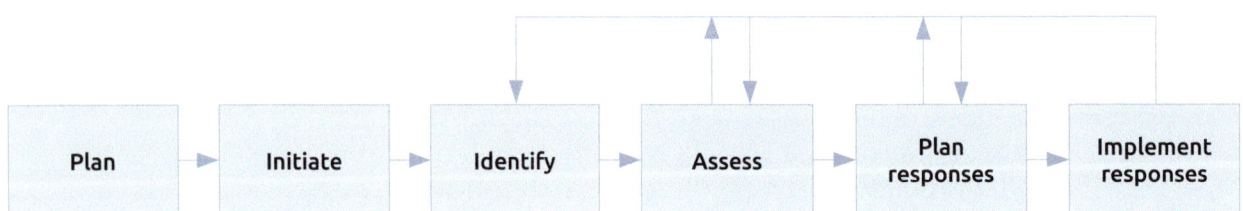

Figure 1.39 Risk management procedure

The initiation step is performed once the work is approved and the resources needed to manage risk are mobilised.

The first specific step of the procedure is to identify risk events and uncertainty. These are documented in the risk register. There are many techniques that aid risk identification but the greatest fault of many P3 managers is to take this step too far. Because risk identification is about thinking of things that might not happen the potential list of risk events is, quite literally, endless. Experienced P3 managers sift out the risks that need to be managed from those that must be left to 'background risk'.

In the next step the nature of the risk is assessed and, where possible, its potential effect on objectives is estimated. A variety of risk techniques are available to assess both risk events and broader uncertainty. These fall into two groups, generally referred to as qualitative and quantitative risk techniques.

Once the risk is understood the management team has to decide on how to respond. Once again there are various approaches to dealing with threats and opportunities and the planned responses are added to the risk register.

Depending upon the nature of the planned responses, some are implemented as part of the delivery plans while others may only come into effect should the risk occur.

The procedure is iterative, with the assessment and response planning steps potentially leading to the identification of more risks.

Risk is inherent in everyday life. All animals have evolved to deal with risk and, naturally, different individuals react in different ways. P3 managers need to identify and manage the behavioural influences of both individuals and groups on the risk procedure. This risk context can have a significant impact on the effectiveness of the procedure.

The management of general health and safety risks (hazards) is usually excluded from P3 risk management, as the management of these risks is traditionally handled by a separate function within the organisation.

Projects, programmes and portfolios

The nature of risk and the principles used to manage it do not vary between projects, programmes and portfolios. In fact it is not very different in P3 management from the rest of human endeavour. However, the specifics do vary in line with the complexity of the work. Risk events become more numerous and diverse, and uncertainty becomes a more influential factor.

As the work becomes more complex its management is distributed. Major projects are subdivided into sub-projects; programmes into projects; portfolios into projects and programmes. As a consequence risk management also becomes distributed and this is the difference between risk management in smaller projects and more complex work.

For example, the management team of a programme has to develop a programme risk management plan that promotes consistency across programme level activity, projects and change management activity. It then delegates responsibility for risk management to the project managers and business change managers. Each project and area of business change will maintain its own risk register.

The challenge for the programme management team arises from the fact that risk does not respect the same boundaries. Risk events often have an impact beyond their host project or business area. The programme management team has to balance the need for delegation with the need for co-ordination. All parts of the programme need to work together to understand which risk events should be recorded in the programme risk register (and managed at that level) and which events should be recorded and managed at a more 'local' level.

The basis for this common understanding is the analysis of risk and uncertainty and, in particular, the objectives the risk affects. Risk that has a local effect on project objectives can clearly be managed at the project level. Risk that directly impacts programme objectives should be part of the programme risk register. The tricky area, as always, is the one in between. Understanding this is the same as understanding the inter-relationships between the component objectives of the programme. If the realisation of a benefit will be adversely affected by a one-month delay in the delivery of an output, then a risk event that could cause a two-month delay in the delivery is clearly a programme-level risk. The teams must also be aware of how risk can move between levels as its impact varies with time.

The same issues apply for large, complex projects and portfolios, albeit with slightly different emphases.

Risk context

General

Risk context addresses the individual and group attitudes and behaviours that affect the way risk arises and how it may be managed.

This context can be viewed as having two components: risk attitude and risk appetite.

Risk attitude describes an individual or group's natural reaction to uncertainty of any type. This is dependent upon people's perception of risk which, in turn, is influenced by a range of factors at both the conscious and unconscious levels.

The effect of risk attitude is most evident during the response planning step in the risk management procedure, where it will influence the way people think a risk should be addressed.

Attitudes can be classified in three ways: risk averse, risk neutral and risk seeking.

As the name suggests, risk averse people do not like taking risks. In some cases this is a positive benefit. When planning work that is risky in a health and safety context, or perhaps when working to provide relief in a war zone, being risk averse is definitely an advantage. It will not eliminate the inherent risk but it means the planner will adopt a very cautious approach to planning risk responses.

In some instances being risk averse is a disadvantage. If a project is developing products for an entrepreneurial technology company in a fast-moving and competitive commercial environment, being risk averse is unlikely to help. In this situation, planners need to be more at the risk seeking end of the spectrum.

Risk attitude can have a major impact on the assessment step, particularly when qualitative risk techniques are being used. Someone who is naturally risk averse may estimate the probability and impact of a risk event as higher than someone who is naturally risk seeking. Where major risks need to be assessed accurately, techniques such as Delphi can help reconcile the different risk attitudes of the individuals involved.

As in so many roles, the task facing the individual is to reconcile their natural predisposition towards uncertainty with the needs of the work at hand. Perhaps being risk neutral is the best personal attribute on the grounds that it will be easier to move to aversion or seeking as the context demands.

Appetite represents the amount of risk that an individual or organisation is prepared to take in order to achieve their objectives and is most evident in the identification step of the procedure. It may be obvious that the entrepreneurial technology company mentioned above will have a high risk appetite in order to achieve its objective of quickly getting innovative new products to market. Less obvious is that the charity that delivers aid to a war zone must also have a high risk appetite. Without it they would stay at home and not risk being shot at.

This highlights the difference between risk attitude and risk appetite. Both must reflect the prevailing context of the work.

A P3 manager needs to understand the host organisation's risk appetite as it applies to the work and the risk attitudes of the team members and stakeholders. During the definition process functions such as solutions development will be heavily influenced by the stakeholders' risk appetite. Some ways of meeting requirements may be delivered quickly or produce high returns but also involve high levels of risk. These would be acceptable to risk seeking stakeholders but not to those who are risk averse. Not all stakeholders will be the same.

Projects, programmes and portfolios

A very obvious difference between small projects at one end of the scale, and portfolios at the other end, is the number of people involved. While the range of people involved in a portfolio is likely to encompass all points on the risk attitude spectrum, a project is very dependent on the attitudes of its manager and sponsor.

Therefore, at the less complex end of the spectrum, the manager and sponsor must be very self-aware and control their instincts to match the needs of the project. At the complex end of the spectrum the management team must work to manage the myriad different attitudes to match the needs of the programme or portfolio.

Where the work involves multiple organisations, the P3 manager will need to balance the needs of different groups of stakeholders. For example, where a project is being delivered by a contractor on behalf of a client, there may be different appetites for risk. The contractor may be risk averse in order to protect profit on the contract, whereas the client may be risk seeking if there are opportunities to increase the value of the project's output.

This can add an ethical dimension to the context. A project manager may identify risk that affects the value of the output to their client but not the contractor's profit. If the means of responding to the risk adversely affects the contractor's profit they may be reluctant to highlight this. It is to be hoped that increasing professionalism in P3 management means that the project manager acts in the best interests of the client and the client recognises this in their dealings with the contractor. The same sort of principle can apply to project managers within a programme.

Programme and portfolio management teams must ensure that the acceptable level of risk for the work as a whole is reflected in the risk management of individual projects and programmes. This does not mean that every project or programme will need to have the same risk appetite, but they must be categorised, prioritised and balanced with the overall acceptable level of risk in mind.

Risk techniques

General

Risk techniques are used in the identification, assessment and response planning steps of the risk management procedure shown in Figure 1.40.

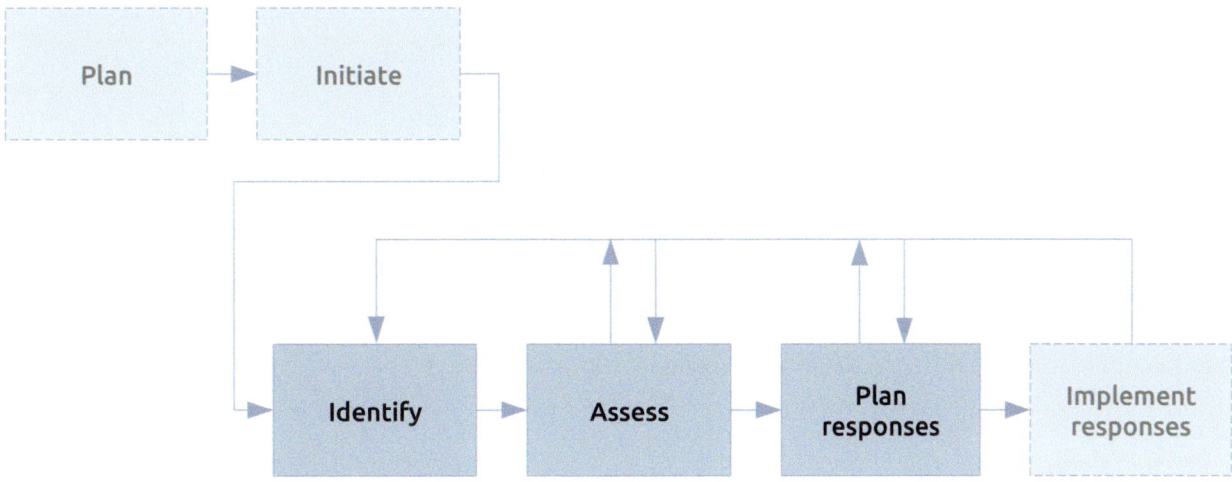

Figure 1.40 Risk management techniques

Few of the techniques described are unique to P3 management but they are all tailored and applied to suit the P3 context.

Identification draws on many different sources of information. All the other P3 management functions will generate risk-related information, and there are techniques in their procedures that are, in effect, about risk management. For example:

- **Stakeholder management** Identifies stakeholders who may be unwilling to support the objectives and may even oppose them. This is a form of risk management as applied to people with influence over the objectives.
- **Schedule management** May identify estimating uncertainties and address these through scheduling techniques such as Monte Carlo or critical chain.
- **Financial management** May similarly identify estimating uncertainties in cost forecasts and accommodate these through contingency and management reserves.

Risk identification needs to acknowledge these elements of risk, integrate with the other functions and pick up all other sources of risk.

Many identification techniques represent different ways of extracting risk-related information from people who have knowledge of the work and its context. This can be on a one-to-one basis or in groups in risk workshops. Individuals with specific knowledge or expertise may be interviewed, while groups can be brought together for brainstorming sessions or co-ordinated using the Delphi technique.

The use of information from previous projects, programmes and portfolios should never be overlooked and involves looking at lessons-learned reports and archived risk registers. In more mature organisations these may have been collated and structured in the form of checklists and prompt lists as part of a knowledge management system.

Techniques for assessing risk are generally divided into qualitative and quantitative, although the line distinguishing the two is sometimes blurred.

Qualitative risk assessment focuses on individual risk events and is primarily based on educated opinion and expert judgement. Qualitative techniques are based on two properties of a risk event: its probability (or the likelihood that it will happen) and its impact on the objectives if it does happen. It is because these properties are difficult to quantify, and often subjective, that techniques based on probability and impact are known as qualitative.

Some approaches to probability-impact assessment introduce increasingly quantitative elements until they potentially produce overtly quantitative date such as expected value. While this is very useful for calculating contingency reserves it should never be forgotten that it is based on qualitative data.

Quantitative risk assessment focuses more on uncertainty and estimating uncertainty in particular. Typical quantitative techniques for addressing uncertainty in schedule and/or cost estimating include PERT, Monte Carlo and sensitivity analysis.

Quantitative techniques can also be used to assess different courses of action that include uncertain external influence. Decision trees can be used to quantitatively compare the effect of a series of events happening or not happening. This can be particularly useful in assessing secondary, or even tertiary, risks and influence the decisions taken in risk response planning.

The principles of response planning are very similar for all types of risk, whether it be general uncertainty or specific risk events (threats or opportunities).

Possible risk responses for threats are to avoid, reduce, transfer or accept them. These act differently on the probability that a risk will occur as opposed to the impact it will have on objectives. If the risk event is an opportunity, the possible responses are to exploit, enhance, share or reject it. The two sets of responses are fundamentally the same, but tailored to minimise the detrimental effect of a threat or maximise the beneficial effect of an opportunity.

Projects, programmes and portfolios

Qualitative risk techniques are generally applicable and scalable to all levels of project, programme and portfolio complexity. A basic risk register as applicable to a simple project can be extended with increasing amounts of information to suit more complex projects.

A small project will make use of probability-impact analysis but is unlikely to warrant quantitative techniques, which require significant effort to use correctly.

> Problems with managing risk can sometimes be incorrectly attributed to the use of risk techniques. A common fault is to employ overly sophisticated techniques to address perceived shortcomings when the real problem lies in understanding the risk context.

Larger, more complex projects will include significant levels of uncertainty; perhaps as a simple accumulation of estimating uncertainty or perhaps because of the use of innovative technology. Even work that uses established technology may be a source of great uncertainty if it is being used in an unusual context or if the delivery teams have no relevant experience. These situations can make good use of techniques such as Monte Carlo, especially since computer software makes these high-volume calculations so much easier.

The main issue that management teams may face when using statistical techniques is communicating the results to stakeholders. When a stakeholder asks the question 'When will my product be delivered?', they anticipate an answer like 'On 12 February', not 'There's a 50% chance it will be by 12 February and a 95% chance it will be by 21 March'.

Stakeholder management needs to decide how such information will be communicated. How easy this is provides a good indication of the maturity of the organisation.

The risk management plan for programmes and portfolios will outline the use of techniques in its component projects, programmes and change management activity. It is important to set guidelines that ensure consistency. Without consistency, it is difficult to aggregate risk from the component parts to get a value for the overall risk of the programme or portfolio.

All identification and response techniques are applicable generally, but it is impractical to apply some quantitative assessment techniques such as network-based Monte Carlo analysis, at the consolidated level.

Portfolios will establish common guidelines for using risk management techniques but they are also able to develop longer-term attitudes and behaviour that ensure that they are used appropriately.

Structured portfolios are directly affected by the external environment. They need to identify risks from the broadest range of sources and may utilise techniques such as PESTLE to assess the external sources of risk to the strategic objectives they are designed to achieve.

Change management

General

The achievement of benefits in a business case often requires changes to the working practices of the host organisation. These changed practices are known as outcomes, and moving from the current practice to the desired outcome is achieved through change management. Outcomes usually involve a section of the organisation adopting and utilising the outputs of one or more projects.

The goals of change management are to:

- define the organisational change required to convert outputs into benefits
- ensure the organisation is prepared to implement change
- implement the change and embed it into organisational practice.

Organisations and individuals respond to change in many different ways. Resistance to change is a natural phenomenon and managing change in a controlled manner is essential if the benefits in a business case are to be realised.

One way of understanding how an organisation may react to change is through metaphors. Morgan identified eight metaphors that liken an organisation to, for example, machines, brains and organisms.

There are many different change management models, such as those devised by Kotter, Carnall and Lewin. Most of these can be identified as being appropriate to one or more of Morgan's metaphors. Carnall's model, for example, is commonly regarded as applicable to organisations that operate like a political system but not those that operate like a machine, whereas Lewin's model is the reverse.

A typical, generic, change management procedure will include the steps shown in Figure 1.41.

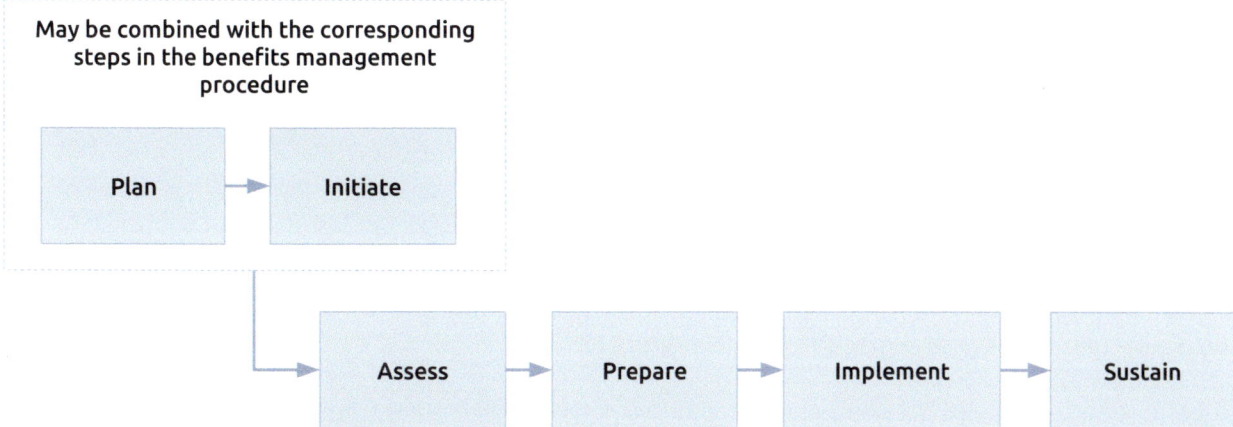

Figure 1.41 Change management procedure

Planning produces the change management plan, which will define the principles of how organisational change should be managed. Since change is both central to the achievement of benefits and simultaneously one of the hardest things to manage well, this is a key document. It must be aligned closely with other management plans such as those for stakeholder management and risk management.

The initiation step makes sure that the resources needed to manage change are in place.

Assessment involves determining the nature of the organisation and predicting its likely response to change. Existing embedded behaviours are considered, along with the organisation's readiness and willingness to implement the required change. Ways of changing and embedding new behaviours are then determined.

Preparation involves promoting a vision and gaining support, and would normally form part of the identification process of a project or programme. This is when stakeholder management is used to gain support for the high-level business case, with particular emphasis on changes required to business as usual. In the definition process it would also include establishing governance and roles to support change, such as the appointment of business change managers.

Implementation is the heart of the procedure. It includes communicating and promoting the benefits of change, removing obstacles and co-ordinating the activities that transform business as usual from the current practices to the required outcomes. Much depends on the organisation's readiness for change, which can be represented by three key factors:

- dissatisfaction with the current situation (A)
- desirability of the proposed change (B)
- practicality of the proposed change (D).

These factors are often shown as having the following relationship:

$$C = (ABD) > X$$

C is the likely success of the change. The more the combination of A, B and D exceeds the cost of the change (X), the more likely it is to succeed.

For changes to deliver the benefits required by the business case they have to be embedded; i.e. they must be stable and become the normal way of working. The sustain step will continue beyond the P3 life cycle to ensure that value is continually realised from the investment in the project, programme or portfolio.

Projects, programmes and portfolios

The inclusion of change management is often seen as the deciding factor in whether something should be considered as a project or a programme. Many sources claim that work including change management leading to benefits must be run as a programme. The same sources maintain that projects deliver outputs and no more.

But the reality is rarely that simple. A piece of work that delivers a single output, leading to small-scale change and a resultant benefit, is probably best considered to be a project. Work that covers multiple outputs, complex change and numerous different benefits is undoubtedly a programme. There is no set point of distinction between the two.

A characteristic of a more complex programme is that it is not easy to predict all the necessary change at the outset. The concepts of a vision and blueprint form an essential part of the assess and prepare steps of the change management procedure with detailed change management plans evolving with the programme.

A frequent obstacle to change arises from the volume of change imposed on individuals, teams or business units from multiple sources. The programme management team should structure the tranches of the programme and co-ordinate the project schedules to ensure that change comes in manageable pieces, interspersed with 'islands of stability'.

Benefits reviews within a programme must focus on embedding change to ensure that long-term benefits are achieved.

Standard portfolios are not normally focused on a co-ordinated set of benefits and in some circumstances may not include any change management at all (e.g. a construction company's portfolio of client contracts).

A structured portfolio involves co-ordinating the change management plans of all component projects and programmes to ensure that they work together effectively. For example, if multiple projects and programmes are imposing change on a single business unit this can have a negative effect, either because the unit cannot accommodate that level of change or because the multiple changes conflict with each other.

Resource management

General

Resource management covers all aspects of the deployment of resources that deliver the project, programme or portfolio. Its goals are to:

- determine the best way to resource the work
- acquire and mobilise the necessary resources
- control resources throughout the life cycle

- demobilise resources at the end of the life cycle
- finalise all contractual arrangements.

The resources needed on a project, programme or portfolio include people, machinery, materials, technology, property and anything else required to deliver the work. Resources may be obtained internally from the host organisation or procured from external sources.

The three main components of resource management are procurement, contract management and mobilisation:

- **Procurement** Is primarily concerned with identifying and selecting external suppliers, but many of the principles can be applied to securing internal suppliers. The degree of formality required will depend upon the complexity of the supply chain and associated risk.
- **Contract management** Deals with the continuing relationship between the management team and suppliers. This may revolve around the terms of a legal contract, an internal service level agreement or may be simple documented agreements for supply.
- **Mobilisation** Is about getting the right resources in the right place at the right time. It also covers the reverse exercise of demobilisation when the resources are no longer required.

A simple procedure for managing resources is shown in Figure 1.42.

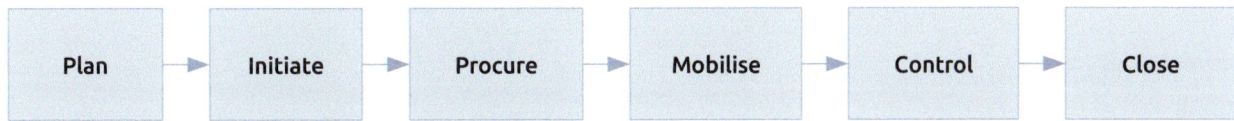

Figure 1.42 Resource management procedure

A resource management plan will initially define how resources should be procured, mobilised and controlled according to organisational policies. This may include policies for tendering, contracting and matrix management of internal resources.

It may be necessary to produce a preliminary management plan and initiate research into resourcing options. Once decisions have been made about how resource management applies to a specific context, the planning and initiation steps can be revisited in more detail.

The procurement step involves an assessment of what resources are needed to complete the scope of work. The work involved can be a significant project in itself and must consider factors such as the:

- decisions to make or buy
- use of single integrated or multiple suppliers
- supplier selection
- supplier relationships
- conditions and forms of contract or agreement
- payment methods, reimbursement and/or internal cross-charging.

The acquisition of external resources will normally be through a procurement procedure that involves tendering and results in a contract for the provision of goods and services.

A P3 manager wishing to procure a solution to complex or innovative requirements may not know exactly how best to meet the requirements and may enter into a dialogue with potential suppliers to help develop a solution. Where this is the case, clear rules on disclosure of information from one potential supplier to another need to be established and maintained, both for the reputation of the purchaser and for legal compliance.

Where resources are acquired internally, there may be service level agreements or terms of reference between the project, programme or portfolio and the department or function providing the resource.

Setting up the management infrastructure and getting resources in place is called mobilisation. Projects and programmes are temporary organisations, whereas a portfolio may be permanent or semi-permanent. Therefore, while the infrastructure for managing a portfolio is mobilised once, project and programme infrastructures are mobilised and demobilised on a regular basis.

> All too often, arrangements for the provision of internal resources are informal and undocumented. This can lead to the P3 manager having no real control over the right resources being available at the right time. Even small projects benefit from some form of documented agreement between the management team and the department providing the resources.

Once in place, resources need to be controlled. This will involve activities such as monitoring progress and rescheduling work, reviewing contracts or service level agreements; responding to resource issues; introducing new resources and closing contracts.

Finally, at the end of the work, the resource infrastructure needs to be dismantled including the disposal of capital assets, closure of contracts and redeployment of internal staff.

Projects, programmes and portfolios

Some projects will be completely internal, drawing purely on the resources of the host organisation. In this situation the project manager may not need significant expertise in formal procurement and contract procedures but will need good negotiation and influencing skills to compete for the limited resource. The project sponsor will have an important role to play in ensuring that the host organisation commits to providing the necessary internal resources. This means that at the end of the identification process there is a firm commitment to provide the resources for the definition process and an agreement in principle to provide the resources necessary for the delivery process.

Larger, more complex projects will utilise a mixture of internal and external resources. The project manager may need support from specialists who have expertise in supplier selection and contract negotiations.

The different elements of a programme will have varying resource needs. It may well be that projects make greater use of external resources while the change management and benefits realisation are primarily done by internal resources. The programme manager should define how the responsibility for managing resources will be shared between project and programme-level management in the programme level resource management plan. The approach should provide co-ordination while delegating sufficient authority to individual projects.

The programme manager will need to consider factors such as:

- elements of the management infrastructure that can be shared between projects
- opportunities for pan-programme procurement
- projects with specialised resource requirements
- structuring tranches to make resource usage more efficient.

Projects and programmes are sometimes initiated without the resource implications being fully understood. Programmes, in particular, have a wide-ranging impact on the host organisation through the need to implement change and realise benefits, as well as deliver project outputs. All aspects of resource management need to be investigated during the definition process and the results widely communicated to stakeholders.

The infrastructure of a portfolio is usually permanent but not necessarily constant. In one planning cycle the portfolio may be very extensive and in another it may be relatively modest. The resource demands of a portfolio will naturally vary according to the number of concurrent projects and programmes. In the managing a portfolio process, the management team must constantly balance the commitment to projects and programmes with the capacity of the host organisation to provide the necessary resources.

Procurement

General

Procurement covers the acquisition from a supplier of the products and services required for completion of a project, programme or portfolio. Its goals are to:

- identify potential external suppliers
- select external suppliers
- obtain commitment to provision of internal resources.

An 'external source' represents any supplier from outside the host organisation. 'Internal sources' are departments or divisions within the host organisation.

Where the external source is a separate legal entity, the terms under which goods and services are procured will be the subject of a legal contract. When the source is part of the same organisation, a less formal approach such as a service level agreement may be used.

Procurement typically incudes the acquisition of:

- 'off-the-shelf' goods and services
- bespoke goods or services designed and provided specifically for the purchaser
- advice or consultancy.

A procurement procedure will contain the steps shown in Figure 1.43.

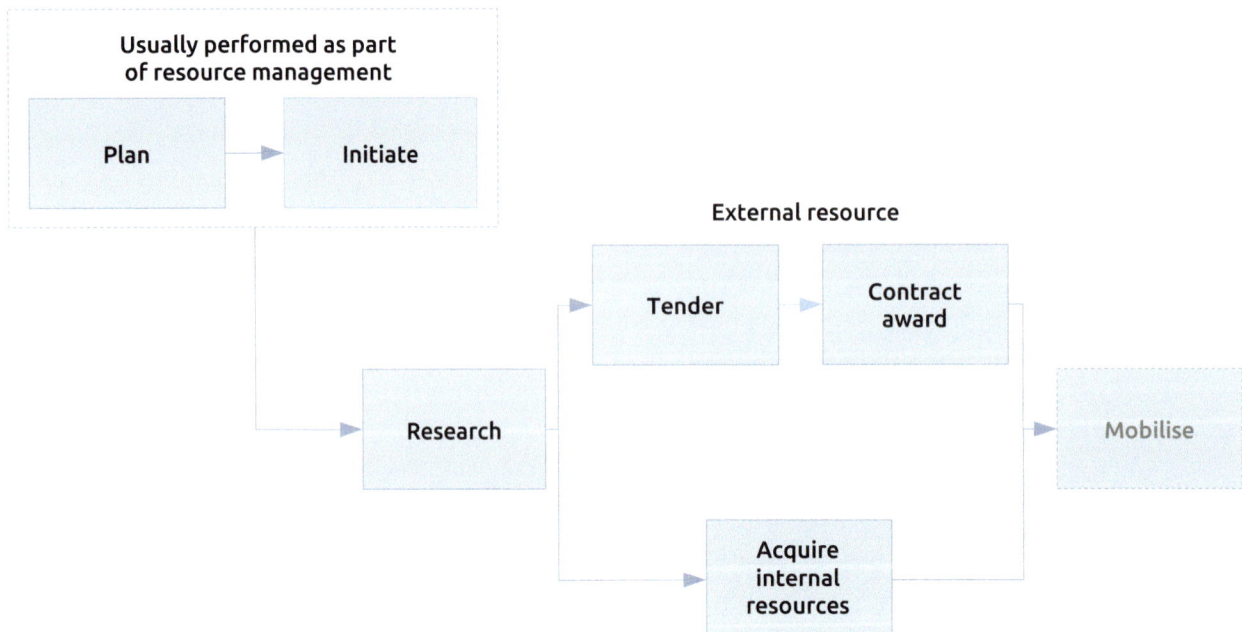

Figure 1.43 Procurement procedure

Research involves identifying the suppliers that have the required capability and may result in a long list of potential suppliers. In some cases the host organisation may have a regularly reviewed and up-to-date approved supplier list that reduces the work needed here.

A pre-qualification exercise aims to reduce the number of potential suppliers to a 'shortlist'. This can be achieved through various means such as sending out a pre-qualification questionnaire. This can clarify the capacity of the supplier, their willingness to tender, their financial stability and technical experience. It may also ask for references for similar work. Other projects or programmes may have experience of the same suppliers and their experience should be researched. In a more mature organisation there should be references to suppliers in the knowledge management system, and lessons learned, in particular, should be reviewed. In a less mature organisation a P3 manager may have to rely on seeking out and talking to other managers with relevant experiences.

Pre-qualification results in a shortlist of suppliers who will be asked to provide a full bid against a defined statement of work, which could be a technical or functional specification. Final selection is often based on a formal tender. Tendering can be an extensive procedure in its own right, especially in some regulated industries, and a P3 manager may need to seek specialist help. It is important that the requirements are clear and all suppliers are given an equal chance of success.

Procurement records must be carefully maintained and archived to mitigate the risk of unsuccessful suppliers challenging the decision. Inputs to selection should include an appropriate risk analysis in addition to cost, time and quality considerations as defined in the resource management plan. Where possible, a reserve supplier should be identified. For critical goods and services the contract may be split among multiple suppliers as a form of risk mitigation.

The contract award step will involve the negotiation and agreement of a contract. Throughout the procurement procedure care must be taken to ensure that a contract is not casually entered into, and it should be made clear in all meetings and in associated documents that the proceedings are 'subject to contract'.

All procurement involves risk and all aspects of the resource management plan must be prepared with risk management in mind. One example of this is the choice of payment methods for external suppliers.

Many resources will not be procured from external suppliers and will not be subject to a formal contract. Acquisition of internal resources is often not seen as a procurement exercise and does not result in a contract award. In some ways, this makes the acquisition of internal resources inherently more risky because the P3 manager is relying on verbal, non-binding commitments from departmental managers to provide the necessary resources when needed.

While tendering and legal contracts are not appropriate for internal resources, the P3 manager must take steps to formalise the relationship with internal suppliers. This may simply be written confirmation of the nature, quantity and timing of the resources being supplied, or it may be a more formal service level agreement. Negotiating and agreeing these contracts should involve the sponsor, who can then provide seniority if there are issues of non-performance.

A package breakdown structure, based on a product or work breakdown structure, shows how work will be arranged in order to procure packages from different suppliers. The allocation of work to these packages is another important mechanism for managing risk.

For each package, the relative importance of time, cost and quality needs to be considered. For example, if a package is on the critical path there will be greater emphasis on time performance. Consciously addressing these factors greatly influences how contract incentives or service levels are designed.

Regardless of the detail of the procurement procedure, the management team must be able to demonstrate that it was conducted ethically.

Projects, programmes and portfolios

Smaller stand-alone projects will not be able to justify a dedicated infrastructure for procurement. If the procurement needs are more complex than the project manager and sponsor can handle, they should use the services of the host organisation.

When a project needs the support of procurement specialists the manager must consider procurement implications as early in the life cycle as is practicable. Waiting until the full approval of the project at the end of the definition process may, for example, result in tender delays and long lead times adversely affecting the schedule. This early procurement is covered by the pre-authorisation work activity in both the definition and boundaries processes.

Managers of smaller projects will have less opportunity to develop relationships with suppliers. In such situations procurement needs to ensure that the mechanisms for supplying the goods or services are as routine and low-risk as possible.

At programme level the management team will need to decide which suppliers are to be managed at project level and which at programme level. Typical situations to consider are:

- suppliers providing goods or services to multiple projects
- specialist suppliers working on one project
- risky contracts that need specialist procurement expertise

- routine supplies
- ongoing maintenance that supports benefits realisation.

All these factors will be taken into account when preparing the resource management plan or, in work involving complex procurement, a specific procurement management plan.

Programmes, portfolios and large, complex projects may enable economies of scale by consolidating and co-ordinating the procurement across otherwise autonomous packages of work. An overall resource management plan will govern how procurement is co-ordinated.

At these larger scales, the management team may be able to make use of partnering and alliancing to create long-term relationships with suppliers. It may also be able to set up framework contracts that agree unit prices for goods and services that can be called off by, for example, individual projects or sub-projects. This greatly reduces the effort required for procurement at the lower levels.

Framework contracts are not appropriate for all goods and services. There will still be many suppliers who have to be locally selected to meet the specific needs of individual projects and programmes. The top-level procurement management plan should set out the basic procedure to be used and maintain a watching brief to identify common needs.

Contract management

General

Contract management includes the negotiation, creation and administration of a contract between two or more parties. Its goals are to:

- support procurement by negotiating terms and conditions
- document contractual agreements
- monitor contractual performance
- conclude contracts.

A typical procedure is shown in Figure 1.44.

The procedure starts with the planning step that defines the scope and objectives of contract management and, if necessary, results in a contract management plan. The initiation step is performed once the work is approved and the resources needed to manage contracts are mobilised. Unless contract management is a major function within a project, programme or portfolio, it is likely that these steps will be part of a broader resource management procedure.

The first specific step is to negotiate contract terms with a supplier. A contract is an agreement made between two or more parties that creates legally binding obligations between them. The contract sets out those obligations and the actions that can be taken if they are not met.

Contracts are covered by contract law. Specialist advice should be sought to ensure that the legal ramifications of any proposed contract are fully understood.

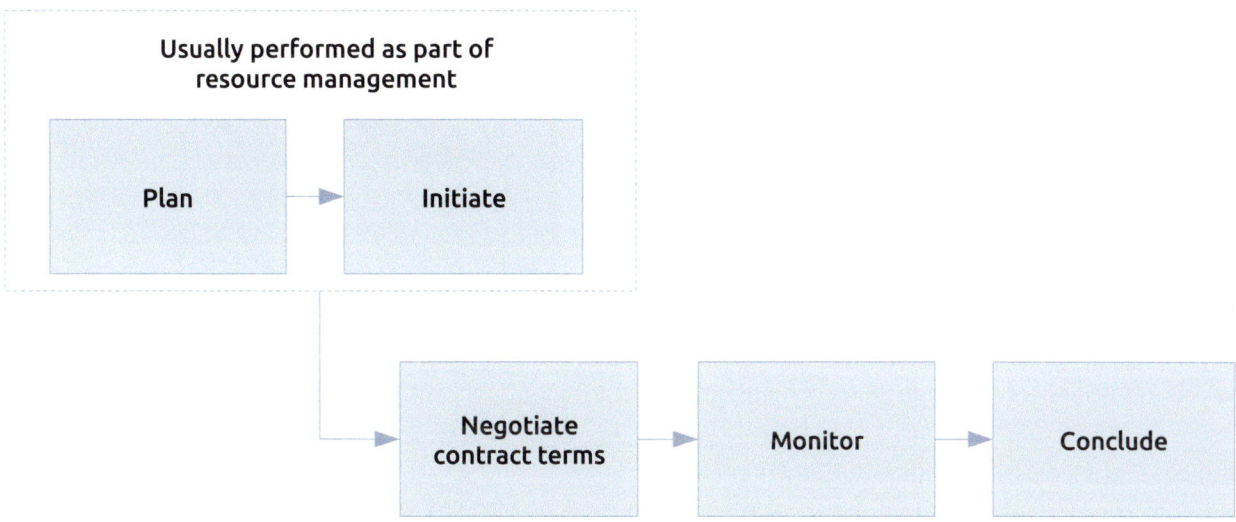

Figure 1.44 Contract management procedure

While the law governing any contract will depend on the applicable jurisdiction, there are general principles that are universal. For example, there must be:

- an offer made by one party, which is accepted by the other party or parties without qualification
- an intention to create a legal relationship between the parties and for the parties to be bound by the obligations in the contract
- a consideration passing from one party to the other in return for the provision of the goods or services covered by the contract
- clear and definite terms describing the conditions to which the parties are agreeing
- legality and lawfulness, with only properly incorporated firms or competent persons entering into the contracts.

A contract is required wherever goods or services are procured from external suppliers. This could simply constitute acceptance of standard terms and conditions or the creation of a specialist contract. The resource management plan should set the high-level conditions that contracts need to implement. For example, if the plan stipulates that risk should be shared between parties, the contract needs to incorporate the relevant payment methods and be drafted to make sure that risk is shared.

Many industries have standard forms of contract, such as the NEC3 range for construction and engineering. Some large organisations, such as the UK's National Health Service, have systems for constructing contracts from standard components. The main advantage of using standard forms of contract is that they take account of established best practice within the particular industry sector or organisation. The disadvantage is that it may not fully address all the areas required by the resource management plan for a particular project or programme.

Standard contracts do not work for all situations. It is often the case that they have to be significantly tailored or a contract has to be built from scratch. These are called bespoke contracts and they are able to reflect the specific context and content of the work. The P3 manager will have to ensure that contracts are properly executed and that they are subject to version control.

Whether standard or bespoke, all contracts have the same typical information and 'conditions', such as:

- general information about the parties to the contract
- a description of the works or services
- the legal system that the contract will use
- the supplier's responsibilities for design, approvals, assignment of such responsibilities and subcontracting
- agreed milestones and completion date
- change control, quality control, testing and defect rectification
- payment methods and procedures
- risk transfer, risk sharing, and insurances
- ownership of assets during the course of the contract, transfer of ownership including intellectual property (IP), and copyright
- dispute management procedures and compensation (e.g. non-performance).

A statement of work (SoW) that defines the activities, deliverables, schedule and pricing can be a useful annex to the main contract (this is often referred to as a schedule and should not be confused with a P3 time schedule). A SoW should be checked to ensure it does not conflict with the main body of the contract and precedence needs to be clear.

If all parties perform as expected, it will not be necessary to resort to the contract to resolve a dispute, but of course relationships do falter and performance sometimes falls short of expectations. For the P3 manager, the contract can become a tool in conflict management, or more specifically, conflict resolution. The P3 manager should not immediately resort to the 'letter of the law' and must approach contractual conflict in the same measured way as any other form of conflict. There may be mitigating circumstances and the impact of destroying the relationship with a supplier must be weighed against the benefits of resolving the dispute in other ways.

The P3 manager must ensure that the management team is aware of how contractual obligations can be created inadvertently by poorly worded communications or inappropriate actions. Case law confirms that changes to a contract can be made without formal legal instructions being issued.

Once the contract is concluded, the P3 manager should confirm that the legal obligations created under the contract have been discharged. Items such as equipment warranties and defect liabilities may need to be administered for months, if not years, after the contract is concluded. The responsibilities for administering such long-term liabilities need to be considered and where appropriate, documented in the follow-on actions report.

Projects, programmes and portfolios

The basic principles of contract law are the same regardless of how the work is managed; i.e. whether it is constituted as a project, programme or portfolio.

Smaller, non-complex projects or work that is performed entirely using internal resources may have no contracts at all. For more complex situations, internal relationships may be defined using service level agreements (SLAs) between an operational department and the project, programme or portfolio. These SLAs may adopt many of the principles of a contract.

As the complexity of the work increases, the P3 manager will need different levels of support in the creation and maintenance of contracts. In many situations procurement specialists will be competent to write and maintain contract documentation. Where the work includes unusual or complex legal issues contract lawyers may be required.

As the scale and complexity of the work develops, co-ordination will be needed between multiple contracts. At programme or portfolio level the work will often be best served by framework contracts with suppliers that cover multiple projects rather than having separately negotiated contracts for a project or work package.

In programmes, portfolios and large projects where there are multiple contracts, the P3 manager must understand the inter-dependencies between them. The actions of one supplier may adversely affect another, leading to a contractual dispute. All inter-dependencies should be considered and the contracts drafted accordingly.

Mobilisation

General

Mobilisation makes sure that appropriate organisational and technical infrastructures are in place for acquiring and deploying resources. It also ensures that these are dismantled or redeployed when no longer required.

The goals of mobilisation are to ensure that:

- capital assets are operational and accessible
- facilities are operational and accessible
- delivery team members are competent and capable
- all resources are redeployed, returned or disposed of at the end of the work.

Mobilisation occurs at various points in the life cycle. The way mobilisation operates within the life cycle processes is covered by the corresponding activities in the definition and boundaries processes.

During the identification and definition processes some mobilisation will be required to put in place teams, and possibly facilities, that can complete the work. Mobilisation of the full project infrastructure will occur once authorisation has been given (although some limited mobilisation may take place earlier to shorten the overall schedule), as shown in Figure 1.45. Mobilisation is also used to a lesser extent as each tranche or stage is started and finished.

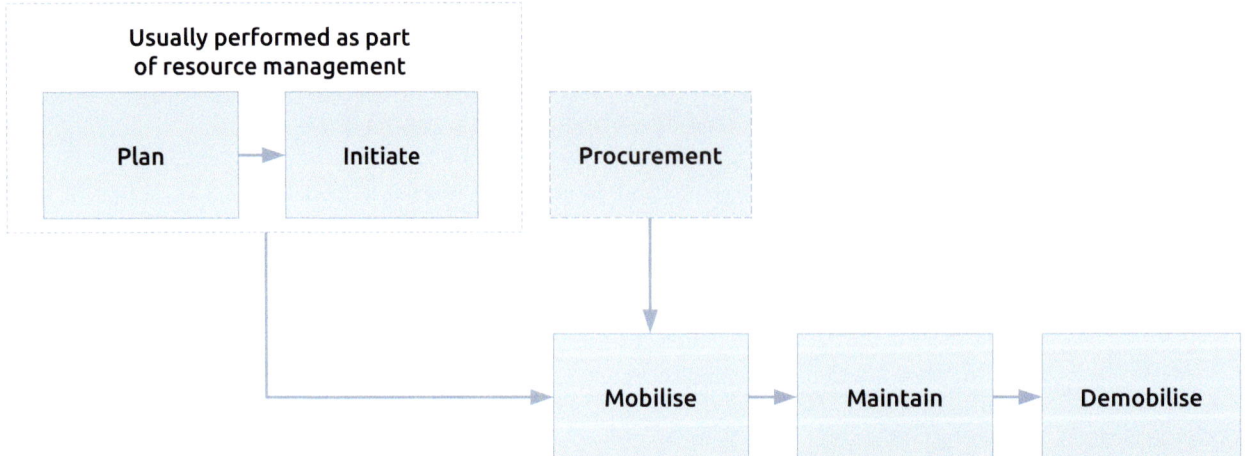

Figure 1.45 Mobilisation procedure

On larger projects or programmes some mobilisation will be performed at the beginning of each stage or tranche. In a portfolio it is simply the decision to operate formal portfolio management that authorises the creation of a suitable infrastructure.

The mobilisation procedure can cover any of the following:

- management team
- premises
- IT hardware, software tools and telecoms
- plant and machinery
- internal and external resources
- governance procedures.

The initial management organisation is put in place to execute the identification and definition phases of a project or programme. The organisation that will manage the delivery phase is designed during 'Define a project or programme' and, after approval of the full business case, the various posts are filled.

In many cases, the management teams will be located in existing premises. These management teams should be co-located whenever possible to improve communication and teamwork. Sometimes co-location is not possible; this may be because multiple companies are working in partnership or because work is managed in different countries. This will put additional pressure on the cohesion of the management team and IT infrastructure that facilitates virtual teams must help alleviate this.

Acquiring resource from internal sources often involves difficult negotiation. In a matrix organisation, for example, resources may retain their departmental home as well as having a role in a project, programme or portfolio. The P3 manager's resource plans may conflict with business-as-usual demands when trying to allocate these resources. That is when good conflict management and influencing skills will come to the fore.

The temporary nature of projects and programmes means that mobilisation will always be followed by demobilisation once the work is complete. This has an impact on widely differing aspects of the work:

- where capital investment in plant and machinery is needed, decisions must be made whether to buy with resale in mind, lease or rent
- when P3 teams are being built, their managers must always bear in mind that approaching demobilisation affects traditional team cycles such as Tuckman.

As the need to demobilise approaches, plans must be drawn up to dispose of assets, redeploy staff and, if necessary, reinstate premises to their previous condition.

Projects, programmes and portfolios

On some small projects very little will be needed in the form of mobilisation. Facilities are all in place and resources do not need to physically move. What needs to be done is more about teamwork than mobilisation. However, models for teamwork are normally based on semi-permanent business-as-usual teams rather than the transient teams found in projects and programmes. Even small projects must consider the demobilisation of the team.

When mobilising programmes and large complex projects, the management team must consider the needs of the component work packages or projects. While the management team and its infrastructure will be in place for the duration of the work, there will be components that need to be mobilised and demobilised during the course of the life cycle.

In these situations the management team must consider the impact of the overall schedule on the infrastructure requirements. Some options for the way the way the work is structured may have a significant impact on the infrastructure costs. For example, the ability to share the costs of mobilisation across multiple projects must be weighed against the impact on benefits and the business case.

A portfolio organisation is more permanent than projects and programmes, although a structured portfolio may go through multiple planning cycles and be reshaped according to the needs of a revised strategic plan. Portfolio mobilisation is typically a one-off project that sets up the infrastructure required to co-ordinate projects and programmes through multiple cycles.

A dedicated portfolio infrastructure forms the basis for an organisation to improve its capability maturity. It may be set up to include permanent organisational structures, such as a project management office (PMO) to provide support and governance. There could also be communities of practice to support the continual improvement of individual competence, or professional development programmes to encourage professionalism.

The mobilisation of a portfolio requires support and commitment at the host organisation's board level to ensure that it is thorough and resilient. Only then will the portfolio infrastructure be embedded in the organisation as the preferred way of delivering projects and programmes.

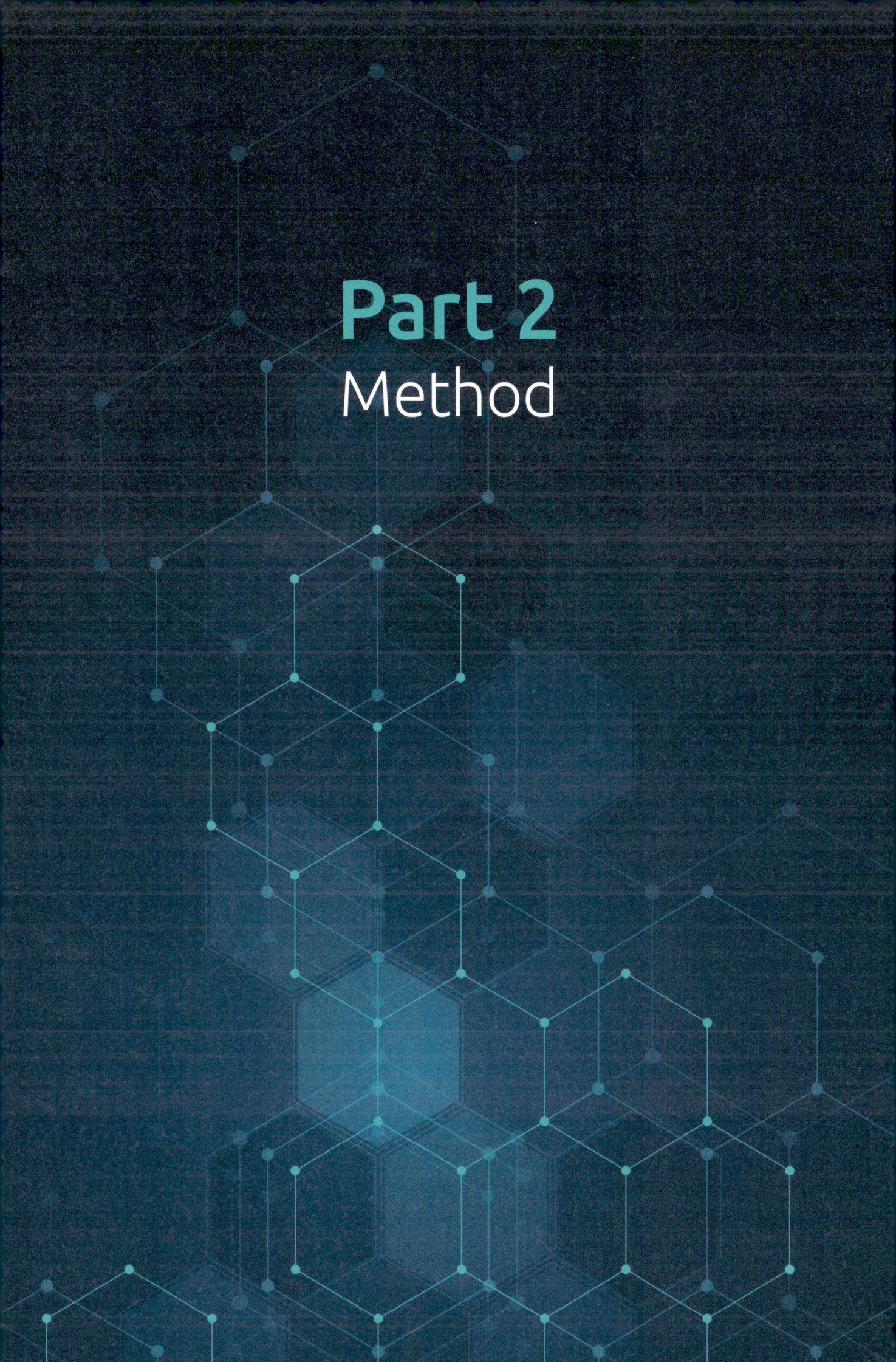

2.1 Overview

The Praxis method comprises process models and descriptions of documentation. These lie at the heart of the governance of a project, programme or portfolio. The individual processes make use of functional procedures, tools and techniques and provide a life cycle-based approach to their application.

The nature of projects and programmes means that they have a very similar life cycle. They can therefore be managed using the same fundamental processes but with adaptations to suit their context and, specifically, their complexity.

While many characteristics of portfolios are shared with programmes, they have a different life cycle. Hence the inclusion in Praxis of two process models: one covering projects and programmes and the other covering portfolios.

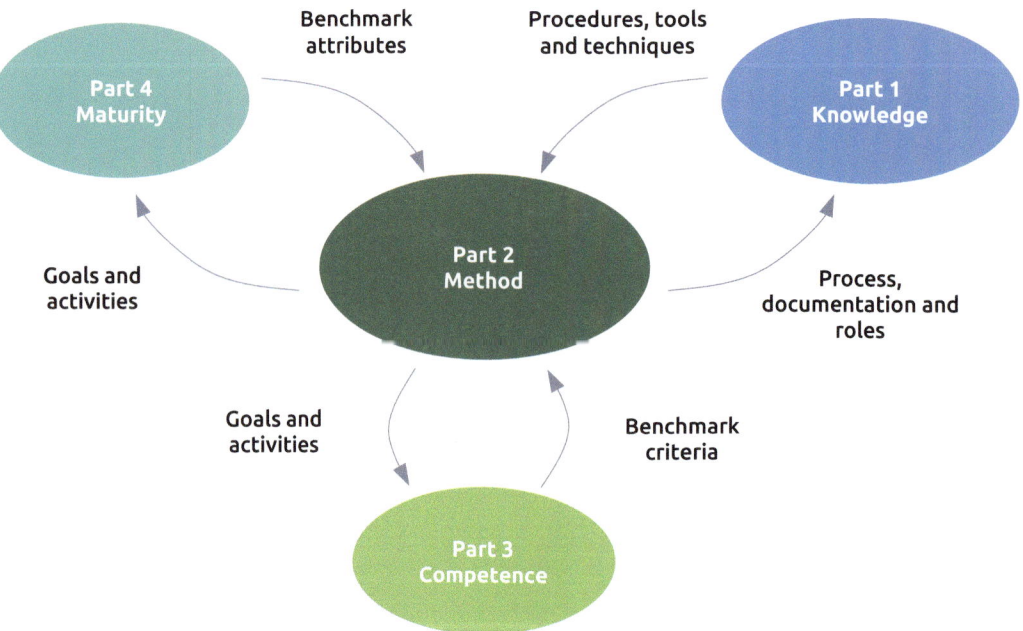

Figure 2.1 Method relationships

The adaptation and implementation of consistent methods is an important factor in developing capability maturity, as shown in Figure 2.1. The processes and documentation in the method provide the mechanism for the integration of functions (and therefore capabilities), which leads to maturity.

The goals and activities of each process provide the basis for defining maturity indicators. In return the maturity model provides attributes that can be used to guide the implementation of the method.

The goals and process activities also provide the structure for knowledge and performance criteria in the competency framework. In return, competency definitions provide a benchmark for individual performance of the processes.

Praxis provides two process models: one for projects and programmes and one for portfolios. Most other guidance describes separate processes for projects and programmes but detailed comparison demonstrates that they are fundamentally the same.

In fact the artificial distinction of 'projects' and 'programmes' as different entities introduces confusion and places constraints on competent project/programme managers when undertaking initiatives that are a combination of the two (as conventionally defined).

Praxis describes the general characteristics of each process and then, as with the functions in Part 1, explains how these can be applied as complexity increases from simple projects to complex programmes. This supports the principle, embraced by Praxis, that describing projects and programmes as two mutually exclusive types of initiative has more to do with human nature than with real, practical differences.

Although Praxis defines two types of portfolio (standard and structured) the process model is the same for both.

2.2 Project and programme processes

The generic process model for both projects and programmes is based on life cycle phases with an additional process to address the sponsorship function. All these can, and should, be tailored to the specific context of the work. Each process is supported by competence and maturity definitions that remain relevant even if the Praxis process is replaced with a corresponding process from another guide, such as PRINCE2® or ISO 21500.

As the scope of the work becomes more complex its primary impact is on the delivery phase. Hence, the reference to multiple delivery process(es) in Figure 2.2. Where the delivery work is delegated to multiple production teams the development process can also be used, and where the delivery phase needs to be segmented into stages or tranches, the boundaries process is required.

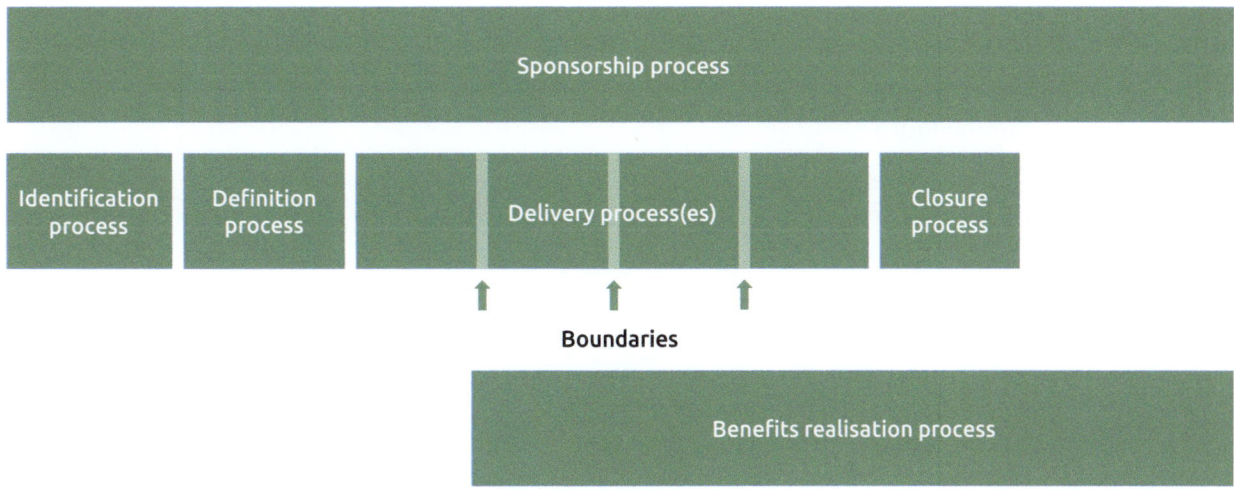

Figure 2.2 Process model for projects and programmes

Just as the functions in Part 1 have an explanation of how they vary according to increasing complexity, each project and programme process has information about its application in situations ranging from small, non-complex projects to large, complex programmes.

This generic model should be adapted in accordance with the context of a project or programme. For example, where a project is part of a programme, the benefits realisation process will usually be performed by the programme. The project identification may also be done at programme level, resulting in a reduced set of processes for the project as shown in Figure 2.3.

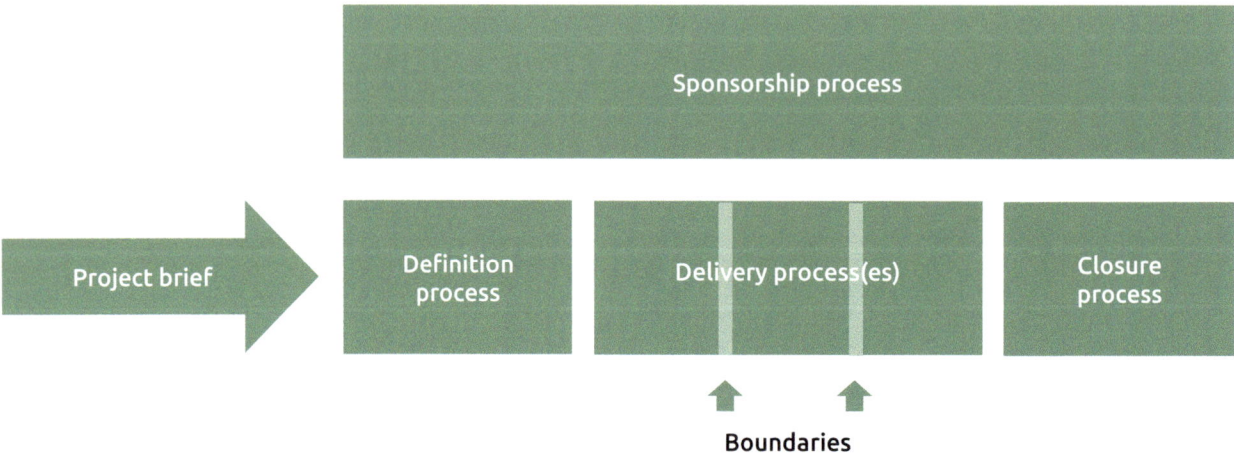

Figure 2.3 Project within a programme or supplier project

A similar approach could be taken for a project or programme that is part of a portfolio. The primary difference between a project and a programme is the complexity of the objectives and this is reflected in the relationship between the delivery process(es) and the benefits realisation process.

The generic model can also be adapted for different environments. For example, where a contracting organisation is delivering a project on behalf of a client organisation the client may perform the identification and benefits realisation processes. They may also perform much of the definition process.

The process model for the contracting organisation would then be limited to the elements shown in the lighter colour in Figure 2.4.

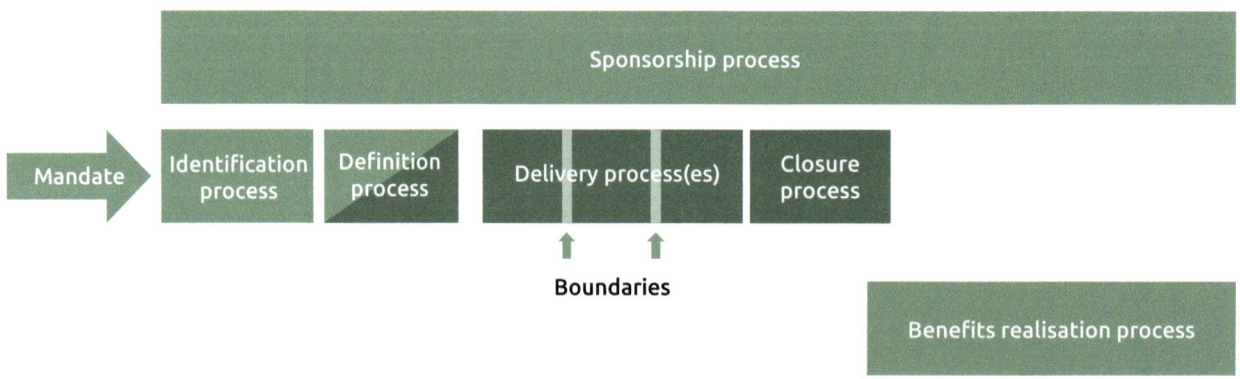

Figure 2.4 Client or contractor project process

2.2.1 Identification process

General

This process manages the first phase of the project or programme life cycle. Its goals are to:

- develop an outline of the project or programme and assess whether is it likely to be justifiable
- determine what effort and investment is needed to define the work in detail
- gain the sponsor's authorisation for the definition phase.

Some initial idea or need for a project or programme will generate a mandate. This can take many forms, ranging from a client's invitation to tender to a strategic objective in a corporate plan, or simply a verbal instruction. The term mandate is applied to whatever information is used to trigger a project or programme.

The first goal is addressed in the form of the brief and the second in the form of the definition plan, as shown in Figure 2.5. At the end of the process these two documents will be presented to the sponsor with a request to authorise the definition process.

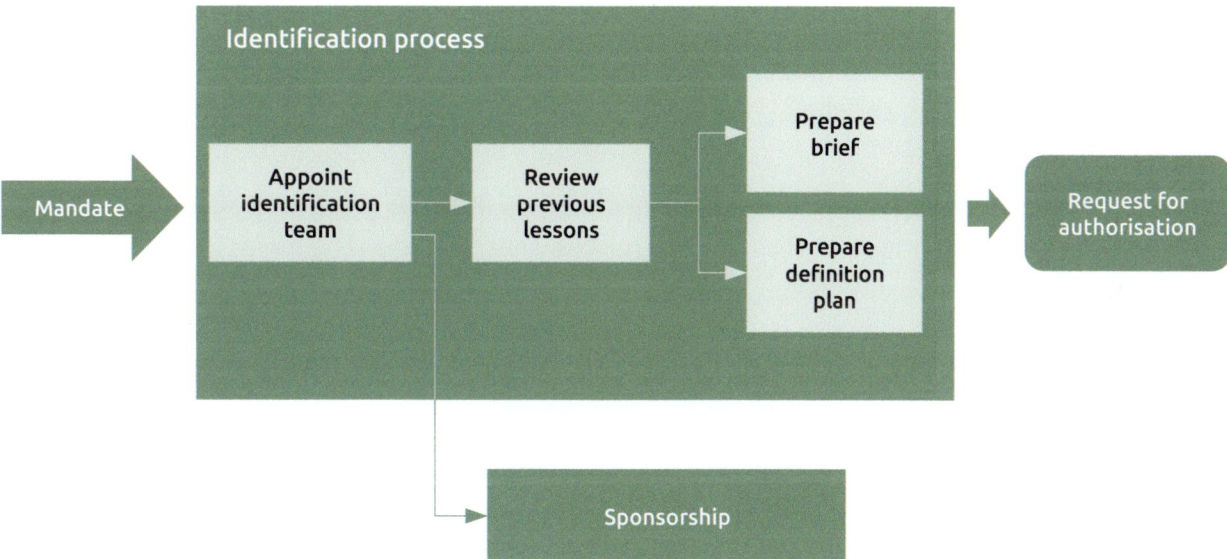

Figure 2.5 Identification process

Appoint identification team

Circumstances at this point will vary enormously according to the context. The work may be triggered by events as diverse as the award of a contract, a decision in a board meeting, a change in regulation or legislation, a market opportunity or any one of a host of other events.

Someone will be the initial recipient of the mandate and must take the necessary actions to formalise the work into a project or programme. This will involve putting together a team that perform the identification activities under the guidance of a sponsor and manager.

In most cases the sponsor and manager appointed here will see the work through the whole life cycle, but in some cases sponsorship and management of the identification and definition processes will be done by different people from those who perform those roles during the delivery process.

The first responsibility of the sponsor and manager will be to check the mandate to fill in any gaps in the information and clarify any ambiguities. They will then need to agree a timescale and budget for the work and assemble the team that will complete the identification activities.

> A property developer may appoint an identification team made up of architects, structural engineers and surveyors. The developer would act as sponsor and may appoint the architect to manage identification and definition. The contract for delivery would be awarded to a construction firm who would then provide a project manager, with the architect providing some aspects of sponsorship on behalf of the developer.
>
> Where a project is part of a programme, the identification team may comprise members of the programme management team, which hands over to a project sponsor and project manager for the definition phase.

During this formative period, information will be gathered for use in the brief and definition plan. This information will be diverse but it is too early to start building individual documents. It is useful for the manager to maintain a diary that is formally known as a daily log. This acts as a repository for information about assumptions, risks, issues, constraints etc., until more formal documentation is established.

Role descriptions for sponsorship and management should be assembled and agreed with the relevant individuals. It is important to confirm that they not only have the necessary competence but also are able to commit sufficient time to the identification process.

Review previous lessons

It is always important to learn from the past. The availability of documented lessons learned will depend upon the host organisation's capability in knowledge management.

Where records of lessons learned are available, the initiation team should review them and identify those that are relevant to the new project or programme. These will be entered into a lessons log along with a description of how they affect the brief and definition plan.

If records are not available, it is still important for lessons to be gathered from previous projects or programmes. This may involve seeking out and interviewing sponsors and managers of previous projects and programmes or organising workshops.

External sources of lessons learned, such as other organisations or professional networks, should also be considered. If the host organisation has not done a project or programme like this one before this activity will rely on such external sources.

Prepare brief

Based on the confirmed mandate, the identification team will start work on the project or programme brief. The purpose of the brief is to provide sufficient information to justify investing in the definition process (the extent of which will be described in the definition plan). The exact content will vary in scope and detail according to circumstances and must be in proportion to the cost and risk of the proposed project or programme.

The key decision made during this process concerns how the work will be governed; i.e. will it be organised as a project or a programme? This is predominantly determined by the early stages of scope management, starting with the capture of requirements. The nature and complexity of the requirements, the scale and complexity of the solution, and the breadth of scope, will collectively indicate how the work should be managed. This decision will, in turn, influence the way that scope management, schedule management, risk management, etc. are covered in the brief.

The brief contains outline information about all of the components of the delivery function. The identification team will:

- work with stakeholders to establish their requirements
- develop a solution and scope of work
- determine whether to manage the work as a project or programme, or a hybrid of the two
- estimate high-level timescales
- identify sources of funding and estimate budgets
- identify and assess the main risks that could affect successful completion
- outline the type and quantity of resource that will be needed and whether it can be sourced internally or externally
- highlight areas of business as usual that will be subject to change (if the need for change is identified as part of the scope)
- identify and assess the most influential stakeholders and propose initial communications.

When determining the extent and detail of information that should be included in the brief, the overriding principle is that it must be sufficient to give the sponsor confidence to authorise the budget for the definition phase.

Preparing the brief will utilise many P3 functions. Each of these includes information on tools and techniques that can be too detailed for use this early in the life cycle. They should be applied at an appropriately high level as each aspect of the work is only documented in outline in the brief.

Prepare definition plan

While the brief outlines the project or programme as a whole, the sponsor will also need to know what is required to produce a full set of detailed documentation. The work required to define the project or programme in detail will range from the concise to the extensive. The definition plan follows the normal format of a delivery plan but has the specific purpose of describing how the definition process will be performed.

The identification team will need to ensure that:

- the scope of the definition work is well defined
- any specialised resources required for detailed definition are identified and available
- any risks specific to the definition work are identified along with proposed responses
- the cost and timescale of the definition phase are estimated as accurately as possible
- arrangements are in place to mobilise the definition team should the definition phase be approved.

Projects and programmes

On small projects the identification activities may be managed and performed by one person, but having a separate sponsor and manager is the minimum requirement. It may also be possible to combine the identification and definition phases into a single process.

In all but the simplest of projects, and all programmes, identification should be a separate phase with a review before proceeding to definition. This can avoid the cost of substantial definition work.

Where a project is part of a programme, the brief may be prepared by the programme management team and the identification process is bypassed at the project level. The same could be true of a programme that is part of a portfolio.

On large, complex projects and programmes, the definition phase may constitute a small project in its own right. Any supporting information should accompany the definition plan, commensurate with the scale and complexity of the definition phase.

2.2.2 Sponsorship process

General

This process, shown in Figure 2.6, does not have an equivalent phase in the project or programme life cycle. It describes the activities that a sponsor must perform to exercise overall control and make key decisions during the life cycle. It also includes aspects of the relationship between the sponsor and the manager.

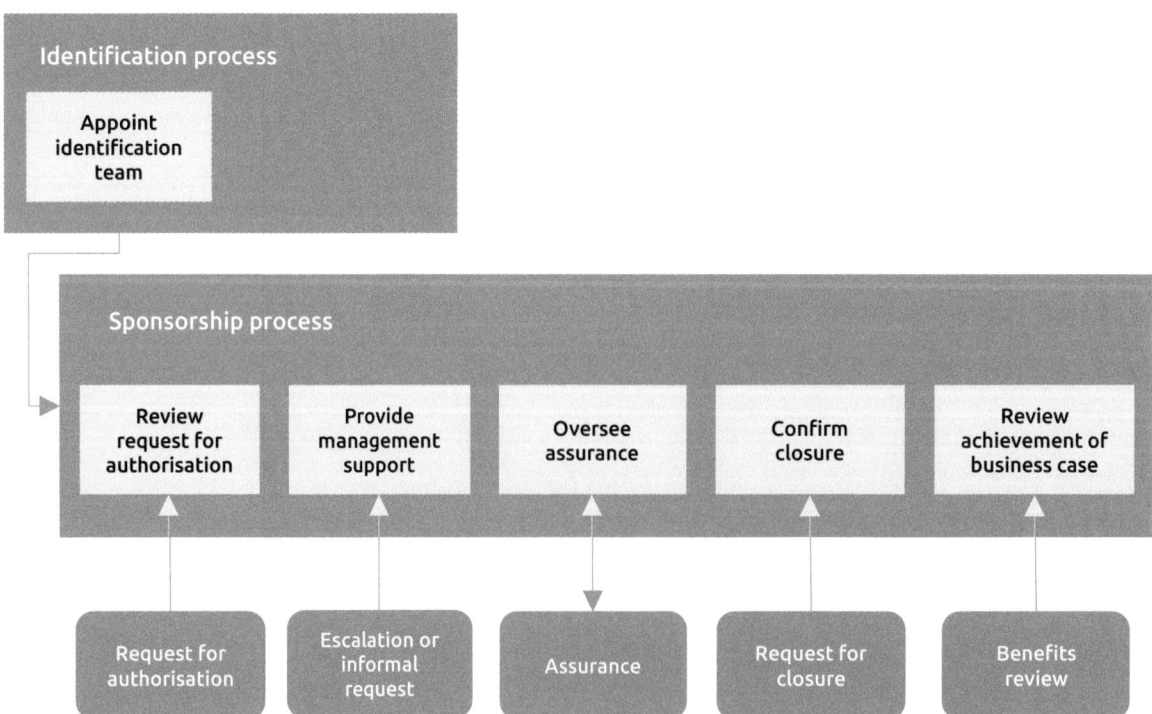

Figure 2.6 Sponsorship process

This process is designed to achieve the goals of the sponsorship function; i.e. to:

- provide ownership of the business case
- act as champion for the objectives of the project or programme
- make go/no-go decisions at relevant points in the life cycle
- address matters outside the scope of the manager's authority
- oversee assurance
- give ad-hoc support to the management team.

Review request for authorisation

Request for authorisation typically occurs at one of three points; i.e. to:

- **Proceed with the definition phase**

    This occurs at the end of the identification process when the sponsor will be presented with a brief and a definition plan. Based on the information provided, the sponsor must decide whether it is worth investing in the definition phase.

    This decision has two aspects:

    > Firstly, the brief and outline business case will give an indication of the viability and practicality of the proposed work. The sponsor must appreciate that this information is based on limited research and is subject to change during definition. The level of certainty in the analysis of viability needs only be sufficient to justify the investment in the definition phase.
    > Secondly, the definition plan will provide detailed information about the duration, cost and resources required to complete the definition. At the end of the definition phase the sponsor will have a further opportunity to authorise or cancel the work.

- **Commence a stage or tranche**

    The first time this occurs will be at the end of the definition process, where the sponsor is provided with a full set of management plans and delivery plans. This is the key decision in any project or programme.

    It may be that considerable effort has been invested in getting to this point and the definition team will certainly be hoping for a positive response. However, the sponsor's decision must be completely objective and thorough. Deciding not to proceed at this point is always a difficult decision to make and communicate, but it is far preferable to authorising work of unproven or dubious viability, desirability or achievability. The sponsor should not be afraid of requesting further information if needed.

    Updated governance documents and delivery information will be reviewed before commencing each subsequent stage or tranche. At this point the sponsor must review what has been achieved, study the detailed plans for the next stage or tranche and take a view on the continuing viability, desirability or achievability of the project or programme as a whole. Only if the sponsor is convinced of the value of the entire project or programme should the next stage or tranche be authorised.

    As the work proceeds it will get harder and harder to refuse authorisation because of the time and money invested so far. Human nature is inclined to be optimistic about the potential to achieve objectives. Failure to terminate projects and programmes that are no longer justifiable is a common cause of wasted investment. Sponsorship requires strong leadership and that can include taking difficult decisions.

- **Implement an exception plan**

    In the authorised plans for a stage or tranche, the manager will have tolerances within which to work. If those tolerances are exceeded, or predicted to be exceeded, the manager will escalate the issue to the sponsor. In some circumstances the sponsor and manager may agree that a revised set of plans is needed to deal with the issue and bring the work back on track. This is known as an exception and when it occurs the manager will produce a revised set of delivery plans that need to be authorised.

    It may well be that a project or programme is well underway but has become less viable or even non-viable in its original form. Rather than terminating the work prematurely, it may be possible to recover sunk costs by reshaping the business case. By amending the scope, adopting a new delivery approach, accepting delays, providing additional investment or a combination of all of these, it may be possible to establish the viability of a significantly revised project or programme. The new delivery plans in this situation will then be submitted for authorisation.

Provide management support

In addition to formal requests such as those to authorise a stage or tranche, the sponsor should provide informal, ad-hoc support to the manager and possibly other members of the management team.

There will be many times during the course of a project or programme where the manager may need to make use of the sponsor's experience or authority within the host organisation. This may arise for many reasons, such as:

- advice on how to deal with a predicted breach of performance tolerances
- help in areas where the manager has limited experience
- resolution of internal conflicts between projects or programmes and business as usual
- clarification of relationships between organisational strategy and the project or programme
- dealing with stakeholder issues or risks that are outside the manager's span of control or influence.

The sponsor should be able to act as coach, mentor and facilitator to the manager on a regular basis.

Oversee assurance

The assurance function is concerned with verifying that management processes are adequate in design and application. Detailed assurance activities will be performed by roles outside of the management team but this work is commissioned and supervised by the sponsor. The assurance role reports to the sponsor.

If assurance reveals any weaknesses or lack of performance in the management of the project or programme, it is the sponsor's responsibility to address and resolve the issues.

Confirm closure

A project or programme is closed when all the outputs have been delivered and the management and delivery teams can be disbanded. The manager will need to present the sponsor with a report showing how products have been handed over and accepted; contracts have been concluded; and infrastructure has been demobilised. A post-project or post-programme review should also be completed. The sponsor may then declare the project or programme closed and inform stakeholders accordingly.

In the real world life is rarely that simple. Projects and programmes do not come to a clean and sudden conclusion. There will always be loose ends to tie up and residual work to be concluded. This should not prevent the formal closure from being confirmed. Outstanding matters should be recorded in a follow-on actions report. Provided the sponsor is content that this report covers all outstanding items and adequate arrangements have been made to ensure they will be completed, then closure can be confirmed.

Review achievement of business case

A business case will contain a list of benefits that justified the project or programme in the first place. In most cases these benefits will not have been achieved when closure is confirmed. The realisation of benefits is usually something that is achieved by the users of the outputs and may continue for some time after the project or programme has been closed.

The sponsor owns the business case and will continue to monitor the achievements of benefits after closure. Sponsors remain in post until a benefits review demonstrates that the business case has either been achieved, will be achieved without further change activity, or demonstrably cannot now be achieved.

The management team will probably have been demobilised before the final benefits review is conducted. It will be necessary for the sponsor to commission the review using business-as-usual resources with external assurance as necessary.

Projects and programmes

As the complexity of the work increases, the sponsor may need to be supported by a programme board. This is useful, for example, where there are joint venture partners in a major infrastructure project or in a programme involving significant cross-departmental change management. In the first example senior representatives of the partner organisation will make up the board, while in the second the board will comprise senior departmental heads.

As complexity increases and the sponsorship process grows, the sponsor may need help from senior members of a support office to whom some responsibilities may be delegated.

Regardless of their makeup, these boards are chaired by the sponsor who retains ultimate accountability for the business case and decisions that affect it.

2.2.3 Definition process

General

This process manages the definition phase of the project or programme life cycle. Its goals are to:

- develop a detailed picture of the project or programme
- determine whether the work is justified
- describe governance policies that describe how the work will be managed
- gain the sponsor's authorisation for the delivery phase.

An authorised brief and definition plan will trigger the process, which is fundamentally the same regardless of whether it has been decided to govern the work as a project or a programme. The output will be a set of documents that describe all aspects of the work, with their content and detail varying to suit the context.

The definition process, shown in Figure 2.7, will plan the management and delivery of the work. A summary of the plans is then presented to the sponsor to gain authorisation for the delivery phase. Although the formal request for authorisation is shown at the end of the process, the manager and sponsor should be in regular communication throughout. When the formal request for authorisation is eventually made, the sponsor should have a good idea of what is being proposed. This is particularly important where some pre-authorisation work may be needed with the agreement of the sponsor.

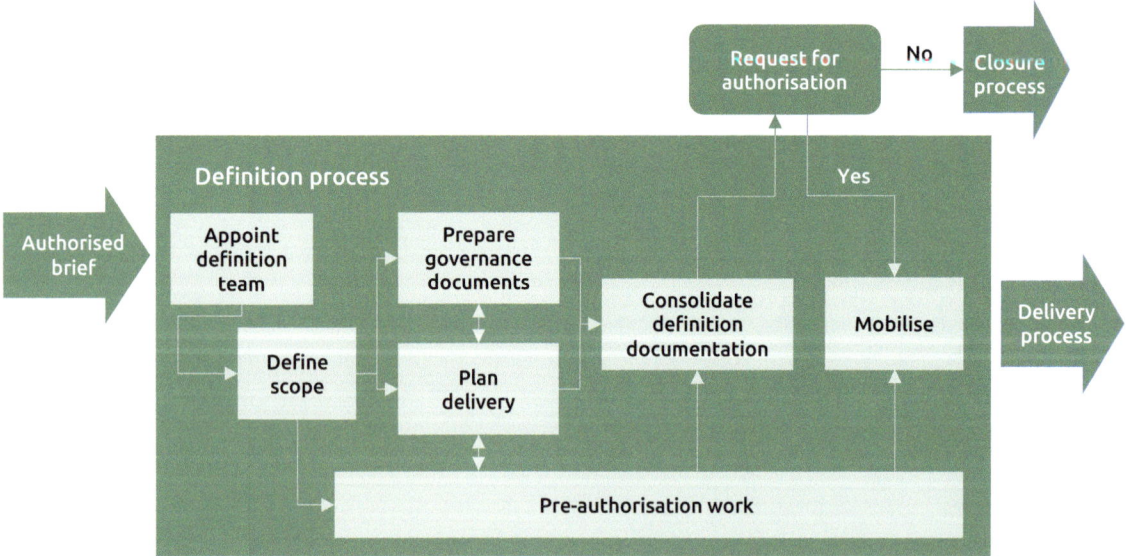

Figure 2.7 Definition process

Planning how the work will be managed involves the development of policies and procedures for all the relevant functions that will be used. What constitutes a 'relevant function' is dependent upon the context of the work.

Planning how the work will be delivered requires the definition team to be competent in all the relevant functions. The resulting delivery documents define the project or programme and how it will be performed. Once authorised they will be baselined to provide a starting point for monitoring and controlling progress.

Thamhain and Wilemon identified that this phase of the life cycle is where conflict is typically at its highest level. If this is combined with the fact that the team is still coming together and probably in Tuckman's 'storming' stage then it is clear that the project or programme manager must be very sensitive to conflict and have good leadership, conflict management and influencing skills.

A well-executed definition process sets the foundation for a successful delivery process.

Appoint definition team

On smaller projects the identification team may have sufficient expertise and capacity to continue and carry out the full definition. On larger projects and programmes it is likely that the identification team will need to be supplemented to provide sufficient resource with the necessary capabilities. A construction project may need to recruit additional specialists such as structural engineers or mechanical and electrical engineers; an IT or business change programme may need to recruit additional business analysts or system architects.

Such technical roles are focused on defining the scope of the work and they will be less involved in the delivery phase of the project or programme. Preparing the management plans and delivery documents is usually done by roles that will go on to form the team that manages the delivery phase.

Define scope

The procedures described in the scope management function will be used to capture stakeholder requirements, develop solutions and define benefits as appropriate. The scope of some projects will only encompass outputs while others will encompass benefits. The scope of programmes will encompass benefits and often significant business change required to achieve them.

Documents that are appropriate to the project or programme could include:

- specifications
- blueprint
- benefits profiles
- vision statement
- product breakdown structures
- work breakdown structures.

The range of scope documents and the detail they contain will also be influenced by the chosen life cycle. Typically, in a serial life cycle the objectives (outputs or benefits) will be defined in greater detail at this stage than in a parallel life cycle. Parallel approaches (such as agile) will continually develop scope throughout the life cycle so the initial definition will be high-level and flexible.

Pre-authorisation work

The conclusion of all planning work before any mobilisation or commencement of any delivery work is often impractical. Specialist materials or equipment may be required that are subject to long lead times; procurement of suppliers through competitive tender may need to start early; applying for statutory or regulatory approvals can be time consuming.

In parallel with planning, the management team should identify any necessary pre-authorisation work that should be done before it is fully defined or authorised. The advantage of placing provisional orders for materials or initiating a tendering process must be weighed against the risk that the next stage or tranche is not authorised.

The performance of pre-authorisation work should be planned and agreed with the sponsor. The completion of this work must be reflected in the plans, but the fact that pre-authorisation work has been completed should not be an influencing factor in judging the viability of the business case when the request for authorisation is made.

Prepare governance documents

Governance documentation includes internally produced management plans and any relevant external policy documents. Management plans can be written for many functions and every functional procedure starts with a step called 'plan'. Some, such as a stakeholder management plan or a risk management plan, are universal since the need to manage stakeholders and risk applies to all projects and programmes. Others, such as a benefits management plan or procurement management plan, are relevant only if the scope of work covers delivery of benefits or external suppliers are used.

Based on the scope of the work, the definition team will decide which functions need a management plan. In more mature organisations there will be standard management plans that can be adapted to the specific context of the work. In less mature organisations management plans tend to be recreated for each new project or programme.

Management plans should not be prepared in isolation. Each one will be influenced by the delivery documents and other management plans. For example, if the stakeholder map identifies potential opposition to the work, the risk management plan must ensure this type of risk is adequately managed.

> In Praxis the independent creation of management plans by projects and programmes is an attribute of level 2 capability.
>
> The creation of centrally controlled management plans that are adapted for the context of each project and programme is an attribute of level 3 capability.

Plan delivery

The content and extent of this activity are unique to each project or programme. Various planning documents will address different aspects. Typical examples include:

- scheduling documents (e.g. activity networks, Gantt charts, milestone plans)
- risk documents (e.g. risk register, risk response plans, Monte Carlo analysis)
- stakeholder documents (e.g. stakeholder register, stakeholder map, communications plan)
- resource documents (e.g. tendering documents, supplier specifications, contracts, service level agreements)
- financial documents (e.g. investment appraisals, cost estimates, budgets, cash flows).

Although these tools and techniques are listed separately, they all interact. It will not be possible to prepare each one in turn. The process will be iterative with, for example, the first draft stakeholder map providing information for the first draft of the risk register, which in turn may affect the initial investment appraisal.

It is not usually necessary, or even desirable, to plan the whole project or programme in detail. In a project the first stage will be planned in detail but the remainder of the work will be planned at a higher level. In a programme the plans for the first tranche will be in greater detail than the rest of the work. This is referred to as rolling-wave planning. The delivery documentation will therefore be in two parts: the overall delivery plans and the detailed delivery plans for the first stage or tranche.

Once the project or programme has been authorised these documents will be 'baselined'. During the delivery phase, progress will be monitored and compared with the baseline documents.

Consolidate definition documentation

At the end of the definition process, a request for authorisation will be submitted to the project or programme sponsor. The decision whether or not to proceed to the delivery phase will be made after a review of the relevant documentation. If authorisation is given the next step is to mobilise the first stage or tranche of the delivery phase. If authorisation is declined a minimal version of the closure process will be performed to demobilise the definition team and archive information.

Although the nature of what is submitted for approval will vary according to the context, it is common to provide three documents:

- **Project or programme management plan**

  This document summarises or brings together all the management plans for the project or programme. It may be a single, self-contained document with a section for each relevant function or a collection of separate management plans.

  In a mature organisation that has standard management plans in use across its portfolio of projects and programmes it will only be necessary for the overall management plan to cross-reference these and highlight the adaptations made for the context of the current work. A sponsor who is familiar with these organisational standards will only need to consider the adaptations to be reassured that the work has the necessary governance in place.

- **Business case**

  The business case explains the justification for the work. It will summarise the scope and balance this against the cost and risk required to achieve it. In doing so it will cross-reference more detailed delivery and content documents such as the specification, budgets and risk register.

- **Project or programme delivery plan**

  The delivery plan shows how the objectives will be achieved. It summarises the delivery documents and will include an overall timescale, resource requirements, cash flow and organisational structures. This plan may cover all the work to be done or it may cross-reference more detailed plans for stages, tranches or functional areas, such as communication, risk or quality.

Mobilise

Once the authorisation is received the project or programme can be mobilised. This puts in place all the equipment, facilities and other resources that are required to deliver the objectives.

Projects and programmes

On small projects the definition activities may be managed and performed by the project manager, but the combination of a separate sponsor and manager is the minimum requirement. It may also be possible to combine the identification and definition phases into a single process.

This process creates a lot of documentation. Too much is just as damaging to the potential success of the work as too little. Section 2.4, Documentation, should not be seen as the set of documents that need to be produced. Rather it is the range of documents that can be used. Deciding on the particular set that best suits the scale and complexity of each project or programme is an important part of this process.

An important element of this is deciding what constitutes relevant documentation for the purpose of requesting authorisation. On small projects the documentation may be distilled into key points in a presentation to the sponsor. On large projects or programmes the governance and delivery documents may be summarised and provided to the sponsor for consideration with the detailed documents being available for inspection as required.

In some contexts, the definition process may be performed by a client organisation. The definition documentation may be given to a contractor organisation that plans the delivery. The definition process is then split between the client and contractor sides of the project.

In larger programmes the definition process may be a small project in its own right. It can be run as a project with the programme definition documentation and delivery plan as the outputs of the project. All aspects of the process model are scalable and smaller versions may be nested inside larger ones.

2.2.4 Delivery process

General

The delivery phase of a small project may comprise only one stage; the delivery phase of a programme may comprise only one tranche. Most projects and programmes will comprise multiple stages or tranches that are conducted in a series or parallel.

Whatever the context, managing each stage or tranche will follow a basic 'plan, do, check, act' cycle, sometimes known as the Shewhart cycle.

In the delivery process:

- 'plan' becomes 'authorise work'
- 'do' becomes 'co-ordinate and monitor progress'
- 'check' becomes 'update and communicate'
- 'act' becomes 'corrective action'.

The goals of delivering a project or programme are then to:

- delegate responsibility for producing deliverables to the appropriate people
- monitor the performance of the work and track it against the delivery plans
- take action where necessary to keep work in line with plans

- escalate issues and replan if necessary
- accept work as it is completed
- maintain communications with all stakeholders.

The cycle will be repeated for the duration of each stage or tranche until a boundary is reached. The management team will operate the cycle within their defined authority; i.e. while the work remains within agreed tolerances. If tolerances are exceeded or are predicted to be exceeded, then issues will be escalated to the sponsor for guidance, supportive action or, in extreme cases, a decision on the continued justification of the work.

The plan, do, check, act cycle and the activities described in Figure 2.8 are shown as discrete steps in a workflow. In reality, a project or programme manager's day will involve elements of all of these activities that are connected in ways not shown in the figure.

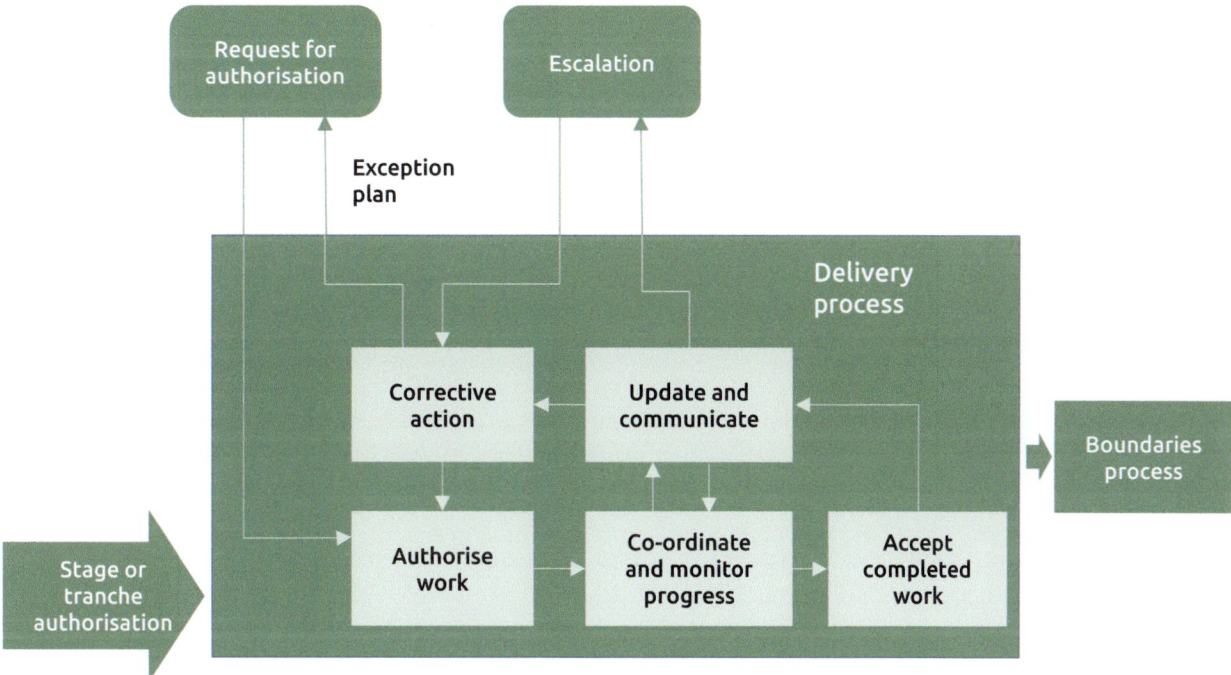

Figure 2.8 Delivery process

Authorise work

Much of the planning work will actually have been completed in the definition process (if this is the beginning of the delivery phase) or in the boundaries process (if this is the second or subsequent stage or tranche).

At this point the previous planning will need to be expanded or enacted depending upon the context. For example:

- A stage in a smaller project may be broken down into work packages that comprise a number of products. These work packages may then be assigned to teams of internal resources.
- A stage in a larger, more complex project may be divided into sub-projects that follow technical specialities, such as groundwork or electrical services in a building project. These sub-projects may be performed by external organisations under contractual terms with associated formal initiation.

- In a programme tranche, the delivery will include projects and business-as-usual work. The authorise work activity at programme level could then equate, for example, to the identification process at project level. The project team will then be given a project brief from which to continue the rest of the project life cycle.

The exact nature of this activity will vary considerably according to the context of the work. However, the basic principles are the same: the stage or tranche is broken down into manageable sections which are documented and delegated to individuals, groups or suppliers.

Delegation requires that those who are being assigned the work are clear about the objectives and how the work will be co-ordinated and monitored. Clear specifications for the delegated work should be accompanied by relevant extracts from the governance documents to ensure that those managing and performing the work understand how the relationship will operate.

Co-ordinate and monitor progress

On all but the smallest of projects, different individuals and teams will be working on different aspects of the project or programme at any one time. This requires co-ordination to ensure that different work packages or sub-projects within a project, or projects within a programme, can co-exist. It may be that two teams in a project need to work in a single physical space; two projects in a programme may require common, but limited resources; two work packages may impact on a common deliverable.

The management team may be able to avoid many potential conflicts in the initial planning and in the way they authorise work. However, there will always be a lot of work conducted in parallel. The greater the complexity, the more closely the work needs co-ordination from the management team. Each delivery team will provide the management team with regular progress reports but must also have clear lines of communication that allow them to escalate issues or ask for guidance at any point.

Progress information may be in the form of regular time-based progress reports or periodic event-based progress reports. The management team must consolidate these reports to understand the overall status of the project or programme. In the process of that consolidation the management team will need to feed information back to delivery teams where they may be affected by progress in other parts of the project or programme.

This activity will utilise many of the specific steps of delivery procedures, such as assessing change requests, implementing risk responses and engaging with stakeholders.

Depending upon the complexity of the work, the responsibility for monitoring and consolidating progress may be given to a separate support function to free up time for the management and delivery teams and probably ensure greater consistency in reporting.

Update and communicate

Documentation will be updated on a regular basis as specified by the relevant management plans. Some documents, such as schedules, will be very dynamic with frequent updates. Others, such as the business case, will be reviewed at significant points such as stage or tranche boundaries.

Of course, the routine update and review documentation should be supplemented by ad-hoc reviews governed by the experience and judgement of the management team. For example, if there is a significant combination of schedule, risk and financial updates that cumulatively impact the business case, the management team must not wait until the next routine review.

Progress will be routinely communicated with stakeholders in accordance with the communications plan. Where any aspect of the work exceeds, or is predicted to exceed, the agreed tolerances, then this must be escalated to the sponsor.

Corrective action

Some degree of corrective action will be happening all the time. This is the essence of co-ordinating work and may be as simple as rescheduling meetings or assigning a task to another person due to illness.

This corrective action activity is about taking more significant action in response to a deviation from the baseline plan. The range of examples of what constitutes corrective action is vast and how it is handled is primarily down to the experience and judgement of the management team.

Two defining characteristics are:

- **Which aspects of the work does the corrective action involve?**

    The action needed may relate to any or all of the fundamental P3 components in any combination. It could be very tangible in that a product has failed its quality control test (scope), material delivery is delayed (schedule) or resources have been underestimated (resource and cost). It could be less tangible where, for example, new risks have been identified that significantly increase the overall risk, or influential stakeholders have changed their position with regard to the work.

    It is important that the way the fundamental components of the work inter-relate is understood. For example, how does a need to discard a product and rebuild affect the schedule? How does a change in schedule affect risks and resource availability? Which stakeholders are affected and how? What are the effects of the revised schedule on the funding arrangements?

    An understanding of these complex inter-relationships comes from thorough planning and maintenance of the delivery documentation. In short, if the work was inadequately planned it will be very difficult to control.

- **How severe is the corrective action?**

    The first and most obvious distinction for severity comes from the tolerances set out in the management plans. When delivery plans are updated with progress they should be able to not just identify that tolerances have been exceeded but also predict that tolerances may be exceeded at some point in the future. If appropriate techniques have been defined and implemented, escalation should occur on the basis that an issue is likely rather than an issue has occurred. The corrective action is therefore something that can be discussed and agreed between the manager and sponsor through the escalation part of the process before implementation.

Even with the best planning and control procedures it is always possible that events will occur that had not been foreseen. The failure of a vital piece of equipment or the insolvency of a supplier can have an immediate and unpredictable effect. In these cases the corrective action needed may involve significant replanning. Delivery plans may not need to be just adjusted but reworked. These are referred to as 'exception plans' and are simply new delivery plans that show how issues will be overcome. Exception plans should be submitted to the sponsor for authorisation.

The ultimate consideration is the effect on the business case. Can the plans be reworked so that the project or programme remains justifiable? If not, the corrective action may be to prematurely close the project or programme to prevent further investment that will not generate an adequate return.

Accept completed work

At some point during the co-ordinate and monitor progress activity a delivery team will say to the management team, 'This piece of work is finished.' Depending upon the context the delivery team may have performed quality control and simply present the results as evidence that the work is complete or it may be that the management team is responsible for quality control and must now test the results of the delivery team's efforts.

This can range from straightforward inspection of standard components to extensive testing and formal, contractual sign-off. Whether formal or informal, acceptance signifies the transfer of ownership of the work and its products from the delivery team to the management team.

Once work has been accepted delivery documentation should be updated and, if required, the acceptance should be communicated to relevant stakeholders.

Projects and programmes

Small projects may simply apply the delivery process, but as the complexity of the work increases it becomes necessary to break it up into manageable pieces. This decomposition takes two main forms: horizontal and vertical.

What may be called 'horizontal' decomposition involves splitting the delivery phase into stages or tranches. These help the management team by enabling techniques such as go/no-go control and rolling-wave planning.

'Vertical' decomposition involves delegating packages of work. This can take the form of sub-projects or work packages within a project or projects within a programme.

This decomposition requires additional processes. Where stages and tranches are created there are boundaries between them. These are managed through the manage boundaries process. Where work is delegated through vertical decomposition it is managed through the development process.

Boundaries process

General

The delivery phase of smaller projects may not be divided into stages. The delivery phase of more complex projects and all programmes will be divided into stages or tranches respectively.

The initial impression of a boundaries process (see Figure 2.9) may be that it all takes place between the end of one stage or tranche and beginning of the next stage or tranche. In reality it is rarely that clear cut. In programmes, tranches of work often overlap and even in projects where stages are sequential, the activities will span the end of one stage and the beginning of the next.

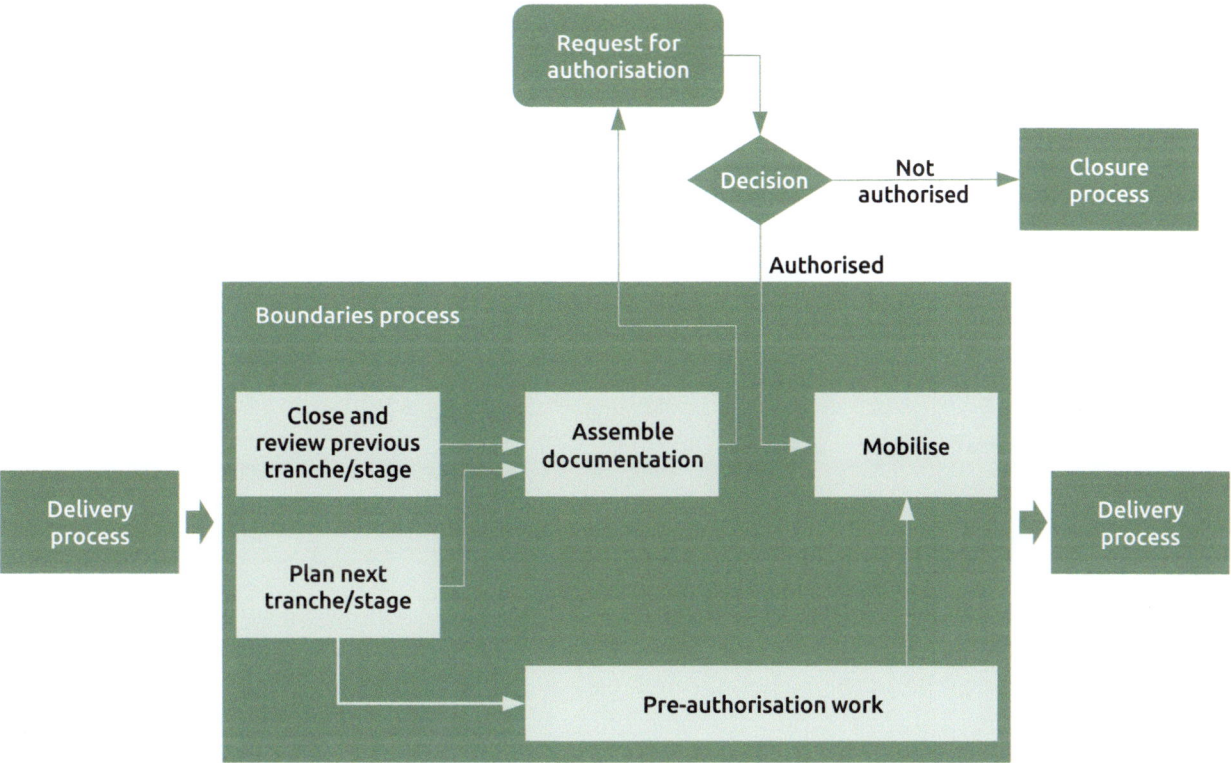

Figure 2.9 Boundaries process

In some cases successive stages or tranches may be largely a continuation of the same type of work. In others they may represent a step change in the type of work being performed, necessitating changes to the management infrastructure and new resources. The process described below will need to be tailored to suit but the main goals of managing boundaries will always be to:

- conclude a stage or tranche in a structured way
- prepare for the next tranche or stage.

The links between the activities are purely indicative. Where stages or tranches overlap, it may be that mobilising later work comes before the closure of earlier work. This is very much a process that must be tailored to the context of the project or programme.

The manager and sponsor should work together closely throughout this process to ensure the smooth transition from one tranche or stage to the next, or possibly terminate the work early if the business case no longer provides justification.

Close and review previous tranche/stage

Closing a stage or tranche may be as simple as reviewing performance, and updating and archiving the relevant delivery documentation. In more complex contexts the conclusion of a stage or tranche may involve demobilising some parts of the project or programme and mobilising new resources.

Common sense dictates that any new work should be planned taking into account the experience gained from the work done so far. The closure of a tranche or stage should include a review of lessons learned, estimating accuracy, effectiveness of risk responses, stakeholder satisfaction and actual compared with planned performance.

The link from this activity to assemble documentation in Figure 2.9 indicates that the documentation pack submitted to the sponsor should demonstrate how plans for the next tranche or stage have taken performance to date into account.

Plan next tranche/stage

Where stages and tranches are employed, the planning done during the definition process will normally take the rolling-wave approach. Therefore, this activity is primarily about taking the high-level project or programme delivery plans and expanding the detail for the next stage or tranche of work.

Looking at the three main areas of documentation in more detail:

- **Project or programme management plans**

    In most cases the policies and procedures that describe the governance of the project or programme will not need to be changed from stage to stage or tranche to tranche. However, there may be circumstances where the environment changes significantly at a boundary and therefore changes are necessary to some management plans.

- **Business case**

    At a stage boundary (i.e. within a project) the project business case should simply need an update based on the latest information and new planning detail.

    Tranches usually have their own business case that is a justifiable subset of the main programme business case. A new tranche business case will be prepared and the main programme business case updated accordingly.

- **Delivery documents**

    The management team must decide whether stage or tranche delivery documents are simply a continuation of the existing project or programme delivery documents, or whether new documents are created. This depends entirely on the context and may be consistent across all functions. For example, a stage may have its own risk register but share its stakeholder register with the project as a whole. Tranches are more likely to have their own set of delivery documents to align with the tranche business case.

All the planning work within this activity should use the experience gained from managing previous stages and tranches to improve the quality of the new or revised plans.

Assemble documentation

The purpose of this activity is to prepare a submission to the sponsor with the objective of having the next stage or tranche authorised.

Care must be taken to provide essential documentation that is not burdened with unnecessary detail. For example, documents that are unchanged since any previous authorisation need not be resubmitted but a note to confirm the lack of change is advisable. Changes to management plans should be summarised rather than resubmitting the changed documents in their entirety.

Detailed delivery documentation will be summarised into delivery plans. Where the delivery plans are produced on a rolling-wave basis it will be necessary to submit the stage or tranche plans in full but only summarise the changes to the top-level project or programme delivery plans. A similar approach will be taken with the business case(s).

Mobilise

In smaller projects most of the mobilisation work will be performed earlier in the life cycle. For larger projects or programmes it may be more efficient to mobilise different resources on a stage-by-stage or tranche-by-tranche basis.

Pre-authorisation work

The conclusion of all planning work before the commencement of any delivery work on the next stage or tranche is sometimes impractical. Specialist materials or equipment may be required that are subject to long lead times; selecting suppliers through competitive tender may need to start early; applying for statutory or regulatory approvals can be time consuming.

In parallel with planning, the management team should identify any necessary pre-authorisation work that should be done before it is fully authorised. The cost of placing provisional orders for materials or initiating a tendering procedure must be weighed against the risk that the next stage or tranche is not authorised.

The performance of pre-authorisation work should be planned and agreed with the sponsor. The completion of this work must be reflected in the plans but the fact that pre-authorisation work has been completed should not be an influencing factor in judging the continuing viability of the business case when the request for authorisation is made.

Projects and programmes

The principles of managing boundaries do not vary greatly according to the complexity of the work. The only significant factor is whether the stages and tranches are serial or parallel. In a less complex project with a small number of stages, they will typically be serial. As one stage comes to a conclusion the next is being started.

On larger, more complex projects, the stages may overlap and in a programme the tranches are usually performed in parallel.

This is because stages tend to reflect areas of work that are naturally sequential for technical reasons, whereas tranches are created for managerial reasons such as quick wins or distributing the impact of change management on business as usual.

Development process

General

This is the process where things actually get produced, as shown in Figure 2.10. It is very simple but very context sensitive. The principles of the develop products process can be applied to any scope of work and in essence it is simply a process for delegation from one level in the organisation structure to another.

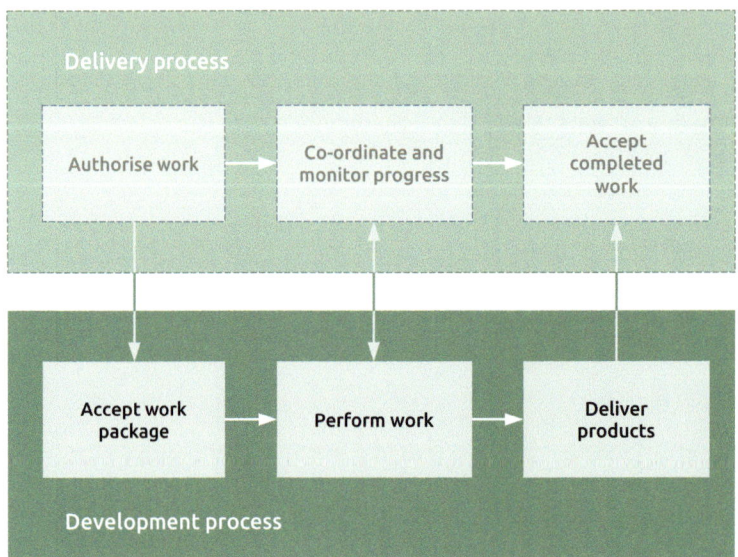

Figure 2.10 Product development process

In some contexts this may be replaced with a specialised approach; for example, in agile projects it may be replaced with a scrum development process.

The goals of the process are to:

- transfer responsibility for a package of work
- execute the package of work
- transfer ownership of the finished products.

Accept work package

A work package can take many forms. It could be an entire project delegated by a programme management team to a project management team; a sub-project delegated by a project management team to a supplier; or a single work package delegated to a small team.

Whatever the scale of the work package the principles remain the same. It must be adequately defined in terms of scope and performance criteria. Both parties to the transfer must be clear on what the work package is and the recipient's ability to perform it.

Where the transfer involves a project being delegated by a programme, the authorise work activity may be the issue of a project mandate or of a project brief. In the latter case, the authorise work activity is effectively the same as the identification process.

Where the transfer involves a project or programme team delegating work to a supplier, there will usually be contractual implications including negotiation of contract terms covering scope and performance.

As the scale of the delegation becomes smaller, it becomes a more personal activity. It depends upon the manager understanding the skills and availability of the team members accepting the work package.

Whatever the context, the team or individual receiving the work package has a responsibility to make sure they understand what is required and have the means to perform the work. A formal acceptance avoids misunderstandings later on.

Perform work

This activity is primarily about the creation of products. Most of the effort will be about technical functions and processes rather than anything uniquely P3 management. The important thing here is the two-way link with co-ordinate and monitor progress.

The person with primary responsibility for the work package will need to plan the work and will have managerial duties appropriate to the scope of the work package. As the work is performed this person will monitor some or all of quality, schedule, resources, cost and risk as specified in the acceptance of the work package. Progress information must be fed back to the level above for consolidation with information from other work packages.

This is a two-way exercise, with information coming from the higher level that may affect the performance of the work; for example, approved changes, delays in connected work and changes in priority.

This connection between monitoring and control at different levels of a project, programme or portfolio is the heartbeat of the management organisation.

Deliver products

The delivery of the products in the work package by the developer is subject to the same contextual variations as the initial delegation. In some cases, the deliver products activity may actually be the entire closure process. In others it will involve concluding a contract or perhaps simply receiving, testing and accepting a product created by a single person.

Records should confirm that the product has been satisfactorily completed and handed over.

Projects and programmes

The project and programme processes in Praxis are designed to be used in different contexts. In small projects a separate development process may not be required. In larger projects, the delivery process can represent work delegated to a team or an external contractor. In a programme the delivery process is, in effect, a summary version of the project life cycle. Figure 2.11 shows that in the programme context the approach is the same but the names have been changed.

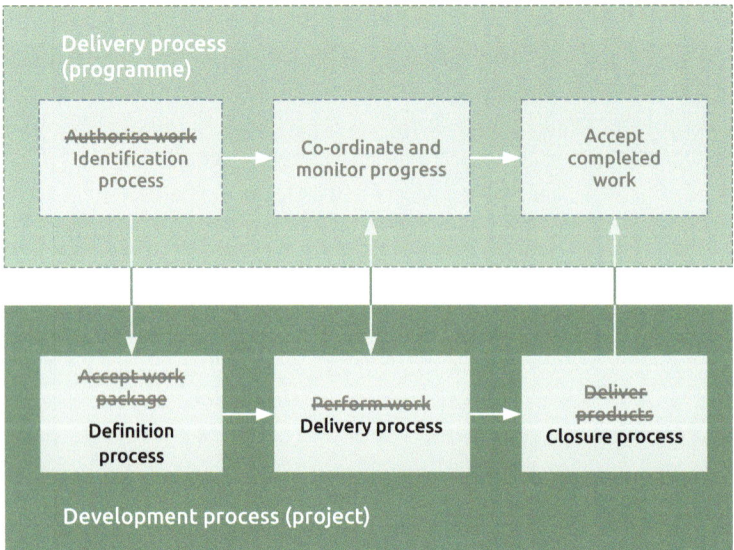

Figure 2.11 Summary of the project life cycle

In this context the authorisation of work at the programme level may be the same as the identification and/or definition process for the component project. Once this has been accepted by the project management team, they start to perform the work; i.e. the delivery process. Finally, the project delivers its products, which are accepted by the programme, and performs the closure process.

This demonstrates that the basic sequence of life cycle phases and their associated processes are common to all contexts. The difference is that in complex work there are more nested levels of life cycles.

2.2.5 Benefits realisation process

General

It is usually the case that simply producing an output does not automatically realise benefits. In most cases an output is used to change some aspect of an organisation's mode of operation or environment. Implicit within the word 'change' is a quantifiable improvement in one or more performance indicators to which value has been assigned.

The goals of this process, as shown in Figure 2.12, are to:

- establish the current state of what is being changed
- co-ordinate the delivery of outputs with the management of change
- ensure changes are permanent
- establish whether benefits have been achieved.

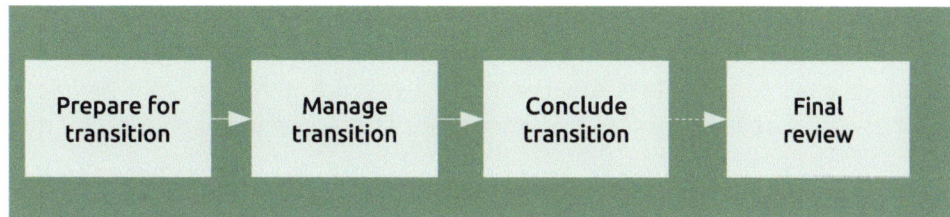

Figure 2.12 Benefits realisation process

In its simplest form, realising benefits is about measuring current performance, helping the people who make up the organisation though the period of change (the transition) and finally, measuring the improvement in performance.

Prepare for transition

The first step in realising benefits must be to assess current performance. The benefit profiles prepared during the definition phase will define the relevant performance indicators.

Establishing the baseline for these performance criteria is the foundation for understanding the business case. Without a starting point improvements cannot be quantified; if improvements cannot be quantified the business case cannot be accurately assessed at the start of the work or reviewed at the conclusion of the work. The data used to baseline performance must be current, accurate and relevant.

Preparing for transition will broadly cover two areas: co-ordinating the delivery of outputs that enable change, and winning the hearts and minds of the people who need to use those outputs to achieve beneficial change.

Planned changes must be effectively communicated to all those affected. Firstly, project management teams need to understand that the delivery of outputs needs to be co-ordinated with change management. This is not the same as delivering as soon as possible, which is often the default position.

Secondly, the effectiveness of any change depends largely on how receptive people in the affected business areas and operational units are to the proposed change. The change management function will ensure that benefits and associated change are communicated, and the 'readiness to change' of all those affected is assessed.

The readiness of the organisation will dictate the ease with which change can be implemented and must be assessed for its impact on schedules, risks and costs throughout the project, programme or portfolio.

Manage transition

Initiating the transition has many principles in common with mobilisation in other aspects of a project or programme. It involves the co-ordination of output delivery with mobilisation of the operational infrastructure needed to realise the benefits.

In this context, mobilisation must include establishing support for those affected by the changes being implemented. This can range from technical support for new systems to HR support for individuals and external support for varied types of stakeholder.

As outputs are accepted they are handed over to staff who have been trained and briefed on follow-on actions. Configuration, risk and quality information is handed over and the planned operational changes are implemented. Any temporary arrangements need to be in place, such as parallel working of two systems, and contingency plans should be in place should any change fail to work.

As changes take effect, the performance criteria are monitored. The full value of benefits may not be achieved during the period of change and will accumulate over a longer period leading up to the final review. However, the significant changes in performance should be observable during this period and these should also provide indications of longer-term success.

During the period of change new opportunities may come to light for additional benefits, which is why the benefits management procedure in Figure 1.29 has the feedback loop to the definition of new benefits.

Conclude transition

Benefits can easily fail to achieve their anticipated value if changes are not embedded into the organisation. New working practices can regress to the previous state if support is not provided. In a programme or portfolio where multiple benefits and associated change are planned, it is particularly important to embed and consolidate one set of changes before considering more.

As the changes take effect it will be possible to decommission the previous systems. Only once the change is well on track to become the normal way of working should the support infrastructure be demobilised.

Final review

The timing of the final benefits review is set according to the original business case. Most benefits are realised continuously once the transition has been embedded into business as usual. On this basis any investment could be justified simply by counting the benefits for a sufficient period of time.

The business case should specify the period over which benefits may be accumulated to generate the value used to justify the work. At the end of this period a final benefits review should be conducted.

In many organisations business as usual is subject to multiple changes that interact and it may be difficult to isolate value generated by specific elements of change. Assessment of benefits should be clear and quantified wherever possible. If this is not possible, then assumptions and subjective judgements used in the review should be clearly documented.

Failure to perform reviews of benefits against business cases makes it impossible to judge the effectiveness of P3 management.

Projects and programmes

The inclusion of this process is often seen as a clear differentiator between projects and programmes. Project management guides do not include benefits realisation on the assumption that that is the responsibility of someone external to the project, typically a client or host programme.

In Praxis, benefits realisation is something that can be part of a project or a programme. The differentiator is the complexity of the relationships between multiple outputs and multiple benefits.

Therefore, at the least complex level, a single output may lead to an easily measured benefit with little need for organisational change. This would be a project that includes benefits realisation. At the other end of the complexity scale, multiple outputs create many outcomes that require significant organisational change. The change may be controversial and involve a diverse array of stakeholders. Benefits may overlap and not always be easy to measure. This is benefits realisation in a programme context.

2.2.6 Closure process

General

The goals of this process are to:

- close a project or programme that has delivered all its outputs
- close a project or programme that is no longer justifiable
- review the management of the work and learn lessons.

Note that the first goal does not identify closure as being when the objectives are complete. Objectives may be described as outputs, outcomes or benefits and these are all achieved at different times. Closure is principally concerned with a temporary organisation handing over responsibility for its objectives and disbanding, as shown in Figure 2.13. Where that occurs in the life cycle will depend on how the project or programme was constituted in the first place.

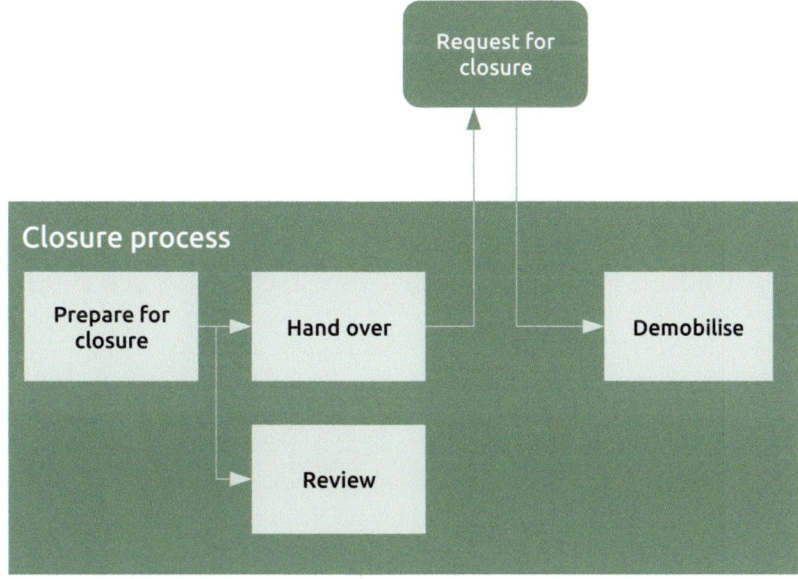

Figure 2.13 Closure process

For example, the realisation of benefits is usually something that is entrusted to business as usual and does not need the project or programme organisation to remain in place. A project or programme may be constituted to end when the final output is delivered; when the change required to realise benefits is concluded; or when the benefits contained in the business case have been achieved. This is one of the choices that will have been made earlier in the life cycle.

The second reason for closure is referred to as 'premature closure' since it occurs earlier than intended. The obvious place for this to occur is at a boundary where the business case is updated and found to be no longer viable, achievable or desirable. That is not to say that the project or programme can only be closed at a boundary. Ongoing control of performance during the delivery phase may reveal serious issues which cannot be satisfactorily resolved. When the issue is escalated to the sponsor the decision may be to prematurely close the project or programme.

Prepare for closure

Closing a project or programme in a controlled way can be an extensive process and needs to be planned in advance. It can be all too easy to focus purely on achieving objectives to the detriment of how they will be handed over, how the organisation will be disbanded and how the administrative loose ends will be tied up.

When closure is in sight, effort must be invested in updating delivery documentation with the closure process in mind. Are there risks specifically associated with the closure? How will stakeholders react and how should they be kept informed? What contractual matters need to be resolved? And how will asset disposal be managed?

> It is in the nature of most project and programme managers that they are motivated by the challenge of the new and solving problems to achieve objectives. The mature organisation must recognise that closure can be seen as tedious and boring; it is probably where project and programme managers need greatest support.

Handover

Who is handing over what and to whom will depend on the context. A contractor may be handing over outputs to a client; a project may be handing over to a programme; a programme may be handing benefits realisation over to business as usual. In the case of a prematurely closed project or programme, outputs that can be salvaged may be handing over to a newly constituted residual project or programme.

Handover can have practical and legal aspects. First and foremost is the need for the receiving organisation to be clear what it is taking over and satisfy itself that everything being handed over is as described and fit for purpose. Conversely there is a responsibility on the delivering organisation to provide everything necessary for the handover to take place successfully.

Handover often constitutes a legal transfer of ownership and this brings additional factors into play ranging from ownership of a physical asset to transfer of employment contracts or other legal responsibilities.

The administrative side of handover must not be overlooked. The project or programme organisation will have records of quality control and configuration management associated with physical assets which should be handed over as well as the assets themselves.

It is not always practical to wait until all deliverables are 100% complete before handing over and demobilising the project or programme organisation. Sometimes deliverables are handed over with some follow-on actions still to be done. One of the outputs of this activity will be the follow-on actions report, which lists any outstanding items.

Review

The second activity in the identification process is 'review previous lessons', which begs the question 'Where do these lessons come from?'

This activity conducts a formal review of the governance and delivery of the project or programme. A key input is the lessons log which will be used to distil lessons learned that will be included in an end project report or end programme report.

> Capturing and utilising lessons learned for individual functions is an attribute of capability level 3.
>
> Incorporating lessons learned into a structured knowledge management system is an attribute of maturity level 4.

Demobilise

During mobilisation a project or programme infrastructure will be assembled, including resources as diverse as premises, software and people. Demobilisation is simply the opposite of that activity.

Physical assets such as buildings, plant and machinery may have been purchased, rented or hired with a subsequent need to sell, redeploy or terminate agreements. Human resources may be contracted or employed. Contract employment may simply require termination of contracts, but redeployment of internal staff needs greater involvement from the project or programme team.

Many projects and programmes are closed before all the benefits in the business case have been realised. This means that while the project and programme managers may have moved on to new ventures, the business change managers (BCMs) still have work to do to complete change in business units. Instead of reporting to a project or programme manager, the BCMs will report directly to the sponsor until the change is completed.

The sponsor will be the 'last person standing'. Where the scope includes benefits, the role of the sponsor does not formally come to a conclusion until a benefits review concludes that the business case has been achieved; achieved to the best degree possible; or will be achieved without further intervention.

Projects and programmes

The principles of closure do not vary with complexity. As complexity increases there is simply more to do to hand over products, demobilise and close contracts.

2.3 Portfolio processes

While project and programme process models are very similar, the portfolio process model is quite different and, at first glance, appears to be much simpler.

Portfolios are very varied in their nature, scale and complexity. A small contracting organisation may have a standard portfolio of a few projects. The reasons for managing these as a portfolio are to co-ordinate resources and embed good practice consistently across all projects. This is sometimes known simply as the 'management of projects'.

At the other end of the scale, a large multinational organisation may have a structured portfolio of projects and programmes designed to meet the strategic objectives of a five-year business planning cycle.

The portfolio process model shown in Figure 2.14 is common to all types of portfolio. Complexity is addressed by the way the process is applied.

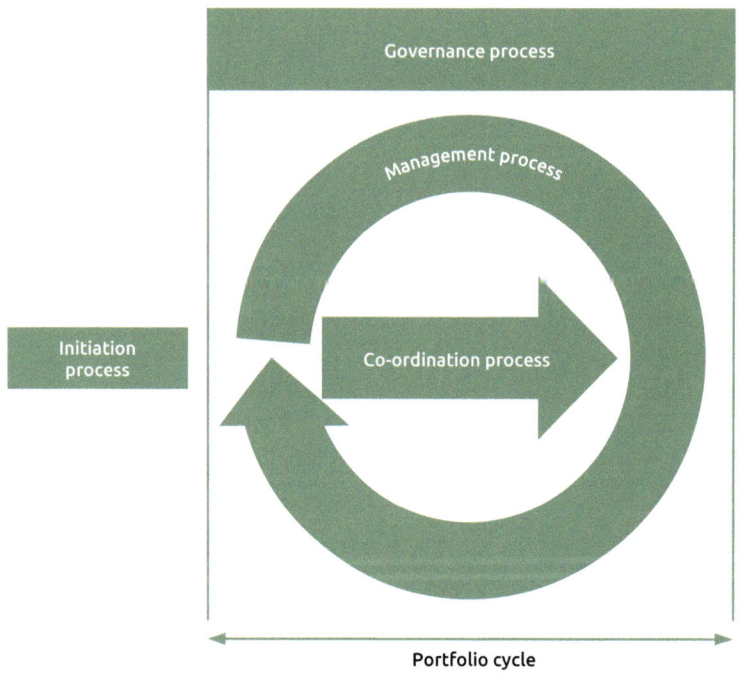

Figure 2.14 Portfolio process model

2.3.1 Initiation process

General

This is usually a one-off process. It represents the point at which the host organisation makes the decision to manage its projects and programmes as a portfolio, as shown in Figure 2.15.

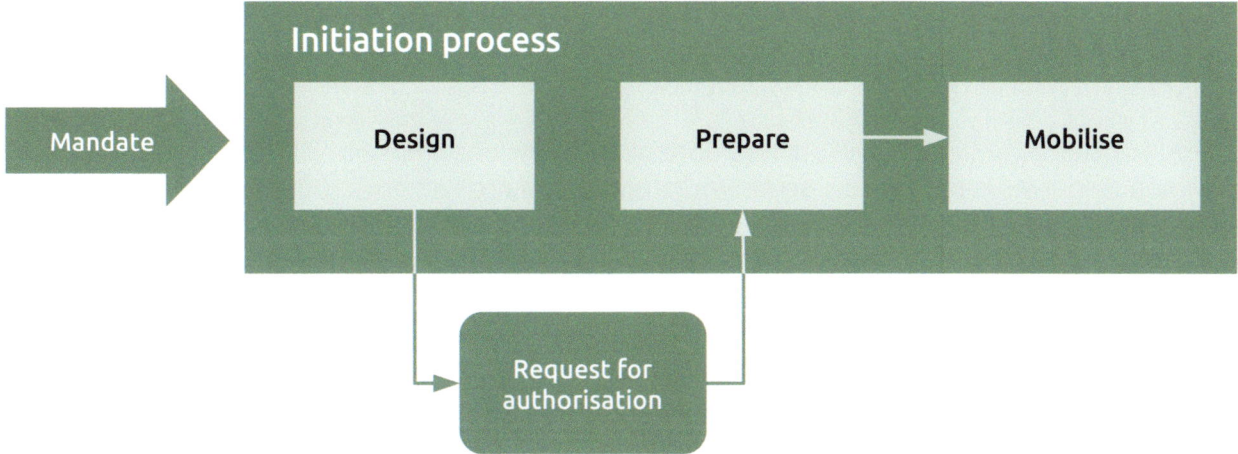

Figure 2.15 Initiation process

The goals of the process are to:

- decide what type of portfolio is required
- design the portfolio infrastructure
- obtain senior-level approval and commitment
- implement the portfolio.

Broadly speaking, the decision to create a portfolio has three purposes:

- To co-ordinate projects and programmes that draw upon a common pool of resource. This is to maximise the efficient use of available resource and avoid conflicts in resource requirements wherever possible.
- To promote a consistent approach to project and programme management. This focuses on developing competency in individuals, capability in functions and maturity of process.
- To manage a set of projects and programmes that collectively achieve a set of strategic objectives.

> Since portfolio initiation is usually a one-off process, Praxis does not contain a corresponding maturity definition. Maturity of portfolio management is assessed by the way the portfolio is governed and managed rather than how it is set up.

The three purposes are by no means mutually exclusive. In fact they are complementary. A 'standard' portfolio will be primarily about the first purpose. It would typically apply to a contracting organisation that delivers projects and programmes on behalf of clients. Although each project and programme is distinct and has a different client, the host organisation that owns the portfolio delivers them using a common pool of resources.

In some cases, multiple clients may stipulate multiple approaches to project or programme management. The contracting organisation has to manage using different client processes and documentation. Where the management approach is chosen by the contracting organisation it makes sense to use the portfolio for the second purpose of managing all projects and programmes in a consistent way. This will make the mobilisation of managerial resources far easier since they will all have common competence and operate common processes.

A structured portfolio is designed to achieve the third purpose: i.e. the delivery of a set of strategic objectives for its host organisation. It is probable that this will require the efficient use of a common pool of resources and will inevitably benefit from a consistent managerial approach.

Therefore, both standard and structured portfolios will be designed with the efficient use of common resources in mind. In a standard portfolio this may be its only purpose. A structured portfolio will primarily be created to achieve a single set of strategic objectives.

Depending on the context, a standard portfolio may be able to apply a consistent managerial approach across all projects and programmes. A structured portfolio will invariably seek to achieve consistency across its component projects and programmes.

Design

Just like projects and programmes, a portfolio will start with some form of mandate. The mandate will give someone the task of initiating a portfolio. This person may be a board member or suitably senior manager who will become the portfolio's sponsor.

The mandate will probably give some indication of whether a standard or structured portfolio is required, but full consideration of that matter is part of this activity.

The 'sponsor designate' will need to assemble a small team to investigate the way a portfolio should be constituted and governed to best suit the needs of the host organisation. The result will be a proposal that is submitted for authorisation to the issuer of the mandate.

Portfolios are rarely created from scratch. It is more likely that an organisation that has several projects and programmes decides to collect these into a portfolio to improve management and/or focus on strategic objectives.

Prepare

If the proposal is accepted preparatory work is commenced. Depending upon the type of portfolio and its context, this could include:

- identifying and documenting managerial processes and documentation for consistent use across all projects and programmes
- preparing standard management plans
- setting up a competency framework to act as the basis of training and role definition
- defining the infrastructure
- reviewing existing projects and programmes to capture good practice and baseline capability maturity
- communicating the impact of portfolio management across the host organisation.

It is highly unlikely that this preparation will start with a totally blank sheet of paper. The organisation will be managing projects, and possibly programmes, and these will already have processes, procedures and

> The 'prepare' and 'mobilise' activities should be run as a project or programme with objectives described in terms of outcomes. These outcomes will define the way the portfolio will work.
>
> In effect, the objectives for this project would be a blueprint for the operation of a portfolio.

documentation standards in place. These existing methods may not be consistent and will be of variable quality.

During this activity all existing methods should be assessed and the current best practice should form the basis of new portfolio-wide standards.

Mobilise

The implementation of a portfolio will often require significant change management. If the systems and processes of portfolio management are to be embedded for long-term benefit, the existing organisation will have to undergo change, not just in terms of physical infrastructure but also in terms of attitude and behaviour.

Mobilisation may include aspects such as:

- setting up governance structures
- initiating training programmes in line with the competency framework and standard processes
- amending recruitment and appointment processes
- implementing information management systems
- adopting existing projects and programmes into the portfolio.

2.3.2 Governance process

General

This process brings together all the governance and professionalism functions and applies them across the portfolio. Its goals are to:

- provide sponsorship of the objectives of the portfolio
- oversee assurance of the portfolio
- promote the discipline and profession of P3 management.

It is misleading to show these functions as a process flow since they are all applied together throughout the life of the portfolio.

Each function is individually described in the functional framework. For the purposes of collecting them together within the portfolio governance process, they can be usefully viewed as three activities, as shown in Figure 2.16.

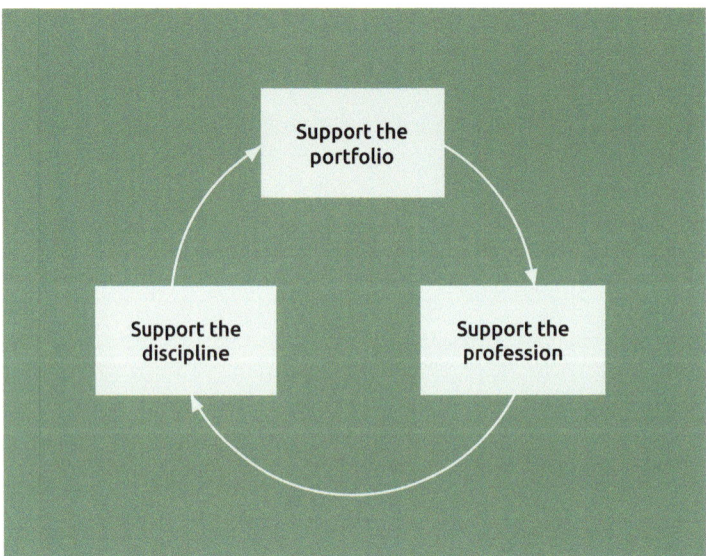

Figure 2.16 Governance process

Support the portfolio

This activity applies the three functions that are concerned with the unique characteristics of each portfolio:

- **Sponsorship**

  Sponsorship of a portfolio covers similar aspects to the sponsorship of projects and programmes, such as considering major authorisation requests and providing support to the people managing the portfolio.

  In addition, portfolio sponsorship must champion the broader aspects of the discipline and profession of P3 management. The sponsor should be someone at board level within the host organisation and represent P3 management in much the same way that a finance director or HR director would represent their departments and professions.

- **Infrastructure**

  The portfolio infrastructure is established to provide resources that perform the management and co-ordination processes. This is often referred to as a PMO, which is variously described as meaning a project management office, programme management office or a combination of both.

  Where the portfolio is deemed to include the entirety of project and programme management within the host organisation, the infrastructure will include the systems and resources needed to support the profession and discipline of P3 management.

- **Assurance**

  Assurance is carried out at many levels, most of which will be within the portfolio. Some level of assurance will also be conducted that is external to the portfolio. This may include third-party accreditation from professional bodies and be based on standards such as a capability maturity model.

Support the profession

The profession of P3 management comprises its people and the way they apply the discipline. If a host organisation defines a single portfolio to encompass all of its projects and programmes, that portfolio will be responsible for all activities that support the profession. If a large organisation defines multiple portfolios (perhaps on geographical or subsidiary company lines), overall responsibility for supporting the profession may sit above the individual portfolios. Where individual portfolios are large and do not share a common context, it may be that they are given responsibility for supporting the profession within their remit and there is no higher-level co-ordination.

Supporting the profession involves applying the functions of:

- **Communities of practice**

  The management of a portfolio will need to decide whether the benefits of communities of practice are best achieved by setting up local communities of practice, encouraging portfolio staff to be involved with external communities, or a combination of both.

- **Competence**

  The portfolio should establish and promote a framework to ensure that all members of staff can identify the competencies that they will need at different stages in their career. The competence framework should be derived from the top-level objectives that the portfolio must achieve and the values that the portfolio wants to promote.

- **Ethics**

  A culture of ethical behaviour should be communicated, promoted and policed throughout the portfolio. As well as generally underpinning the working environment this may be designed to ensure that the portfolio conforms to legislation and regulation applicable to its context.

- **Learning and development**

  A comprehensive approach to learning and development will incorporate various forms of training, coaching and mentoring. The approach should be based on the competence framework and ensure that every role within the portfolio is performed by someone with the necessary competencies.

Support the discipline

The discipline of P3 management comprises the tools, techniques and procedures that collectively make it distinct from other forms of management. Supporting the discipline of P3 management involves:

- **P3 management**

  Although projects have been around for millennia and formalised P3 management has existed for decades, there is still a tendency in some organisations to see it as subordinate to other disciplines and unworthy of specific attention.

  The portfolio must promote the clear benefits of a structured and disciplined approach to the delivery of projects and programmes.

- **Knowledge management**

    The host organisation may already have knowledge management systems in place, in which case the portfolio simply needs to apply these to P3 management. If these do not exist then the portfolio must set up and maintain its own systems.

- **Capability maturity**

    The portfolio should adapt the principles of capability maturity to create a model for organisational learning and development in much the same way that competencies are used to create a framework for individual learning and development.

    The portfolio will monitor the development of project and programme management and may combine this with assurance. The portfolio may perform self-assessment of its own capability maturity.

    The need for external assessment and certification depends upon whether this has commercial benefits for the host organisation.

- **Life cycle**

    The life cycle of projects and programmes acts as the skeleton on which process is built and methods defined. The portfolio must promote adaptable but consistent life cycles for its component projects and programmes. Through assurance, the portfolio will monitor the application of life cycle-based processes.

2.3.3 Management process

General

This process, shown in Figure 2.17, deals with the high-level management of the portfolio. The activities will be applied according to the type of portfolio and its context. Its goals are to:

- assess the suitability of projects and programmes for inclusion in the portfolio
- maintain a beneficial and manageable mix of projects and programmes.

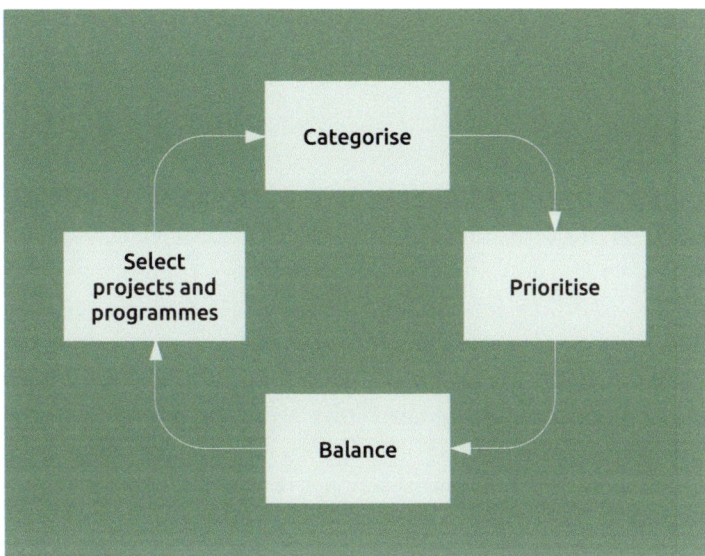

Figure 2.17 Management process

Although primarily a portfolio management process, the activities described here are also relevant to a version of the delivery process for large, complex programmes.

Select projects and programmes

The main criterion for inclusion of a project or programme in a standard portfolio may be simply that it exists. This is the case where the host organisation has created a standard portfolio with the primary purpose of improving the effectiveness of project and programme management through consistency and co-ordination.

Structured portfolios may have a quite sophisticated system for selecting projects and programmes. In this case the portfolio is designed to achieve strategic organisational objectives that could be achieved by various means. Some structured portfolios may have a top-down approach to defining the projects and programmes they will contain. However, many more will have a more bottom-up approach where the host organisation as a whole is able to identify potential pieces of work and present these to the portfolio management team for inclusion.

In this latter case, the portfolio must have a filtering procedure aligned with the project and programme life cycle. Many ideas will be mandated; some of these will be rejected at the end of the identification process. More will be rejected at the end of the definition process, with the remaining projects and programmes being re-evaluated at the end of each stage or tranche.

The portfolio must be rigorous in testing business cases for their ability to deliver benefits that are consistent with the strategic objectives. In large portfolios a scheme of delegation may be used to allow decisions to be made at different levels of authority. For example, at a lower level a senior manager or panel may have authority to approve projects up to £1 million in value to a total of £10 million, whereas project or programmes above that value would have to be approved by the portfolio sponsor.

The remaining activities in this process are all designed to help with maintaining a viable portfolio of projects and programmes. While these are most applicable to a structured portfolio that is defined by strategic objectives, available resources and possibly regulatory or legislative factors, they can also be useful in the context of a standard portfolio.

Categorise

Categorisation is useful on particularly large portfolios. Categories are defined to make it easier for senior decision makers to understand the nature of the portfolio. Typical categories might align with specific strategic objectives; alternatively they may identify characteristics such as mandatory or discretionary, short- or long-term investments, high-or low-risk, or significant or marginal change. Each project or programme may belong to multiple categories, giving the opportunity to review the portfolio components according to different criteria. This is particularly useful when considering the balance of the portfolio.

The procedures used in selecting projects and programmes may differ for different categories as may the approach to governing them.

Prioritise

All portfolios are subject to finite resources, whether they be financial, logistical, mechanical or human. When multiple initiatives compete for finite resources, conflicts will occur and choices will need to be made.

Prioritisation helps with making the right choices. The priority of any organisation is to continue to exist. Naturally, for example, any project that is designed to comply with new legislation, without which a company would be unable to continue trading, will be given high priority.

Work may be prioritised based on measures of financial return, both in terms of the value of benefits, the timescale in which they will be realised and the certainty associated with achieving them.

In a structured portfolio, the strategic objectives may have different priorities. Projects and programmes will inherit the priority of the objectives they fulfil.

Whatever prioritisation mechanism is used, the result will guide the initial selection of projects and programmes and subsequently the management of resource conflicts between multiple projects and programmes.

Balance

Categorisation and prioritisation help the management team and senior managers (perhaps board members) understand the dynamic nature of the portfolio. This, in turn, should help with balancing the portfolio.

For example, categorisation may identify that too many initiatives are in the 'high risk' category. It may be that this comes about as a consequence of prioritising high-reward projects and programmes. Prioritisation may identify the high-priority strategic objectives but the categorisation may show that these are receiving a disproportionate amount of the investment available.

Whereas categorisation and prioritisation can be relatively objective, finding the right balance can be more subjective. It is driven by the context and values of the host organisation. In a young and dynamic business it may be acceptable and feasible to have a high proportion of the portfolio generating significant change. In an entrepreneurial organisation it may be desirable to have high overall levels of risk (with associated potential for high return). In more established organisations, regulated industries or not-for-profit organisations these approaches may be unacceptable.

Ultimately, every organisation must adjust the portfolio of projects and programmes to have a balance of factors with which it is comfortable.

Even in a portfolio that is carefully balanced at the outset, it is possible that it can become unbalanced over time. This could conceivably lead to premature closure of a project or programme. If aspects of the associated business case remain justifiable, ways should be sought to retain the most valuable benefits while restoring the balance of the portfolio.

2.3.4 Co-ordination process

General

While the management process shapes and adjusts the portfolio, this process deals with the day-to-day co-ordination of its component projects and programmes. The two processes are closely aligned. While management process sets parameters within which the co-ordination is performed, the information produced by the co-ordination will inform the ongoing prioritisation and balancing.

The goals of this process are to:

- consolidate information from the component projects and programmes to understand the portfolio as a whole
- monitor the performance of the portfolio against its objectives
- manage the inter-relationships between projects and programmes.

At any given point in time, the portfolio will contain inter-related projects and programmes at all stages of the life cycle. In reality, the co-ordination involves projects in definition, programmes in delivery, projects in closure and programmes in identification.

Figure 2.18 and the activities described below are a simplification of the process designed to facilitate discussion of what needs to be done.

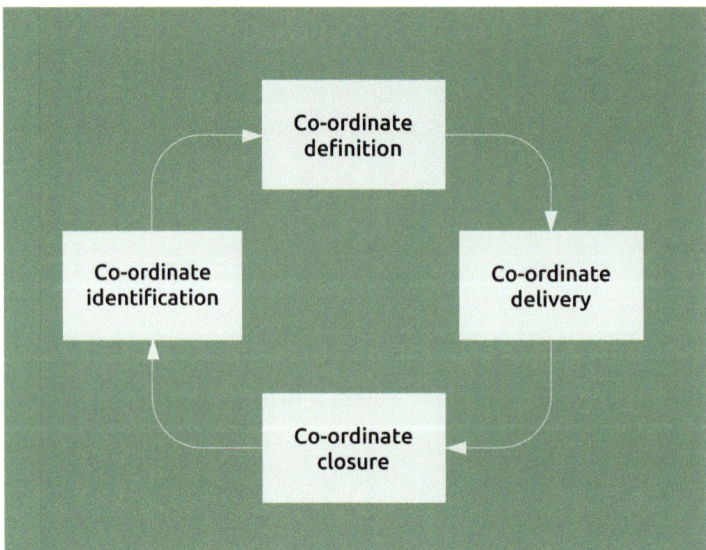

Figure 2.18 Co-ordination process

Co-ordinate identification

The project or programme identification process starts with a mandate and concludes with a brief. This will include high-level requirements management and solutions development where project and programme teams are working with stakeholders. The portfolio may need to co-ordinate this to ensure stakeholders are not burdened with simultaneous demands from multiple projects.

In some contexts this is entirely handled by client organisations; the portfolio management team simply has to review externally produced briefs (or their equivalent) and integrate these into the portfolio.

In structured portfolios the portfolio management team will need to decide whether they simply issue a mandate or perform identification themselves and kick projects and programmes off with a brief; i.e. start projects and programmes at the definition phase.

This depends entirely on the context. Some portfolios have a set of high-level strategic objectives and will delegate much of the responsibility for designing ways of achieving those objectives. Others will have more clearly defined and delineated objectives where it makes more sense to start work off with highly co-ordinated project and programme briefs.

Where the project and programme briefs are produced by the corresponding project and programme management teams, the portfolio management team must review these in the context of all other projects and programmes in the portfolio.

High-level plans and business cases must be reviewed for their impact on other plans and business cases. What may work perfectly well in isolation may not work so well in concert with the rest of the portfolio. Conversely, the portfolio management team may identify opportunities in a new brief to enhance other projects or programmes.

Co-ordinate definition

In some cases the definition phase is also performed by a client organisation, in which case the portfolio management team must review the definition documentation and consider the impact on the existing portfolio.

The definition of a project or programmes can be a substantial piece of work in its own right. Where this is performed within the portfolio, the management team must confirm that competent resources can be made available since this may impact on other projects and programmes.

As with identification, the portfolio management team needs to monitor the impact that combined definition phases may have on individual or small groups of stakeholders.

Co-ordinate delivery

This is where the bulk of co-ordination will take place. The portfolio management team must retain an overview of progress across all projects and programmes and have a clear understanding of any inter-dependencies between them.

Once issues and their impact are understood, the portfolio management team must act accordingly. This can involve adjusting budgets, redeploying resources, accelerating or decelerating work or even recommending the termination of a project or programme.

Co-ordinate closure

A key part of closure is the demobilisation of a project or programme's infrastructure, including disposal of assets and redeployment of staff. The portfolio management team should work closely with the project and programme management teams leading up to closure so that this is managed to the benefit of other projects and programmes in the portfolio.

2.4 Documentation

Documents fall into three categories: governance, scope and delivery.

Governance documents set out policies, standards and guidelines for the management of the work. Some of these may be specialist documents provided by the host organisation, a client or a regulatory body. Praxis only deals with the management plans that reflect how elements of P3 management will be managed.

Scope documents describe the objectives in terms of outputs, outcomes and benefits.

Delivery documents are the largest and most diverse group. They describe what needs to be done, when it will be done and by whom. They also support the management processes and procedures.

2.4.1 Management plans

For a portfolio, governance documents will be created in the initiation process. In projects and programmes they are prepared in the definition process.

High-level scope and delivery documents are produced in the identification process; i.e. the first phase of the project or programme life cycle.

> The document descriptions in this section are generic and will need to be tailored to suit the context. For example, where references are made to programme- and portfolio-level information these may not be appropriate for a project.

Since guidelines for the format and usage of these documents are set out in the governance documents it may seem odd that the governance documents are apparently not prepared until after these initial content and management documents.

In a more mature organisation governance documents will exist in a standard form ready to be adapted to different contexts. The standard governance documents will be used by competent members of the identification team to guide their documentation during the identification process. During definition, the standard governance documents will be tailored to the context of each project and programme, thus providing guidance for the detailed management and content documents thereafter.

These documents set out the way a function will be managed. The two main sections cover the policy and procedure of the function with the detail being adapted to the context of the work. This is distinct from a delivery plan, which explains the detail of how a specific piece of work will be delivered.

Policy includes sections on roles and responsibilities, information management, assurance, budget and interfaces to other functions.

Procedure begins with defining the steps to be used in performing the function, followed by detailed recommendations on the tools and techniques to be used in each step.

Management plans are created according to the needs of the work. If appropriate, functions may be merged into one plan or a function may be subdivided. There is a danger that the following list of management plans appears highly bureaucratic and time-consuming to prepare. The principle is simply that there are many functions that need to be managed and it is important to think about how that will be done. The range and detail of management plans should be consistent with the complexity of the work.

Organisation management plan

The need for an organisation management plan increases as the complexity of the work increases. On small projects an organisation will be in place before any management planning takes place so there is little point in developing an organisational management plan. At any point in time in a major portfolio there will be new project or programme organisations being set up, existing ones being adjusted or management teams being demobilised. In this case policies and procedures promote consistency and efficiency in the way organisations are managed.

Policy

Introduction
The type of organisation required by a project, programme or portfolio is highly sensitive to the context and scope of the work. A P3 organisation may be wholly internal to the host organisation or may include partner organisations; it may include main contractors and sub-contractors; it could be physically co-located or virtual. All these factors will be explained in the introduction.

Roles and responsibilities
This section is not about roles and responsibilities of people within the P3 organisation. It describes who is responsible for designing, recruiting and demobilising the P3 organisation itself.

Information management
For any organisation to function effectively, each individual within the organisation must understand how they fit in and how they should interact with others. This section will describe how these factors will be documented and communicated to all involved.

Assurance
The criteria for successful organisation management that will be used in any assurance reviews will be described here.

Assurance of organisation management function will review how the policies and procedures are initiated and operated.

Budget
The cost of the management team is often absorbed as a corporate cost or, in a contract environment, as an on-cost of the activities that make up the delivery work.

In some cases the cost of managing a project, programme or portfolio will be budgeted and controlled separately. This may be because a mature organisation measures the performance of its P3 management function, or it may be that a form of contract is used that pays for management activity and delivery activity in different ways.

Interfaces
There will be interfaces between the organisation management plan and other management plans, but in this case interfaces could also cover relationships between different departments, companies or individuals working within the overall organisation.

Procedure

Design
This section will set out how the management team should be designed in response to its context.

Identify
Ideally, all members of a management team are chosen based on their suitability for the specific project, programme or portfolio, including their competence in the relevant functions and experience of the context. However, simple availability is often a more influential factor.

This section should describe how individuals should be recruited and appointed given the context of the work.

Maintain
The organisation is neither constant nor permanent. This section should set out how the management team should be adjusted throughout the life cycle and describe the mechanisms for introducing new team members and redeploying those who are no longer required.

Stakeholder management plan
The stakeholder management plan sets out the preferred procedures, tools and techniques to be used in managing stakeholders.

Policy

Introduction
The document must take into account the context of the work. A stakeholder management plan produced for a small project conducted with the confines of an organisational department will be quite different from one for a major programme in the public eye.

The introduction will describe the background to the work and make it clear how this document relates to other relevant documents, such as risk management plans or policies of the host organisation, parent programme or portfolio.

Roles and responsibilities
Overall responsibility for stakeholder management may lie with the project manager in smaller projects or a dedicated team of specialists in a large programme or portfolio, but many people will have stakeholder management responsibilities. An important aspect of engaging with some stakeholders is assigning an appropriate member of the team to maintain the relationship. The principles for how that is done should be described here. It may also show paths of escalation and communication within the P3 organisation structure.

Information management
The composition and format of the stakeholder register and communication plan will be defined here, along with any other specialist stakeholder management documents. It is important to tailor the scope of the stakeholder register and communications plan to the needs of the work.

Any required progress reports should be described together with their purpose, timing and intended recipients.

Assurance
The criteria for successful stakeholder management that will be used in any assurance reviews will be described here.

Assurance of the stakeholder management function will review how the policies and procedures are initiated and operated.

Assurance may also audit the end results of stakeholder management by surveying stakeholders and their attitudes towards the project, programme or portfolio.

Budget

Communication with stakeholders will incur costs and these should be included in budgets. The stakeholder management plan will not contain these budgets but will describe whether they exist, how they are managed and where the figures are located.

Interfaces

Stakeholders must be considered in all aspects of managing a project, programme or portfolio. Stakeholder information will have links to documents on benefits, issues, risk etc. How these interfaces and cross-references will be managed should be defined in this section.

Procedure

Identify

This section will recommend the techniques that should be used to identify stakeholders and the sources of information available.

Where lessons have been captured from previous work, they may be available as checklists of typical stakeholder groups that need to be included.

Assess

Stakeholders will be assessed in terms of their areas of interest, levels of interest and influence. These would typically be represented as stakeholder maps and influence/interest matrices. The choice and format of such documents will be defined here, along with parameters for the scales to be used for interest and influence.

Care must be taken to ensure stakeholder information is secure and confidentiality is maintained.

Plan communications

The channel, frequency, format and content of communication with stakeholders will be designed to suit their interest and influence. The policies set out in this section will provide guidance on all these factors.

Technical projects may need guidance on standard terminology and multinational programmes or portfolios may need guidance on the language to be used.

Communication activities may be included within general delivery plans or may warrant a separate communication plan. The preferred approach should be defined here.

Engage

The allocation of responsibilities for engaging with stakeholders must reflect interest and influence. The levels of management seniority that should be involved with different stakeholders should be defined.

Guidelines for managing feedback, and particularly for dealing with objections or negative publicity, must be considered.

Control management plan

Control is one of the central functions of P3 management. It is concerned with performing work in accordance with delivery documents and updating them based on actual performance.

Policy

Introduction

The introduction will describe the background to the work and make it clear how this document relates to other relevant documents, such as the policies of the host organisation, parent programme or portfolio.

Roles and responsibilities

Roles and responsibilities in relation to control are very diverse. They will range from the sponsor's responsibilities in assessing exceptions and authorising new plans to a team member's responsibility to accurately report progress. There may also be specialist roles in assessing the impact of progress or quality control.

Information management

Control will generate a lot of reports including, for example, progress reports, event reports, earned value reports, and issue registers.

Consistency is vitally important to the smooth running of the control systems. The purpose and format should be described here (possibly by simply referring to standard templates that should be used).

Assurance

The criteria for successful control that will be used in any assurance reviews will be described here.

Budget

The management effort used in controlling the work is part of the cost of setting up a management team and is not costed separately. However, there may be cost associated with acquiring certain systems to facilitate control, ranging from specialist software to quality testing equipment.

Interfaces

The control function interfaces with all other aspects of delivery. Performance of the schedule, risk, quality, cost, change and resource functions are co-ordinated as described by this document. This plan therefore has relevance to most other management plans.

This section will describe how the control management plan works in conjunction with the other management plans.

Procedure

Monitor performance

Any aspect of delivery must be controlled. Some functions will have control mechanisms defined in their respective management plans; for example, cost control methods may well be defined in a financial management plan. Any function that does not have its own specialist controls defined should be covered here.

This section should specify how performance data will be captured and what reports will be used to communicate progress. There should be reports that are both event-driven and time-driven, covering both cybernetic and go/no-go types of control.

Assess performance

Various techniques for assessing performance are described in the control function. This section will specify which ones are to be used in which circumstances.

Performance should also be judged against tolerances, which may also be defined here and trigger escalation in the delivery process.

Corrective action

Progress will never be precisely according to plan. Different levels of corrective action will inevitably be needed. This section should describe the approach to how plans will be updated and changes communicated. It will set out the principles for escalation of issues between different levels of the management team and how these issues should be resolved.

Information management plan

There is an information management element to all other management plans that deals with the format and distribution of specific documentation. This management plan should not duplicate those policies. Rather, it is about general approaches to the creation, storage and dissemination of information.

Policy

Introduction

The introduction will describe the background to the work and make it clear how this document relates to other relevant documents, such as the policies of the host organisation, parent programme or portfolio.

Roles and responsibilities

Responsibilities for information management will be widespread since many people will be involved in the management of information in one form or another. However, there must be some core responsibility for ensuring that information is correctly stored, accessed and archived or destroyed.

This will often fall to a support function but on small projects it will default to the project manager.

Assurance

The criteria for successful information management that will be used in any assurance reviews will be described here.

Budget

A separately identifiable budget for information management is only likely where there are complex or unusual information management requirements.

Interfaces

All functions are dependent upon information and, therefore, interface with the function of information management. Some specific interfaces may be worth defining, such as how information management relates to configuration management; i.e. which documents should be included in a configuration management system and which are subject to simpler policies for version control.

Procedure

Collect data and create information

This section will define how data will be collected and any specific techniques to be used in creating information from the data. This should ensure consistency across data capture activities in different functions such as monitoring progress and quality control.

Document and store information

Duplication of document descriptions in the information management section of other management plans should be avoided. This plan is concerned with establishing consistency across the specific requirements of all other functions. It may set out policies in areas such as formats of paper and electronic documents, secure storage or backup.

Access and disseminate

Access may be of particular concern in situations where different levels of security are applied. Members of the management team may need access to some documents but be excluded from access to others.

This section would cover, for example, security clearances or authorisations procedures for access to information. Similarly, it may set out policies for who may receive certain information or who should be notified when information is released.

Archive

Superseded documents are usually archived rather than destroyed in order to retain an audit trail of revisions. Once the work is finished, contracts closed and the post-project/programme reviews completed, the bulk of delivery information will be archived, with anything that remains live being handed over to business as usual.

Destroy

Most P3 information will conform to organisational standards for the period of storage, which will be longer than the duration of a project or programme.

In some cases there may be security or contractual reasons for the management team to have some responsibility for the destruction of information within the life of their work.

Assurance management plan

Policy

Introduction

The introduction will describe the background to the work and make it clear how assurance supports sponsorship and delivery.

Roles and responsibilities

Internal assurance may be performed by members of the management team, provided they are not assuring their own work. External assurance must be carried out by a person or team who is not connected with the day-to-day management of the project, programme or portfolio.

This section must clearly identify roles and responsibilities, taking into account the importance of effective and ethical assurance to the sponsorship and delivery of a project, programme or portfolio.

Information management

The composition and format of assurance reports will be described here, together with the principles of how these should be communicated to the management team and other stakeholders.

Assurance

This section will explain the operational relationship between internal and external assurance.

Budget

Internal assurance is usually performed by people who have other roles and responsibilities on the management team and separate identification of the cost of assurance activity will only be necessary in complex, rigorously assured contexts.

External assurance is usually covered by an external budget. However, this means that, for example, a programme would have a budget for assurance of its component projects and a portfolio would have a budget for assurance of its component programmes.

Procedure

There is no standard procedure for assurance since the specific steps are entirely dependent upon the context of the work. In principle the procedure must include steps that fulfil the goals of the assurance function.

Scope management plan

Scope is the defining characteristic when choosing to manage work as a project or a programme. The more complex the scope, the more extensive the range of management plans needed to describe how it will be managed.

An all-encompassing scope management plan, as described here, will work for less complex scope. As the complexity increases some parts of scope may need their own management plan, such as a benefits management plan. Ultimately, the scope management plan may be replaced by management plans for each aspect of managing scope.

Broadly speaking a scope management plan will exist for projects, whereas a programme will have separate management plans for the different components of scope management. Naturally there will be points in between where there is an umbrella scope management plan supported by more detailed management plans as required.

Policy

Introduction

The introduction will describe the background to the work and make it clear how the governance of scope is documented. If aspects of scope management are taken out of this document and expanded into their own management plans, they should be listed here.

Roles and responsibilities

At its simplest, one person (maybe the project manager) will be able to perform the managerial and technical aspects of scope. At its most complex, scope will need specialists in different functions (e.g. requirements management or configuration management) or specialists in different technical disciplines (e.g. architects, electrical engineers or aeronautical engineers).

This section may contain the detail of roles and responsibilities or it may just contain an overview with more detail in each of the relevant 'procedure' sections of the plan.

Information management

The composition and format of scope documents may be defined here. Alternatively, this section may contain an overview of scope documentation with more detail in each of the relevant 'procedure' sections of the plan.

Assurance

The criteria for successful scope management that will be used in any assurance reviews will be described here. If necessary, detailed criteria can be included in the 'procedure' sections of the plan.

Budget

The cost of scope management is to a large extent the cost of the project or programme. This section should not attempt to deal with the entire budget but concentrate on certain specialist areas. For example, there may be a specific budget for feasibility studies or scope changes.

If necessary, detailed criteria can be included in the 'procedure' sections of the plan.

Interfaces

This section is particularly important if the scope management plan is an umbrella document for more detailed management plans such as a benefits management plan or a configuration management plan.

It should also provide cross-references to other functions to highlight areas of scope that have higher levels of risk or particularly influential stakeholders. If necessary, detailed criteria can be included in the 'procedure' sections of the plan.

Component procedures

The composition and detail of this part of the plan is entirely dependent on the scale and complexity of the scope. One simple overall procedure many be appropriate or a number of more specialised procedures may be defined.

Requirements management
The extent of requirements management must be consistent with the complexity of the scope of work and stakeholder involvement.

Solutions development
The solutions development procedure and techniques will be defined in accordance with the complexity of the outputs required.

Benefits management
It is likely that a scope management plan will only contain a section on benefits if the number of outputs and benefits is small. Otherwise a full benefits management plan will be used.

Change control
Changes to scope can be a major influence on the success of projects and programmes. This section must define clear procedures including levels of authority, change budgets and assessment techniques. It should also describe how associated communications should be handled.

Configuration management
By definition, the more complex the scope of a project or programme, the more inter-relationships there are between outputs, outcomes, benefits and their component products. Configuration management may also cover management documentation.

Benefits management plan

A separate benefits management plan (as opposed to a benefits section in the scope management plan) will often be required where there are multiple benefits, significant change and the relationships between outputs and benefits are more complex; i.e. a benefits management plan is usually appropriate where the work is managed as a programme rather than a project.

Policy

Introduction
The introduction will describe the background to the work and make it clear how this document relates to other relevant documents, such as a scope management plan or policies of the host organisation, parent programme or portfolio.

Roles and responsibilities
Responsibility for benefits management lies primarily with the business areas that have to realise the benefits through outputs and change. The people who represent these business areas on the project or programme management team are called business change managers (BCMs). Project

and programme managers have responsibility for co-ordinating their outputs with the BCMs' change activities and the sponsor has overall responsibility for achieving the benefits in the business case.

This section of the management plan must clearly describe these roles and their responsibilities for benefits management. It will also show paths of escalation and communication within the P3 organisation structure.

Information management

The composition and format of benefits documents (such as benefit profiles) will be defined here.

Any required progress reports should be described together with their purpose, timing and intended recipients.

Assurance

The criteria for successful benefits management that will be used in any assurance reviews will be described here.

Budget

The costs of achieving benefits include the cost of developing the outputs and the cost of implementing change in business as usual.

The former is typically easier to quantify as it is the budget for the project producing the relevant output. The latter can often be hidden and harder to attribute. This section must make it clear how benefit costs will be accounted for, how budgets will be set and where the figures are located.

Interfaces

The achievement of benefits is the fundamental reason for investing in projects and programmes. They are, among other things, impacted by stakeholders, affected by risk and dependent upon schedule.

The interfaces and cross-references between individual benefits and other aspects of the project or programme should be defined in this section.

Procedure

Quantify

This section will set out the methods and techniques to be used in quantifying benefits. Guidance should be particularly thorough in areas where quantification is more difficult.

Value

This section of the management plan must set out the rules that will be used to value the benefits. Historically many projects and programmes have been approved on the basis of over-optimistic valuations of benefits and/or undervaluation of dis-benefits. This section is therefore central to the success of the business case.

The methods for allocating costs to benefits, especially where multiple outputs and multiple benefits have complex inter-relationships, may also be defined here.

Plan benefits realisation

This section will set out how the benefits realisation work will be co-ordinated with the delivery of outputs; how communications will be maintained and how the organisation should prepare for change.

The first step in realising benefits is to measure the 'before' state. This section should define the performance indicators that will be used to measure the before state. The same parameters will be used to measure the end state to confirm whether the stated value of benefits has been achieved. The timing of these measurements and any interim measurements should be defined here.

Realise benefits

This section should explain how the transition will be managed. This will include the approach to co-ordinating output delivery with organisational change activities and the preferred approaches for change management.

> On complex programmes this section will be expanded and may be supplemented with a separate change management plan.

Schedule management plan

Scheduling is often taken for granted as a routine, well established procedure that would not justify a management plan of its own. Where simple projects are regularly performed this may well be the case, although scheduling approaches should still be documented at an organisational or portfolio level and assured against this standard.

As more complex projects and programmes are undertaken, more thought should be given to the range of techniques available for both time scheduling and resource scheduling. This is particularly important where different parts of the work may need to use different techniques but still facilitate consolidation to produce high-level schedules.

Policy

Introduction

The introduction will describe the background to the work and make it clear how this document relates to other relevant documents, such as a scope management plan or policies of the host organisation, parent programme or portfolio.

Roles and responsibilities

Allocation of responsibility for schedule management may range from the project manager in smaller projects to a dedicated team of specialists in a large programme or portfolio. This section of the management plan must clearly describe which roles have which responsibilities for schedule management. It will also show paths of escalation and communication within the P3 organisation structure.

Information management
The composition and format of schedule reports such as Gantt charts, milestone plans or resource histograms will be described here.

Assurance
The criteria for successful schedule management that will be used in any assurance reviews will be described here.

Budget
Any expenditure attributable to schedule management should be noted here, such as purchase of scheduling software.

Interfaces
Schedules will include activity aimed at producing outputs, outcomes and benefits but may also include management activity for areas such as risk management and stakeholder management. Schedules can interface with all other aspects of P3 management and how cross-references will be handled should be explained here.

Procedure

Identify and estimate
Identification and estimating of items to be included in a schedule covers a wide range of production and managerial activity with different levels of complexity. The use of techniques to document activity (e.g. work breakdown structures) and estimating techniques for time and resource (e.g. comparative or analytical approaches) should all be specified here.

Build model
Modelling can be as simple as a Gantt chart or as complex as probabilistic networks. The techniques and methods to be used are defined here including, where appropriate, how the outputs of different methods and techniques may be consolidated to produce an overall schedule for a complex piece of work.

Analyse
Analysis may be as simple as the drafting of a linked bar chart or as complex as Monte Carlo analysis. The techniques and methods to be used are defined here including, where appropriate, how the outputs of different methods and techniques may be consolidated to produce an overall schedule for a complex piece of work.

Report
Different modelling and scheduling techniques result in different types of output. Communication of the schedule is a key part of ensuring all members of the management team, delivery team and stakeholders have a common understanding of the progress and predicted performance of the work.

> If a schedule management plan does not exist this information should be covered by the stakeholder management plan.

Reports should be carefully tailored to their recipients and be as consistent in approach as possible. How that will be achieved is defined here.

Finance management plan

Not all aspects of this plan will be relevant in some contexts. In other contexts it may be necessary to expand this into multiple management plans.

Projects that are part of a programme may not need to perform investment appraisal or establish funding. Major infrastructure programmes may need to develop a management plan for funding that is separate to the management plan for financial control.

Policy

Introduction

The introduction will describe the background to the work and make it clear how this document relates to other relevant documents, such as a scope management plan or policies of the host organisation, parent programme or portfolio.

Roles and responsibilities

Allocation of responsibility for finance management may range from the project manager in smaller projects to a dedicated team of specialists in a large programme or portfolio. This section of the management plan must clearly describe which roles have which responsibilities for financial management.

It will also show paths of escalation and communication within the P3 organisation structure.

Information management

The composition and format of financial reports such as cash flows, funding schedules or management accounts will be described.

Assurance

The criteria for successful finance management that will be used in any assurance reviews will be described.

Budget

Any expenditure attributable to finance management should be noted here, such as centrally provided accounting resources or specialist software.

Interfaces

All aspects of the work will need funding. Interfaces will show how costs are aggregated from different aspects of the work.

Procedure

Estimate costs

Estimating can be conducted in a variety of ways according to the context of the work and the progression of the life cycle. The approach to estimating costs, sources of information and techniques to be used should all be defined.

Investment appraisal

Investment appraisal techniques vary, as do the parameters that can be applied. As a project or programme becomes larger there may be multiple instances of investment appraisal being applied. It is important that the approach is consistent and well defined.

Establish funding

It may be that funding is in place before the point where management plans are developed. It may also be the case, on larger projects or programmes, that the acquisition of funding is phased throughout the life cycle. If that is the case this section should describe the procedures to do this.

Develop budget

This section should describe how budgeting should be performed and how it should be maintained as progress is recorded. The approach to contingency reserves and management reserves should also be defined here.

Financial control

Only the largest of projects or programmes will be independent of corporate accounting systems. Financial information must often be extracted from corporate systems that are more tuned to business as usual than project or programme work. This section will explain how that situation is to be managed.

It will also contain levels of authority for approving expenditure and tolerances that should be applied to financial plans.

Risk management plan

Policy

Introduction

The document must take into account the context of the work. For example, a risk management plan produced for a small stand-alone construction project will be quite different from one for a large IT project that is part of a business change programme.

The introduction will describe the background to the work and make it clear how this document relates to other relevant documents, such as a stakeholder management plan or the policies of the host organisation, parent programme or portfolio.

The risk appetite may be described to ensure an understanding of how much risk is acceptable in pursuit of the objectives.

Roles and responsibilities

Allocation of responsibility for risk management may range from the project manager in smaller projects to a dedicated team of specialists in a large programme or portfolio. This section of the management plan must clearly describe which roles have which responsibilities for risk management.

It will also show paths of escalation and communication within the P3 organisation structure.

Information management
The composition and format of a risk register will be defined here, along with any other specialist risk management documents. It is important to tailor the scope of the risk register to the needs of the work. For example, some fields in the register are important if aggregating risk across multiple projects or programmes is necessary, but otherwise they overcomplicate the document and appear to add bureaucracy.

Any required progress reports should be described together with their purpose, timing and intended recipients.

Assurance
The criteria for successful risk management that will be used in any assurance reviews will be described here.

Budget
There are two financial aspects to risk management. Firstly, there is the budget for the management of risk (e.g. external resources, software and internal resources). Secondly, there is the budget that covers the cost of risk responses.

The risk management plan will not contain these budgets but will describe whether they exist, how they are calculated and managed, and where the figures are located.

Interfaces
Risk is inherent in all aspects of a project, programme or portfolio. Risk events and overall risk have links to documents on benefits, issues and stakeholders. How these interfaces and cross-references will be managed should be defined in this section.

Procedure

Identify
This section will recommend the tools and techniques that should be used to identify risk events. These should reflect the nature of the work (e.g. routine or innovative) and the resources available.

Where lessons have been captured from previous work, they may be available as checklists and prompt lists of risk events or risk categories that need to be considered.

Assess
The field of risk assessment has a broad range of tools and techniques, ranging from relatively simple qualitative analysis techniques to highly sophisticated quantitative analysis techniques and associated software applications.

Care must be taken in ensuring that this guidance includes those tools and techniques that are appropriate to the work being undertaken. Too much risk assessment can detract from making common-sense decisions about the level and extent to which risk should be managed.

This section may also describe the parameters for the way some techniques are used; for example, it may define the scales to be used for probability and impact in qualitative analysis, the statistical distributions to be used in Monte Carlo analysis or the preferred method for calculating expected value.

Plan responses

The preferred responses to risk will depend upon the risk context and in particular the risk attitude of the organisation. For example, it may be corporate policy to transfer as much threat as possible through insurance or suitable contract terms with suppliers. Conversely, an organisation may prefer to retain control over all threats for security or confidentiality reasons and bias responses towards reduction and avoidance.

Approaches to opportunities will also vary. In some environments (e.g. a contractor delivering an output) it is far less important to invest resource into identifying opportunities than in others (e.g. a pharmaceutical research project).

Implement responses

Guidance for the selection of risk owners and actionees will be described here. The way that response actions will be monitored and controlled will also be described, and this should ensure that the information required to complete the previously defined reports is collected.

Change management plan

The effective management of change is vital in order to generate benefits from outputs. Changes to business as usual will be included in the scope of most projects, programmes and portfolios. There will always be resistance to change and implementing a clearly documented and consistent approach contributes to dealing with this resistance.

> In projects that include benefits management (i.e. non-complex change), the contents of this document will probably be covered by the benefits management plan.

Policy

Introduction

The generic change management procedure will need to be adapted to the context of the work. Various models for change can be used and these use different techniques. This section should define the context, describe the procedure and define preferred techniques.

Roles and responsibilities

Change management will include people within the P3 organisation and people within the business-as-usual organisation. This section should define the responsibilities of all those involved.

Information management

Effective communication is key to overcoming resistance to change. This section should explain how information management will be used to prepare and disseminate all types of communication.

Assurance

The criteria for successful change management that will be used in any assurance reviews will be described here.

Budget

This section should define budgets for the management of change that are held within the overall project, programme or portfolio budget.

There should also be budgets held within business as usual that are not included here. These should be identified so that members of the P3 management team can ascertain that all necessary budgets are in place. It also needs to be clear what expenditure is covered by the project, programme or portfolio, and what is covered by business as usual, so that nothing is underfunded.

Interfaces

The way change needs to be managed can impact on P3 schedules, risk registers, communications plans and many other areas. How these cross-references will be managed should be explained here.

Procedure

Assess

The preferred mechanisms for assessing the nature of the organisation and its readiness to change are described here. Techniques for implementing change will also be covered.

Prepare

This section of the change management plan must be carefully integrated with stakeholder management and communications. It will describe how the management team must generate support for change, break down barriers and improve the organisation's readiness to change.

> At the project level the plan can focus on relatively narrow change. At the programme or portfolio level the plan must take into account the effects of cumulative change and different types of change being implemented by multiple projects on a single area of business as usual.

Implement

This section describes how change should be managed. It will include references to stakeholder management and communications during the period of change. It may also describe or link to corporate policy for areas such as redundancy, relocation and recruitment.

Sustain

For benefits to be continually realised, change must be embedded. This section will describe ongoing actions designed to support the changed organisation until such time as the changes cease to be seen as change and are accepted as being the normal way of operating.

Resource management plan

Policy

The policy for managing resources may be largely dictated by organisational standards. It may well be that most of the resource management plan simply references organisational standards. Where the work simply applies these organisational standards a P3-specific resource management plan may be deemed unnecessary, provided an understanding of organisational standards is written into the roles of the management team.

Where specific policies have to be developed it may be necessary to perform some of the research first. This will reveal the mix between internal and external resources and identify what procurement approaches will be necessary. The results of the research may then be incorporated into a refined version of the plan.

Introduction
The context of the work and the decisions made on how to resource the work will be explained here.

Roles and responsibilities
Allocation of responsibility for resource management may range from the project manager in smaller projects to a dedicated team of specialists in a large programme or portfolio. This section of the management plan must clearly describe which roles have which responsibilities.

It will also show paths of escalation and communication within the P3 organisation structure.

Information management
As the range of resources and procurement procedures becomes more complex, the extent of the supporting information will expand.

Managing resources is one of the defining functions of P3 management and has the potential to be the source of most of the issues a management team has to resolve. It is important to thoroughly document all decisions and agreements to avoid scope for disagreement during delivery.

This section will advise on the extent, content and use of a wide range of documents.

Assurance
The criteria for successful resource management that will be used in any assurance reviews will be described here.

Budget
Specialist advice may be needed for certain aspects of resource management (e.g. legal input on contracts). While most costs associated with managing resources are part of the general management overhead, specific budgets may need to be identified.

Interfaces
Resources will have specific links to stakeholders, associated risks and specific schedules. How these cross-references will be managed is detailed here.

Procedure

Research
The research into resource options could be a blank sheet of paper, but if not the help available to the P3 management team should be described here. This could include approved suppliers lists, existing framework agreements or outsourcing arrangements.

Tender

Tendering must be transparent, ethical and effective. This section will define the procedures to be used and guidelines to be followed.

Contract award

Only the very largest projects, programmes or portfolios will be legal entities in their own right. Most contracts will be signed by members of the P3 management team. It is important for the management plan to set out the host organisation's policies for entering into contracts, and who is entitled to do so on the organisation's behalf.

Mobilise

This section will describe any guidelines for mobilising all forms of resource. It could be anything from procedures for installing new software on the host organisation's servers, through mechanisms for seconding internal personnel, to security protocols for contract staff. Much of this will probably be in the form of references to organisational policies.

Manage

How resources should be administered and controlled will also be a varied topic. This could be anything from how to insure capital items; how line management of seconded staff is to be handled; or how contractor performance will be monitored.

Close

Closing the resource management procedure will cover disposal of assets, redeployment of internal resources and formal closure of contracts. Policies for any aspect of closing down resourcing arrangements will be described here.

2.4.2 Scope documents

Scope documents describe the objectives of the work. In many cases it is possible to define standard documentation that is independent of the environment; for example, a business case or benefit profile. In others, the content is entirely dependent upon the technical nature of the work and so Praxis simply describes what is to be achieved by the document but cannot define any detail, such as a specification.

Mandate

The term mandate applies to whatever information is used to trigger the initiation process. It could be a minute in a management meeting, the award of a contract to supply or simply an email from a senior manager.

Vision statement

A vision statement is a brief description of the end goal of a complex project or programme. A succinct and memorable description is necessary where there are many stakeholders who need to gain an insight into the end result of a complex piece of work. The purpose of this document is similar to that of an artist's impression of a major construction project. It does not provide much detail but gives a good understanding of what the work is all about.

Often seen as something peculiar to programmes, the vision statement can be equally applicable to a project, particularly larger or more complex projects where stakeholders need to be engaged early in the life cycle.

There are no standard sections to a vision statement but it is important that it promotes the justification for the work as well as the outputs, changes and benefits that will arise.

Specification

Specifications define outputs and are created by the solutions development procedure. The structure and content of a specification is entirely dependent on the context. In construction a specification may comprise layouts, elevations, bills of quantities and structural details. In IT, a specification could be functional or technical.

The specification is whatever is required by good practice in the relevant context. In many contexts, the specification for an output may be formed from a series of descriptions of individual products. Some of these products may be deliverables in their own right and some tracked as configuration items in a configuration management system.

> Since stakeholders are interested in the progress of their deliverables it makes sense for deliverables to automatically be considered as configuration items to ensure that progress and quality information is readily available.

Product documents

The extent and detail of product documentation is very dependent upon the context of the work. Rather than prescribe separate documents, Praxis provides a list of fields from which suitable documents should be constructed according to the needs of the project or programme. This may result in a simple approach, with one document per product, or a more extensive approach, with separate documents for product descriptions, configuration items and quality records.

For convenience, the fields have been listed in three sections. Where these are expanded into separate documents fields will often need to be duplicated across the separate documents.

Descriptive information

Identifier
A unique identifier that may be made up of components such as a project or programme code, product code and version number.

Title
The name by which the product is known.

Description
A description of the product, possibly including its purpose and how it fits into the overall output.

Composition
For a simple product, this section may be enough to describe the components and nature of the product. More complex products will need cross-references to technical specifications.

Owner

If the product is a deliverable the owner will be the stakeholder to whom the product is handed over. Otherwise it will be a member of the management team who is responsible for accepting the product before it is integrated into the output as a whole.

Cross-references

Links to other documents that provide further information about the product (e.g. risk register, stakeholder map and lessons log).

Development information

Developer

The person, team, department or contractor that is responsible for the development of the product.

Planned dates

When the product is planned to be developed.

Actual dates

When the product was actually developed.

Quality criteria

These are the quality criteria that will be tested in quality control. This could be references to external quality standards, criteria unique to the product or a combination of both.

Quality tolerances

For each quality criterion the range of measurements within which the product would be acceptable should be listed.

Quality control methods

The control methods that should be used will be defined here. These could range from qualitative user reviews to mechanical inspection and statistical analysis.

Quality control responsibilities

The individuals or groups that are responsible for implementing the quality control methods.

Test dates

The planned and forecast dates for most testing or review activities are entirely dependent upon a delivery schedule that is being updated on a regular basis. To avoid duplication of effort, the planned and forecast dates may simply be covered by a cross-reference to the appropriate delivery plan. Such cross-references may be supplemented with information such as, 'product must be tested within one week of completion'.

Test results

The results of quality control could be as simple as a pass/fail or extensive test data. Either way, the consequence of the test results should be documented. If the quality is acceptable the product may be passed on for integration with other products or it may be handed over to the owner. If the quality is unacceptable the product may be reworked or discarded. In some circumstances it may be possible or necessary to accept a product that has not met its criteria but that is a decision that will have to be made by the sponsor.

Cross-references

Typically these cross-references will be to delivery plans that show the context of the planned and actual dates.

Configuration information

Current version

An identifier indicating the most recent version of the product. The configuration management section of the scope management plan will define the system for incrementally labelling the versions of a product.

Status

A classification of the current status as defined in a configuration management plan (e.g. in development, under review, approved or handed over).

Date of last change

When the latest version of the product was released for test or handover.

Previous versions

When the date of the latest version is recorded, it does not replace previous dates. Each 'current version' identifier and 'date of last change' remain in the document to show the product's development timeline.

Location

Where the item is situated or stored. This is applicable to a 'soft product' such as an electronic file or a physical component that can be moved around prior to installation. It is not relevant to products that are built into the overall output, such as the foundations of a building or the keel of a ship.

Current holder

The current version of a product may be with the original producers or a test team. Where the product is physical and uncopiable this is simply useful information.

In the case of electronic files (e.g. documents or computer code) where a download or email attachment creates a copy, it is vital to understand who has the sole authority to work on the product. This is essential to ensure that there are not multiple people making simultaneous changes to a product.

Relationships

This section explains how the product works with other products. It is the key field when assessing a change request as it identifies how a change to this product may affect other products.

Typical documents

Many different types of document can be assembled from the menu of product information. The ones described below are chosen on the basis that they commonly occur in guides and methods for P3 management. This is not intended to be a definitive or prescriptive list.

Product description

A mini-specification for a particular component of the project, programme or portfolio's objectives. It enables people to understand the detailed nature, purpose, function, appearance and acceptance criteria of the product. It should contain sufficient information to identify: what activities will be needed to develop, test and approve the product; the resources needed to develop it; the costs of the product; and where further information may be found.

> Typical contents of each document are summarised in Table 2.1.

Product register

Summarises information from the product descriptions to provide an index of products and a quick overview of their status. Sometimes referred to as a product checklist.

Quality register

Summarises quality control activities for all products and provides a central reference for a potentially very varied portfolio of quality control documentation.

Configuration item

Provides a record of an item that has been placed under configuration management. It covers information such as history, current status, version and connections to other items.

Status account

Summarises information about the current state of a defined set of configuration items; for example, 'all products due for completion in the next month' or 'all products being developed by XYZ contractors Ltd.' The scope of the status report should be described before listing the information shown in Table 2.1.

Table 2.1 Suggested contents of each document

Field	Product register	Product description	Quality register	Configuration item	Status account
Identifier	✓	✓	✓	✓	✓
Title	✓	✓	✓		
Description		✓		✓	
Composition		✓			
Owner				✓	✓
Description cross-references	✓	✓	✓	✓	✓
Developer				✓	✓
Planned dates	✓		✓		✓
Actual dates	✓		✓		✓
Quality criteria		✓			
Quality tolerances		✓			
Quality control methods		✓	✓		
Quality responsibilities		✓	✓		
Test results				✓	✓
Development cross-references	✓	✓	✓	✓	✓
Current version	✓			✓	✓
Status				✓	✓
Date of last change				✓	✓
Previous versions				✓	
Location				✓	
Current holder				✓	
Relationships				✓	

Blueprint

A blueprint is a form of specification. It is applicable to programmes of business change where the ultimate objective is a changed organisation and working methods. The blueprint represents the sum of all outcomes resulting from the outputs of projects and the change activity performed by business as usual. The benefits in the business case should be capable of being realised as a result of achieving the blueprint.

Typical sections include:

- **Operational models** Including business models and processes including operational costs and performance criteria
- **Organisation structure** Including staffing levels, skill requirements and possibly cultural change

- **Infrastructure** Including plant, machinery, IT systems and buildings, highlighting what is reused and what is new.

Within these sections the blueprint may show the pre-programme state and the state at the end of each tranche as well as the final end-of-programme state.

Benefits map

A benefits map is a form of influence diagram and is needed where there are complex relationships between multiple outputs, benefits and the strategic objectives that the benefits support. Within these relationships there may be dis-benefits and outcomes that form a bridge between outputs and benefits.

The map will take the form of a chart that illustrates:

- outputs
- outcomes
- benefits and dis-benefits
- strategic objectives
- dependencies between outputs, outcomes and benefits/dis-benefits.

Benefit profile

A benefit profile is used to define both benefits and dis-benefits. It is typically developed during the definition process of a project or programme following requirements management. The profile includes sections that describe the benefit or dis-benefit and how it will be realised and measured. A benefit profile typically contains the following sections:

- **Identifier**

  Each benefit or dis-benefit should have a unique identifier. This is primarily used for cross-referencing in reports and supporting documentation.

- **Description**

  A description of the benefit, or dis-benefit, and how it will be observed.

- **Assumptions**

  Any assumptions made in estimates of cost or value, design of change required or availability of resources.

- **Dependencies**

  Benefits usually depend upon outputs and therefore the projects that produce them. A benefit may depend upon multiple outputs or even products and events external to the current project or programme. All such dependencies should be documented here.

- **Business area**

  The business area affected by benefit or dis-benefit should be identified along with a description of the following:

- outcomes necessary to enable benefits realisation
- change that will need to be implemented to achieve the necessary outcome
- performance indicators associated with the benefit (before and after values)
- impact and mitigation actions for a dis-benefit.

- **Costs**

  All costs associated with the benefit should be described, with care taken to avoid double counting in complex circumstances.

  Ideally it should be possible to perform a value for money calculation for a benefit, but complex dependencies (i.e. many-to-many relationships between outputs and benefits) may render this impractical. If necessary this section may simply provide links to specialised financial analysis documentation.

  Since dis-benefits are unavoidable negative consequences of change, they will not have costs associated with achieving them, although there may be costs associated with mitigating the effects of the dis-benefit.

- **Value**

  If at all possible a benefit should be valued in financial terms to facilitate a value for money calculation but this is not always possible, leading to a subjective assessment of the benefit's viability.

  This calculation will be subject to the same complexity as the cost calculations, resulting in this section containing links to specialised financial analysis documentation.

  Any 'value' associated with a dis-benefit is effectively a cost that should be accounted for in the business case.

- **Cross-references**

  It is dangerous to consider any document in isolation as all aspects of a project, programme and portfolio are inter-related. Cross-references could mark the link between a benefit or dis-benefit and, for example, any risk events that may affect it. Relevant parts of a blueprint or benefit realisation plan may also be referenced.

- **Resources**

  Ownership will typically fall to the business change manager for the business area affected by the corresponding change. This section should describe the resources needed to implement the change and realise the benefit.

- **Supporting documentation**

  Links to any supporting information should be listed in the profile. This could include information used in arriving at estimated cost and value, plans and records of staff consultations regarding implementing the change or any other relevant information.

Business case

The business case is the central document to a project or programme life cycle. The reason for defining a life cycle with phases, tranches and/or stages is to enable go/no-go decisions to be made that prevent wasted investment. These decisions are primarily made based on the viability of the business case. A business case typically contains the following sections:

- **Background**
  This initial section will explain the context of the project or programme. Any assumptions made in preparing the business case will be documented here along with constraints and dependencies on other projects or programmes. Any impact that this work will have on other projects or programmes should also be noted.

  > In the outline version of the business case that forms part of the project or programme brief the background section will not be necessary as it is covered by the corresponding section in the brief.

- **Project or programme summary**
  All aspects of project or programme delivery will be summarised at a sufficient level to enable the justification for the work to be understood.

  The summary will typically comprise:

  > **Scope** Summary of objectives, in terms of outputs, outcomes and benefits as appropriate
  > **Schedule** High-level schedule with start and finish dates for major sections of work such as phases, tranches, stages or projects within a programme
  > **Finance** Funding arrangements and a summary cash flow
  > **Risk** Major risk events and the overall risk profile
  > **Resource** Sources of resource, contract arrangements, and summary volumes
  > **Change** Breadth and depth of change required
  > **Stakeholders** Key supporters and opponents.

- **Justification**
  This is the key section. It weighs the benefits of the work against the investment needed to achieve them. In this context the terms 'benefits' and 'investment' can be broadly interpreted.

  The simplest justification will be purely financial. If the benefits have a certain cash value and the investment cost is less, then the work can be justified.

  However, justification is often not that simple. A project or programme will have to balance the 'investment' in terms of risk taken; it may need to consider ecological 'costs'; intangible benefits may need complex valuations; it may simply be that the 'do nothing' option has unacceptable consequences.

One of the tricky parts of writing a business case is where to place all the information. For example, should:

- an assumed constraint be placed in assumptions or constraints?
- an uncertainty about funding be placed in the finance or risk section?
- a reference to another project that affects the benefits be placed in dependencies or the change section?

In the outline business case it does not matter too much as long as all the information is in there somewhere. When it comes to the full business case, the document is summarising other more detailed documents. The allocation of information in the business case must therefore reflect those detailed documents. For example, anything derived from the risk register should be summarised in the risk section of the business case.

Brief

The project or programme brief is created by the identification process and is one of the documents submitted to the sponsor to seek approval to start the definition process.

During the definition process each section of the brief will be used as a basis for development of multiple specialist documents. The version of the brief used for authorisation will then be archived.

A brief typically contains the following sections:

- **Background**

    This will initially be drawn from the mandate supplemented with additional research to establish the context of the project or programme. Any assumptions made in preparing the brief will be documented here, along with constraints and dependencies on other projects or programmes. Any impact that this work will have on other projects or programmes should also be noted.

- **Outline business case**

    This section will follow the structure of the business case but in a different context to the separate business case document used throughout the rest of the project or programme. The business case produced at the end of the definition phase is a 'bottom-up' document that summarises many detailed delivery documents. This outline business case is an initial 'top-down' estimate of how the project or programme will develop.

    The nature of the estimating funnel means that the possible spread of estimates for schedule, cost, resource, risk, etc. is at its broadest in the outline business case. Stakeholder expectations must be managed and the possible estimating spread explained.

    A key difference between the outline and full business case is the treatment of scope. In the context of the brief, the summary of scope should include the different options that arose from the initial solutions development. The justification section will look at the preferred option but the other options should be summarised, including the 'do nothing' option.

- **Governance**

    The first question to be answered here is whether the work is to be managed as a project or a programme (or possibly a combination of the two). The components of Praxis are designed to be as independent of this decision as possible, but the two areas immediately impacted by this decision are the organisation structure and the delivery phase of the life cycle.

    The brief must contain a draft organisation structure that is appropriate for the context, environment and complexity of the work. Wherever possible, individuals will be identified to fulfil the identified roles.

If the work is a typical project this section will identify the probable stages of delivery and any interim outputs. In a typical programme, a list of probable projects and tranches will be identified.

2.4.3 Delivery documents

While the management plans set out the governance principles for how the work will be managed and the scope documentation defines what should be achieved, the delivery documents are at the heart of actually doing the work.

Which delivery documents are to be used and what their format will be is defined in the management plans. They are primarily used in the delivery, development and boundaries processes.

Delivery documents are the most dynamic of the three documentation groups and should be maintained in accordance with the principles of information management and configuration management.

Definition plan

The definition plan is created in the identification process and, alongside the brief, is one of the documents submitted to the sponsor to seek approval for the definition process.

This document is based on the general delivery plan format and adapted to suit the context of the work. Since this plan only exists in conjunction with a project or programme brief, its content can be simplified to avoid duplication.

Communication plan

The communication plan is based on the general delivery plan format with the scope being stakeholder communications.

While focusing on the timing of communications, the plan may also include their cost, how they will be controlled and how they link to other delivery plans.

Stakeholder register

The stakeholder register records information about individuals and groups who have an interest in the work being performed.

Typical headings in the register include:

- **Title**
  The name of the stakeholder, whether an individual or group.

- **Contact details**
  As well as listing points of contact with the stakeholder, this section could also express the stakeholder's preferred methods of contact and reasons for the preferences.

- **Area and level of interest**

    The areas of the project, programme or portfolio in which the stakeholder is interested and an estimate of their level of interest.

    The area of interest could be expressed in terms of any aspect of the work. A stakeholder may be interested in specific outputs or benefits, the impact on them of the activity that produces outputs and benefits or a combination of both.

    The level of interest could be in explanatory form or simply an estimate on a scale of high, medium and low.

- **Influence**

    The first point to note is whether the stakeholder is generally supportive of, or opposed to, the work. The level of influence should then be assessed and how that influence may be manifested.

- **Communications log**

    A record of communication with the stakeholder.

- **Cross-references**

    Specific stakeholders may be associated with particular aspects of delivery (such as risks, contracts and products) that are documented elsewhere. This section should include useful cross-references to other documentation.

    The most affected and/or influential stakeholders may have individual stakeholder profiles containing the above information in more detailed form. These stakeholders should be included in the register with a cross-reference to their individual profiles.

- **Supporting information**

    It is often useful to view stakeholder information as a whole rather than on a stakeholder-by-stakeholder basis. For example, supporting information may include:

    › A stakeholder map which shows a matrix of stakeholders and areas of interest. This makes it easy to see all the areas of interest of a particular stakeholder; all the stakeholders interested in a particular area; common grouping of stakeholder and interest.
    › An interest/influence matrix which plots stakeholders on a matrix that has scales of influence and interest (typically high, medium and low). This quickly identifies the key influencers and assists in deciding how communications will be managed.

Risk register

The purpose of the risk register is to record information about identified risk events. The amount of information that needs to be recorded will depend upon the context of the work.

In its simplest form (in a small self-contained project) the register will be a list of risk events and the results of qualitative analysis. A much more sophisticated risk register will be designed to enable aggregations across multiple projects and programmes. It will also record, or cross-reference to, more specialised documentation showing quantitative analysis of general uncertainty (e.g. Monte Carlo analysis or sensitivity analysis).

A general structure for the risk register will follow the risk management procedure. The fields used within that structure will be selected from those described below. (Note: the procedural headings would not normally appear in the risk register.)

Identify

Identifier

Each risk should have a unique identifier. This is primarily used for cross-referencing in reports and supporting documentation.

Author

The person or entity that identified the risk. In many cases this will be an individual but a programme-level risk may have been identified by a project team or a project risk identified by a sub-contractor.

Date registered

The date the risk was first entered into the register.

Category

If required by the risk management plan, the register should categorise the risks. There could be multiple types of category; for example, a risk could be categorised as a threat or opportunity and then further categorised as legal, schedule or financial.

This information can be used if it is necessary to review risk by category; for example, all schedule risk or all regulatory risk. It is also useful post-project, programme or portfolio when compiling check lists of risks for use in future risk identification.

Description

A full description of the risk, possibly following a 'cause; event; effect' structure; i.e. what causes the risk, how will the event be observed and what effect would it have?

Cross-references

It is dangerous to consider any document in isolation as all aspects of a project, programme and portfolio are inter-related. Cross-references could mark the link between a risk and the relevant product documents or benefit profile that it affects. It could reference a specific activity in a schedule or provide a link between a programme-level risk and related project-level risks.

Assess

Probability

The probability of a risk occurring will be estimated according to the preferred scales set out in the risk management plan.

Impact

The impact of a risk occurring will be estimated according to the preferred scales set out in the risk management plan. The areas affected by the risk event should also be noted, typically in terms of scope, schedule and cost, but also (if appropriate) the stage, tranche or business area.

Expected value

The cost impact of a risk event can be used to calculate an expected value. In the simplest approach the cost impact is multiplied by the probability (assuming probability has been estimated on a numeric scale) to give the expected value. The expected value of more complex risk events may be calculated using tools such as decision trees.

Expected value provides a target cost for any response activity and also provides a useful mechanism for quantifying and aggregating overall risk. This can be used as one measure for risk appetite.

Proximity

The predicted timing of the risk event, should it occur.

Assumptions

The estimation of probability, impact, expected value and proximity may be based on certain assumptions. For example, the impact of delay in an activity in the schedule may be assessed on the basis that that activity lies on the critical path. It should be noted that the impact will be different, should the schedule change and the activity no longer sits on the critical path.

Supporting documentation

Risk registers are most suited to recording individual risk events and the results of qualitative risk analysis. For complex risk situations, the fields of the risk register may be inadequate to store all the relevant information. For instance, if a particularly complex risky situation was assessed using the Delphi technique, the detail would not be stored in the risk register, but in supporting documentation.

In some cases quantitative analysis techniques may be appropriate. For example, a decision tree may be used to analyse alternative scenarios or Monte Carlo analysis will be used to address general estimating uncertainty of innovative work.

These techniques will generate working papers and reports that are important in understanding the overall risk associated with a project, programme or portfolio and should be referenced in the risk register.

> One way of including the analysis of broader uncertainty within the risk register is to create a pseudo risk event such as 'estimating uncertainty'. This appears as an entry in the risk register with relevant information that fits the register's format but with most information referenced as supporting documentation.

Other risk-related information that may need to be referenced could be financial (risk budgets), schedules (contingency plans) and stakeholder details.

Ensuring that all references to risk are located in one place ensures that any risk aggregation, particularly across programmes and portfolios, does not miss anything.

Plan responses

Type

The type of risk response may be annotated here. The nature of the response will probably be evident from its description, but noting the category can aid analysis of overall risk in terms, for example, of how much threat has been transferred or what proportion of opportunity has been exploited.

Response

The actions chosen in response to the risk event and their effect (e.g. a reduction in probability, impact, or both).

The cost of implementing the response should be estimated to ensure it does not exceed the expected value of the risk itself and that the total cost of risk responses fits within the risk budget.

Residual and secondary risk events

Despite best efforts to deal with a risk event, the planned response may leave some residual risk or create a new, secondary risk. In some cases this can be covered by explanatory text; in others it may be necessary to create a new risk event with cross-references to the original risk.

Implement responses

Owner

The person responsible for managing the risk.

Actionee

The person who will implement the response. This may, or may not, be the same person as the owner.

Status

A simple statement of whether the risk event is active (default situation) or closed. A risk event may be closed if its probability or impact has greatly reduced (and it has been accepted), work has progressed beyond the cause of the event or it occurred and has been dealt with.

Delivery plan

Delivery plans come in various shapes and sizes. The first delivery plan to be prepared will be the project or programme definition plan. Subsequently, delivery plans can be prepared to cover a part of the life cycle (e.g. a stage or tranche plan), a delivery component (e.g. a benefits realisation plan or communication plan) or a specialist plan (e.g. an exception plan or contingency plan).

It is useful for all types of delivery plan to follow a consistent format, although this should be adapted as necessary and not followed slavishly.

Typical sections include:

- **Description**
  Covering a brief description of what the plan encompasses; for example, project, tranche, stakeholder communications, benefits realisation and programme definition.

- **Dependencies**
  Any external factors upon which this plan is dependent. This could include factors as diverse as approvals, links to other projects or programmes, legislation and market research.

- **Assumptions**
  Any assumptions upon which the plan is based.

- **Lessons incorporated**
  Details of relevant lessons from previous similar work that has been reviewed and accommodated within this plan.

- **Scope**
  The scope of the plan expands on the description to define the objectives it covers. It can be useful to explicitly state what is not included as well as what is.

- **Schedule**
  Scheduling techniques appropriate to the context and detail of the plan will generate various types of report that can be included in this section.

  The schedule can encompass activities that generate outputs, implement change, realise benefits and manage the work.

- **Finance**
  The main concern of this section is the budget. The estimated costs of all the resources involved in the schedule will be included, alongside management budgets for factors such as change control, risk responses and management reserves.

- **Control**
  Details of how the plan will be monitored and controlled, including tolerances for all relevant components of delivery.

- **Complementary documentation**
  A plan does not exist in isolation and will inevitably have close links to other documents. Rather than duplicate information, this section of the plan should direct the reader to other documents and the information they contain that is relevant to this plan; for example, the risk register or specification.

Issue register

The issue register records all problems that need to be escalated from one level of management to another.

Typical headings in the log include:

- **Identifier**
  Each issue should have a unique identifier. This is primarily used for cross-referencing in reports and supporting documentation.

- **Date**

  The date the issue was first raised.

- **Raised by**

  The details of the person or group raising the issue.

- **Escalated to**

  The details of the person or group that the issue is raised to.

- **Description**

  A description of the issue including cause and effect. Cause will explain how the issue came about and the effect will describe its impact on the objectives in terms of scope, schedule, finance, risk and resource.

- **Solution**

  Wherever possible, issues should be accompanied by options and recommendations for their resolution.

- **Decision**

  The nature of any decisions required, timescales for decision making and, potentially, the consequences of delay.

  Subsequently updated to document the decisions made.

- **Status**

  The current status of the issue.

- **Date closed**

  The date when the decision was reached and implemented.

- **Cross-references**

  Cross-references could identify detailed information about the effect of the issue or about any exception plans that have been prepared to deal with it. Once the issue is closed there could be, for example, a cross-reference to the lessons learned log.

Lessons log

A lessons log for a particular project or programme will have two distinct sections. The first is created in the review previous lessons activity during the identification process, where lessons learned from previous work that are applicable to the current work are logged. The second section records lessons that have arisen in the conduct of the current work and may be applicable in the future.

The capture and use of lessons learned is a dynamic process and any project or programme may generate experience that is applicable to other projects and programmes at any time. How these experiences are transferred is the subject of knowledge management and a key component in gaining level 4 maturity.

Typical headings in the log include:

- **Lesson type**

  The way lessons may be categorised would be defined in the organisation's knowledge management strategy. Categories need to help users of the knowledge management system identify the lessons that would be of use to them. It may be that lessons could be classified by function or process; by type of project or programme; or by business areas affected. Knowledge management supports the development of professionalism so classification may reflect communities of practice that are responsible for particular areas of professional development.

- **Lesson detail**

  The detail should follow a simple format of cause and effect; i.e. what was the event and how was it first identified; what impact did it have and on what areas of work.

  The entry should include the actions that the team took as a result of the event and include any recommendations on how the lesson should be incorporated into the governance of projects, programmes and/or portfolios in the future.

- **Date logged**

  The date the lesson was recorded.

- **Logged by**

  The name of the person or team that identified the lesson.

Daily log

A daily log is a personal document that records informal information that is not stored in any of the other defined documentation. It is primarily a diary of events that its owner can use as an *aide-memoire* of conversations and decisions. It can also be a note of ideas or comments that will need to be recorded elsewhere at some point in time. For example, an initial thought about a new risk or an idea for a lesson to be recorded.

While informal, the log should have some structure for ease of use and reference. For example, typical headings for entries may be:

- date of entry
- description
- action arising
- target action date
- result.

Change log

The change log records all requests for change and their progress through the change control procedure.

Typical headings in the log include:

- **Identifier**

  Each change request should have a unique identifier. This is primarily used for cross-referencing in reports and supporting documentation.

- **Date**

  The date the request was first received by the management team.

- **Requested by**

  The name and details of the stakeholder making the change request.

- **Description**

  A description of the change being requested. This may be the request in full or may reference more detailed specifications of proposed changes to a product or products.

- **Status**

  The current status of the request within the change control procedure and predictions of when the procedure will be completed.

- **Decision**

  A note of whether the request was accepted or rejected and a summary of the reasons why.

- **Date closed**

  The date when the decision was reached.

- **Communication**

  Confirmation that the decision has been communicated to all relevant stakeholders with feedback where appropriate.

- **Cross-references**

  Cross-references could identify detailed information about the nature of the request or about the assessment process. It is useful for assurance purposes to indicate which delivery plans have been updated to reflect any accepted change requests.

Progress report

Progress needs to be communicated at regular intervals. This may be, for example, from an individual to their team manager; from a contractor to a project manager; or from a project manager to a programme manager. A progress report may cover a small work package, change management activity in a business area or an entire programme in a portfolio.

Regardless of the scale or context, the principles are the same. The report needs to explain what has been done compared with what was planned; what comes next; what problems need attention; and what lessons have been learned.

A progress report is a time-driven control document used in the delivery process. The content of an effective progress report is dependent upon the judgement of a competent manager who understands the needs of the report's recipient.

Content should reflect the context of the work and target audience, but the primary categories of information are:

- **Date**
  The date of the report.

- **Period**
  The period covered by the report.

- **Summary**
  An overview of progress, highlighting the key points in the report and any actions or decisions required by the recipients of the report.

  This section may also include a follow-up from previous reports, including actions completed or decisions outstanding.

- **This reporting period**
  Progress in all elements of delivery should be reported according to the control management plan and the scope of work covered by the report. Detailed progress will be contained in other documents, such as schedules, accounts and configuration records. This report should summarise progress and focus on key performance indicators. It should also cross-reference the detailed documents in case further information is required by the recipients of the report. The type of information that should be included could be:

  > **Scope** Deliverables completed and accepted; changes authorised; quality control results.
  > **Schedule** Summarised actual vs. baseline schedules; key performance indicators such as schedule performance index.
  > **Finance** Actual vs. baseline cash flow; key performance indicators such as cost performance index.
  > **Risk** New risks; actual occurrence of risks events; response activities completed; increase/decrease in overall risk.
  > **Resource** Actual vs. baseline resource usage; contracts let or completed.
  > **Change** Readiness for change indicators; change objectives completed.
  > **Stakeholders** Communications completed; stakeholder reaction; new stakeholders.

- **Next reporting period**
  Summary of what will be covered by the next progress report and when it will be issued.

- **Tolerance status**
  Tolerances exceeded or in danger of being exceeded. Issues to be escalated, guidance needed.

- **Lessons report**
  A review of what went well, what went badly and suggestions for lessons to be included in the lessons log.

Event report

In addition to time-driven progress reports, progress may be reported at a particular event. This may be more applicable to certain stakeholders and will also be an input to the go/no-go decision process at the end of a defined segment of work; for example, the end of a stage within a project; the end of a contractor's work package; the end of a tranche within a programme or the end of a project within a portfolio.

Regardless of the scale or context, the principles are the same. The report needs to explain what has been done compared with what was planned; what, if anything, comes next; and what lessons have been learned.

The content of an effective event report is dependent upon the judgement of a competent manager who understands the needs of the report's recipient.

Content should reflect the context of the work and target audience, but the primary categories of information are:

- **Date**
  The date of the report.

- **Event**
  The segment of work covered by the report.

- **Summary**
  An overview of performance, highlighting the key points in the report and any actions or decisions required by the recipients of the report.

- **Performance**
  Performance in all elements of delivery should be reported according to the control management plan and the scope of work covered by the report. Detailed progress will have been covered by the time-driven progress reports. This report can have two main functions. Firstly, it informs stakeholders of performance in a segment of work that has been completed. This may simply be a matter of good communication and stakeholder relations. Secondly, it may be a key part of deciding whether to continue with the next segment of work.

  In either case it should summarise performance in the areas of:

  > **Scope** Deliverables completed and accepted; changes authorised; quality control results.
  > **Schedule** Summarised actual vs. baseline schedules; key performance indicators such as schedule performance index.
  > **Finance** Actual vs. baseline cash flow; key performance indicators such as cost performance index.
  > **Risk** Were risk responses effective, were there major risks that occurred and had not been foreseen?
  > **Resource** Actual vs. baseline resource usage; contract performance.
  > **Change** How has change been received; were change objectives completed?
  > **Stakeholders** Communications completed; stakeholder reaction.

- **Next event report**
  If the segment of work covered by this report is followed by another related segment that should be described here. If there are elements of the completed segment of work that are outstanding these should be detailed in a follow-on actions report.

- **Lessons report**
  A review of what went well, what went badly and suggestions for lessons to be included in the lessons log.

Follow-on actions report

The nature of a follow-on actions report will vary considerably according to its context. In simple terms it must list the actions that remain outstanding when the project or programme team is demobilised. Such actions could relate to unfinished deliverables, corrective action on existing deliverables, or tidying up managerial loose ends such as final payments.

As a minimum the report should contain:

- description of the outstanding action
- owner
- planned date for resolution
- actual date of resolution.

3.1 Overview

Praxis contains three groups of competencies. Delivery competencies are based on section 3.3; process competencies are based on individual processes defined in Part 2; and interpersonal competencies are addressed in the corresponding sections of Part 1.

There is only one competency for each function or process and in practice each of these will need to be adapted to suit the setting in which it is to be applied. That means that a competency must be aligned with the complexity and the environment of the work and whether it is to be managed as a project, programme or portfolio. Some suggestions on tailoring are included alongside each competency but these are simply indicative and not comprehensive. There is more information about adapting competencies in the article on tailoring Praxis (**https://www.praxisframework. org/en/resource-pages/tailoring-praxis**).

The level of individual performance is aligned with level 2 in the capability maturity model since this requires competent staff. Competencies are aimed primarily at a P3 manager role and will need to be adapted for other roles such as sponsor, assurance or support.

The maturity model shown in Figure 3.1 provides an organisational context in which the individual competencies need to be applied.

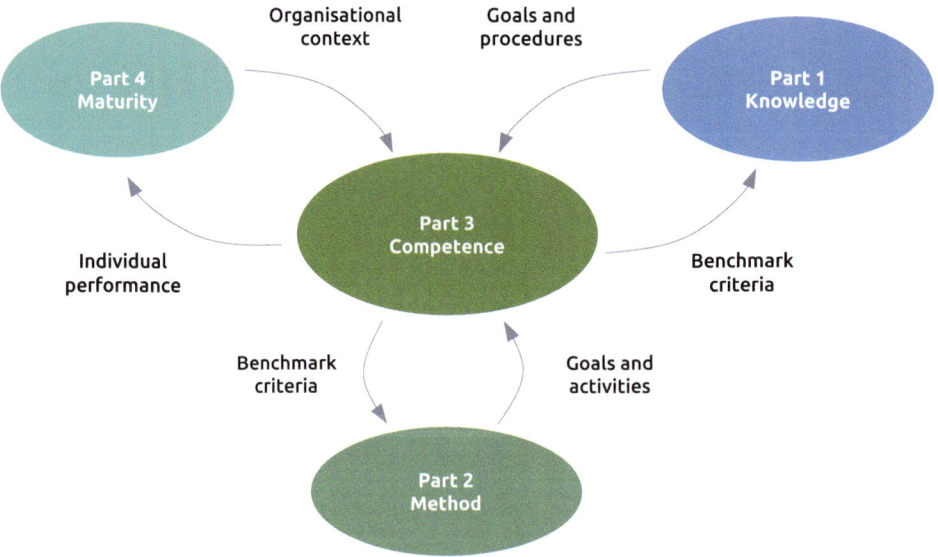

Figure 3.1 Competence relationships

Part 1 (Knowledge) and Part 2 (Method) provide the overall structure of the competency framework and more detailed information for the knowledge and performance criteria. In return the performance criteria defined in the competencies provide benchmarks of individual performance.

Competencies are divided into three types:

- **Objectives**
  This section lists the specific goals that the competency is designed to achieve.

- **Performance criteria**

    These are the criteria that someone must effectively perform to be deemed competent in achieving the goals.

- **Knowledge and understanding**

    In order to effectively exhibit the performance criteria someone must have knowledge and understanding of the relevant principles, procedures, tools and techniques.

3.2 Management competencies

This section includes competencies that relate to appropriate functions in section 1.3.

The context functions do not have corresponding competencies, with one exception. The sponsorship function has an equivalent process of the same name. The process competency for sponsorship, therefore, covers the sponsorship function.

As with section 1.3, these competencies are divided into two types: delivery (section 3.3) and interpersonal (section 3.4).

3.3 Delivery competencies

Delivery competencies align with the delivery functions in Part 1. The titles reflect the fact that competency is about implementing the functions rather than simply describing what the functions are. Hence the competency 'manage stakeholders' is the application of the function 'stakeholder management'.

3.3.1 Provide assurance

Objectives	The purpose of this competency is to: • review management planning • monitor effectiveness of functions and processes • give stakeholders confidence that the work is being managed effectively and efficiently.

Performance criteria *You must be able to*	P1 plan and initiate assurance P2 review the design and implementation of life cycle-based processes P3 review the design and implementation of management plans P4 audit the performance of quality control activities and review any resulting corrective action P5 maintain assurance documentation P6 communicate the outcomes of assurance to stakeholders.
Knowledge and understanding *You need to know and understand*	K1 the goals of assurance K2 responsibilities for assurance K3 the context of the work and its impact on assurance K4 assurance procedures and techniques K5 the purpose and content of assurance documentation K6 the principles of the P3 functions and processes being assured K7 how to adapt assurance throughout the life cycle K8 how to communicate assurance outcomes to stakeholders.

This is the only competency that does not have a performance criterion that starts with 'assure the quality of …' because that would be a circular reference.

This competency may be applied by someone acting internally or externally to the management team. When applied as external assurance, it would include the checking of any previous internal assurance; for example, programme assurance may check that project assurance is being conducted correctly.

Where the context of the work requires particularly rigorous assurance (e.g. legislative or regulatory requirements or high-risk environments) the knowledge criteria may be expanded to include specific assurance techniques.

3.3.2 Manage the organisation

Objectives	The purpose of this competency is to: • design an organisation appropriate to the scope of work to be managed • identify and appoint members of the management team • maintain and adapt the organisation throughout the life cycle.

Performance criteria *You must be able to*	P1 design an appropriate organisation in accordance with the context of the work P2 recruit competent staff P3 lead, motivate, communicate and resolve conflict P4 maintain the organisation throughout the life cycle P5 demobilise the organisation P6 assure the maintenance of the organisation.

Knowledge and understanding *You need to know and understand*	K1 the principles and goals of organisation management K2 responsibilities for organisation management K3 the context of the work and its impact on organisation design K4 how to define roles and assess the suitability of potential team members K5 the skills required to lead and support an effective management team K6 how to respond to changing organisational requirements during the life cycle K7 how assurance applies to the organisation K8 the principles of staff redeployment.

This competency may be applied to someone who has to decide whether work is to be managed as a project or programme. In this case P1 requires an understanding of both projects and programmes. In less complex situations it may be applied to someone who is given a project and simply has to design a project organisation to suit the circumstances. While P1 works in both contexts the knowledge criteria may be expanded for clarification.

In an ideal world a manager can recruit their own team but management team members are often appointed on the basis of availability. If the manager has no control over recruitment P2 may be omitted.

3.3.3 Manage stakeholders

Objectives	The purpose of this competency is to: ● ensure that the views and attitudes of all stakeholders are understood ● influence stakeholders to be supportive of the work wherever possible ● maximise the impact of supportive stakeholders ● minimise the impact of unsupportive stakeholders.

Performance criteria *You must be able to*	P1 plan and initiate stakeholder management P2 identify stakeholders P3 assess stakeholders' interests and influence P4 influence and communicate with stakeholders P5 maintain stakeholder management documentation P6 adapt communications throughout the life cycle P7 monitor and control stakeholder management P8 assure the quality of stakeholder management.

Knowledge and understanding *You need to know and understand*	K1 the principles and goals of stakeholder management K2 responsibilities for stakeholder management K3 the context of the work and its impact on managing stakeholders K4 a procedure for stakeholder management K5 the purpose and content of stakeholder management documentation K6 methods for identifying stakeholders and appropriate sources of information K7 techniques for assessing and documenting stakeholder interest and influence K8 communication channels and how to use them K9 how to influence stakeholders and negotiate with them K10 how stakeholders and their interest and influence may change during the life cycle K11 how assurance applies to stakeholder management.

Multiple projects or programmes may share stakeholders. The co-ordination of stakeholder management across these projects and programmes may be deemed to be covered by P7 but an additional explicit performance criterion may be added if necessary. At portfolio level it may be appropriate to just 'monitor' and omit the 'control'.

Similarly, some environments (particularly those that are heavily regulated) may have very specific types of communication that are sufficiently important to constitute additional performance criteria.

Techniques for identifying and assessing stakeholders are entirely subjective. It is not the case that there are complex stakeholder analysis techniques for work that has larger numbers of stakeholders or more influential stakeholders. The difference between stakeholder management techniques in simple or complex contexts is more about the effort put into the procedure and the detail in the documentation.

3.3.4 Manage the business case

Objectives	The purpose of this competency is to: • summarise context and delivery in a single document • explain the desirability, achievability and viability of the proposed work • develop the primary document that will be used to support a go/no-go decision at all gates in the life cycle • update and maintain the business case throughout the life cycle.	
Performance criteria *You must be able to*	P1 perform high-level planning (to develop an outline business case) P2 summarise the output of detailed delivery documents (to develop a detailed business case) P3 use appropriate techniques to justify the project or programme P4 prepare and present the business case in a way that is likely to gain the support of stakeholders P5 develop arguments that justify the project or programme to stakeholders P6 respond to requests for additional information in a clear and timely way P7 monitor factors that influence the viability of the business case P8 assure the quality of the business case.	Since the business case is primarily a summary and presentation of more detailed information, the difference between a simple and a complex context is covered by adaptations of the competencies that create the detailed information. This competency can be interpreted for all levels of complexity without any significant adjustment. In owning the business case, the sponsor is accountable for all these performance criteria but may be more actively involved in areas such as P5 and P7.

Table continues

3.3.4 Manage the business case, *continued*

Knowledge and understanding *You need to know and understand*	K1	the principles and goals of business case management
	K2	responsibilities for business case management
	K3	the context of the work and its impact on managing the business case
	K4	general principles and processes for developing a business case
	K5	the structure and content of the business case document
	K6	how to summarise stakeholder requirements to represent desirability
	K7	how to summarise detailed delivery documents covering scope, schedule, finance, risk, resource and change to represent achievability
	K8	how to summarise detailed investment appraisal information to represent viability
	K9	how to present the business case to relevant stakeholders to support decision making
	K10	how the integrity of a business case is affected by progress
	K11	how the integrity of the business case is affected by external factors
	K12	how assurance applies to the business case.

3.3.5 Plan governance

Objectives	The purpose of this competency is to:
	- describe the principles that should be used to manage the work
	- provide consistency with flexibility across multiple projects and programmes.

Performance criteria *You must be able to*	P1 identify external policy documents that will form part of the governance documentation P2 produce management plans to suit the context of the work P3 develop new management plans where organisational standards are not available P4 maintain management plans throughout the life cycle P5 assure the quality of management plans.	Since competencies are aimed at level 2 capability, P1 simply requires the competent person to produce a management plan. If the host organisation is operating at level 3 centrally defined documents should be available and tailored to the context of each piece of work. In this case 'produce' may be replaced with 'tailor' and P2 used to plug any gaps.
Knowledge and understanding *You need to know and understand*	K1 the principles and goals of management planning K2 responsibilities for management planning K3 the context of the work and its impact on management plans K4 the purpose and content of a typical management plan K5 how standard management plans may be tailored K6 how management plans may be adjusted during the life cycle K7 how assurance applies to management plans.	

3.3.6 Plan delivery

Objectives	The purpose of this competency is to:
	- describe the objectives of the project, programme or portfolio
	- define the work required to achieve the objectives and describe how it will be performed
	- estimate the resources and finance needed to perform the work
	- document the plans and update them throughout the life cycle.

Performance criteria *You must be able to*	P1	prepare specifications that describe the scope of the work	Most of the criteria in this competency are covered by other more detailed competencies; i.e. where planning is described for each function. The primary use for this competency is on smaller projects or where a role does not include detailed planning criteria from other functional competencies.
	P2	prepare delivery plans for all aspects of the work, including schedule, finance, resources, risk and change	
	P3	update plans throughout the life cycle	
	P4	assure the quality of delivery planning.	
Knowledge and understanding *You need to know and understand*	K1	the principles and goals of delivery planning	
	K2	responsibilities for delivery planning	
	K3	the context of the work and its impact on delivery planning	
	K4	the way in which delivery plans should be prepared and presented	
	K5	estimating techniques applicable to different components of delivery	
	K6	modelling techniques applicable to schedules, finances, resources, risk and change	
	K7	how delivery plans are connected and how updates on plans impact on other plans	
	K8	how assurance applies to delivery planning.	

3.3.7 Exercise control

Objectives	The purpose of this competency is to: • review performance against baselines • evaluate the effect of actual performance on future plans • take action as required to achieve planning targets or agree revised targets.

Performance criteria *You must be able to*	P1 plan and initiate control P2 co-ordinate the activity of the delivery team(s) P3 monitor progress P4 evaluate the impact of actual progress on the objectives P5 resolve issues and replan accordingly P6 maintain control documentation P7 assure the quality of the control procedure.	Control techniques vary considerably according to the complexity and context of the work. This general competency could be used as a basis for several context-sensitive competencies within a single tailored version of Praxis. For example, 'Exercise project control' or 'Exercise programme control' could be significantly different; or perhaps control on traditional (waterfall) projects will focus on schedule and cost, whereas control of agile projects will focus on deliverables within time boxes.
Knowledge and understanding *You need to know and understand*	K1 the principles and goals of control K2 responsibilities for control K3 the context of the work and its impact on control K4 a range of techniques for monitoring and reporting progress K5 how to predict future performance based on actual progress K6 the principles and application of tolerances K7 the purpose and content of control documentation K8 how assurance applies to control.	

3.3.8 Manage information

Objectives	The purpose of this competency is to:
	- capture data accurately and consistently
	- develop usable information from raw data
	- maintain information securely and accessibly during its useful life
	- support effective decision making and communication.

Performance criteria *You must be able to*	P1 plan and initiate information management
	P2 collect data from a variety of sources
	P3 transform data into information
	P4 store, access and disseminate information
	P5 archive and destroy information as required
	P6 assure the quality of information management.

Knowledge and understanding *You need to know and understand*	K1 the principles and goals of information management
	K2 responsibilities for information management
	K3 the context of the work and its impact on managing information
	K4 a procedure for information management
	K5 methods for data capture and analysis
	K6 techniques for presenting information
	K7 information storage and access methods including version control
	K8 how to tailor information to meet different needs
	K9 how and when to archive or destroy information
	K10 how assurance applies to information management.

The larger and more complex a piece of work, the more data it is possible to collect and the more information that can be disseminated.

However, the success of information management is not judged by the volume of information managed. The focus of these performance criteria should be on the need for accurate and usable information in support of decision making.

In an environment that is subject to security constraints, performance criteria related to clearances and authorisations may be needed.

The context of some projects, programmes and portfolios may mean that certain information has statutory, contractual or regulatory significance.

In those contexts it may be appropriate to add relevant specific knowledge criteria.

3.3.9 Manage scope

Objectives	The purpose of this competency is to:
	- identify stakeholder wants and needs - specify outputs, outcomes and benefits that meet agreed requirements - maintain scope throughout the life cycle.

Performance criteria *You must be able to*	P1 plan and initiate scope management P2 work with stakeholders to determine and agree scope P3 accurately document, baseline and communicate scope P4 monitor work and ensure it accords to agreed scope P5 control changes and maintain scope documentation P6 assure the quality of scope management.
Knowledge and understanding *You need to know and understand*	K1 the principles and goals of scope management K2 responsibilities for scope management K3 the context of the work and its impact on managing scope K4 an overall procedure for managing scope K5 the purpose and content of scope documentation K6 product definition techniques K7 the principles of requirements management and solution development K8 the principles of benefits management K9 the principles of change control and configuration management K10 how assurance applies to scope management.

Scope is the primary factor in deciding whether to manage work as a project or programme. While the performance criteria are applicable in all situations, the knowledge criteria may be adjusted (for example, benefits management may not be within the scope of a non-complex project).

This competency summarises several others and should be adjusted according to the set of scope-related competencies used.

Manage requirements

Objectives	The purpose of this competency is to:
	- ensure that all relevant stakeholders have the opportunity to express their wants and needs
	- reconcile multiple stakeholder requirements to create a single viable set of objectives
	- achieve stakeholder consensus on a baseline set of requirements.

Performance criteria *You must be able to*	P1	plan and initiate requirements management
	P2	capture requirements from stakeholders
	P3	review the requirements to distinguish wants from needs
	P4	assess the requirements to look for overlaps, gaps and conflicts
	P5	evaluate requirements and select those that can most effectively satisfy the majority of stakeholder requirements
	P6	develop a set of objectives that reflect stakeholders' requirements
	P7	baseline the requirements
	P8	assure the quality of requirements management.

Knowledge and understanding *You need to know and understand*	K1	the principles and goals of requirements management
	K2	responsibilities for requirements management
	K3	the context of the work and its impact on managing requirements
	K4	a procedure for managing requirements
	K5	the purpose and content of requirements management documentation
	K6	how to work with stakeholders to gather requirements
	K7	the sources of information that will support requirements management
	K8	how to assess stakeholder wants and needs
	K9	how to manage stakeholder expectations
	K10	how to prioritise and agree requirements with stakeholders
	K11	the relationship between requirements, objectives and acceptance criteria
	K12	how assurance applies to requirements management.

Determining requirements is the first step to determining the complexity of the work but the basic performance criteria are equally applicable to simple and complex contexts.

If the requirements are anticipated to be particularly complex it may be appropriate to specify performance of particular techniques, such as value management, although care should be taken to follow this through to other aspects of scope management and control.

It may also be appropriate to address the need to assemble and manage specialists in the field of requirements management.

Where there are multiple stakeholders with potentially differing views on requirements it may be appropriate to include elements of influencing, negotiation and conflict management in the knowledge criteria.

Develop solution

Objectives	The purpose of this competency is to:
	• evaluate baseline requirements and alternative solutions to achieve them
	• select the optimum solution
	• create a specification for the solution.

Performance criteria *You must be able to*		
	P1	mobilise the necessary expertise to support the development of solutions
	P2	involve stakeholders in the evaluation of potential solutions
	P3	agree the optimum solution with stakeholders
	P4	clearly document the agreed solution in a specification
	P5	assure the quality of solutions development.

Knowledge and understanding *You need to know and understand*		
	K1	the principles and goals of solution development
	K2	responsibilities for solution development
	K3	the context of the work and its impact on developing a solution
	K4	the relationship between solutions and requirements
	K5	a procedure for developing solutions
	K6	the purpose and content of solutions development documentation
	K7	the sources of information and expertise for the development of solutions and how to analyse such information (including using lessons learned)
	K8	how to work with stakeholders to develop solutions
	K9	the reasons for developing a range of solutions and how these should be presented
	K10	how to manage stakeholder expectations
	K11	how assurance applies to solutions development.

The 'necessary expertise' is dependent on the context of the work and this may be replaced with specific references to roles from a particular sector (e.g. architects, structural engineers and services engineers).

If a broadly applicable technique such as value management has been introduced in requirements management it should also be included here.

The solution is, in effect, the technical design of an output. Naturally, the knowledge criteria could be expressed in terms that are far more specific to the technical environment as long as the generic principles are covered.

Manage benefits

Objectives	The purpose of this competency is to:
	- define benefits and dis-benefits of the proposed work
	- establish measurement mechanisms
	- implement any change needed in order to realise benefits
	- measure improvement and compare with the business case.

Performance criteria *You must be able to*	P1	plan and initiate benefits management
	P2	define, document and communicate benefits and dis-benefits
	P3	define measurement mechanisms and implement them throughout the life cycle
	P4	initiate and manage change
	P5	review achievement of benefits in the business case
	P6	assure the quality of benefits management.

Knowledge and understanding *You need to know and understand*	K1	the principles and goals of benefits management
	K2	responsibilities for benefits management
	K3	the context of the work and its impact on managing benefits
	K4	a procedure for managing benefits
	K5	the purpose and content of benefits management documentation
	K6	mechanisms for quantifying and valuing benefits and dis-benefits
	K7	how to measure benefits
	K8	the impact of change on stakeholders
	K9	different approaches to managing change
	K10	the relationships between outputs, outcomes and benefits
	K11	how assurance applies to benefits management.

This competency covers the whole benefits management procedure but different people will be involved at different stages. For example, while a P3 manager may be involved in defining benefits, they will usually not be in post when the final benefits review is performed, which will be led by the sponsor. Where they exist, business change managers will be the main role for P4 with the manager having a more co-ordinating role.

Benefits management and change management usually go hand in hand so these two competencies should be tailored in tandem.

Control scope change

Objectives	The purpose of this competency is to:
	• capture stakeholders' requests to make changes to scope
	• ensure that requests are only approved if viable and achievable
	• integrate changes into the existing scope.

Performance criteria *You must be able to*	P1 plan and initiate change control P2 capture and assess change requests P3 decide whether to accept change requests P4 implement accepted change requests P5 keep stakeholders informed P6 take action to manage any issues that arise P7 assure the quality of change control.

This competency is closely linked to configuration management.

On complex projects and programmes the two functions will probably be performed by different people and it will be appropriate to have separate competencies for controlling scope change and managing the configuration.

On simpler projects it may be better to combine them into a single competency for inclusion in a role that is responsible for both.

Knowledge and understanding *You need to know and understand*	K1 the principles and goals of change control K2 responsibilities for change control K3 the context of the work and its impact on controlling scope change K4 a procedure for change control K4 the purpose and content of change control documentation K6 the types of change requests that may emerge K7 the reasons for scope change K8 the need to record project changes and the impact of such changes on delivery plans K9 the importance of communicating decisions to stakeholders K10 the issues that may emerge and how these can be managed K11 how assurance applies to change control.

Manage the configuration

Objectives	The purpose of this competency is to:
	- identify the products that will be treated as configuration items
	- support the assessment of change requests and document the results of change control
	- maintain the validity of the configuration and the accuracy of the configuration management system.

Performance criteria *You must be able to*	P1	plan and initiate configuration management
	P2	identify configuration items
	P3	use configuration records to support all aspects of scope management
	P4	maintain configuration management documentation
	P5	assure the quality of configuration management.

Knowledge and understanding *You need to know and understand*	K1	the principles and goals of configuration management
	K2	responsibilities for configuration management
	K3	the context of the work and its impact on configuration management
	K4	a procedure for configuration management
	K5	the purpose and content of configuration management documentation
	K6	how the configuration management system supports change control
	K7	how to perform status accounting
	K8	how to verify and audit a configuration
	K9	how assurance applies to configuration management.

At programme or portfolio level the focus is on major deliverables and co-ordination of lower-level configuration management. This may be reflected in the performance criteria for people operating at programme or portfolio level.

Configuration management systems will vary according to the nature of the configuration items.

If it is necessary to include use of specific systems they can be included here as knowledge criteria.

3.3.10 Manage the schedule

Objectives	The purpose of this competency is to:
	- determine timescales for the work
	- calculate profiles of resource demand
	- present schedule reports suitable for different stakeholders.

Performance criteria *You must be able to*	P1	plan and initiate schedule management
	P2	identify the work that must be performed to achieve objectives
	P3	model the way work will be performed
	P4	determine and apply suitable estimating methods for time and resource
	P5	schedule the work
	P6	agree schedules with stakeholders
	P7	determine and apply suitable reporting methods
	P8	assure the quality of schedule management.

Knowledge and understanding *You need to know and understand*	K1	the principles and goals of schedule management
	K2	responsibilities for schedule management
	K3	the context of the work and its impact on managing the schedule
	K4	a procedure for schedule management
	K5	the purpose and content of schedule documentation
	K6	techniques for identifying work components
	K7	methods for modelling the performance of work
	K8	time and resource estimating techniques
	K9	analysis techniques and reporting formats
	K10	the importance of maintaining and updating the schedule
	K11	how assurance applies to schedule management.

Scheduling approaches are closely linked to all aspects of the context of the work. There are various ways in which this competency can be tailored.

For example, performance criteria may be added or extended to cover:

- consolidation and maintenance of multiple schedules for programmes or complex projects
- audit and approval of contractor schedules.

There is a wide range of methods and techniques that can be used in schedule management. Additional knowledge requirements may be added to cover specific techniques, particularly where more sophisticated scheduling (e.g. Monte Carlo analysis) or industry-specific approaches (e.g. line of balance) are required.

3.3.11 Manage finance

Objectives	The purpose of this competency is to:
	- estimate the cost of achieving the objectives
	- assess the viability of achieving the objectives
	- secure funds and manage their release throughout the life cycle
	- set up and run financial systems
	- monitor and control expenditure.

Performance criteria *You must be able to*	P1	plan and initiate financial management
	P2	ensure the cost of the work is understood
	P3	identify the best means of funding the work
	P4	apply principles of financial and management accounting
	P5	maintain financial documentation
	P6	assure the quality of financial management.

Knowledge and understanding *You need to know and understand*	K1	the principles and goals of financial management
	K2	responsibilities for financial management
	K3	the context of the work and its impact on financial management
	K4	a procedure for managing finance
	K5	the purpose and content of financial management documentation
	K6	the principles of investment appraisal
	K7	the principles of funding
	K8	the principles of budgeting and cost control
	K9	how assurance applies to financial management.

This competency summarises several others and should be adjusted according to the set of financial functions relevant to the context.

Managing finance in a P3 environment inevitably links to, and possibly overlaps with, corporate finance systems. When applying this competency to a P3 role it must reflect what is, and what is not, within the authority of the P3 organisation and what is controlled by the host organisation's financial systems.

Develop investment appraisal

Objectives	The purpose of this competency is to:
	● assess the viability of achieving the objectives ● support the production of a business case.

Performance criteria *You must be able to*	P1 determine factors affecting the appraisal P2 identify suitable appraisal techniques P3 perform an investment appraisal P4 present investment appraisal information as part of a business case P5 maintain investment appraisal documentation P6 assure the quality of investment appraisal
Knowledge and understanding *You need to know and understand*	K1 the principles and goals of investment appraisal K2 responsibilities for investment appraisal K3 the context of the work and its impact on the investment appraisal K4 objective appraisal techniques K5 subjective appraisal techniques K6 the importance of maintaining and updating the appraisal K7 methods for presenting investment appraisal information K8 how assurance applies to investment appraisal.

Investment appraisal approaches are closely linked to complexity and environment.

It may be that investment appraisal is normally performed before the management team is formed. It then only needs to understand and review the appraisal.

In some environments the investment appraisal may have regulatory or statutory implications that are significant enough to need specific reference in the performance criteria.

Additional knowledge requirements may be added to cover specific techniques, particularly where more sophisticated appraisal (e.g. environmental impact analysis) or industry-specific approaches are required.

Manage funding

Objectives	The purpose of this competency is to:
	- determine the best way to fund the work
	- secure commitment from the fund holders
	- manage the release of funds throughout the life cycle.

Performance criteria *You must be able to*	P1	identify suitable sources of project or programme funds
	P2	compare different sources of funds and select the optimum combination
	P3	negotiate the terms and conditions for the provision of funds
	P4	co-ordinate drawdown of funds with expenditure
	P5	maintain funding documentation
	P6	assure the quality of the funding procedure.

Knowledge and understanding *You need to know and understand*	K1	the principles and goals of funding
	K2	responsibilities for funding
	K3	the context of the work and its impact on funding
	K4	a procedure for funding
	K5	the benefits and drawbacks of different sources of funding
	K6	how to synchronise funding and expenditure
	K7	the purpose and content of funding documentation
	K8	how assurance applies to funding.

The adaptation of this competency is primarily influenced by whether the funds are provided internally or externally.

Where internal funds are allocated it is usually unnecessary to compare different methods and the administration of the release of funds will be simpler.

Some large projects or programmes may utilise multiple sources of funds and specialised approaches (such as the various public/private arrangements). In these contexts the knowledge criteria should be extended to cover these specialised approaches.

Develop budgets and control costs

Objectives	The purpose of this competency is to:
	• determine the income and expenditure profiles for the work
	• develop budgets and align with funding
	• implement systems to manage income and expenditure.

Performance criteria		
You must be able to	P1	refine cost estimates and allocate costs to budgets
	P2	calculate values for contingency and management reserves
	P3	set up and manage cost control systems
	P4	co-ordinate expenditure with the availability of funds
	P4	maintain budget and cost control documentation
	P5	assure the quality of budgets and cost control.

Knowledge and understanding		
You need to know and understand	K1	the principles and goals of budgeting and cost control
	K2	responsibilities for budgeting and cost control
	K3	the context of the work and its impact on budgets and cost control systems
	K4	a procedure for developing budgets and controlling costs
	K5	how to estimate and operate contingency and management reserves
	K6	cost attributes and payment types
	K7	the purpose and content of budgetary and cost control documentation
	K8	how assurance applies to budgeting and cost control.

Cost control systems must reflect the scale and complexity of the work. On programmes, portfolios and larger projects there will be procedures for setting budgets for component parts and consolidating actual costs across those component parts. In a portfolio there may be a scheme of delegation for the approval of budgets.

Therefore, multiple competencies may have to be developed in this area to accommodate the responsibility and authority of different roles within the system.

3.3.12 Manage risk

Objectives	The purpose of this competency is to: <ul><li>ensure that levels of overall risk within a project, programme or portfolio are compatible with organisational objectives</li><li>ensure that individual risks and responses are identified</li><li>minimise the impact of threats to objectives</li><li>optimise opportunities within the scope of work.</li></ul>

Performance criteria *You must be able to*	P1 plan and initiate risk management P2 identify risk events P3 assess the probability and impact of risk events P4 plan responses to risk events P5 implement responses to risk events and maintain acceptable levels of overall risk P6 maintain risk management documentation P7 monitor and control risk management P8 assure the quality of risk management.	The approach that an organisation takes to managing risk is dependent upon its risk context. The competency will have to be adjusted to meet different appetites and attitudes in different aspects of the work. For example, a small entrepreneurial company working in leading-edge technology projects has a very different risk profile from a charity delivering an aid programme in a war-torn country and this needs to be reflected in the competency of its staff.
Knowledge and understanding *You need to know and understand*	K1 the principles and goals of risk management K2 responsibilities for risk management K3 the context of the work and its impact on risk management K4 a procedure for risk management K5 the purpose and content of risk management documentation K6 methods for identifying risk and appropriate sources of information K7 techniques for assessing threats and opportunities K8 types, and appropriate use, of risk response actions K9 risk attitude and risk appetite K10 how risk events and overall risk may change during the life cycle K11 how assurance applies to risk management.	

3.3.13 Manage change

Objectives	The purpose of this competency is to: • define the organisational change required to convert outputs into benefits • ensure the organisation is prepared to implement change • implement the change and embed it into organisational practice.
Performance criteria *You must be able to*	P1 plan and initiate change P2 identify the change required to existing practices P3 assess the organisation's readiness to change P4 communicate and implement change P5 ensure that new practices are embedded in business as usual P6 maintain change management documentation P7 assure the quality of change management.
Knowledge and understanding *You need to know and understand*	K1 the principles and goals of change management K2 responsibilities for change management K3 the context of the work and its impact on change management K4 a procedure for change management K5 the purpose and content of change management documentation K6 how to specify change K7 models that describe the nature of organisational change K8 how to communicate change K9 techniques for assessing readiness to change K10 methods for overcoming resistance to change K11 how to ensure changes are embedded in business as usual K12 how assurance applies to change management.

The amount of organisational change required by a project, programme or portfolio varies considerably, as do the consequences of managing change badly.

This competency is also relevant to several roles that have a different perspective on change management.

It is important, therefore, to ensure that this competency matches the importance of change management in the context of the work and also the role to which it is applied.

3.3.14 Manage resources

Objectives	The purpose of this competency is to:
	- determine the best way to resource the work
- acquire and mobilise the necessary resources
- manage resources throughout the life cycle
- demobilise resources at the end of the life cycle
- finalise all contractual arrangements.

Performance criteria *You must be able to*	P1	plan and initiate resource management
	P2	identify the best resourcing method for delivering the scope of work
	P3	negotiate the provision of internal resources
	P4	select and appoint external suppliers
	P5	mobilise resources throughout the life cycle
	P6	administer and control resources
	P7	maintain resource management documentation
	P8	assure the quality of resource management.

Knowledge and understanding *You need to know and understand*	K1	the principles and goals of resource management
	K2	responsibilities for resource management
	K3	the context of the work and its impact on resource management
	K4	a procedure for managing resources
	K5	the purpose and content of resource management documentation
	K6	the principles of procurement
	K7	the principles of contract management
	K8	the principles of mobilisation
	K9	how assurance applies to resource management.

This competency summarises several others and should be adjusted according to the set of resource related competencies used.

The nature of these performance criteria can vary considerably according to the context of the work. When applied to small internal projects, the references to external resources may be omitted.

On more complex projects and programmes (and almost certainly on all portfolios) it is likely that this competency will be supplemented or replaced by more detailed competencies for procurement, contract management and mobilisation.

Knowledge criteria will be adapted to match the performance criteria, but not necessarily on a one-to-one basis. For example, where suppliers may be selected and appointed at programme level, it may be necessary for a project manager using those suppliers to be familiar with contract law.

Procure resources

Objectives	The purpose of this competency is to:
	- identify potential external suppliers
	- select external suppliers
	- acquire commitment to provision of internal resources.

Performance criteria *You must be able to*	P1	plan and initiate procurement
	P2	identify potential suppliers
	P3	tender for external supplies
	P4	negotiate for internal resources and develop service level agreements
	P5	maintain procurement documentation
	P6	assure the quality of procurement.

This competency covers the procurement of both internal and external resources. It may be that in some contexts the work is resourced from only one of these sources and the competency could be adjusted accordingly.

Knowledge and understanding *You need to know and understand*	K1	the principles and goals of procurement
	K2	responsibilities for procurement
	K3	the context of the work and its impact on procurement
	K4	a procedure for procurement
	K5	the purpose and content of procurement documentation
	K6	how to identify and shortlist suppliers
	K7	how to conduct a tendering procedure
	K8	how to secure internal resources in a matrix organisation
	K9	how assurance applies to procurement.

Manage contracts

Objectives	The purpose of this competency is to:
	- support procurement by negotiating terms and conditions
	- document contractual agreements
	- monitor contractual performance
	- conclude contracts.

Performance criteria		
You must be able to	P1	plan and initiate contracts
	P2	negotiate contract terms and conditions
	P3	adapt standard terms and conditions
	P3	develop and maintain contract documentation
	P4	assure the quality of contract management.

Knowledge and understanding		
You need to know and understand	K1	the principles and goals of contract management
	K2	responsibilities for contract management
	K3	the context of the work and its impact on contracts and contractual relationships
	K4	a procedure for managing contracts
	K5	the purpose and content of contract documentation
	K6	relevant standard forms of contract
	K7	legal terminology such as 'offer and acceptance' and 'consideration'
	K8	how assurance applies to contract management.

In more complex situations a P3 manager may need advice on contract law from lawyers. The more critical and complex the legal relationships, the more dependent the manager will be on this advice. The key word here is 'advice'; it will still be the manager's responsibility to decide how to act upon the legal advice.

Depending upon the context, this competency may need to be amended to reflect the relationship between the manager and the legal advisors.

Mobilise resources

Objectives	The purpose of this competency is to ensure that: • capital assets are operational and accessible • facilities are operational and accessible • delivery team members are competent and capable • all resources are redeployed, returned or disposed of at the end of the work.

Performance criteria *You must be able to*	P1 plan and initiate mobilisation P2 mobilise resources at relevant points in the life cycle P3 demobilise resources at relevant points in the life cycle P4 maintain relevant documentation P5 assure the quality of mobilisation and demobilisation.	Mobilisation can range from ensuring that internal resources are available and inducted onto a small project to setting up the infrastructure to manage a programme like the Olympic Games. While all the criteria in this competency apply to all situations regardless of the context and complexity, they will probably need to be supplemented with specific references to the extent of resource and infrastructure that needs to be mobilised.
Knowledge and understanding *You need to know and understand*	K1 the principles and goals of mobilisation K2 responsibilities for mobilisation K3 the context of the work and its impact on mobilisation and demobilisation of resources K4 procedures for mobilisation and demobilisation K5 the purpose and content of the relevant documentation K6 how to work with other managers in a matrix organisation K7 how to co-ordinate multiple suppliers K8 relevant employment legislation K9 mechanisms for disposal of capital assets K10 how assurance applies to mobilisation and demobilisation.	

3.4 Interpersonal competencies

Interpersonal is one of three groups of competencies, the other two being delivery (section 3.3) and process (section 3.5).

Interpersonal competencies align with the interpersonal functions in Part 1. The titles reflect the fact that competency is about implementing the functions rather than simply describing what the functions are. Hence the competency 'manage conflict' is the application of the function 'conflict management'.

Interpersonal competencies are by no means unique to P3 management and may often be expressed in terms of personal behaviours and personality characteristics.

The interpersonal competencies in this section focus on how the functions need to be implemented in the P3 context. Additional behaviours could be added as part of tailoring Praxis.

3.4.1 Communicate

Objectives	The purpose of this competency is to: • impart relevant information • ensure the information is understood.	
Performance criteria *You must be able to*	P1 determine what needs to be communicated and its context P2 identify the target audience and establish any preferred methods and language P3 identify potential barriers to communication and seek to reduce them P4 deliver communication in an effective and timely way P5 ensure that team members and stakeholders have the opportunity to communicate their views P6 seek feedback on the effectiveness of communication and act accordingly.	This competency is about what makes someone a good communicator. The procedural and documentation aspects of communication are covered by stakeholder management and information management.
Knowledge and understanding *You need to know and understand*	K1 the goals of communication K2 the context of the work and its impact on communication K3 different forms of communication K4 factors that affect the effectiveness of communication K5 potential barriers to communication K6 how to tailor a message to its intended audience K7 the media available and their advantages and disadvantages.	

3.4.2 Manage conflict

Objectives	The purpose of this competency is to:
	- utilise the positive aspects of conflict
	- resolve organisational and interpersonal conflict
	- minimise the impact of conflict on objectives.

Performance criteria *You must be able to*	P1	identify potential areas of conflict and, if necessary, take action to prevent or mitigate these
	P2	encourage team members and stakeholders to resolve conflict among themselves
	P3	examine the conflict from all parties' viewpoints
	P4	consider how to resolve the situation and seek external help where appropriate
	P5	negotiate and communicate the agreed solution.

Knowledge and understanding *You need to know and understand*	K1	the goals of conflict management
	K2	the context of the work and its impact on conflict management
	K3	conflict as a normal element of team development
	K4	typical causes and sources of conflict
	K5	the relationship between magnitude and frequency of conflict
	K6	models for conflict resolution
	K7	relevant and available external resources for conflict resolution.

This competency is primarily written from the point of view of a manager who needs to resolve a conflict between others.

However, all members of the team should be aware of the principles of conflict management and seek to prevent negative conflict before it gets to the point where formal resolution is required.

3.4.3 Delegate

Objectives	The purpose of this competency is to: • allocate work effectively to individuals, teams and suppliers within the project, programme or portfolio • use delegation as a motivation and development tool.

Performance criteria *You must be able to*	P1	decide which tasks and responsibilities need to be delegated
	P2	choose people who are competent and available to do the work
	P3	describe and explain the targets and scope of the work
	P4	make sure people understand what needs to be done
	P5	encourage progress by giving advice, support and training
	P6	suggest ways to solve any problems that arise
	P7	monitor delegated work to check that agreed targets are met.

Because delegation is built into P3 management structures and processes, there is a danger that this important skill is taken for granted.

Outside of the explicit delegation situations (e.g. the delegation of responsibility for preparing a business case from sponsor to manager) the general conduct of the work constantly depends upon delegation of work from one party to another.

Knowledge and understanding *You need to know and understand*	K1	the goals of delegation
	K2	the context of the work and its impact on delegation
	K3	how to select and define work for delegation
	K4	when not to delegate
	K5	how to set targets and monitor progress towards them
	K6	how to support those to whom work has been delegated
	K7	the broader impact of delegation on the project and project management team.

3.4.4 Lead

Objectives	The purpose of this competency is to:
	- provide focus and promote commitment to objectives
	- inspire team members to successfully achieve the objectives.

Performance criteria *You must be able to*	P1	clearly communicate a team's collective and individual objectives
	P2	involve team members in planning how to achieve objectives
	P3	adopt a leadership style appropriate to the circumstances
	P4	seek feedback and adapt behaviours accordingly
	P5	encourage and motivate the team
	P6	behave ethically and professionally.

Knowledge and understanding *You need to know and understand*	K1	the goals of leadership
	K2	the context of the work and its impact on leadership
	K3	different styles of leadership and your own natural style
	K4	how leadership can adapt with the development of the team
	K5	the principles of motivation
	K6	the principles of ethical and professional behaviour.

Leadership comes in many forms and is affected by many factors. This competency will need to be adapted for different circumstances. For example, leading a small team with ample opportunity for face-to-face contact requires a different approach to providing 'visionary' leadership to a broad stakeholder community.

Adaptations will also need to take into account the positional power of the individual and their role in the P3 organisation.

3.4.5 Influence

Objectives	The purpose of this competency is to:
	- develop and maintain a high-performing team
- persuade stakeholders to support the objectives
- persuade stakeholders to support the achievement of the objectives.

Performance criteria *You must be able to*	P1 identify ways in which you can best meet the needs of others while meeting your own objectives P2 maintain effective working relationships P3 secure champions for particular aspects of the work P4 develop and present convincing arguments for the principles underlying the objectives P5 communicate persuasively to gain support for the objectives.

Knowledge and understanding *You need to know and understand*	K1 the goals of influencing K2 the context of the work and its impact on influencing K3 how behaviour influences others K4 how to identify people who will positively influence others K5 how to identify obstacles and ways to overcome them K6 ways of assessing the success of influence.

There will be many people at different levels within an organisation that the management team needs to influence.

Inevitably, positional power will be a significant factor for some stakeholders; i.e. the influencing communication needs to come from someone of perceived authority.

Achieving the performance criteria of this competency across the project, programme or portfolio will be a joint effort between the sponsor and manager.

3.4.6 Negotiate

Objectives	The purpose of this competency is to:
	- find solutions to issues involving two or more parties
	- develop beneficial relationships between two or more parties.

Performance criteria *You must be able to*	P1 initiate and conduct a negotiation P2 decide on the desired outcome and minimum acceptable position P3 determine a negotiation strategy P4 use bargaining techniques to reach a mutually acceptable conclusion P5 use external parties if appropriate P6 ensure the implementation of the negotiation's outcomes.

Negotiation is often primarily associated with contract negotiation but it is a skill equally applicable to areas such as conflict resolution and delegation.

Negotiation will be concentrated around the early stages of the life cycle and in the mobilisation activities in particular.

Knowledge and understanding *You need to know and understand*	K1 the goals of negotiation K2 the context of the work and its impact on negotiation K3 different types of negotiation K4 how to plan for negotiation K5 bargaining techniques K6 the role of external parties in areas such as mediation and arbitration K7 how to document the outcomes of the negotiation.

3.4.7 Work within a team

Objectives	The purpose of this competency is to: • create a team from a collection of individuals • develop and maintain the performance of the team.

Performance criteria *You must be able to*	P1 work with others to maximise your and their contribution to team objectives P2 help the team work through the phases of team development P3 demonstrate commitment to the team's objectives P4 manage personal objectives, keep promises and highlight issues as soon as possible.
Knowledge and understanding *You need to know and understand*	K1 the goals of teamwork K2 the context of the work and its impact on teamwork K3 the roles that different individuals perform within a team K4 the typical development phases that a team goes through K5 how a team is affected by the different phases of the life cycle K6 the impact of working as a virtual team K7 the importance of developing mutual respect and trust.

The P3 environment has teams at various levels. Different roles are often team members at one level and team leaders at another level. For example, a project manager leads a project team but may be a member of a programme management team.

Most teams now have some element of virtual working but K5 can always be removed if necessary.

Additional knowledge criteria may be required for situations such as international teams.

3.5 Process competencies

Process is one of three groups of competencies, the other two being delivery (section 3.3) and interpersonal (section 3.4).

Process competencies align with the processes in Part 2. The titles reflect the fact that competency is about implementing the processes rather than simply describing what the processes are. Hence the competency 'identify a project or programme' is the enactment of the 'identification process'.

3.5.1 Identify a project or programme

Objectives	The purpose of this competency is to:
	- develop an outline of the project or programme and assess whether it is likely to be justifiable
	- determine what effort and investment is needed to define the work in detail
	- gain the sponsor's authorisation for the definition phase.

Performance criteria *You must be able to*		
	P1	perform initial requirements management
	P2	identify and review lessons learned and prepare high-level delivery plans
	P3	assess whether the project or programme is justifiable
	P4	decide whether to govern the work as a project or a programme
	P5	plan the definition phase
	P6	prepare and present the brief and definition plan to the sponsor
	P7	assure the quality of the process.

This process may well be omitted from some life cycles, usually where a client or a parent programme has already done the identification.

However, it is likely that any project or programme manager will have to perform this process in some form or other during their career. Even though this competency may not be applicable in every context it is applicable to every manager.

Knowledge and understanding *You need to know and understand*		
	K1	the goals of the process
	K2	the typical activities that make up the process
	K2	the context of the work and its impact on the process
	K3	how to apply the relevant functional procedures at an appropriate level of detail
	K4	the difference between a project and a programme, and the circumstances in which either form of governance is applied
	K5	the purpose and content of a brief and definition plan
	K7	how assurance applies to the process.

3.5.2 Sponsor a project or programme

Objectives	The purpose of this competency is to: • provide ownership of the business case • act as champion for the objectives of the project or programme • make go/no-go decisions at relevant points in the life cycle • address matters outside the scope of the manager's authority • oversee assurance • give ad-hoc support to the management team.

Performance criteria *You must be able to*	P1	communicate the objectives of the project or programme
	P2	oversee the creation of the management team
	P3	motivate and support the management team
	P4	influence stakeholders
	P5	resolve issues outside the manager's control
	P6	make informed decisions about whether the work should be continued or closed
	P7	ensure the work is being managed effectively
	P8	assure the quality of the process.

Knowledge and understanding *You need to know and understand*	K1	the goals of the process
	K2	the typical activities that make up the process
	K3	the context of the work and its impact on the process
	K4	how to assure effective governance
	K5	how to lead, motivate and influence team members and stakeholders
	K6	the principles of project and programme delivery
	K7	a life cycle-based process for the management of projects and programmes.

Not everyone who needs to be competent in sponsorship is called a sponsor. For example, a programme manager may act as sponsor to some of a programme's component projects.

The worst situation for any project, programme or portfolio is that someone has the title 'sponsor' but does not have the skill or time to exhibit this competency.

Since the assurance of P3 management is a responsibility of the sponsor, it may seem odd that this competency includes assurance of sponsorship. It implies the sponsor is assuring themselves. This criterion applies primarily to the situation where a programme or portfolio sponsor needs to assure the sponsorship of component projects or programmes.

3.5.3 Define a project or programme

Objectives	The purpose of this competency is to:
	- develop a detailed picture of the project or programme
	- determine whether the work is justified
	- describe governance policies that set out how the work will be managed
	- gain the sponsor's authorisation for the delivery phase.

Performance criteria *You must be able to*		
	P1	obtain appropriate resources for detailed scope definition
	P2	research, describe and document scope
	P3	plan the governance and delivery of the work
	P4	maintain communication with the sponsor
	P5	consolidate, summarise and present information to the sponsor for authorisation
	P6	perform any pre-authorisation work as necessary and mobilise the project or programme after authorisation
	P7	assure the quality of the process.

Knowledge and understanding *You need to know and understand*		
	K1	the goals of the process
	K2	the typical activities that make up the process
	K3	the context of the work and its impact on the process
	K4	how to perform the relevant functions to suit the context of the work.
	K5	the purpose and content of both governance and delivery plans
	K6	how to identify pre-authorisation work and agree it with the sponsor
	K7	how to mobilise for the first stage or tranche of work
	K8	how assurance applies to the process.

This process can range from a simple exercise performed predominantly by a project manager to, in effect, a project in its own right. These performance criteria are relevant to any scale of work and the competency can be tailored to suit a manager preparing a short document for approval to a team doing extensive research, testing prototypes and managing a complex approval procedure.

The principles also apply to contexts that approach scope in a different way. Agile projects may not require such detailed scope definition at the start of the work but they still need some clear objectives and documented plans – albeit in the agile form.

The knowledge of relevant functions refers to areas as diverse as requirements management, risk management, financial management, organisation management and mobilisation, since they can all have a role in this process.

3.5.4 Deliver a project or programme

Objectives	The purpose of this competency is to: • delegate responsibility for producing deliverables to the appropriate people • monitor the performance of the work and track it against the delivery plans • take action where necessary to keep work in line with plans • escalate issues and replan if necessary • accept work as it is completed • maintain communications with all stakeholders.

Performance criteria *You must be able to*	P1 define, delegate and accept work packages P2 monitor and co-ordinate progress across work packages P3 review and accept completed work P4 predict issues, take corrective action and escalate as required P5 prepare exception plans and submit for authorisation P6 maintain effective communication at all times P7 assure the quality of the process.	When executing this process a manager may be managing a handful of part-time resources or a large and diverse range of internal and external resources. Either way, the principles remain the same but the competency will need to be adapted to reflect how the criteria manifest themselves in a particular context. For example, this could include reference to functional competencies such as manage contracts or manage funding. It could also include reference to specific control techniques such as earned value management if these are required by the context of the work.
Knowledge and understanding *You need to know and understand*	K1 the goals of the process K2 the typical activities that make up the process K3 the context of the work and its impact on the process K4 how to create and delegate work packages K5 techniques for tracking progress including, if required, consolidation across multiple work packages K6 how to identify potential issues and resolve or escalate them K7 how to communicate progress K8 how assurance applies to the process.	

Develop products

Objectives	The purpose of this competency is to: • transfer responsibility for a package of work • execute the package of work • transfer ownership of the finished products.	
Performance criteria *You must be able to*	P1 understand the work package specifications P2 plan the performance of the work P3 ensure the work is performed to the required standard and report progress P4 hand products over to the originator of the work package P5 assure the quality of the process.	This competency covers the P3 management aspects of creating products that achieve objectives. Clearly, it must be complemented by the technical competencies involved in actually performing the work.
Knowledge and understanding *You need to know and understand*	K1 the goals of the process K2 the typical activities that make up the process K3 the context of the work and its impact on the process K4 how to receive a work package K5 planning a work package K6 monitoring and reporting progress K7 the technical skills required to perform the work K8 how to hand over completed products K9 how assurance applies to the process.	

Manage boundaries

Objectives	The purpose of this competency is to: • conclude a stage or tranche in a structured way • prepare for the next tranche or stage.	
Performance criteria *You must be able to*	P1 prepare for the closure of a stage or tranche of work P2 review the previous stage or tranche P3 review governance and plan delivery of the next stage or tranche based on previous performance P4 submit documentation for approval of the next stage or tranche P5 mobilise the next stage or tranche P6 assure the quality of the process.	The criteria for this process are very similar to those in the definition and closure processes. In effect the manage boundaries process is a combined and reduced version of the definition and closure processes as applied to the beginning and end of stages and tranches.
Knowledge and understanding *You need to know and understand*	K1 the goals of the process K2 the typical activities that make up the process K3 the context of the work and its impact on the process K4 how to identify pre-authorisation work and agree it with the sponsor K5 how to submit an authorisation request to the sponsor K6 procedures for mobilising and demobilising resources K7 how assurance applies to the process.	

3.5.5 Close a project or programme

Objectives	The purpose of this competency is to close a project or programme that: • has delivered all its outputs • is no longer justifiable.

Performance criteria *You must be able to*	P1 prepare for the closure of the project or programme P2 hand over products to the appropriate stakeholders P3 review the conduct and performance of the project or programme P4 demobilise the organisation and infrastructure P5 assure the quality of the process.

A project or programme is often closed when all the specified outputs have been produced. That does not necessarily mean that the business case has been achieved, so this competency covers not only the handover of products but also the responsibility for whatever comes after the project or programme has been closed.

The competency should therefore be tailored to reflect whether the project or programme team is responsible for planning follow-on work and handing over responsibility for implementing these plans.

Knowledge and understanding *You need to know and understand*	K1 the goals of the process K2 the typical activities that make up the process K3 the context of the work and its impact on the process K4 how to successfully hand over products K5 how to document and hand over follow-on actions K6 how assurance applies to the process.

3.5.6 Realise benefits

Objectives	The purpose of this competency is to: ● establish the current state of what is being changed ● co-ordinate the delivery of outputs with the management of change ● ensure changes are permanent ● establish whether benefits have been achieved.

Performance criteria *You must be able to*	P1 agree the responsibilities for benefits realisation with relevant stakeholders P2 control output delivery to optimise transition P3 ensure that current performance is benchmarked P4 manage the transition from the current state to that defined by the blueprint P5 embed change and measure the end state performance P6 assure the quality of the process.

To be successful this process requires close co-ordination between those responsible for delivering outputs and those responsible for managing change. On all but the simplest of projects, these are likely to be different people.

When applying this competency to different roles (such as the programme manager or business change manager) it can be tailored to place an emphasis on those parts of the process that are of particular importance to each role.

Knowledge and understanding *You need to know and understand*	K1 the goals of the process K2 the typical activities that make up the process K3 the context of the work and its impact on the process K4 the principles of benefits management K5 the principles of change management K6 how to integrate benefits realisation with project and programme control K7 how assurance applies to the process.

3.5.7 Initiate a portfolio

Objectives	The purpose of this competency is to: • decide what type of portfolio is required • design the portfolio infrastructure • obtain senior-level approval and commitment • implement the portfolio.

Performance criteria *You must be able to*	P1	match the type of portfolio to the host organisation's needs
	P2	provide business justification for the implementation of a portfolio
	P3	submit the case for a portfolio to strategic management
	P4	set up and mobilise the portfolio management infrastructure
	P5	assure the quality of the process.

Knowledge and understanding *You need to know and understand*	K1	the goals of the process
	K2	the typical activities that make up the process
	K3	the context of the work and its impact on the process
	K4	the difference between a standard and a structured portfolio
	K5	the ways in which a portfolio may be governed
	K6	how a portfolio should function alongside business as usual
	K7	the resources needed to support discipline and profession of P3 management
	K8	how to develop a business justification for investment in portfolio management
	K9	how assurance applies to the process.

Initiating a portfolio is not something that is done on a regular basis. In terms of longer-term professional development it is not necessary to have a competency in a process that is only executed once.

However, this competency is useful as a basis for defining an appropriate role and helping to identify the best person to execute the process.

3.5.8 Govern a portfolio

Objectives	The purpose of this competency is to: ● provide ownership of the objectives of the portfolio ● oversee assurance of the portfolio ● promote the discipline and profession of P3 management.

Performance criteria *You must be able to*	P1	champion the objectives of the portfolio
	P2	demonstrate commitment to the discipline and profession of P3 management
	P3	influence senior executives to support the portfolio's objectives
	P4	motivate and support the management team
	P5	resolve issues outside the manager's control
	P6	assure the quality of the process.

Knowledge and understanding *You need to know and understand*	K1	the goals of the process
	K2	the typical activities that make up the process
	K3	the context of the work and its impact on the process
	K4	how to lead, motivate, influence and support the P3 community and stakeholders
	K5	the principles of project and programme delivery
	K6	the importance of organisational culture in the success of portfolios
	K7	the role of strategic functions such as knowledge management, capability maturity, ethics and professionalism
	K8	how assurance applies to the process.

The objectives referred to in the goals may relate to a standard or structured portfolio.

Governing a portfolio will include many people with different roles. This competency is aimed at someone who is accountable for the governance. The detailed responsibilities will be delegated to others.

This is the portfolio equivalent of project and programme sponsorship.

3.5.9 Manage a portfolio

Objectives	The purpose of this competency is to: • assess the suitability of projects and programmes for inclusion in the portfolio • maintain a beneficial and manageable mix of projects and programmes.

Performance criteria *You must be able to*	P1 operate a project and programme selection process P2 create categories of projects and programmes that align with the portfolio objectives P3 prioritise projects and programmes in accordance with the portfolio objectives P4 maintain a balance of projects and programmes in accordance with the defined profile P5 assure the quality of the process.	This competency applies to the whole management team as responsibility for selection, prioritising, etc. will be spread across different roles. The portfolio manager will have accountability for the performance criteria. A performance criterion for the portfolio manager that covers the definition of supporting roles and consequent delegation could be added.
Knowledge and understanding *You need to know and understand*	K1 the goals of the process K2 the typical activities that make up the process K3 the context of the work and its impact on the process K4 schemes of delegation for selection of projects and programmes K5 characteristics used in categorising projects and programmes K6 mechanisms for prioritising projects and programmes K7 tools that assist with balancing a portfolio K8 how assurance applies to the process.	

3.5.10 Co-ordinate projects and programmes

Objectives	The purpose of this competency is to: • consolidate information from the component projects and programmes to understand the portfolio as a whole • monitor the performance of the portfolio against its objectives • manage the inter-relationships between projects and programmes.

Performance criteria *You must be able to*	P1 co-ordinate governance across the component parts of the portfolio P2 consolidate and co-ordinate plans across the portfolio P3 manage overall resource and financial capacity P4 assure the quality of the process.
Knowledge and understanding *You need to know and understand*	K1 the goals of the process K2 the typical activities that make up the process K3 the context of the work and its impact on the process K4 tools and techniques for normalising data K5 effective methods for summarising and consolidating progress information K6 how to manage complex inter-relationships between multiple projects and programmes K7 how assurance applies to the process.

This competency applies to the whole management team as responsibility for complex co-ordination will be spread across different roles.

The portfolio manager will have accountability for the performance criteria. A performance criterion for the portfolio manager that covers the definition of supporting roles and consequent delegation could be added.

The co-ordination of projects is clearly something that portfolio management has in common with programmes. This competency could be adapted for use in a programme management role – perhaps a member of a PMO responsible for assisting the programme manager with the mechanics of co-ordinating multiple projects.

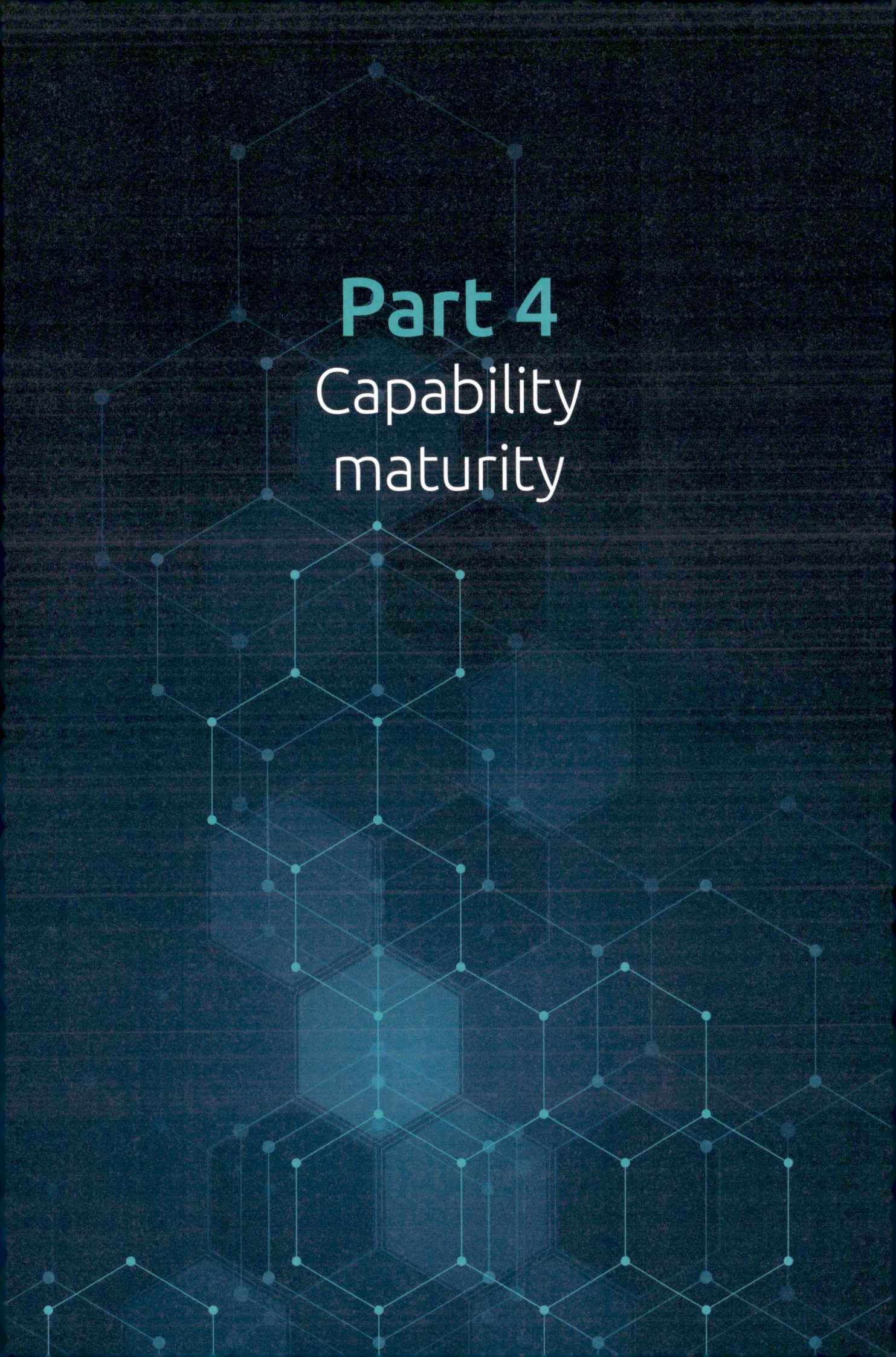
Part 4
Capability maturity

4.1 Overview

The purpose of a capability maturity model is to provide guidance in the development of an organisation's ability to deliver projects, programmes and portfolios effectively and efficiently. This can be viewed in two ways: internally or externally.

Viewing capability maturity internally is simply about developing the organisation's ability so that more projects and programmes deliver their objectives (effectiveness) and less investment is wasted (efficiency). A large proportion of the benefit of developing capability maturity for internal purposes is achieved simply by examining internal processes and making sure they are embedded in the culture of the organisation. Even a poor or inappropriate maturity model can act as a catalyst for this improvement, although the more appropriate the model the greater the stability and effectiveness of the resulting improvement.

Viewing capability maturity externally concerns the reassurance of stakeholders. For example, where a customer is about to invest in a project or programme that is to be delivered by a third party, they will be more confident in the performance of a third party that has demonstrably achieved a high level of capability maturity. This external view implicitly requires the capability maturity of different organisations to be compared; i.e. they should have been assessed against the same model.

Clearly, the best use of capability maturity would be where organisations were assessed against the same model for external purposes but there was sufficient flexibility within that model to account for the difference in context of each organisation's P3 management.

The underpinning principle of Praxis is that P3 management comprises a broad set of components that are assembled and tailored to suit the context of each unique piece of work. The Praxis capability maturity model aims to be flexible enough to be adaptable to different contexts while being consistent enough to allow comparison between different organisations.

> The high-level attributes in the capability descriptions should be read in conjunction with the corresponding function, particularly when interpreting the attributes in the context of the difference between projects, programmes and portfolios.

This is achieved by setting the attributes that describe different levels of maturity at a fairly high level. These attributes are supplemented with advice on their application. The result is not dissimilar to the approach taken by ISO 9000, where each organisation can develop a quality system to suit its own context but, provided the quality system aligns with the ISO 9000 principles, it can still be accredited to a universally accepted standard.

The Praxis maturity model adapts the principles of the CMMI® model by applying separate measures for capability and maturity. Figure 4.1 illustrates the matrix of capability and maturity; only a sample of the functional framework is shown.

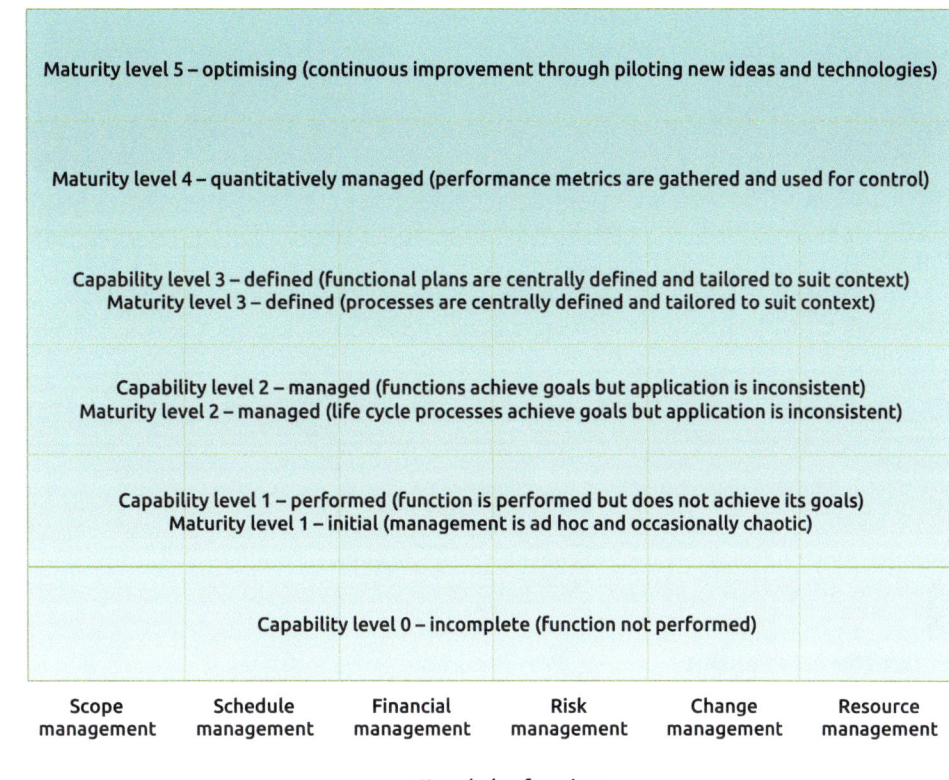

Figure 4.1 The matrix of capability and maturity

The capability side of the model follows the structure of the functional framework, so that capability can be developed and assessed on a function-by-function basis. An organisation will identify the functions that are appropriate to its context and develop its capability accordingly.

Maturity is achieved by developing capability and then implementing the life cycle processes that apply the functions in an integrated and co-ordinated way. Maturity is increased by developing capability in the relevant functions and then embedding the appropriate methods (project, programme or portfolio).

To aid with improvement, Praxis describes each function using a set of indicators. For each indicator, attributes are described that illustrate the different levels of capability. Because the fundamental principles of managing functions are very similar a large proportion of the indicators and attributes are common to all functions. These are collected together as the generic goals of capability. Indicators and attributes that relate to specific goals are then described for each function.

Maturity levels are described for each life cycle process. This does not imply that an organisation's maturity can be defined for individual processes. An organisation will tailor its overall life cycles according to the context of its projects, programmes and portfolios. Maturity is then judged to be the level achieved in all the appropriate processes, as shown in Figure 4.2.

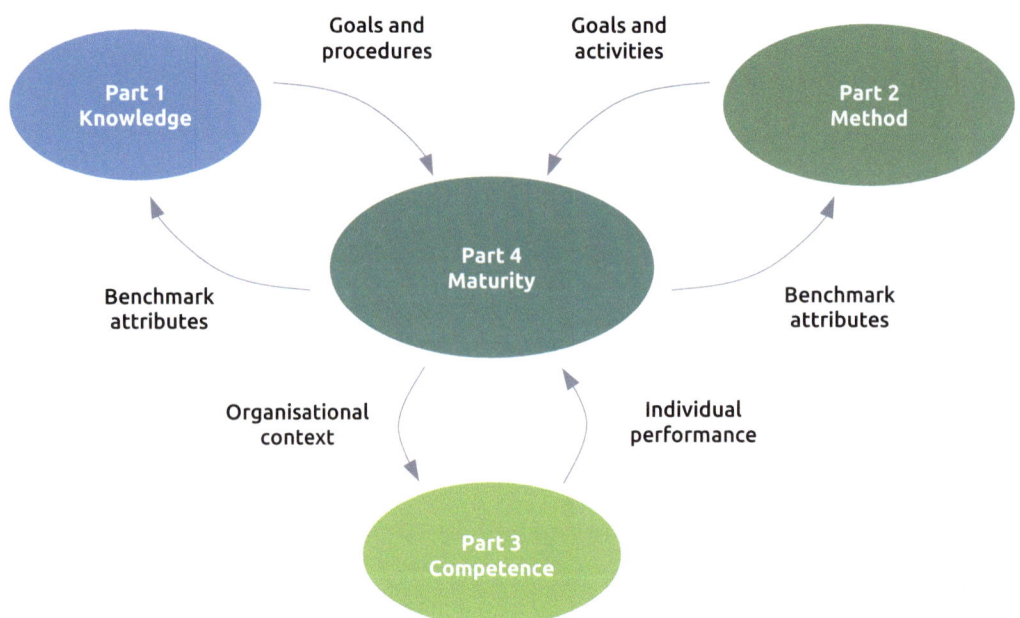

Figure 4.2 Maturity relationships

The capability maturity model derives its structure from Parts 1 (Knowledge) and 2 (Method). In return it describes a series of attributes that describe a standard development path for functions and processes.

Capability and maturity at level 2 require competent people so the competencies in Praxis (Part 3) are pitched at this level. The maturity model provides an organisational context for the development of individual competencies.

4.2 Capability

To reach a level of capability for a function, the organisation must achieve the appropriate generic goals as they relate to the function, as well as the specific goals of the function. The goals are cumulative; for example, to reach level 3 in risk management the organisation must have achieved the generic goals and risk management specific goals at levels 2 and 3, as demonstrated through the attributes listed.

Specific attributes are only described for levels 2 and 3:

- **At level 0** The function is rarely, if ever, performed in a way consistent with its description in Part 1. This level represents a lack of formal P3 management.
- **At level 1** The function achieves its goals in an ad-hoc manner. This is the key factor regardless of any specific attributes. Level 1 represents an organisation that manages to achieve goals through the work of a few talented individuals.
- **At level 2** The goals are generally achieved using competent people as described in Part 3. P3 management is effective but could be more efficient.
- **At level 3** The organisation co-ordinates P3 management to achieve efficiencies and ensure that good practice is consistent and embedded in the organisational culture.

4.2.1 Generic goals

Level 2

- Establish an organisational policy for performing the function
- Develop and maintain a plan for the function
- Provide sufficient, competent resources for performing the function
- Assign responsibility and authority for performing the function
- Monitor and control the function
- Perform assurance of the function.

Level 3

- Establish centrally defined procedures and practices
- Tailor procedures and practices to suit the context
- Perform independent assurance of the function
- Collect and utilise lessons learned.

Generic attributes

	Level 1	Level 2	Level 3
Description	The function is either not performed or is only partially performed. Where it is partially performed, the approach is ad hoc and succeeds through individual effort.	An organisational policy exists that requires the function to be performed. The function is performed by competent people and plans exist for how the function will be performed. The procedure is monitored and controlled.	The plan for performing the function is based on a centrally defined approach that is tailored for each project, programme and/or portfolio. Lessons learned are collected and utilised.
Indicators	**Level 1 attributes**	**Level 2 attributes**	**Level 3 attributes**
Roles and responsibilities	No formal responsibilities are assigned for the function.	Role descriptions contain responsibilities for the function.	Role descriptions conform to organisational standards, tailored to the context. Statements of authority and accountability are documented.
Information management	There is some ad-hoc documentation relating to the function but it is incomplete.	There is sufficient documentation relating to the function.	All documentation is based on organisational standards, has been tailored to the context of the work and is under configuration control.

Table continues

	Level 1	Level 2	Level 3
Assurance	The function is not assessed for the achievement of the specific goals.	The function is checked to ensure that it is being performed effectively; i.e. that the specific goals are being met.	The function is independently checked to ensure that it is based on organisational standards, has been tailored to the context of the work and is being performed effectively throughout the life cycle.
Budget	There is no identified budget for performing the function.	Budgets exist for all aspects of the function.	Budgets exist and include costs that have been estimated according to organisational standards.
Interfaces	The interfaces between this and other functions are not understood.	The interfaces between this and other functions are understood and documented.	The interfaces between this and other functions are understood, documented and acted upon in a consistent manner.
Plan	There is some evidence of relevant tools and techniques being used but no formal procedures are applied.	A management plan exists for the performance of the function.	The management plan is based on an organisational standard with adjustments to suit the context of the work. This is continually reviewed throughout the life cycle.
Initiate		Members of the management team are competent in the function.	All roles that may be involved in the function include appropriate responsibilities and performance criteria in their descriptions.
Specific goals		The procedural attributes designed to achieve the specific goals of the function are described in sections 4.2.2 to 4.2.14.	

4.2.2 Assurance

Assurance should:

- review management planning
- monitor effectiveness of functions and processes
- give stakeholders confidence that the work is being managed effectively and efficiently.

Indicators	Level 2 attributes
Process	The overall management of a project, programme or portfolio is reviewed to ensure it is fit for purpose. This includes life cycle-based processes and organisation structure.
Planning	The existence of effective management plans is checked.
Control	Quality control activities and results are reviewed to ensure plans are being implemented.
Report	The results of assurance are communicated to stakeholders.

Indicators	Level 3 attributes
Process	The overall management of a project, programme or portfolio is reviewed to confirm that it accords to organisational standards and has been effectively tailored to match the context of the work.
Planning	Management plans are reviewed against organisational standards and the context of the work. An independent review is conducted of whether all appropriate management plans exist.
Control	The use of quality control results to record and refine lessons learned is reviewed. An independent review is conducted of whether all appropriate control documentation exists.
Report	The assurance management plan is discussed with stakeholders and regular updates ensure high levels of confidence in the management of the work.

The primary concern of assurance at level 2 is to confirm that the P3 management team is applying good practice to the management of the work.

The assurance resources may not be sufficiently experienced to challenge the management team about the processes, procedures, techniques and documentation used.

Note: assurance is a generic attribute of all functional capabilities. No individual function can be claimed to be at level 2 unless assurance is at level 2.

At level 3 the assurance resources should be able to critically review the processes, procedures, techniques and documentation used by the management team.

This review will include comparison with organisational standards and lessons learned from previous projects and programmes. There will be particular emphasis on how the management team has tailored the organisational standards to its own context.

The assurance reviews will also check that new lessons learned are being recorded and input to the knowledge management function.

Stakeholders will be consulted to determine their levels of confidence in the management of the work.

Note: assurance is a generic attribute of all functional capabilities. No individual function can be claimed to be at level 3 unless assurance is at level 3.

4.2.3 Support

Support should:

- provide administrative support to P3 managers
- support the governance of P3 management
- provide specialist technical support
- conduct assurance.

Indicators	Level 2 attributes
Administrative support	Resources are available to provide assistance that allows P3 managers to spend more time on management rather than administration.
Support of governance	Resources are available to assist in the development of management plans and maintain lessons learned.
Technical support	Technical specialists in different P3 management functions are available to provide advice and guidance.
Assurance	Resources are available to conduct assurance reviews and audits.

Indicators	Level 3 attributes
Administrative support	Support offices are constituted at appropriate levels for projects, programmes and portfolios within the host organisation.
Support of governance	Support offices provide assistance in the development of the discipline and profession of P3 management.
Technical support	Technical specialists are integrated into P3 management teams as experts in specific functions.
Assurance	Assurance resources provide consultative support to P3 management teams who need to act on the findings of assurance reports.

There is a multitude of ways in which a support infrastructure can be constituted. It would be misleading to suggest that one set of indicators and attributes represents good practice in P3 support.

More than any other, this capability should be seen as a starting point for the development of a capability that matches the way support is constituted in any given organisation.

4.2.4 Organisation management

Organisation management should:

- design an organisation appropriate to the scope of work to be managed
- identify and appoint members of the management team
- maintain and adapt the organisation throughout the life cycle.

Indicators	Level 2 attributes
Initiate	An organisation structure is designed, team members are assigned and roles are documented.
Maintain	Ad-hoc and reactive adjustments are made to the management team.
Close	Members of the management team are released back to business as usual.

Indicators	Level 3 attributes
Initiate	A procedure is followed that identifies potential team members and adheres to an appropriate selection process.
Maintain	The organisation is formally reviewed at appropriate points in the life cycle with structure adapted and roles adjusted as necessary. New appointments follow the selection process.
Close	The performance of management team members is reviewed and communicated back to line managers.

At level 2 members of the management team are often assigned based purely on availability rather than through a selection process (which is a characteristic of level 3).

4.2.5 Stakeholder management

Stakeholder management should:

- ensure that the views and attitudes of all stakeholders are understood
- influence stakeholders to be supportive of the work wherever possible
- maximise the impact of supportive stakeholders
- minimise the impact of unsupportive stakeholders.

Indicators	Level 2 attributes
Identify	Key stakeholders are identified and documents exist with adequate information to achieve specific objectives.
Assess	Stakeholders are assessed for interest and influence, and the results are documented.
Plan communications	Communications are planned and communication activities are adequately resourced.
Engage	Stakeholders are engaged according to the communications plan.

Indicators	Level 3 attributes
Identify	A range of techniques is utilised to ensure all stakeholders are identified. Stakeholder checklists are available derived from lessons learned.
Assess	Stakeholders are assessed using consistent techniques in accordance with the management plan. Standard documentation is adapted to suit the context.
Plan communications	Communications are planned according to organisational policies that have been adapted as necessary. Plans are reviewed throughout the life cycle. All appropriate channels of communication are utilised; supportive stakeholders with appropriate seniority are available and assigned to communication activities.
Engage	Stakeholders are engaged according to the communications plan. Effectiveness is monitored and results fed back into revised plans.

The underlying techniques of stakeholder management are not greatly affected by the setting of the work.

At level 2, stakeholder management is deemed adequate if the key stakeholders are identified and communications are sufficient to keep them engaged.

It is recognised that some less influential stakeholders may be missed and the focus will be on minimising the impact of unsupportive stakeholders rather than maximising support from supportive stakeholders.

The management team provide the resource for engagement and may not always encourage supportive stakeholders to influence unsupportive stakeholders.

At level 3, stakeholder management is comprehensive. The identification of stakeholders is thorough and covers both supportive and unsupportive stakeholders equally.

Stakeholder information is regularly updated and appropriate people from outside the management team are utilised to engage with stakeholders.

Communications are also thorough and all appropriate channels are used to maximum effect.

4.2.6 Business case management

Business case management should:

- summarise context and delivery in a single document
- explain the desirability, achievability and viability of the proposed work
- develop the primary document that will be used to support a go/no-go decision at all gates in the life cycle
- update and maintain the business case throughout the life cycle.

Indicators	Level 2 attributes
Summarise and present the desirability of the work	Stakeholder requirements for the chosen solution are summarised to clearly demonstrate why the work is desirable. This always includes the 'do nothing' option.
Summarise and present the achievability of the work	Planning is performed to level 2 capability and delivery documentation for the chosen solution is summarised to clearly demonstrate how the work is achievable.
Summarise and present the viability of the work	Investment appraisal is performed to level 2 capability and the results summarised to clearly demonstrate the viability of the work.
Update the business case	The business case is reviewed, updated and used to support key decision points.

Indicators	Level 3 attributes
Summarise and present the desirability of the work	Stakeholder requirements in relation to all solutions considered are summarised. This clearly demonstrates why the work as specified is the most desirable approach.
Summarise and present the achievability of the work	Planning is performed to level 3 capability and delivery documentation for the chosen solution is summarised to clearly demonstrate how the work is achievable.
Summarise and present the viability of the work	Investment appraisal is performed to level 3 capability and the results summarised to clearly demonstrate the viability of the work.
Update the business case	The business case is under constant review and issues that will potentially impact the business case are forecast in advance.

A business case is fundamental to any project or programme, whatever the level of capability maturity. There has to be a good and demonstrable reason for investing in the work. For that reason, the differences between level 2 and level 3 capability are, at first sight, quite subtle.

The principal differences are the amount of background information given (with respect to options considered but not recommended) and the frequency with which the business case is reviewed.

4.2.7 Control

Control should:

- review performance against baselines
- evaluate the effect of actual performance on future plans
- take action as required to achieve planning targets or agree revised targets.

Indicators	Level 2 attributes
Monitor performance	Performance of key delivery functions is monitored (e.g. delivery schedule, scope and cost). Reports are prepared and communicated to relevant members of the management team.
Assess performance	Performance is assessed on a function-by-function basis (e.g. Gantt based slip charts for schedule impact).
Corrective action	Corrective action is taken on a function-by-function basis with escalation being ad hoc.

Indicators	Level 3 attributes
Monitor performance	Performance of all delivery functions is monitored (e.g. communications; consideration of change requests). Integrated reports are prepared and communicated to relevant members of the management team.
Assess performance	Performance is assessed on an integrated basis (e.g. earned value analysis combining schedule and cost).
Corrective action	Corrective action is taken on an integrated basis with escalation being based on tolerances and clear escalation procedures. Exception plans are formally assessed and authorised or the work terminated.

All functions of a project, programme or portfolio must be controlled. The key difference between level 2 and level 3 capability is the degree to which data from the functions is combined to provide a more integrated approach.

4.2.8 Information management

Information management should:

- capture data accurately and consistently
- develop usable information from raw data
- maintain information securely and accessibly during its useful life
- support effective decision making and communication.

Indicators	Level 2 attributes
Collect and create data	All necessary data is collected or created.
Document and store information	Data is presented as information that supports decision making processes and keeps stakeholders informed. Version control and ownership of documents is clear.
Access and disseminate	Documentation is accessible but controlled. Dissemination is recorded and traceable.
Archive	Documents are archived when no longer required.
Destroy	Destruction of information is ad hoc unless required for contractual or legal reasons.

Indicators	Level 3 attributes
Collect and create data	All necessary data is collected or created in a demonstrably consistent manner.
Document and store information	Presentation standards are implemented across all documentation. Key documents are subject to full configuration management. Systems exist to support workflow, secure storage and backup.
Access and disseminate	Levels of access are defined and controlled. There are systems in place to manage authorisations and check dissemination before release.
Archive	Documents are archived when no longer required but document histories are retained.
Destroy	Storage is periodically reviewed and unnecessary documentation destroyed.

The need for assessing capability in information management is less about the inherent complexity of the work and more about its external environment. A large and highly complex piece of work may be very open and straightforward from an information point of view, whereas a small project may be commercially sensitive and in need of careful information management.

In an environment where security is important it may be a necessity to have level 3 maturity in information management – nothing less would be adequate.

4.2.9 Scope management

Scope management should:

- identify stakeholder wants and needs
- specify outputs, outcomes and benefits that meet agreed requirements
- maintain scope throughout the life cycle.

Indicators	Level 2 attributes
Manage requirements	Requirements are captured from key stakeholders.
Develop solution	A solution is developed from the documented requirements.
Implement solution	Change requests are logged and assessed with results communicated to the requesting stakeholder. Version control of products is maintained.
Manage benefits	Benefits are identified, documented and their implementation is planned.

Indicators	Level 3 attributes
Manage requirements	A variety of techniques are used to capture requirements from all stakeholders, fully analysed and baselined.
Develop solution	There is evidence that a range of solutions has been considered and the specification is thorough.
Implement solution	Change requests are logged and all aspects of their impact on the work thoroughly assessed. Responsibility for change approval is clearly defined and budgets allocated. Where appropriate the development of products is recorded within a configuration management system.
Manage benefits	Standard format profiles exist for benefits and dis-benefits. Quantitative metrics are used to confirm the achievement of benefits.

This scope management capability summarises the capabilities for the functions that make up scope management.

As it stands this capability is suited to an organisation that runs less complex projects that include benefits management.

In situations where an organisation does not operate all the scope management functions (e.g. a contracting organisation) or where scope is complex (e.g. business change programmes), it will be better to use the relevant individual scope management functions.

Requirements management

Requirements management should:

- ensure that all relevant stakeholders have the opportunity to express their wants and needs
- reconcile multiple stakeholder requirements to create a single viable set of objectives
- achieve stakeholder consensus on a baseline set of requirements.

Indicators	Level 2 attributes
Capture	Key stakeholders are consulted about requirements.
Analyse	The viability of all requirements is assessed.
Consult	Where necessary, clarification is sought and feedback provided to stakeholders.

Indicators	Level 3 attributes
Capture	All requirements are captured from appropriate stakeholders using a range of techniques. Stakeholders have confidence that their wants and needs will be considered fully and fairly.
Analyse	The implications of stakeholder wants and needs are fully understood with gaps, overlaps and conflicts removed.
Consult	All appropriate stakeholders are consulted. The best possible level of consensus is achieved and documented in a set of well specified baseline requirements.

At level 2 requirements management this may be more focused on responding to stakeholders who actively involve themselves in the procedure.

As a result some less proactive stakeholders may be missed, resulting in some complexity being missed in the early stages.

It could also be the case that less influential stakeholders are not involved and some others may not have full confidence in the procedure.

At level 3 the input from proactive stakeholders will be the starting point for the involvement of less active stakeholders by the management team.

Appropriate techniques could include surveys and benefit identification workshops. This may also be illustrated by the implementation of structured requirements management techniques such as value management.

Solutions development

Solutions development should:

- evaluate baseline requirements and alternative solutions to achieve them
- select the optimum solution
- create a specification for the solution.

Indicators	Level 2 attributes
Evaluate and select	Alternative solutions are evaluated.
Assess value improvements	There is consideration of how value may be optimised.
Produce specification	Comprehensive specifications exist.

Indicators	Level 3 attributes
Evaluate and select	A range of alternative solutions is fully evaluated, including innovative approaches.
Assess value improvements	A range of formal value improvement techniques is applied in order to arrive at the preferred solution.
Produce specification	Specifications are complete, thorough and appropriate to the planned development method.

At level 2 the management team may focus on the more obvious solutions that can be assessed more quickly using existing knowledge, expertise and/or technology.

At level 3 more time is spent on considering less obvious or more innovative solutions.

This may be illustrated by the implementation of structured requirements management techniques such as value management.

Benefits management

Benefits management should:

- define the benefits and dis-benefits of the proposed work
- establish measurement mechanisms
- implement any change needed in order to realise benefits
- measure improvement and compare it with the business case.

Indicators	Level 2 attributes
Quantify	Benefits are quantified and documented. There is evidence supporting the estimates of benefit quantities.
Value	Financial benefits are valued and documentation shows the reasoning behind the valuations.
Plan benefits realisation	Plans for realising benefits exist and are updated throughout the life cycle.
Plan benefits realisation	There is some measurement of pre-change metrics but this may be inconsistent. Benefits reviews may be left to individual business-as-usual units.

Indicators	Level 3 attributes
Quantify	Full benefit profiles are prepared for benefits. These are reviewed throughout the life cycle. New benefits profiles are produced throughout the life cycle as new benefits are identified. There is a clear link between updated benefit profiles and the business case.
Value	Sophisticated techniques are used to value non-financial benefits and documentation shows the reasoning behind the valuations.
Plan benefits realisation	All benefits realisation activities are included in a separate benefits realisation plan or as a section of the main project or programme delivery plan. These plans are regularly updated and interfaces maintained.
Realise benefits	Metrics affected by change are baselined before change is applied and tracked throughout the realisation period. A full benefits review is conducted on completion and actual net benefit is compared with the original business case.

As is the case with all references to benefits, dis-benefits are deemed to be covered as well.

The complexity of the benefits management function is a defining factor in deciding whether a piece of work is a project or a programme.

On projects where there is a simple relationship between a small number of outputs and a benefit, level 2 will be perfectly adequate.

At level 2, identification of new benefits during the life cycle may not be comprehensive.

Where there is a many-to-many relationship between multiple outputs and benefits the work will most likely be run as a programme and level 3 capability will be more appropriate.

Change control

Change control should:

- capture stakeholders' requests to make changes to scope
- ensure that requests are only approved if viable and achievable
- integrate changes into the existing scope.

Indicators	Level 2 attributes
Request	Change requests are submitted and logged.
Review	All change requests are reviewed against high-level objectives and stakeholders informed of results.
Assess	All change requests that pass the review are assessed.
Decision	A decision is made and documented for all assessed requests.
Implement	All approved changes are implemented.
Feedback	Stakeholders who originate requests are informed of the final decision.

Indicators	Level 3 attributes
Request	Change requests are submitted and logged in a consistent format fully describing the nature of and reason for the change.
Review	All change requests are reviewed for consistency with high-level objectives. Changes that are not consistent with high-level objectives are rejected.
Assess	All change requests that pass the review are objectively assessed in detail for their viability, desirability and practicality. Recommended action is documented and submitted for a decision.
Decision	A group or individual has clear accountability and responsibility for the final decision. Decisions for assessed requests are made in a timely manner.
Implement	Approved changes are built into all scope and delivery documentation.
Feedback	Stakeholders who originate requests are kept informed of progress and the rationale behind the decision. All relevant stakeholders are kept up to date with scope changes.

Scope change requests can apply to any objective; i.e. outputs, outcomes or benefits.

Change control is most easily applied to outputs, and physical products in particular. Where the change control procedure is applied more broadly to benefits there must be evidence that all consequences for business as usual, change management activity and the business case have been considered.

Configuration management

Configuration management should:

- identify the products that will be treated as configuration items
- support the assessment of change requests and document the results of change control
- maintain the validity of the configuration and the accuracy of the configuration management system.

Indicators	Level 2 attributes
Identify	The configuration covers the key technical deliverables.
Control	Configuration management covers version control and basic configuration records.
Status accounting	Status accounts are produced on an ad-hoc basis and focus on the statistics of the configuration management system.
Verification and audit	Physical and functional audits are performed.

Indicators	Level 3 attributes
Identify	A configuration that fully covers the outputs is identified and indexed. Inter-relationships between configuration items are fully and consistently documented. Key P3 management documents are included in the configuration. The configuration is baselined.
Control	Configuration records are regularly updated with information from change control and quality control.
Status accounting	Status accounts are produced on a regular basis and are used to highlight management issues.
Verification and audit	Regular physical and functional audits are performed and reported against the baseline configuration.

At level 2 management documents may not be included in the configuration and audits may be ad hoc rather than planned.

The type of management issues highlighted in a status report at level 3 could be, for example, that a small number of stakeholders produce the majority of change requests, or one part of the specification is particularly targeted by change requests. In either case action may be appropriate to address a possible stakeholder issue or weakness in the specification respectively.

4.2.10 Schedule management

Schedule management should:

- determine timescales for the work
- calculate profiles of resource demand
- present schedule reports suitable for different stakeholders.

Indicators	Level 2 attributes
Identify work	Work required to deliver objectives is identified and documented appropriately. This is updated regularly with a frequency that matches the scale and complexity of the work.
Time scheduling	Single or multiple models are built that are adequate for the context and complexity of the work. These are periodically updated as the work is monitored and controlled. Time estimates are mainly subjective and only single-point estimates are used. The model is analysed using methods adequate for the context and complexity of the work. Analyses are repeated to reflect progress.
Resource scheduling	Resource estimates are mainly subjective and based on a general knowledge of the types of resource employed. The model is analysed using methods adequate for the context and complexity of the work. Analyses are repeated to reflect progress.
Report	Standard reports are distributed at regular intervals.

Indicators	Level 3 attributes
Identify work	Activities required to manage functions are identified and included in the scheduling model.
Time scheduling	Schedules are updated at regular, frequent intervals as the work is monitored and controlled. All technical and managerial activity is included in the models. Time estimates are based on objective data wherever possible. Analyses are repeated to reflect progress and test 'what-if' scenarios.
Resource scheduling	Resource estimates are based on objective data wherever possible and on a specific knowledge of the resources employed. The influence of different resources on the schedule is understood. Analyses are repeated to reflect progress and test 'what-if' scenarios.
Report	Stakeholders are regularly provided with schedule reports that are tailored to their differing needs.

Scheduling approaches are closely linked to scope complexity, which means there is a wide range of 'appropriate' methods.

As complexity increases, different modelling techniques may be required to match the needs of different sections of work. For example, programme scheduling will cover a greater breadth and focus on the consolidation and summarisation of multiple project and business change schedules.

It is recognised that at level 2 the modelling and scheduling should be adequate but less sophisticated than it could be. It is also likely that scheduling focuses on the activity required to deliver outputs and may not apply the same rigour to management activities such as communication, risk response and procurement.

At level 3 the organisation is expected to use approaches that are more than just adequate and introduce sophistication that reduces risk and increases shareholder satisfaction.

The management activities involved in areas such as communications, risk responses and procurement should be modelled and scheduled with the same rigour as the production activities and integrated with them.

Having built an accurate model of the schedule a level 3 organisation will use it to test alternative scenarios, not only to solve issues but also constantly refine the schedule.

Stakeholders will be able to obtain up-to-date schedule information that is tailored to their requirements rather than relying on standard schedule reports.

4.2.11 Financial management

Financial management should:

- estimate the cost of achieving the objectives
- assess the viability of achieving the objectives
- secure funds and manage their release throughout the life cycle
- set up and run financial systems
- monitor and control expenditure.

Indicators	Level 2 attributes
Estimate costs	Top-down estimates are performed early in the life cycle and refined bottom-up as specifications become available.
Investment appraisal	Simple appraisal techniques are documented in the business case.
Secure funding	Routine sources of funding are confirmed.
Develop budget	An overall budget for the work is documented and progress reports track against this budget.
Financial control	Actual costs are accurate and used to track against budget.

Indicators	Level 3 attributes
Estimate costs	Cost estimates are reviewed throughout the life cycle and plans updated.
Investment appraisal	Detailed quantitative techniques are used to assess the viability of the work.
Secure funding	A variety of funding mechanisms is considered and the optimum approach is chosen.
Develop budget	Separate budgets are identified for different aspects of the work. Contingencies and management reserves are used.
Financial control	Financial systems are able to track actual costs against categories of cost as defined in a cost breakdown structure.

This financial management capability summarises the capabilities for the functions that make up financial management. This summary capability will typically be more relevant for projects that are entirely funded from a single source and use existing financial control systems.

The more detailed subsidiary capabilities should be used where:

- funding is external and/or comes from multiple sources
- the business case requires more sophisticated investment appraisal
- the scale and complexity of the work requires dedicated financial control systems.

Investment appraisal

Investment appraisal should:

- assess the viability of achieving the objectives
- support the production of a business case.

Indicators	Level 2 attributes
Collect inputs	Stakeholders are informed of the criteria to be appraised.
	All objective data is collected. Where subjective data is used it is identified as such and appropriately structured.
Appraise	Appraisal techniques are adequate for the justification of the work.
Report	The appraisal is communicated to stakeholders as appropriate and is the primary input to go/no-go decisions by the sponsor.

Indicators	Level 3 attributes
Collect inputs	Stakeholders are involved in determining the criteria to be appraised.
	All objective and subjective data are collected. Subjective data is quantified wherever possible.
Appraise	Appraisal techniques are sophisticated and cover all aspects of the data collected.
	Multiple techniques will probably be used to confirm viability from differing perspectives.
Report	The appraisal is continually reviewed throughout the life cycle. There are agreed tolerances for controlling escalation of deviation from baselined appraisal.

Level 2 capability is concerned with ensuring appraisal supports go/no-go decisions with acceptable reliability.

At level 3 there should be consistent principles guiding investment appraisal across the range of complexity.

Stakeholders will be actively involved in determining the criteria for appraisal and all subjective data will be subject to analysis.

The investment appraisal will be regularly reviewed as delivery documentation is updated with progress.

Funding

Funding should:

- determine the best way to fund the work
- secure commitment from the fund holders
- manage the release of funds throughout the life cycle.

Indicators	Level 2 attributes
Identify sources	Regular funding sources are investigated and qualitatively assessed.
Negotiate terms	Usual terms are accepted with limited negotiation.
Administer funding	Funding is drawn down according to approved budgets and cash flow forecasts.

Indicators	Level 3 attributes
Identify sources	All possible sources of funding are investigated and quantitatively compared. The benefits of the chosen funding approach over others are demonstrable.
Negotiate terms	Specialist resources are employed to negotiate optimum terms and conditions.
Administer funding	Systems to administer the drawdown of funds are fully integrated with cost control systems.

The provision of internal funding for less complex projects is normally more straightforward and level 2 maturity is adequate.

Level 2 is also representative of circumstances where multiple projects, and possibly programmes, are consistently funded in the same way.

Level 3 maturity is more appropriate to external funding of larger projects and programmes where the arrangements are often unique to the specific context.

Greater integration between the administration of funds and control of expenditure is required at this level to ensure efficient use of facilities provided.

Budgeting and cost control

Budgeting and cost control should:

- determine the income and expenditure profiles for the work
- develop budgets and align them with funding
- implement systems to manage income and expenditure.

Indicators	Level 2 attributes
Refine base estimates	Cost estimating is performed bottom-up for all aspects of delivery.
Estimate reserves	Sums are set aside for contingency reserve and management reserve.
Accounting control	Cost control systems are able to track actual costs in multiple categories and report these against baseline.

Indicators	Level 3 attributes
Refine base estimates	Cost estimates are allocated to categories of cost in a cost breakdown structure.
Estimate reserves	There is a quantifiable link between the risk responses and the contingency budget. Management reserves are based on previous experience and analysis of the specific requirements of the project or programme.
Accounting control	Cost control systems are able to track and report by cost attribute, category and steps in the payment process.

At level 2 a more qualitative approach to estimating is allowable for less complex projects. The key factors are that the detailed estimating is performed and the reserve budgets exist.

Actual vs. budget reports may be based purely on total expenditure and not broken down further.

At level 3 the management team should be able to report on costs in multiple ways and demonstrate that reserve budgets have been quantitatively estimated.

4.2.12 Risk management

Risk management should:

- ensure that levels of overall risk within a project, programme or portfolio are compatible with organisational objectives
- ensure that individual risks and responses are identified
- minimise the impact of threats to objectives
- optimise opportunities within the scope of work.

Indicators	Level 2 attributes
Identify	There is identification of both threats and opportunities.
Assess	Risk events are assessed in terms of probability, impact and timing.
Plan responses	Risk responses are planned and response activities are adequately resourced.
Implement responses	Risk responses are implemented.

Indicators	Level 3 attributes
Identify	A range of techniques is used to identify appropriate threats and opportunities. These are continually reviewed throughout the life cycle.
Assess	Risk assessment is conducted from a number of perspectives, including strategic, operational, commercial and internal to the initiative. A range of qualitative and quantitative techniques is used as appropriate. Overall risk is matched to the organisation's risk appetite.
Plan responses	Risk responses are planned according to organisational policies that have been adapted as necessary. Plans are reviewed throughout the life cycle. All appropriate response types are utilised and management team members with appropriate seniority are available and assigned to response activities. Responses are developed in line with the organisation's risk attitude.
Implement responses	Risk responses are implemented in accordance with the risk response plan. Effectiveness is monitored and results fed back into revised plans.

Risk management probably has the broadest range of techniques of all the delivery functions. It is not uncommon for risk management to be over-complicated in relation to the complexity of the work.

A key difference between level 2 and level 3 is that techniques are appropriately applied.

For example, at level 2 there may be over-zealous identification of minor risks that can reduce the effectiveness of the function even though the goals are achieved. At level 3 better weighting and analysis ensures that response planning is proportionate.

4.2.13 Change management

Change management should:

- define the organisational change required to convert outputs into benefits
- ensure the organisation is prepared to implement change
- implement the change and embed it into organisational practice.

Indicators	Level 2 attributes
Assess	The areas of the organisation that are subject to change are assessed for their readiness to change.
Prepare	Change plans are communicated and stakeholders are influenced to support change.
Implement	Change is implemented in accordance with the organisation's readiness and change plans. Progress is monitored and communicated.
Sustain	Representatives of organisational areas that have changed are assigned responsibility for supporting and maintaining new management processes and behaviours.

Indicators	Level 3 attributes
Assess	The underlying characteristics of the organisation are assessed and the likely reaction to change is predicted.
Prepare	Preparation for change is clearly sensitive to the characteristics of the organisation and takes predicted responses into account.
Implement	Individuals affected by change are supported and the approach to change is amended as work proceeds. There are clear links between the control systems within the project, programme or portfolio and the control systems within the organisational area subject to change.
Sustain	Plans exist describing how change will be supported until it is deemed to be embedded in business as usual. The effectiveness of change is periodically assessed alongside benefits realisation.

Capability in change management cannot be achieved by the P3 organisation alone. Inevitably, it will involve people in business as usual who do not regard themselves as part of the project, programme or portfolio.

Level 2 is likely to be sufficient for projects implementing non-complex change.

Level 3 is an important goal for programmes with complex objectives.

4.2.14 Resource management

Resource management should:

- determine the best way to resource the work
- acquire and mobilise the necessary resources
- control resources throughout the life cycle
- demobilise resources at the end of the life cycle
- finalise all contractual arrangements.

Indicators	Level 2 attributes
Procure	A procurement procedure exists to identify suppliers and acquire resources.
Mobilise	Plans exist to show how the infrastructure will be mobilised and how these plans are implemented.
Control	Resource usage is monitored and plans updated accordingly.
Close	Demobilisation is planned.

Indicators	Level 3 attributes
Procure	Standard procedures are tailored to suit the context of the work. External resources are acquired through tendering and contract terms are negotiated. The management team works with operational departments to agree service levels for internal resources.
Mobilise	The infrastructure is adjusted throughout the life cycle and mobilisation is performed at the beginning of each stage or tranche.
Control	Plans for consumable resources are reviewed regularly and estimates revised. Capital assets are maintained throughout.
Close	Staff are formally redeployed, the value of capital assets is realised and contracts are closed formally.

This resource management capability summarises the capabilities for the functions that make up resource management.

If the project or programme makes use of both internal and external resources, and involves letting contracts for goods or services, it would be more appropriate to use the individual capabilities.

Procurement

Procurement should:

- identify potential external suppliers
- select external suppliers
- acquire commitment to provision of internal resources.

Indicators	Level 2 attributes
Research	Research is conducted but is often limited to known suppliers.
Tender	Tendering procedures exist but are informal. The approach is demonstrably legal and ethical.
Contract award	Contract award may comprise a relatively simple exchange of letters.
Acquire internal resources	Internal resources are acquired on an informal basis with negotiations between the management team and line managers being conducted on an ad-hoc basis.

Indicators	Level 3 attributes
Research	Thorough research is conducted and may be based on organisation-wide framework agreements.
Tender	Tendering activity follows a formal procedure tailored to the context of the work.
Contract award	Contract award includes formal negotiation of terms and conditions. An audit trail of the procedure is available to demonstrate that ethical, legal and regulatory standards have been met.
Acquire internal resources	The plans for internal resource usage are discussed with line managers in the early phases of the work. Service level agreements formalise the commitment of departments to provide internal resource.

Procurement is something that can, and often is, performed relatively informally. This is especially the case with internal resources.

The difference between levels 2 and 3 is the formality with which the procurement is conducted and documented. Formalised procurement is a classic 'insurance' activity. It probably will not be valued until something goes wrong.

Programme-level procurement is often about economies of scale. This will mean that some procurement responsibility is not devolved to projects and therefore requires high levels of co-ordination at the programme level. In these circumstances, contracts may be 'framework agreements' which allow programme-level negotiation with project-level scheduling.

Contract management

Contract management should:

- support procurement by negotiating terms and conditions
- document contractual agreements
- monitor contractual performance
- conclude contracts.

Indicators	Level 2 attributes
Negotiate contract terms	Standard terms and conditions are in place and deemed to be adequate.
Monitor	Contracts are only considered when a breach is suspected.
Conclude	Contracts are closed with confirmation that delivery is complete and final payment made.

Indicators	Level 3 attributes
Negotiate contract terms	Standard terms and conditions are reviewed and, if necessary, amended subject to negotiation.
Monitor	Contracts are reviewed to ensure they remain fit for purpose at key points in the life cycle.
Conclude	Contracts are reviewed and a post-contract report is produced that evaluates performance and makes recommendations for future contracts.

The difference between level 2 and 3 is not about the quality of individual contracts as they all need to be robust and fit for purpose.

It is more about consistency across multiple contracts and the degree to which they are treated as working documents.

Mobilisation

Mobilisation should ensure that:

- capital assets are operational and accessible
- facilities are operational and accessible
- delivery team members are competent and capable
- all resources are redeployed, returned or disposed of, at the end of the work.

Indicators	Level 2 attributes
Mobilise	Mobilisation is based primarily on availability.
Maintain	Assets and facilities are maintained on an ad-hoc basis.
Demobilise	Assets are disposed of and internal resources are released back to business as usual.

Indicators	Level 3 attributes
Mobilise	All resources are confirmed as being available and effective before being implemented according to plan.
Maintain	Maintenance of assets is planned and reliable performance ensured.
Demobilise	Disposal of assets and facilities is managed to realise full value. The performance of internal resources is reviewed and communicated back to line managers.

On low-complexity projects, mobilisation and demobilisation will often only cover small numbers of internal resources.

As scale and complexity increases, this capability may have to cover procurement and disposal of significant capital assets and services. It will link closely with the procurement and contract management capabilities.

4.3 Maturity

Many guides describe five very similarly structured levels in their maturity models. Praxis does not see the growing maturity of an organisation as simply executing each and every process in an increasingly rigorous way. There are more fundamental differences between immature and mature organisations, as shown below.

Level 0	Level 0 is simple. An organisation does not formally recognise the existence of projects, programmes or portfolios.
	Projects may be mentioned in name but individuals simply manage them intuitively and without any formal structure.
	Since this level represents the absence of P3 management, there is no need to define indicators or attributes.
Level 1	At level 1 an organisation recognises projects, programmes or portfolios and may apply some functions and processes.
	Goals are achieved, but this is usually through individual effort and heroics rather than a formal approach.
	Once again, there is no need to define indicators and attributes at this level because it simply represents an organisation that runs projects, programmes or portfolios but has not reached level 2.
Level 2	Maturity levels 2 and 3 are defined in the Praxis capability maturity model.
Level 3	These levels represent an organisation that recognises the need to develop and support competent P3 managers and provide them with the structures that consistently achieve the goals of the life cycle processes.
Level 4	At maturity levels 4 and 5, an organisation is regularly achieving the goals of the life cycle process in a measurable and repeatable way.
Level 5	
	These levels describe how the organisation embeds these practices into the organisation's way of working. Effective P3 management in these organisations is resilient and resistant to the pressures of political, economic and environmental change.

4.3.1 Maturity levels 2 and 3

This section describes maturity of P3 management at levels 2 and 3.

The characteristics of level 1 are common to all three; i.e. where goals are achieved it is often through individual effort and heroics rather than a formal approach.

To reach maturity levels 2 and 3, the organisation must demonstrate a corresponding level of capability in the relevant functions and the ability to co-ordinate these in each of the relevant life cycle processes.

The generic indicators apply to project, programme and portfolio processes. To reach a level of maturity for programme management, project management of the component projects must be at a similar level.

To reach a level of maturity for portfolio management, programme and project management of the component programmes and projects must be at a similar level.

Generic attributes

Indicators	Level 2 attributes	Level 3 attributes
Goals	The goals of the process are achieved, although some elements of level 1 heroics may still be observed.	The goals of the process are achieved through effective application of the process.
Functions	All functions used to conduct the processes are performed to capability level 2.	All functions used to conduct the processes are performed to capability level 3.
Assurance	The process is checked to ensure that it is being performed effectively.	The process is checked to ensure that it is based on organisational standards, has been tailored to the context of the work and is being performed efficiently.
Improvement	Improvements to processes and procedures are opportunistic and informal.	Processes and procedures are regularly reviewed; improvements are made as necessary and formally disseminated throughout the P3 management community.

Identification process

The goals of this process are to:

- develop an outline of the project or programme and assess whether is it likely to be justifiable
- determine what effort and investment is needed to define the work in detail
- gain the sponsor's authorisation for the definition phase.

Indicators	Level 2 attributes
Description	A separate identification phase is recognisable and there is an identifiable mandate that triggers the start of the phase.
Appoint identification team	Responsibilities for achieving the goals of the process are included in management team roles.
Review previous lessons	The manager or identification team accesses informal sources of information to identify lessons that may be relevant.
Prepare brief	A document is prepared that is sufficient for the sponsor to reliably judge whether or not the project or programme will be desirable, viable and achievable.
Prepare definition plan	A document is prepared that is sufficient for the sponsor to understand the scope and timescale of the definition phase.

On smaller projects the 'identification team' may simply be the project manager (applicable to level 2 or 3).

It is not necessary for the name 'identification team' to be used as long as there is a team that has responsibility for the goals of the process.

At level 2 the identification team may be appointed, based more on availability than technical competence.

Indicators	Level 3 attributes
Description	A process for the identification phase is centrally defined. This is tailored to suit the context of projects and programmes.
Appoint identification team	Resources with the necessary technical competencies are made available to join or advise the identification team.
Review previous lessons	The organisation's records enable the manager or identification team to research lessons learned and capture relevant lessons, which are then documented in a lessons log.
Prepare brief	The brief conforms to organisational standards with adaptations appropriate to the context of the work. There is evidence that the decision to manage the work as a project or programme has been made rationally and objectively.
Prepare definition plan	The definition plan conforms to organisational standards with adaptations appropriate to the context of the work.

Sponsorship process

The goals of this process are to:

- provide ownership of the business case
- act as champion for the objectives of the project, programme or portfolio
- make go/no-go decisions at relevant points in the life cycle
- address matters outside the scope of the manager's authority
- oversee assurance
- give ad-hoc support to the management team.

Indicators	Level 2 attributes
Description	Sponsors are appointed and are competent in sponsorship.
Review request for authorisation	Sponsors are presented with adequate information when authorisation is required and have sufficient resource to effectively assess that information.
Provide management support	Sponsors are available to the management team as and when required.
Confirm closure	Sponsors are requested to confirm closure and have adequate information on which to base the decision.
Review achievement of business case	Sponsors initiate and preside over a review of the business case at the appropriate time.

Indicators	Level 3 attributes
Description	Sponsors adhere to the centrally defined role and the sponsorship process as tailored to suit the context of the work.
Review request for authorisation	Sponsors are involved in the preparatory work leading up to a request for authorisation to ensure that the management team are clear about the sponsor's requirements.
Provide management support	Sponsors take an active role in coaching and mentoring members of the management team.
Confirm closure	Sponsors are actively involved in preparing for closure.
Review achievement of business case	Sponsors maintain active involvement in the period between the closure of the project or programme and the point at which the business case is due to be reviewed.

Sponsors at level 2 tend to be reactive. Although they perform the sponsorship role and process, this is largely done in response to prompts from the management team.

Sponsors at level 3 are more proactive. They are involved in the work leading up to major decision points so that they are fully conversant with the information that will be formally assessed. They also make sure that the management team are aware of their requirements in terms of the level of detail and format of information provided.

Level 3 sponsors are also active in developing members of the project management team, providing coaching and mentoring to promote the smooth running of the project or programme.

Definition process

The goals of this process are to:

- develop a detailed picture of the project or programme
- determine whether the work is justified
- describe governance policies that describe how the work will be managed
- gain the sponsor's authorisation for the delivery phase.

Indicators	Level 2 attributes
Description	A separate definition phase and process is recognisable and the goals are achieved.
Appoint definition team	Responsibilities for achieving the goals of the process are included in management team roles.
Define scope	Documentation is prepared that is sufficient for the management team, stakeholders and sponsor to understand the scope of the work.
Pre-authorisation work	If necessary, pre-authorisation work is performed with the agreement of the sponsor.
Prepare governance documents	Documentation is prepared that is sufficient for the sponsor to understand how the work will be managed and assured.
Prepare delivery documents	Delivery documents are prepared that are sufficient for the sponsor to understand all relevant delivery aspects of the work (e.g. scope, timescale and risk).
Consolidate definition documentation	Governance and delivery documentation is combined to enable the sponsor to make an informed decision about progression to the delivery phase.
Mobilise	The equipment, facilities and other resources required to deliver the objectives, or the first stage or tranche of work, are mobilised.

Indicators	Level 3 attributes
Description	A process for the definition phase is centrally defined. This is tailored to suit the context of the work.
Appoint definition team	Resources with the necessary technical competencies are made available to join or advise the definition team.
Define scope	Scope documentation conforms to organisational standards with adaptations appropriate to the context of the work.
Pre-authorisation work	The impact of performing pre-authorisation work is assessed and incorporated into delivery documentation.

On smaller projects the 'definition team' may simply be the project manager (applicable to level 2 or 3). In this case it may well be that the identification and definition processes are combined. If so, this maturity level should be used for assessment purposes as the outputs of the combined process should be the same as for the definition process.

It is not necessary for the name 'definition team' to be used as long as there is a team that has responsibility for the goals of the process.

At level 2 the definition team may be appointed, based more on availability than technical competence.

Indicators	Level 3 attributes
Prepare governance documents	Governance documentation conforms to organisational standards with adaptations appropriate to the context of the work.
Prepare delivery documents	Delivery documents conform to organisational standards with adaptations appropriate to the context of the work.
Consolidate definition documentation	Governance and delivery documentation is combined, rationalised and summarised in accordance with organisational standards with adaptations appropriate to the context of the work.
Mobilise	Mobilisation takes the stage or tranche structure into account to ensure mobilisation is as efficient as possible.

Delivery process

The goals of this process are to:

- delegate responsibility for producing deliverables to the appropriate people
- monitor the performance of the work and track against the delivery plans
- take action where necessary to keep work in line with plans
- escalate issues and replan if necessary
- accept work as it is completed
- maintain communications with all stakeholders.

Indicators	Level 2 attributes
Description	The delivery phase is managed separately from definition. Where appropriate the phase is divided into stages or tranches.
Authorise work	Work is divided into packages that are formally assigned to teams with performance criteria.
Co-ordinate and monitor progress	Progress is recorded and its impact is assessed and acted upon. Teams working on different work packages are co-ordinated.
Update and communicate	Documentation is regularly updated and disseminated in accordance with the communications plan.
Corrective action	Exception plans are produced where necessary and work is terminated when a business case is no longer achievable.
Accept completed work	Deliverables are formally accepted by the management team.

Indicators	Level 3 attributes
Description	A process for the delivery phase is centrally defined. This is tailored to suit the context of the work.
Authorise work	The impact of new work packages on the performance of existing work packages is assessed.
Co-ordinate and monitor progress	Progress information from multiple work packages is consistent and consolidated. Plans are regularly reviewed and updated information fed back to the work packages.
Update and communicate	Adherence to the communications plan is monitored and controlled. Key documents are subject to configuration management.
Corrective action	Systems are in place to identify the need for corrective action in advance.
Accept completed work	Deliverables are subject to a consistent acceptance procedure including sign-off and handover.

How the process, and therefore this competency, is implemented will depend upon the complexity of the work being managed.

Less complex projects will have few work packages while programmes and complex projects will have many. Where there are many work packages, these are likely to vary in terms of their scale and whether they are performed by internal teams or external suppliers.

More complex work will require more complex techniques. Whereas Gantt-based slip charts may be adequate in a non-complex situation, other circumstances may require more sophisticated techniques such as earned value management.

All these contextual factors must be taken into account when considering maturity for this process.

Where the work includes delegated work packages and the use of the development process, the maturity of the two processes should be the same; i.e. the delivery process cannot be at level 3 if the development process is only at level 2.

Development process

The goals of this process are to:

- transfer responsibility for a package of work
- execute the package of work
- transfer ownership of the finished products.

Indicators	Level 2 attributes
Description	The formal definition and allocation of work packages to teams, suppliers or individuals is recognised and documented.
Accept work package	Recipients of delegated work formally acknowledge receipt of the work package scope and performance criteria.
Perform work	The team or individuals performing the work are technically competent and provide regular progress updates.
Deliver products	All products are formally handed over with accompanying documentation.

Indicators	Level 3 attributes
Description	A process for delegating work packages is centrally defined and tailored to suit the context.
Accept work package	Recipients of delegated work are involved in refining the work package scope and performance criteria.
Perform work	The team or individual performing the work uses monitoring and reporting procedures that are consistent with those used to consolidate progress information at the higher level. There are regular updates from the higher level covering any external influences on the performance of the work.
Deliver products	Product handover is consistent for all work packages across the project or programme.

This maturity should be developed and assessed according to the context in which it is being used. It may be appropriate to have multiple versions, for example:

- where a programme is delegating work to a project this process is effectively a summary of the project life cycle
- where a project or programme delegates work packages to suppliers who perform according to a negotiated contract
- where managers of smaller projects allocate work to internal teams or individuals.

Boundaries process

The goals of this process are to:

- conclude a stage or tranche in a structured way
- prepare for the next tranche or stage.

Indicators	Level 2 attributes
Description	Phase, tranche and/or stage boundaries are recognised and formal approval is sought before commencing new sections of work.
Close and review previous stage/tranche	Key lessons from earlier stages or tranches are documented. Stakeholders are informed of the closure of the previous tranche or stage.
Plan next stage/tranche	Stages and tranches are planned using progress information from previous work.
Assemble documentation	Documentation is assembled that will enable the sponsor to make an informed decision about the authorisation of the stage or tranche.
Mobilise	Most resources are mobilised at the start of the work.
Pre-authorisation work	Work that would significantly delay the work if left until authorisation is agreed and performed.

Indicators	Level 3 attributes
Description	A process for managing tranche and stage boundaries is centrally defined. This is tailored to suit the context of the work.
Close and review previous stage/tranche	A formal review of a tranche or stage is conducted. The tranche or stage is formally closed including any necessary demobilisation. Lessons learned are added to the organisation's knowledge management system.
Plan next stage/tranche	Performance metrics and lessons learned from previous stages or tranches are used to refine plans for subsequent stages or tranches.
Assemble documentation	Evidence is provided that demonstrates how performance metrics have been used to improve performance in subsequent stages or tranches.
Mobilise	Care is taken to maximise the efficient use of resources by mobilising them on a stage-by-stage or tranche-by-tranche basis.
Pre-authorisation work	Pre-authorisation work is planned and controlled to a level consistent with the rest of the work.

The principles of managing boundaries between tranches and stages are largely independent of the scale and complexity of the work.

While stages tend to be sequential, tranches typically overlap so that the activities related to boundaries can be chronologically spread out. This should be taken into account when assessing attributes of tranche boundaries.

Closure process

The goals of this process are to:

- close a project or programme that has delivered all its outputs
- close a project or programme that is no longer justifiable.

Indicators	Level 2 attributes
Description	Projects and programmes are formally closed, with the goals of closure usually achieved.
Prepare for closure	Closure activities, including handover, review and demobilisation, are planned in advance of closure.
Hand over	All deliverables are handed over, with the relevant stakeholders confirming that specifications have been met. Follow-on actions reports may be used to agree actions required to finalise deliverables after closure.
Review	The management and governance of the project or programme is reviewed and a post-project or post-programme review is prepared, with lessons learned highlighted. If appropriate, achievement of the business case is reviewed.
Demobilise	All physical assets are sold, redeployed or hire contracts closed. Contracts for services are closed. Internal human resources are released to their home departments or redeployed to other projects or programmes.

Activities such as handover will vary in detail depending upon whether performance is subject to contractual terms.

Responsibilities for demobilisation will be affected by whether a project or programme is stand-alone or part of a portfolio.

Indicators	Level 3 attributes
Description	A process for managing closure is centrally defined. This is tailored to suit the context of projects. Projects and programmes are terminated when no longer justifiable.
Prepare for closure	Specialist resources are available to work with the management team while closure is planned in parallel with project or programme delivery.
Hand over	Stakeholder satisfaction with deliverables is followed up post-handover to confirm that both handover and any follow-on actions were successful.
Review	Lessons learned are consistently recorded and disseminated. Recommendations for the improvement of standard processes and procedures are made.
Demobilise	In the case of redeployment of physical assets or release of internal human resource, demobilisation is performed with the requirements of other projects and programmes in mind and not as an isolated activity.

Benefits realisation process

The goals of this process are to:

- establish the current state of what is being changed
- co-ordinate the delivery of outputs with the management of change
- ensure changes are permanent
- establish whether benefits have been achieved.

Indicators	Level 2 attributes
Description	The need to manage the transition from existing to new modes of operation is recognised and managed.
Prepare for transition	Performance criteria are baselined in accordance with benefits profiles. Changes are communicated and readiness for change is qualitatively assessed.
Manage transition	Competent resources are in place to manage the change. Outputs are formally handed over to operational teams. A support infrastructure is in place.
Conclude transition	New working practices are supported until deemed to be embedded as normal operation. Pre-change systems are decommissioned.
Final review	Final reviews are conducted against authorised business cases.

Indicators	Level 3 attributes
Description	A process for realising benefits is centrally defined. This is tailored to suit the context of projects and programmes.
Prepare for transition	Standard approaches exist for the measurement of performance criteria and these are tailored to the context of the work. Readiness for change is quantitatively assessed.
Manage transition	Performance criteria are monitored throughout the transition. New benefits are identified and introduced if viable and practical.
Conclude transition	The impact of the changes is reviewed and related benefit plans are updated. Performance improvements are measured and predictions made with respect to planned benefit value.
Final review	Final reviews are conducted with quantifiable measurement of benefits wherever possible. All qualitative measurements are supported by clear and justifiable assumptions.

This process is often seen as being unique to programmes, but where the relationship between outputs and a benefit are non-complex it can be applied through a small extension to the traditional project life cycle.

When assessing an organisation's maturity in realising benefits it is advisable to qualify the maturity level with some explanation of the context in which this has been achieved.

Governance process

The goals of this process are to:

- provide ownership of the objectives of the portfolio
- oversee assurance of the portfolio
- promote the discipline and profession of P3 management.

Indicators	Level 2 attributes
Description	An infrastructure exists that includes competent individuals with responsibility to govern the portfolio.
Support the portfolio	A senior manager has responsibility for sponsorship of the portfolio. A portfolio infrastructure exists and has responsibility for co-ordinating all projects and programmes within the host organisation.
Support the discipline	Formal approaches are promoted for the management of projects and programmes. Preferred tools and techniques are defined for relevant functions. The host organisation understands its capability level in all relevant functions.
Support the profession	The portfolio manages learning and development programmes for project staff, including knowledge and competency development. The host organisation understands its capability level in the application of all relevant functions.

The principles of governance maturity are the same for a standard or structured portfolio. They will simply be applied in a different context with a structured portfolio having the additional focus of a defined set of strategic objectives.

Indicators	Level 3 attributes
Description	The governance infrastructure is established as the centre of excellence for the discipline and profession of P3 management.
Support the portfolio	The portfolio infrastructure is formally constituted as a permanent organisation (such as a PMO). This includes formal approaches to sponsorship, assurance and project or programme support across the portfolio.
Support the discipline	Standard life cycle processes and tailoring guidelines are implemented. Knowledge is captured and used on new projects and programmes. The host organisation understands its maturity level in the application of all relevant processes.
Support the profession	Communities of practice are set up, ethical standards are established and P3 management is seen as equivalent to other professions within the business.

Management process

The goals of this process are to:

- assess the suitability of projects and programmes for inclusion in the portfolio
- maintain a beneficial and manageable mix of projects and programmes.

Indicators	Level 2 attributes
Description	The portfolio organisation is responsible for selecting, categorising and prioritising projects and programmes. It is also responsible for balancing the overall portfolio.
Select projects and programmes	A board exists within the portfolio that has responsibility for reviewing business cases and making go/no-go decisions.
Categorise	Projects and programmes are categorised according to their main characteristics.
Prioritise	Projects and programmes are prioritised according to simple characteristics such as business return.
Balance	Objectives are defined with regard to the required balance of the portfolio. The portfolio is regularly assessed against these objectives.

Indicators	Level 3 attributes
Description	A process for managing the portfolio is defined, implemented and regularly reviewed.
Select projects and programmes	Boards exist within a scheme of delegation that enables them to give authorisation within defined limits. Briefs and project or programme management plans are assessed against available capacity and strategic objectives.
Categorise	Projects and programmes are categorised according to multiple characteristics, allowing complex analysis of the portfolio.
Prioritise	Projects and programmes are prioritised according to multiple weighted characteristics, allowing complex analysis of the portfolio.
Balance	The characteristics of a balanced portfolio are defined in inter-related and weighted terms. The portfolio is regularly assessed against these objectives.

> The difference between a standard and structured portfolio is primarily that in a structured portfolio the prioritisation and balancing activities must be aligned with the strategic objectives.

Co-ordination process

The goals of this process are to:

- consolidate information from the component projects and programmes to understand the portfolio as a whole
- monitor the performance of the portfolio against its objectives
- manage the inter-relationships between projects and programmes.

Indicators	Level 2 attributes
Description	The portfolio organisation is responsible for co-ordinating the life cycles of component projects and programmes.
Co-ordinate initiation	The portfolio organisation issues and co-ordinates the issue of mandates. Specialist resources required for identification are co-ordinated at portfolio level.
Co-ordinate definition	Management plans exist for all projects and programmes. Specialist resources required for definition are co-ordinated at portfolio level.
Co-ordinate delivery	Resource and funding requirements are co-ordinated at portfolio level.
Co-ordinate closure	The portfolio management team plans ahead for the reuse of demobilised resources on new projects and programmes.

The difference between a standard and structured portfolio is simply that in a structured portfolio the co-ordination activities must be aligned with the strategic objectives.

Indicators	Level 3 attributes
Description	A process for co-ordinating project and programme life cycles is defined, implemented and regularly reviewed.
Co-ordinate initiation	Where appropriate, project and programme briefs may be prepared at portfolio level to ensure integration and co-ordination.
Co-ordinate definition	Standard management plans are defined, regularly reviewed and updated by the portfolio management team. Project and programme delivery plans are aggregated at portfolio level and assessed.
Co-ordinate delivery	Progress information is aggregated to assess overall impact on inter-related projects and programmes. Guidance and recommendations are fed back to project and programme management teams.
Co-ordinate closure	Consolidated plans are reviewed to assess the impact of demobilising projects and programmes. The portfolio management team co-ordinates project and programme demobilisation and mobilisation to maximise efficient working.

4.3.2 Maturity levels 4 and 5

To reach maturity levels 4 and 5 the organisation must be able to quantitatively assess its performance and use this information to improve continuously.

The guiding principle of level 4 is that performance is measured quantitatively. In progressing from level 3 to level 4 maturity, an organisation is moving from a focus on being effective to a focus on becoming efficient, while remaining effective.

It would be possible to identify attributes for individual processes at level 4 but the principles of quantitatively measuring performance are common to all processes.

Praxis uses the four high-level functions from Part 1 listed below to assess maturity at levels 4 and 5. These address broad aspects of the setting of individual projects, programmes and portfolios, together with the professionalism of those who deliver them.

In the Praxis approach to assessing capability maturity, these high-level functions are assessed as part of the portfolio management processes.

Indicators	Level 4 attributes	
P3 delivery performance	A body exists that is accountable for the performance of projects, programmes and portfolios across the host organisation. Delivery of objectives is quantitatively measured and recorded.	The body that 'owns' all projects, programmes and portfolios within the organisation can take many forms. It could be a company board, a portfolio board or a specially constituted group such as a P3 management office (PMO).
Communities of practice	A community of practice exists for P3 management. This community has responsibility for defining and measuring P3 management performance criteria.	In smaller organisations a single community of practice covering all of P3 management will suffice. As the complexity of projects, programmes and portfolios increases it may be appropriate to have communities that cover specialist areas such as risk management or assurance.
Knowledge management	The knowledge management system records data from the quantitative measurement of functions and processes. It can identify strengths, weaknesses and trends.	Many knowledge management systems are designed to manage textual information such as lessons learned. At level 4 the system needs to enable the quantitative analysis of performance data.
Learning and development	Learning and development programmes include formal assessments to quantify levels of individual knowledge and performance.	This is not referring to tests or qualifications that develop competent people as they are a requirement of level 2. Level 4 learning and development is about collective assessment to confirm that levels of knowledge and competence are being maintained and the return on investment is understood.

The guiding principle of level 5 is that performance metrics are used to continuously improve the delivery of projects, programmes and portfolios. Continuous improvement can be slow and incremental or achieved in significant steps. The latter will usually come through significant innovation and change to the management processes.

Indicators	Level 5 attributes	
P3 delivery performance	A body exists that is responsible for the continuous improvement of the delivery of projects, programmes and portfolios across the host organisation. This body has authority in areas within the host organisation that constitute the environment of each project programme or portfolio.	The ability to deliver objectives is often affected by factors outside the core P3 discipline and profession. To achieve continuous improvement the body that 'owns' all projects, programmes and portfolios must have some degree of authority in the environment outside the P3 domain.
Communities of practice	The community of practice is actively involved in similar communities external to the host organisation. It is involved in benchmarking, identification of innovative approaches and implementation of changes to the host organisation's systems and processes.	The community (or communities) of practice will maintain external links to other organisations and professional bodies to identify innovations that may deliver step change in the continuous improvement.
Knowledge management	The knowledge management system is used to identify areas for improvement and track the effect of changes to the host organisation's systems, procedures and processes.	The knowledge management system may not include analysis tools but must allow interrogation that delivers suitable data to analysis tools.
Learning and development	Learning and development programmes include formal CPD processes.	At this level the organisation will expect P3 managers to take responsibility for their personal development and will track the effort put into CPD.

References

Adair, J (revised 2009). *Effective Team Building*. Pan MacMillan, London

Belbin, M (1981). *Management Teams*. Heinemann, London

Berlo, D (1960). *The Process of Communication: An Introduction to Theory and Practice*. Holt, Rinehart and Winston, New York

Blake, R; Mouton, J (1964). *The Managerial Grid*. Gulf Publishing, Houston

Carnall, C (2007). *Managing Change In Organisations*. Prentice Hall, London

Cialdini, R B (1995). *Influence: the Psychology of Persuasion*. Quill, New York

Cohen, A R; Bradford, D L (2005). *Influence Without Authority*. Wiley, Hoboken

Corporate Governance Code (UK) https://www.frc.org.uk/directors/corporate-governance-and-stewardship/uk-corporate-governance-code. Financial Reporting Council, London

Furlong, G (2005). *The Conflict Resolution Toolbox*. Wiley and Sons, Ontario

Hersey, P; Blanchard, K H (1969). 'Life Cycle Theory of Leadership'. *Training and Development Journal* 23 (5)

Herzberg, F (1959). *The Motivation to Work*. Wiley, New York

Katzenbach, J R; Smith, D K (1993). *The Wisdom of Teams: Creating the High-performance Organisation*. Harvard Business School, Boston

Kotter, J P (1995). *Leading Change*. Harvard Business School Press, Boston

Lewin, K (1951). *Field Theory in Social Science*. Harper and Row, New York

Maccoby, M; Scudder, T (2011). *Leading in the Heat of Conflict*. ATD Magazine, Alexandria

Margerison-McCann https://www.teammanagementsystems.com/tms-profiles/team-management-profile-tmp/

Maslow, A H (1943). 'A Theory of Human Motivation'. *Psychological Review*, 50 (4): 370–96

McGregor, D (1960). *The Human Side of Enterprise*. McGraw-Hill, New York

Montana, P; Charnov, B (2008). *Management*. Barron's Educational Series, Hauppauge, New York.

Morgan, G (1986). *Images of Organisation*. Sage, Thousand Oaks

NEC3 range (contract management) https://www.neccontract.com/products/contracts/nec3/engineering-and-construction-contract/nec3-ecc

Nonaka, I; Takeuchi, H (1995). *The Knowledge Creating Company: How Japanese Companies Create the Dynamics of Innovation*. Oxford University Press, New York

Sarbanes-Oxley (USA) (2002) **https://www.govinfo.gov/content/pkg/COMPS-1883/pdf/COMPS-1883.pdf**

Shell, G R (2006). *Bargaining for Advantage.* Penguin Books, New York

Shewhart, W A (1939). *Statistical Method from the Viewpoint of Quality Control.* Department of Agriculture. Dover, New York, 1986, page 45

Software Engineering Institute (SEI) Capability Maturity Model CMMI-DEV v1.3 (2010). *Improving Processes for Developing Better Products and Services.* Carnegie Mellon University, Pittsburgh

Tannenbaum, R; Schmidt, W (1973). 'How to Choose a Leadership Pattern'. *Harvard Business Review*

Thamhain, H J; Wilemon, D L (1975). *Conflict Management in Project Life Cycles.* Sloan Management Review

Thomas, K W; Kilmann, R H (1978). 'Comparison of Four Instruments Measuring Conflict Behavior'. *Psychological Reports.* 42 (3_suppl): 1139–1145

Tuckman, B W (1965). 'Developmental Sequence in Small Groups'. *Psychological Bulletin* 63 (6): 384–399

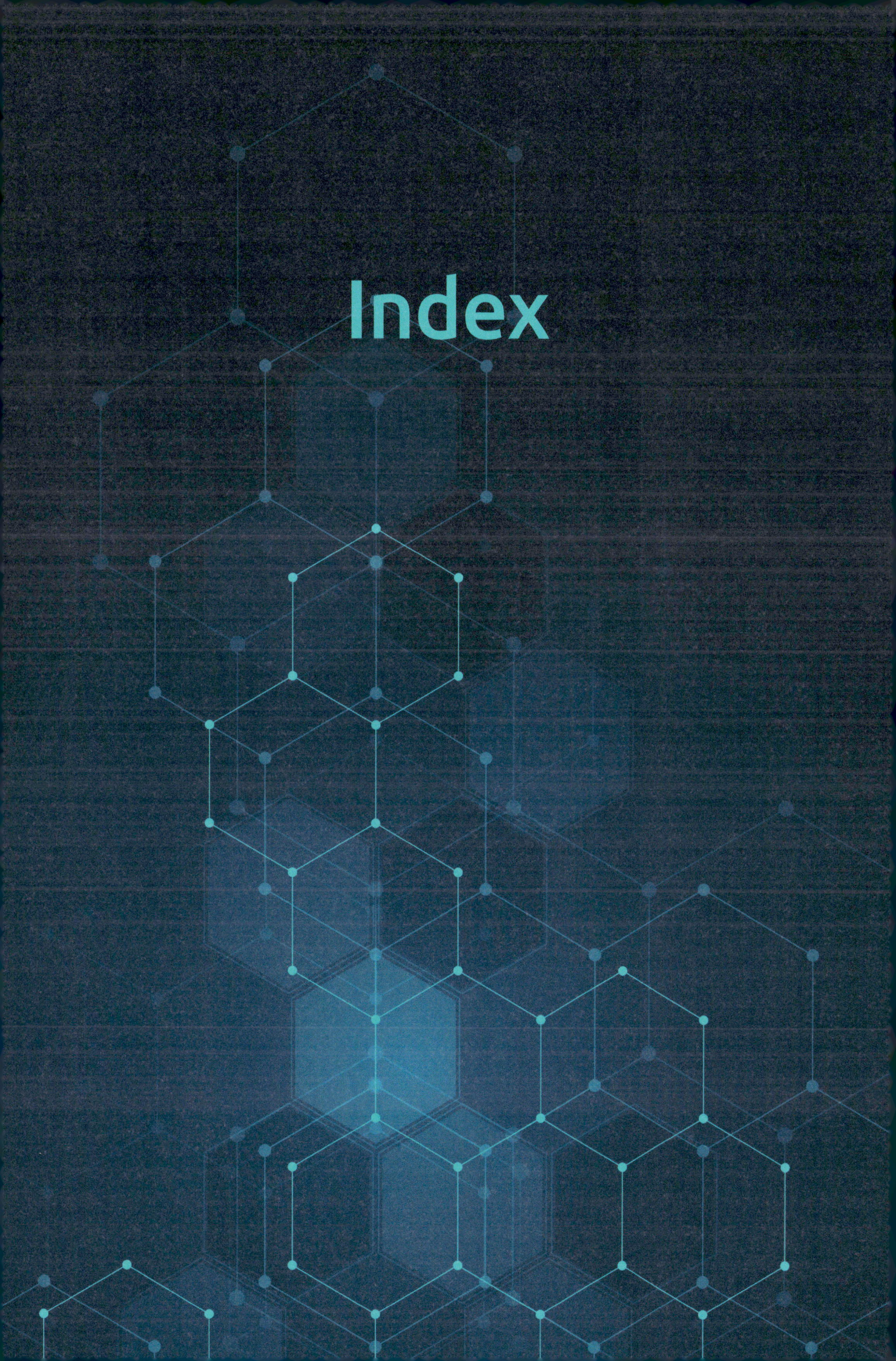
Index

A

acceptance of work 152
assurance 73–75, 142, 168, 220, 271
assurance competency 220
assurance management plans 183
authorisation of work 149–150

B

BCMs (business change managers) 60
benefit profiles 201–202
benefits management 85–88, 281
benefits management competency 232
benefits management plans 185–187
benefits maps 201
benefits realisation 18
benefits realisation competency 260
benefits realisation process 158–161, 305
blueprints 200–201
BOOT (build, own, operate, transfer) projects 107
boundaries process 153–156, 303
boundary management competency 258
briefs 138–139, 204–205
budgeting and cost control 108–111, 239, 288
budgeting and cost control competency 239
build, own, operate, transfer (BOOT) projects 107
business case management 64–65, 275
business case management competency 223–224
business cases 143, 147, 154, 203–204
business change managers (BCMs) 60

C

capability 268–294
capability maturity 29–32, 170, 266–310
Capability Maturity Model® Integration (CMMI) 30–31
change 12
change control 91–93, 282
change logs 212–213
change management 118–120, 290
change management competency 241
change management plans 192–193
close a project or programme competency 259
closure 143, 154
closure process 161–163, 304

CMMI (Capability Maturity Model® Integration) 30–31
communicate competency 246
communication 39–41, 150–151
communication plans 205
communities of practice (CoPs) 33–34, 169
competence 34–35, 169
 see also delivery competencies; interpersonal competencies; process competencies
complexity 11–13
configuration management 88–91, 283
configuration management competency 234
conflict management 41–43
conflict management competency 247
contract management 121, 126–129, 293
contract management competency 244
control 68–71, 276
control competency 227
control management plans 180–181
control scope change competency 233
co-ordinate projects and programmes competency 264
co-ordination process 173–175, 308
CoPs (communities of practice) 33–34, 169
corrective action 151–152
cost control 108–111, 288
cost control competency 239

D

daily logs 212
define a project or programme competency 255
definition documentation 147
definition plans 139, 205
definition process 144–148, 299–300
definition teams 145
delegate competency 248
delegation 43–45
deliver a project or programme competency 256–258
delivery
  assurance 73–75
  benefits management 85–88
  business case management 64–65
  change control 91–93
  change management 118–120
  configuration management 88–91

contract management 121, 126–129
control 68–71
cost control 108–111
financial management 100–102
funding 105–108
information management 71–73
integrative management 55–57
investment appraisal 102–105
mobilisation 121, 129–131
organisation management 57–61
planning 66–68, 146–147
planning competency 226
procurement 121, 123–126
requirements management 80–83
resource management 120–123
resource scheduling 98–100
risk context 113–115
risk management 111–113
risk techniques 115–118
schedule management 93–96
scope management 75–79
solutions development 83–85
stakeholder management 61–64
time scheduling 96–98
delivery competencies
    control scope change 233
    develop budgets and control costs 239
    develop investment appraisal 237
    develop solution 231
    exercise control 227
    manage benefits 232
    manage business cases 223–224
    manage change 241
    manage configuration 234
    manage contracts 244
    manage finance 236–239
    manage funding 238
    manage information 228
    manage organisations 221
    manage requirements 230
    manage resources 242–245
    manage risk 240
    manage schedules 235
    manage scope 229–234
    manage stakeholders 221
    mobilise resources 245

plan delivery 226
plan governance 225
procure resources 243
provide assurance 220
delivery documents 154–155, 175, 205–216
    change logs 212–213
    communication plans 205
    daily logs 212
    definition plans 205
    delivery plans 209–210
    event reports 215–216
    follow-on actions reports 216
    issue registers 210–211
    lessons logs 211–212
    progress reports 213–214
    risk registers 206–209
    stakeholder registers 205–206
delivery plans 209–210
delivery process 148–158, 300–301
demobilisation 163
develop budgets and control costs competency 239
develop investment appraisal competency 237
develop products competency 257
develop solution competency 231
development 36–37, 169
development process 156–158, 302
documentation
    delivery documents 205–216
    management plans 176–195
    scope documents 175, 195–205
    update and review 150–151
dynamics 12

E

earned value management (EVM) 110–111
environments 8–9
ethics 35–36, 169
event reports 215–216
EVM (earned value management) 110–111
exercise control competency 227

F

finance management 100–102, 285–288
finance management competency 236–239

finance management plans 189–190
follow-on actions reports 216
funding 105–108, 287
funding management competency 238

G

goals 269–270
govern a portfolio competency 262
governance 13–32
governance documents 146, 175
governance planning competency 225
governance process 167–170, 306

H

handover 162–163

I

identification process 137–140, 297
identify a project or programme competency 253
influence competency 250
influencing 46–47
information management 71–73, 277
information management competency 228
information management plans 181–182
initiate portfolio competency 261
initiate portfolio process 164–167
innovation 12
integrative management 55–57
interpersonal competencies
    communicate 246
    delegate 248
    influence 250
    lead 249
    manage conflict 247
    negotiate 251
    work within a team 252
interpersonal skills
    communication 39–41
    conflict management 41–43
    delegation 43–45
    influencing 46–47
    leadership 47–50
    negotiation 50–52
    teamwork 52–54
investment appraisal 102–105, 286

investment appraisal development competency 237
issue registers 210–211

K

knowledge management 28–29, 170

L

lead competency 249
leadership 47–50
learning and development 36–37, 169
lessons learned 28, 138
lessons logs 211–212
life cycles 17–24, 170

M

manage a portfolio competency 263
manage benefits competency 232
manage boundaries competency 258
manage business case competency 223–224
manage change competency 241
manage configuration competency 234
manage conflict competency 247
manage contracts competency 244
manage finance competency 236–239
manage funding competency 238
manage information competency 228
manage organisation competency 221
manage requirements competency 230
manage resources competency 242–245
manage risk competency 240
manage schedule competency 235
manage scope competency 229–234
manage stakeholders competency 221
management
    delivery 54–131
    interpersonal skills 38–54
    of projects, programmes and portfolios 15–17, 37–131
management plans
    assurance management plans 183
    benefits management plans 185–187
    change management plans 192–193
    control management plans 180–181
    finance management plans 189–190
    information management plans 181–182

organisation management plans 176–178
resource management plans 193–195
risk management plans 190–192
schedule management plans 187–188
scope management plans 183–185
stakeholder management plans 178–179
management process 170–173, 307
mandates 195
maturity levels 295
   2 and 3 296–308
   4 and 5 309–310
mobilisation 121, 129–131, 155, 167, 294
mobilise resources competency 245

N

negotiate competency 251
negotiation 50–52

O

OBS (organisational breakdown structures) 60
organisation management 57–61, 221, 273
organisation management plans 176–178
organisational breakdown structures (OBS) 60

P

P3 *see* projects, programmes and portfolios
plan delivery competency 226
plan governance competency 225
planning 66–68
PMOs (project management offices) 14, 61
portfolio governance competency 262
portfolio initiation process 261
portfolio life cycles 23–24
portfolio management 16–17, 170–173
portfolio management competency 263
portfolio processes
   co-ordination process 173–175, 308
   governance process 167–170, 306
   initiation process 164–167
   management process 170–173, 307
portfolios 10–11, 166–168
   see also projects, programmes and portfolios
Praxis method 134–135
pre-authorisation 145–146, 155

process competencies
   close a project or programme 259
   co-ordinate projects and programmes 264
   define a project or programme 255
   deliver a project or programme 256–258
   develop products 257
   govern a portfolio 262
   identify a project or programme 253
   initiate a portfolio 261
   manage a portfolio 263
   manage boundaries 258
   realise benefits 260
   sponsor a project or programme 254
process models 134–135
procure resources competency 243
procurement 121, 123–126, 292
product development competency 257
product development process 156–158
product documentation 196–199
professionalism 32–37
programme briefs 138–139, 204–205
programme delivery plans 147
programme life cycles 22–23
programme management 15–16
programme management plans 147, 154
programme processes 135–136
programmes *see* projects, programmes and portfolios
progress co-ordination and monitoring 150
progress reports 213–214
project briefs 138–139, 204–205
project delivery plans 147
project life cycles 19–22
project management 15–16
project management offices (PMOs) 14, 61
project management plans 147, 154
project processes 135–136
projects, programmes and portfolios (P3)
   assurance 75
   benefits management 87–88
   budgeting and cost control 110–111
   business case management 65
   capability maturity 31–32
   change control 92–93
   change management 120
   communication 40–41

projects, programmes and portfolios (P3) *continued*
    configuration management 90–91
    conflict management 43
    contract management 128–129
    control 70–71
    cost control 110–111
    delegation 45
    financial management 102
    funding 107–108
    governance 14–15
    influencing 47
    information management 73
    investment appraisal 105
    knowledge management 29
    leadership 49–50
    life cycles 17–24
    management 15–17
    management discipline 169–170
    management profession 169
    mobilisation 131
    negotiation 51–52
    organisation management 59–61
    planning 68
    procurement 125–126
    requirements management 81–83
    resource management 122–123
    resource scheduling 100
    risk context 115
    risk management 113
    risk techniques 117–118
    schedule management 95–96
    scope management 78–79
    solutions development 84–85
    sponsorship 25
    stakeholder management 63–64
    support 27
    teamwork 53–54
    time scheduling 97–98
    use of terms 9–11
provide assurance competency 220

Q

qualitative risk assessment 116, 117
quantitative risk assessment 116–117

R

RAM (responsibility assignment matrix) 60
realise benefits competency 260
requests for authorisation 141–142
requirements management 80–83, 279
requirements management competency 230
resource management 120–123, 291–294
resource management competency 242–245
resource management plans 193–195
resource mobilisation competency 245
resource procurement competency 243
resource scheduling 98–100
responsibility assignment matrix (RAM) 60
risk context 113–115
risk management 111–113, 289
risk management competency 240
risk management plans 190–192
risk registers 206–209
risk techniques 115–118

S

schedule management 93–96, 283–284
schedule management competency 235
schedule management plans 187–188
scope 11
scope change control competency 233
scope definition 145
scope documents 175, 195–205
scope management 75–79, 278–283
scope management competency 229–234
scope management plans 183–185
SEI Capability Maturity Model 30
service level agreements (SLAs) 129
settings 7–13
SLAs (service level agreements) 129
solutions development 83–85, 280
solutions development competency 231
SoWs (statements of work) 128
specifications 196
sponsor a project or programme competency 254
sponsorship 24–25, 168, 219
sponsorship process 140–143, 298
stakeholder management 61–64, 274
stakeholder management competency 222
stakeholder management plans 178–179

stakeholder registers 205–206
standard portfolios 10
statements of work (SoWs) 128
structured portfolios 10
support 26–27, 272

T

teamwork 52–54
teamwork competency 252
time scheduling 96–98
transition 159–160

U

uncertainty 11–12

V

value management 81
vision statements 195–196

W

work packages 156–157
work within a team competency 252